Si ... ON

ILE RPG

RPG IV BY EXAMPLE

GEORGE FARR
SHAILAN TOPIWALA

A Division of
DUKE COMMUNICATIONS INTERNATIONAL

Loveland, Colorado

Library of Congress Cataloging-in-Publication Data

Farr, George, 1961-
   RPG IV by example / by George Farr and Shailan Topiwala.
     p. cm.
   Includes index.
   ISBN 1-882419-34-0
   1. RPG (Computer program language) I. Topiwala, Shailan.
  II. Title.
  QA76.73.R25F37 1996
  005.2'45—dc20   96-10035
                                                     CIP

Virgil Green, Technical Editor

Copyright © 1996 by DUKE PRESS
DUKE COMMUNICATIONS INTERNATIONAL
Loveland, Colorado

It is the reader's responsibility to ensure procedures and techniques used from this book are accurate and appropriate for the user's installation. No warranty is implied or expressed.

This book was printed and bound in the United States of America.

ISBN 1-882419-34-0

1 2 3 4 5 EB 9 8 7 6

I can think of no other deserving this honor
than my wife Diana and my children
Angelica, Michael, and AnnaLisa

In addition
I would like to dedicate this book
to my mother Angelica Farr
and my in-laws John and Anna Zissaros.
Thank you for all your continuous support and encouragement.

— George Farr

For my three beautiful children
Keirtan, Maya, and Dhavita,
who have all missed having me around.

I also wish to thank
my darling Carolyn
for her support throughout this project.
It would not have been possible without you.

— All my love, Shailan

Acknowledgments

We would like to take this opportunity to thank several people for their valuable contribution to the text.

Jon Paris	Ron Rose
Susan Gantner	Russ Popeil
Claus Weiss	Ming Ho
Hermas Lo	Brad Doyle
George Voutsinas	Chi Wai Cheung
Ibrahim Batthish	Hin Chui
Inge Weiss	Barry Sears

Above all, we must thank the "By Example" series editor, Virgil Green, for his invaluable contributions to this book. Without Virgil's unfailing eye for accuracy, patience, guidance, understanding of programmers' everyday work environment, and amazing programming expertise, we could never have made this book as practical and useful as it is. We owe Virgil a great debt of gratitude for all the work he put into our book.

Foreword

Many years in the making and not without a little controversy along the way, RPG IV represents a major change to RPG. Some consider RPG IV to be the biggest change ever, possibly even greater than the change from RPG II to RPG III that came with the System/38. Certainly, RPG IV will be the biggest change for the majority of the RPG programming community, many of whom have grown up with RPG III.

One fact is clear: the introduction of RPG IV has produced an enormous demand for education on the capabilities and facilities of the new language. We, along with many of our colleagues at IBM and other AS/400 educators, have devoted a considerable portion of our working lives over the year or so to trying to meet this demand. From writing magazine articles to presenting at user group meetings and conferences, we have tried to help quench the thirst for knowledge. Now, as RPG IV becomes available to more and more AS/400 users when they move to V3R1, that demand is skyrocketing.

One piece missing from the educational puzzle has been a guide to complete RPG IV language. With this book, George and Shailan fill that gap. No matter what aspect of the language interests you, you'll find the answers here. From understanding how D(efinition) specs let you define tables and arrays, you'll find it all here, clearly explained in George and Shailan's usual straightforward manner.

If you've been lucky enough to catch George in one of his public speaking engagements, or have read some of his earlier writings, you'll already be familiar with his ability to explain the complex in a straightforward manner. If you haven't been so lucky, you're in for a real treat. Read and enjoy.

Jon Paris and Susan Gantner
Technical Associates
AS/400 AD Marketing Support
IBM Toronto Laboratory

About the Authors

George Farr joined the IBM Toronto Laboratory in 1985 and worked with the RPG development team for seven years. As part of this team, he developed many functions, including release 3.0 string support. After spending a year with the AS/400 languages architecture and planning team, George joined the visual development organization as the compiler development team leader for the first release of VRPG. Since the start of the second release of VRPG (V3R6), he has been the VRPG development manager.

George has a specialized honors degree in computer science from York University in Toronto. He is a frequent speaker at COMMON, at other conferences, and at user groups. He has published numerous articles on the subject of AS/400 languages and environments, and he is the co-author of *ILE: A First Look*. George can be reached at gfarr@vnet.IBM.com

Shailan Topiwala worked for IBM for six years (from 1989 through 1995), first in development of the RPG and PL/I compilers for the AS/400; and then as a member of the development team responsible for VRPG, a client/server product designed for the OS/2 platform.

In 1995, Shailan left IBM to join InviTech Corporation of Toronto, a company focused on SAP and AS/400 systems. He is the accounts manager for the AS/400 and Visual Solutions team at InviTech.

Shailan holds a Bachelor's degree in mathematics from Saint Mary's University in Halifax, Nova Scotia, and a Master's degree in computer science from the Technical University of Nova Scotia where he completed thesis work specializing in pictorial languages. He is the co-author of *ILE: A First Look*. Shailan can be reached at sct@invitech.com.

Table of Contents

CHAPTER 1

Introduction

Over the years, RPG programmers have been asking for many changes to the language. These requests have ranged from increasing the size of field names to having free-form specifications. In response, IBM has continuously been enhancing the language since its inception. For example, named constants became available with Version 1 Release 2 (V1R2) and string operation codes and initialization support arrived with V1R3. In addition, V1 and V2 provided several structured operation codes.

Even with all these enhancements, more improvement was necessary. However, the way RPG was defined made more enhancements difficult. RPG was reaching the end of its life, and the only way to revive it was to re-examine the language definition. These considerations led from RPG III to the development of the Integrated Language Environment (ILE) and ILE RPG IV.

RPG IV includes such changes as specifications that are new, redefined, eliminated, and changed in function. Also, mixing uppercase and lowercase characters is allowed. New operation codes in RPG IV, operation code extenders, and free-form expressions are further changes. Other changes include extended keyword support, the ability to continue specifications over multiple lines and to indent lines to show structure, additional data types, built-in functions, ILE source types, and other ILE enhancements. The following table summarizes the main changes from RPG III to RPG IV.

Summary of Changes in RPG IV

Specification Changes
    Elimination of E-specifications and L-specifications
    Addition of Definition specifications
    Addition of keywords to H- and F-specifications
    Elimination of File-continuation specifications
    Alteration of C specifications to allow fixed-form and free-form calculations
    Expansion of columns to accommodate new length limits and sizes

Acceptability of mixed uppercase and lowercase in source code

Inclusion of new operation code functions
    Acceptability of longer field names for readability
    Introduction of operation code extenders

Introduction of new operation codes

Introduction of free-form expressions

Extension of keyword support

Acceptability of continuation from one line to the next

CONTINUED

Summary of Changes in RPG IV

Acceptability of indentation
Introduction of new data types
        Pointers
        Date
        Time
        Timestamp
Introduction of built-in functions
Introduction of new source types
Integration in ILE
Provision of two types of program calls
        CALL
        CALLB

RPG III Versus RPG IV Specifications

For an overview of specification differences between RPG III and RPG IV, you can begin by comparing the specifications of the two versions. The table below lists the RPG III and RPG IV specifications. On the left are the familiar specifications. The right side lists the RPG IV specifications.

RPG III Specification Types	RPG IV Specification Types
Header specifications (H-specs)	Header specifications (H-specs)
File specifications (F-specs)	File specifications (F-specs)
Extension specifications (E-specs)	Definition specifications (D-specs)
Line specifications (L-specs)	
Input specifications (I-specs)	Input specifications (I-specs)
Calculation specifications (C-specs)	Calculation specifications (C-specs)
Output specifications (O-specs)	Output specifications (O-specs)

RPG IV eliminates E- and L-specs. All functions that you previously coded on these specs are now in other specifications. For example, you previously defined an array on the E-specs. This function is now part of the D-specs. In RPG III, L-specs identify the name of the printer file, the number of lines per page, and the overflow line number for program-defined printer files. In addition, the L-specs provide values for the lines per page, forms length, overflow line number, and overflow line for a specific printer file. In contrast, RPG IV keywords provide all these values. With the E- and L-specifications dropped, the new order of the RPG IV specifications is

1. H-specs (control specification)
2. F-specs
3. D-specs
4. I-specs
5. C-specs
6. O-specs
7. ** records
   File translation records
   Alternate collating sequence records
   Compile-time array or table data

EXPANDED LIMITS

One important change in RPG IV is new specification limits. RPG IV allows larger size limits for names, the number of files and subroutines, and the size of fields. The table below compares the limits between RPG III and RPG IV.

	RPG III Limits	RPG IV Limits
Length of names, including file, field, data structure, and array names	6	10
Length of record format names	8	10
Number of files allowed in a program	50	no limit
Number of subroutines allowed in a program	256	no limit
Size of character fields	256	32767
Number of decimal places	9	30
Size of data structure	9999	32767
Number of array elements	9999	32767
Size of named constant	256	no limit

UPPERCASE AND LOWERCASE SPECIFICATIONS AND VALID CHARACTERS

Unlike RPG III, RPG IV accepts specifications in mixed case, which means the compiler's first task on its first pass is to convert all the specifications to uppercase. So, if source contains a field name CUSTNO, CustNo, or custno, the compiler will turn the name into uppercase, CUSTNO, and all three variations will refer to the same field and the same storage location.

RPG IV increases the number of valid characters for symbolic names. For example, in RPG IV you can define a name with a dollar sign ($) or an underscore. These characters were not valid in the past. The valid character set for RPG IV symbolic names is

- the uppercase alphabet letters, A B C D E F G H I J K L M N O P Q R S T U V W X Y Z

- the lowercase alphabet letters (RPG IV translates them to uppercase during compilation)
- the numbers 0 1 2 3 4 5 6 7 8 9
- the characters $ # @ _ %

RPG IV has several rules for defining symbolic names (such as field and data structure names).

1. The first character of the name must be alphabetic (including the characters $, #, and @).

2. The remaining characters must be alphabetic or numeric (including the underscore character).

3. The name must be entered left adjusted on the specification, except in specifications (such as D-specs) that allow the name to float within the defined name specification positions..

4. The name cannot be an RPG IV special word.

5. The symbolic name can be 1 to 10 characters long.

6. The symbolic name must be unique in a program.

OPERATION CODES AND OPERATION CODE EXTENDERS

Because of the new lengths that RPG IV allows, operation code names have changed from the abbreviated RPG III version. You can now spell out the full name of most operations. This innovation adds to the readability of RPG code, but it means changing some old habits if you're an RPG III programmer. The table below lists the old and new operation code names.

RPG III	RPG IV
BITOF	BITOFF
CHEKR	CHECKR
COMIT	COMMIT
DEFN	DEFINE
DELET	DELETE
EXCPT	EXCEPT
LOKUP	LOOKUP
OCCUR	OCCUR
REDPE	READPE
RETRN	RETURN
SELEC	SELECT
SETOF	SETOFF
UNLCK	UNLOCK
UPDAT	UPDATE
WHxx	WHENxx

Note that the RPG IV compiler will accept only the new names. Do not use the old RPG III names for these operations, or the compiler will flag the old name with a syntax error.

Operation Code Extender

In addition to renaming operation codes, RPG IV introduces a new concept: the operation code extender, which provides additional information about an operation. The operation code extender adds function to an operation. In RPG III, column 53 is overloaded with options such as P for padding and N for no-locking on reads. To eliminate this overloading, RPG IV lets you specify an operation code extender after the operation code. For example, you can now code READ(N), the operation code with the N (No lock) extender, to read a record from an update file without locking the record for update. Certain operations, such as DIV (Divide) and CAT (Concatenate), support operation code extenders. The following table lists the operation code extenders and the operations that you can use them with.

Extender	Explanation	Valid Operation Codes
H	Half adjust	Arithmetic operations: ADD, DIV, EVAL, MULT, SQRT, SUB, XFOOT, Z-ADD, and Z-SUB
N	No lock	Input/Output operations: READ, READE, READP, READPE, and CHAIN
P	Pad	Character operations: CAT, MOVE, MOVEA, MOVEL, SUBST, and XLATE
D	Test for date field	Operational descriptor: CALLB and TEST
T	Test for time field	Operational descriptor: TEST
Z	Test for timestamp field	Operational descriptor: TEST

The operation code extender must appear to the right of the operation code and is enclosed in parentheses. Blanks between the operation code and the operation code extender are allowed but not required.

KEYWORDS

A major innovation in RPG IV is the availability of keywords to perform functions that require coding in RPG III. Not only do keywords simplify programming, but they will also be a vehicle for future enhancements to the language, so you'll want to pay attention to them.

RPG IV keywords, which you can specify in the H-, F,- and D-specs, are similar to DDS keywords. To specify an RPG IV keyword, you enter the keyword in the keyword section of the specification, followed immediately by parentheses enclosing the keyword's parameters. When you have multiple parameters for a keyword, you separate them by colons.

Continuation

RPG IV has enhanced the ability to continue specifications over more than one line. You can enter a plus sign or a hyphen to continue a literal to the next line. In addition, you can continue the extended Factor 2 on the C-specs and constants/edit word fields on O-specs. You do not need continuation characters with keywords on H-, F-, and D-specs or on continued C-spec-extended Factor 2 entries for the new free-form expressions.

Indentation

Indentation support has been available since V2 and is carried over with RPG IV. You specify indentation using the *INDENT parameter on the CL create commands for compiling RPG source. The default is *NONE (No indentation). The following screen illustrates the use of this parameter with the CRTBNDRPG (Create Bound RPG Program) command.

```
                   Create Bound RPG Program (CRTBNDRPG)

  Type choices, press Enter.

  Optimization level . . . . . . .    *NONE        *NONE, *BASIC, *FULL
  Source listing indentation . . .    ' | '        Character value, *NONE
  Type conversion options  . . . .    *NONE        *NONE, *DATETIME, *GRAPHIC...
                  + for more values
  Sort sequence  . . . . . . . . .    *HEX         Name, *HEX, *JOB, *JOBRUN...
    Library  . . . . . . . . . . .                 Name, *LIBL, *CURLIB
  Language identifier  . . . . . .    *JOBRUN      *JOB, *JOBRUN...
  Replace program  . . . . . . . .    *YES         *YES, *NO
  User profile . . . . . . . . . .    *USER        *USER, *OWNER
  Authority  . . . . . . . . . . .    *LIBCRTAUT   Name, *LIBCRTAUT, *ALL...
  Truncate numeric . . . . . . . .    *YES         *YES, *NO
  Fix numeric  . . . . . . . . . .    *NONE        *NONE, *ZONED
  Target release . . . . . . . . .    *CURRENT     *CURRENT, V3R1M0
  Allow null values  . . . . . . .    *NO          *NO, *YES
```

RPG lets you select the character to denote continuation in structured operation clauses. You can select any character string up to two characters long. If you use a blank character, you must enclose the string with quotation marks. This example uses the bar character (|) to specify indentation. All structured constructs, such as IF and loop constructs, will use this character to line up the start and end of each construct. This character will appear in the source listing to show the program's structure.

The program fragment below uses the | option on the indent parameter. The DOU / ENDDO construct has the | to line up the start and end and improve readability and maintainability.

```
*...1....+....2....+....3....+....4....+....5....+....6....+....7....+
C        KEYS         KLIST
C                     KFLD                         FIRSTK
C                     KFLD                         SECONDK
C*****
C                     EXCEPT    HEADING
C                     DOW       NOT *IN55 AND NOT *IN12
C                     |MOVE     FIRST       FIRSTK
C                     |MOVE     LAST        SECONDK
C        KEYS         |SETLL    DBKEYS
C                     |READ     DBKEYS
C   N55               |EXFMT    CUSTINFO
C                     |EXCEPT
C                     ENDDO
C                     EXCEPT    FEEDBACK1
C                     EXCEPT    FEEDBACK2
```

Note that any indentation that you see in source code will not be reflected in the listing debug view, which you create by specifying DBGVIEW(*LIST). Also note that the indentation may not appear as expected if errors occur in the program.

NEW DATA TYPES

RPG III has four data types: binary, packed, zoned, and character. In addition to these data types, RPG IV adds date, time, timestamp, and pointers. The date, time, and timestamp types let you manipulate dates and times. For example, you can calculate durations easily.

One new data type that requires some immediate explanation is the pointer data type. A pointer's value represents an address in memory for a particular structure, function, program, register, or field. As a field of type character contains a character value and a field of type numeric contains a numeric value, a structure of type pointer contains an address as its value. The pointer data type includes the basing pointer and the procedure pointer.

BUILT-IN FUNCTIONS

Built-in functions (BIFs) are also new in RPG IV. You use a BIF as part of a free-form expression to get a value. BIFs are similar to operation codes in that they perform operations on data you specify. Unlike operation codes, however, BIFs return a value for the expression to use, rather than placing a value into a Result field. All BIFs have the percent symbol (%) as their first character.

As an example, instead of issuing the SUBST (Substring) operation code to retrieve a substring and then an IF construct to compare the extracted string, you can enter a free-form expression and %SUBST on an IF operation code. You see how this approach works in the following fragment.

```
*...1....+....2....+....3....+....4....+....5....+....6....+....7....+
C                IF        %SUBSTR(NAME:1:20)='GEORGE FARR'
```

%SUBST is only one BIF available in RPG IV. Others include %ADDR (to retrieve the address of a field) and %INDEX (to change the index of a table or a multiple-occurrence data structure). The table below lists all the built-in functions in RPG IV.

Name	Description
%ADDR	Address of a variable
%ELEM	Number of elements or occurrences
%PADDR	Address of a procedure
%SIZE	Size of variable or literal
%SUBST	Substring (similar to SUBST opcode)
%TRIM	Trim leading and trailing blanks from string
%TRIML	Trim leading (left) blanks from string
%TRIMR	Trim trailing (right) blanks from string

CALL AND CALLB

In RPG III only one type of call is available, and you specify it with the CALL operation code. CALL lets an RPG program execute a different program object and return to the calling program after the called program is finished.

This type of call is a dynamic call, which means that the system finds the called program at runtime. With this type of call, the program being called does not have to exist at compile time. The called program has to be in your library only at runtime, when the program starts executing. This type of call is expensive because all program resolution has to happen at runtime, which affects performance.

ILE RPG IV institutes a new type of call, the bound call, with the CALLB (Call Bound) operation code. CALLB lets you execute a function or procedure that is bound (compiled) into the application that issues CALLB. It is available only in ILE programs that you compile by means of the CRTPGM (Create Program) or CRTSRVPGM (Create Service Program) command and that have more than one module object bound into them. The type of call that CALLB performs is "static calling." That is, CALLB references procedures that are linked, or bound, into the executing application.

RPG IV Specifications

RPG IV is still specification based and has six specifications for coding different parts of the program. The Header specification (H-spec) lets you define global information, such as date formats and compile options, that pertains to the entire program. The File specification (F-spec) declares the database, display, and printer files that the program will process. The Data Definition specification (D-spec) describes the program's data, including standalone fields, data structures, and arrays. Calculation specifications (C-specs) are where you define all the calculations and processing that must occur. The Input specifications (I-specs) let you define the layout of program-described files and override external data definitions. The Output specification (O-spec) defines the output's appearance, including the positioning of data on a report and the layout of files that the program defines.

The RPG compiler takes the information you code on the various specifications and builds a program that the program cycle processes. The RPG cycle determines the processing flow for reading records from the files you declare on F-specs or define on I-specs, incorporating data you define on the D-specs, performing the calculations you code in the C-specs, and outputing what you define on the O-specs. In RPG's early years, programmers had to spend a good deal of intellectual energy on understanding how the cycle functions.

Modern iterations of the language, and especially RPG IV, however, take much of the control of the program flow out of the RPG cycle and put it in your hands. This book will mention the RPG cycle seldom. Good RPG programming technique uses the F-, I-, D-, and O-specs to define information essential to your program but keeps control of the processing flow in the C-specs.

RPG has always been a fixed-form, positional language. Each specification has a fixed layout with defined positions for each entry. For example, on the F-spec you enter the file name in positions 7 through 16, the file type in position 17, and the file designation in position 18. RPG IV retains this structure but adds some free-form expressions and keywords to simplify coding, to add function, and to facilitate structured programming technique. The discussion of each specification will point out where you can use these new facilities.

The Header Specification

In RPG IV, the Header specifications (H-specs) provide general information about the program. Here, you specify such entries as the program's name and default formats for dates and times.

To enter H-specs, as with all RPG specifications, you can put a sequence number in positions 1 through 5 to identify each line of code. Then, the first coding entry goes in the sixth position to tell the compiler the type of specification that follows. For an H-spec, you must put an H in position 6. You cannot code comments in positions 7 through 80, the *non-commentary* portion of the

H-specs, unless you code an asterisk in position 7. Otherwise, RPG IV reserves positions 7 through 80 for H-spec keywords. The *commentary* portion, where you can enter documentation comments, spans from position 81 through 100. Here's a summary of H-spec entries.

Position	Description
1-5	Sequence number
6	Specification type: H
7-80	Free-form keywords
81-100	Comments

The H-specs are free form and keyword driven. In fact, H-specs are the first and only RPG IV specifications that are free form and keyword driven. Whereas you previously had to specify each option in a designated position, you now use new keywords with parameter values. Here is a sample H-spec.

```
*...1....+....2....+....3....+....4....+....5....+....6....+....7....+
H DFTNAME(ITEMLIST) TIMFMT(*ISO)
```

Limiting H-spec entries to keywords makes RPG IV H-specs easy to read and easy to specify. The DFTNAME (Default Name) keyword specifies a parameter value of ITEMLIST, which gives this program its name. The TIMFMT (Time Format) keyword's *ISO parameter value determines that the program's time format is the International Standards Organization (ISO) format. Notice that you can put more than one keyword on a line, or you can code multiple H-spec lines to improve readability. The table below lists and describes all H-spec keywords and their parameters.

Header-Specification Keywords

Keyword	Parameters	Description
ALTSEQ	*NONE, *SRC, *EXT	Specifies a collating sequence. The default is *NONE.
CURSYM	'sym'	Specifies a character to use as the currency symbol in editing. The symbol must be a single character enclosed in quotes. All characters are valid except 0, *, period, comma, &, –, C, R, and blank.
DATEDIT	Format{separator}	Specifies the format of numeric fields when the Y edit code is used.
DATFMT	Format{separator}	Specifies the date format for date literals and default formats for date fields.
DEBUG	*YES, *NO	*YES causes a DUMP operation.
DECEDIT	'value'	Specifies the character to use as the decimal point for edited decimal numbers. The possible values are period, comma, '0.', and '0,'

CONTINUED

Keyword	Parameters	Description
DFTNAME	program name	Specifies the default program or module name.
FORMSALIGN	*YES, *NO	Lets you repeatedly print the first line of an output file conditioned with the 1P indicator, allowing you to align the printer.
FTRANS	*NONE, *SRC	Performs file translation if specified with *SRC, and translation table must be specified in the program.

Specifying H-Spec Information in a Data Area

You can supply the information from the H-spec to the compiler through a data area. Using a data area means that you can have a default source for header information, for example. All RPG IV programs can use the same H-specs, so you don't have to specify the same information for every program you write. In addition, putting header information in a data area reduces the overhead associated with creating an H-spec in each member.

The compiler searches for H-spec information in a particular order. First, the compiler looks in the source file being compiled. Then, the compiler tries to find a data area named RPGLEHSPEC in any library on your library list (*LIBL). Finally, the compiler looks for a data area named DFTLEHSPEC in QRPGLE.

To create a data area to store H-specs, you use the OS/400 CRTDTAARA (Create Data Area) command. This sample code illustrates how to specify this command to create the data area ALLPGM in library FARR. This example specifies the DECEDIT (Decimal Edit) keyword with a period as the decimal point character for the program.

```
CRTDTAARA   DTAARA(FARR/RPGLEHSPEC)               +
               TYPE(*CHAR)                        +
               LEN(50)                            +
               VALUE('DECEDIT('.')'               +
               TEXT('default H specification for my program')
```

The File Specification

RPG IV File specifications (F-specs) are where you declare to your program the data files and device files that the program will use. F-specs provide such information as the file name, whether the file is externally described or program-described, record length, whether the file is input or output, any sequencing, and whether a file is a device file and what type of device file it is. The F-spec is an RPG IV specification that is partially fixed form and partially free form (Keywords provide some F-spec information).

To identify an F-spec, you enter an F in position 6. Positions 7 through 80 are the noncommentary portion of this specification. The commentary portion is from position 81 through 100. Positions 44 through 80 on the F-spec are the keyword positions. If you run out of room to enter keywords on one line, you can continue on the next F-spec line by entering a keyword in the keyword section, starting at position 44. The following table lists all the positional entries for F-specs.

Position	Description
1-5	Sequence number
6	Form type
7-16	File name
17	File type I - Input file O - Output file U - Update file C - Combined file for input and output
18	File designation Blank - Output file P - Primary file S - Secondary file R - Record address file T - Array or table file
19	End of file (E)
20	File addition Blank - No additions allowed A - Allow addition
21	Sequence A/blank - Match fields are ascending or descending D - Match fields are descending
22	File format E - Externally described file F - Program described file
23-27	File record length
28	Limit processing L - Sequential within limits Blank - Sequential or random processing
29-33	Length of key or record address
34	Record address type A - Character P - Packed G - Graphic K - Key values are used to process the file D - Date keys T - Time keys Z - Timestamp keys
35	File organization I - Indexed file T - Record address file

CONTINUED

Position	Description
36-42	Device type
	DISK, PRINTER, WORKSTN, SPECIAL, SEQ
43	Reserved
44-80	Keywords

The sample code below shows how to specify F-specs to declare files. This example declares two files — an externally described database file, ItemMast, and a program-defined printer file, QPrint. The F-spec demonstrates both fixed-format and free-format file declaration. The I in position 17 on line 02 declares this file as an input file, and the O in position 17 on line 03 declares the printer file as output. The E and the F in position 22 declare these files as externally (free format) and program-defined (fixed format), respectively.

```
*...1....+....2....+....3....+....4....+....5....+....6....+....7....+
FItemMast  IF   E           K DISK
FQPrint    O    F    8Ø        PRINTER OFLIND(*INOF)
```

In addition to the positional entries on these F-specs, you see a free-form keyword. OFLIND(*INOF) defines the indicator that will be turned on when the printer file encounters the overflow line for the form. A complete list of keywords for F-specs follows.

File-Specification Keywords

Keyword	Parameters	Explanation
COMMIT	RPG-Name	Lets you process the file under commitment control
DATFMT	Format {Separator}	Gives the F-spec a default date format
DEVID	Fieldname	Specifies the name of the program device that supplied the record processed in the file
EXTIND	*INUx	Determines that the file is a candidate for OPEN only if the external indicator is set in the job
FORMLEN	number	Indicates the form length for a printer file
FORMOFL	number	Specifies the overflow line number
IGNORE	record-format	Lets the program ignore a record format from an externally described file
INCLUDE	record-format	Lets you include the record formats you list as parameters of this keyword
INFDS	data-structure-name	Gives a data structure name to associate with the file for feedback information
INFSR	subroutine-name	Names a subroutine to take control in case of an exception/error during file processing
KEYLOC	number	Gives the start position of the key in a program-described file

Continued

Keyword	Parameters	Explanation
MAXDEV	*ONLYI*FILE	Specifies the maximum number of devices for a WORKSTN file
OVFIND	*INxx	Determines which lines in a printer file will print when overflow occurs
PASS	*NOIND	Lets the program take responsibility for passing indicators on input and output
PGMNAME	program-name	Specifies the program name
PLIST	PLIST-name	Names the parameter list to pass to the program for a special file
PREFIX	prefix-name	Lets you prefix a character to the names of all fields defined in all records of the file specified in positions 7 through 16
PRTCTL	Data structure{:*COMPAT}	Specifies the use of dynamic printer control
RAFDATA	file-name	Names the input or update file that contains the data records to process
RECNO	field-name	Specifies processing by relative record number
RENAME	DDS-name:new-name	Lets you rename record formats used within this program
SAVEDS	data-structure-name	Lets you save and restore a data structure for the file
SAVEIND	number	Saves and restores indicators 01 to the number you specify here for each device
SFILE	record-format:RRN field	Lets you define the subfiles to use in the file
SLN	number	Determines where a record format is written to the display
TIMFMT	format{separator}	Allows a default time format for this specification
USROPN	no parameter	Specifies that you will use the OPEN operation to open the file explicitly

Most F-spec entries are easy to understand. One entry, however, requires some explanation. The file designation entry (position 18) tells the RPG IV compiler how to process the file you are declaring. The file designation determines whether RPG's program cycle or the C-specs you provide will process that file. An F in position 18 tells the RPG compiler that this data file is designed as *full procedural* and not to let the RPG cycle process it. When you define a file as full procedural, the program will handle the reading and writing of the file explicitly.

The RPG program cycle has many complexities that are not pertinent here, but note that the cycle is not a conventional construct. It can hinder readability, and the cycle requires coding practices that result in unclear logic and logic constructs that other languages cannot easily accommodate. In other words, RPG's cycle is a part of the language that you need to avoid.

RPG IV provides looping structures in the C-specs that produce more readable and maintainable programs than programs that depend on the RPG cycle. RPG's looping structures replace the cycle for file processing. In contrast to the RPG cycle, these loop structures allow logic that is easy to read, follow, and maintain.

The Definition Specification

The new RPG IV Definition specification (D-spec) lets you define named constants, standalone fields, data structures, data structure subfields, arrays, and tables and specify data type. You identify a D-spec by entering a D in position 6. A D-spec consists of two basic sections: fixed-form entry (positions 7 through 42) and free-form keyword entry (positions 44 through 80). The following table lists all D-spec positional entries.

D-Spec Positional Entries

Position	Description	Entries
7 - 21	Name	**Valid RPG name** (no reserved words or figurative constants) of data structure, data structure subfield, standalone field, or constant. Note that the name's start position is irrelevant as long as the name does not extend beyond position 21 of the specification
		Blanks for unnamed storage for a filler subfield in a data structure definition or an unnamed data structure
22	External Description	**Blank** if the data structure or data structure subfield is not externally described, but it is program described
		E if this D-spec is declaring a data structure or data structure subfield that is externally described. Note that for data structure subfields, an E in position 22 means that the subfield you're defining is externally described
23	Data Structure Type	**S** for a program status data structure
		U for a data area data structure
		Blank for a user-defined data structure
24	Definition Type	**C** to define a named constant
		S to define a scalar field, array, or table (with S, a valid RPG data type and a length entry are required)
24 - 25	Definition Type	**Blanks** to define a data structure subfield
		DS to define a data structure of any type
26 - 32	From Position	**Blank** to define a subfield by length only (the length will be in positions 33 through 39)
		Numeric literal to define the start position of a data structure subfield (value must be from 1K to 32K for a named data structure and 1K to 9,999,999K for an unnamed data structure; right justified; no decimal points or positions)

CONTINUED

Position	Description	Entries
		RPG reserved word (left justified) For a program status data structure: *STATUS, *PROC, *PARM, *ROUTINE For a file information data structure: *FILE, *RECORD, *OPCODE, *STATUS, *ROUTINE
33 - 39	To Position	**Blank** to define a named constant a standalone field or subfield that has an implied length a standalone field or subfield containing the LIKE D-spec keyword a subfield that is defined elsewhere a data structure
		Unsigned numeric literal to define a named data structure (enter a value between 1 and 32,767, right justified) an unnamed data structure (enter a value between 1 an 9,999,999) Signed numeric literal to create a definition using the LIKE keyword (if the value is negative, the length value will be deducted from the size of the field given as a parameter for the LIKE keyword. If the value is positive, it will be added to the size of the field you specify with LIKE)
		Reserved word
40	Internal Data Type	**Blank** to define a program field definition that is LIKE that of another program field in the same RPG program a data type numeric definition a data type character definition **A** to define data type character **G** to define data type graphic **T** to define data type time **D** to define data type date **Z** to define data type timestamp **P** to define numeric data type of packed decimal **B** to define numeric data type of binary **S** to define numeric data type of zoned decimal ***** to define data type basing pointer or procedure pointer
41 - 42	Decimal Positions	**Blank** to indicate a data type character field, or to indicate the LIKE keyword is present **Numeric value from 0 to 30** (positions 26 through 39 must also contain a value to provide the overall width of the numeric field you are defining)
43	Reserved	**Blank** is required for this IBM-reserved position
44 - 80	Keyword Entry	Valid D-spec keywords

D-Spec Keywords

Keywords are valid in D-specs in addition to the positional entries. The following table lists and explains all the D-spec keywords.

D-Spec Keywords

Keyword	Description	Parameters	Explanation
ALT	alternating array name	array-name	Defines a compile-time or pre-runtime array in alternating format. The array with which you specify ALT is the alternate array. Its method of loading is defined by the main array which you specify as the parameter of ALT. The two arrays are then loaded in alternating order, starting with the main array.
ASCEND	ascending sequence	no parameters	Specifies that any array or table element data stored for the array with which this keyword is specified will be stored in ascending sequence.
DESCEND	descending sequence	no parameters	Specifies that any array or table element data stored for the array with which this keyword is specified will be stored in descending order.
BASED	basing pointer	basing-pointer-name	Specifies a basing pointer.
CONST	constant	constant-value	Defines a named constant.
DTAARA	data area	data-area-name	References an external data area from within the RPG program by creating an association between that data area and a standalone field, data structure, or data structure subfield.
DATFMT	date format	format{separator}	Specifies the format and separator character for data type date fields.
DIM	dimension	number-of-elements	Specifies how many elements are in the array this D-spec is defining. The required number-of-elements parameter must be a previously defined numeric constant or literal. This value must be positive in sign and have zero decimal positions.
EXPORT & IMPORT	data structure export or import	no parameters	Let a program or module reference a field or data structure defined in a different source module. The D-spec containing the EXPORT keyword (the export definition) defines a field or data structure as available for use in a different program or module. The D-spec containing the IMPORT keyword defines the field or data structure as one that uses an export definition.
PREFIX	subfile prefix	prefix-string	Prepends the names of each subfield in an extracted data structure with a string given as PREFIX's parameter value. *CONTINUED*

Keyword	Description	Parameters	Explanation
EXTNAME	externally defined file	filename {format name}	Renames an entire external data structure.
EXTFLD	externally defined field	field-name	Renames a subfield contained in an externally described data structure.
EXTFMT	externally defined format	code	Lets you specify the external data type for compile-time and pre-runtime numeric arrays and tables.
FROMFILE	array from-file	file-name	Lets you specify the file with input data for the pre-runtime array or table being defined.
TOFILE	array to-file	file-name	Lets you specify a target file to which a pre-runtime or compile time array or table is to be written.
INZ	initialize	constant-value	Initializes a standalone field, data structure, or data structure subfield. The optional constant-value parameter value can be a literal, named constant, figurative constant, or built-in function. When you do not provide the parameter value, the compiler will initialize the field being defined to the default value for the internal data type (i.e., zeroes for data type numeric, blanks for character). Subfields of data structures are always initialized to blanks.
NOOPT	no optimization	no parameters	When used in the definition of a critical standalone field, data structure, or data structure subfield, ensures that the compiler's runtime always maintains the most recent data value for that field. Lets you use any data associated with a nonoptimized field during exception handling.
CTDATA	compile-time data	no parameter	Specifies that the array this D-spec is defining is a compile-time array, and its data is at the end of the source.
LIKE	like	RPG-field-name	The field being defined takes on the attributes and the length of the variable specified as a parameter.
OCCURS	occurs	numeric constant	The OCCURS keyword allows the specification of the number of occurrences of a multiple occurrence data structure.
OVERLAY	overlay	name {:position}	The keyword is allowed only for data structure subfields. The subfields overlays the storage of the subfield specified by the parameter name at the position specified by the parameter position. The default for position is 1.
PACKEVEN	pack even	no parameter	This keyword indicates that the packed field or array has an even number of digits. The

Continued

Keyword	Description	Parameters	Explanation
			keyword is only valid for packed program described data structure subfields defined using FROM/TO positions.
PERRCD	number of elements per record	numeric constant	This keyword allows you to specify the number of elements per record for a compile-time or pre-runtime array or table. If not specified the default is 1.
TIMFMT	time format	format {separator}	This keyword allows the specification of a time format, and optionally the time time separator for a standalone field or data-structure subfield of type time.

D-Specification Coding Example

Below, you see three examples of D-specs to define a named constant, a character field, and a packed-decimal numeric field. On each line, following the specification-identifying D in position 6, is the name of the item being defined. On the line defining CoName, you see a C in position 24, which means CoName is a named constant. The definition of CoName is completed with the keyword CONST (Constant) in positions 44 through 80 to initialize this named constant with a value of *'Books'*. The definition for Work makes this field a standalone character field of length 5. The INZ (Initialize) keyword gives this field an initial value of blanks. TaxRate is also a standalone field. Its length is 5. Its data type is packed decimal, and it has 4 decimal positions. The INZ keyword gives this field an initial value of 0.0725.

```
*...1....+....2....+....3....+....4....+....5....+....6....+....7....+
D CoName         C                   CONST('Books')
D Work           S                 5A  INZ(*BLANKS)
D TaxRate        S                 5P 4 INZ(.0725)
```

The Input Specification

Originally, the purpose of the Input-specs (I-specs) was to define the layout of fields in records and specify these fields' data types. However, the function of the I-specs expanded to include defining data structures and named constants and initializing fields. One of IBM's design goals for RPG IV was to eliminate the need to define data structures and named constants on the I-specs. Consequently, in RPG IV, data-structure and named-constant definition is in the new D-specs. RPG IV I-specs are solely for defining the layout of program-described files and for overriding specifications of externally described data. If you never use program-described database files, you will never need I-specs for defining them. This is the preferred way to program.

The other uses for I-specs are almost as out of date as program-described files. In the I-specs, you can rename database fields that come from externally described files, but a much better way to ensure unique field names is to use RPG's prefix capability when you define the file in the F-specs. Another reason some programmers use I-specs with externally described files is to define level breaks based on fields that come from the externally described file. This programming method is outdated, and you will want to handle such situations with structured programming constructs in the C-specs. The remaining reason for possibly including I-specs in a program is the questionable practice of using multi-format logical files. Most programmers will agree that this technique is not a good programming solution.

Because of the limited use for I-specs and because program-described files are bad programming practice, this book does not cover the I-specs in depth. However, if you are maintaining *someone else's* RPG IV program with program-described files, you will need to know what the specifications look like. These tables show I-spec positional entries.

I-Specs for Program-Described Files	
Position	**Description**
Record Identification Entries	
6	I
7-16	File name
16-18	Logical relationship
17-18	Sequence
19	Number
20	Option
21-22	Record identifying indicator
23-46	Record identification codes
47-80	Reserved
Field Description Entries	
6	I
7-30	Reserved
31-34	Date/Time external format
35	Date/Time separator
36	Date format
37-46	Field location
47-48	Decimal positions
49-62	Field name
63-64	Control level
65-66	Matching fields
67-68	Field record relation
69-74	Field indicators
75-80	Reserved

I-Specs for Externally Described Files	
Position	**Description**
Record Identification Entries	
6	I
7-16	File name
17-20	Reserved
21-22	Record identifying indicator
23-80	Reserved
Field Description Entries	
6	I
7-20	Reserved
21-30	External file name
31-48	Reserved
49-62	Field name
63-64	Control level
65-66	Matching fields
67-68	Reserved
69-74	Field indicators
75-80	Reserved

The Calculation Specification

Calculation specifications (C-specs) contain the instructions you want executed to accomplish the tasks that your program must complete. These tasks include reading records, performing arithmetic calculations, manipulating data, writing information to a database, and processing display files. The C-specs are where IBM has most significantly enhanced RPG.

To identify a C-spec, you enter a C in position 6. Positions 7 through 80 are the noncommentary portion of this specification. The commentary area is in positions 81 through 100.

C-specs are now a combination of fixed-form and free-form entries. The free-form entries are new to RPG IV. The free-form entries let you write expressions like those that most programming languages include and thus make RPG both easier to use and more universally understandable than before. The fixed-form entries are in the following table.

Fixed-Form C-Spec Positional Entries

Position	Description	Entries
6	Spec. definition	**C**
7-8	Control-level indicators	**blank** The specification will execute at detail calculation time for every program cycle if the condition specified in positions 9 through 11 is satisfied, or if this specification is part of a subroutine.
		L0 The specification will be performed at total calculation time for every program cycle.
		L1 - L9 When an indicator L1 through L9 is specified, the operation code in the same specification will execute at total calculation time if the specified indicator is on. A level break or an input or output operation sets on the L1 through L9 indicators.
		LR When the LR indicator is a control-level indicator, the C-spec will execute during the last calculation time of the RPG program cycle.
		SR Only for documentation within a subroutine. Subroutine specifications must follow total calculation specifications.
		And/or Creates complex indicator test conditions, with positions 9 through 11. Positions 7 and 8 of a specification that precedes an AND/OR specification applies to all the AND/OR specifications that follow.
9-11	Conditioning indicators	**Blank** The C-spec will be processed unconditionally.
		01 - 99 Useful in simulating IF-THEN-ELSE structures.
		KA - KN and KP - KY Function key indicators that you can use as condition indicators for display and workstation files.
		L1 - L9 Control-level indicators that you can set on via an input or output operation or, a level break.
		LR The last-record indicator can cause the C-spec to be performed at total calculation time.

CONTINUED

Position	Description	Entries
		MR Allowed if one or more of the M1 through M9 indicators are defined for the primary, and at least one secondary, file in the program.
		H1 - H9 Halt indicators cause the particular C-spec to be executed, if it will be encountered by the compiler's runtime before the *GETIN step of the program cycle.
		RT The return indicator can condition C-specs and will signal to the compiler's runtime that program execution needs to return to the calling program. This test for the RT indicator occurs after the check for the LR indicator but before the program cycle processing the next record. Note that the RT indicator will be set off when the RPG program is called again.
		U1 - U8 The external indicators are accessible in CL programs and RPG IV programs.
		OA-OG, OV The overflow indicators are defined by the OFLIND keyword on an F-spec and are set on whenever the last line on a page of output has been printed or passed via line feed.
12-25	Factor 1	**Field name** The value of the specified field (which you must declare on a D-spec in the same program) can provide a value for an operation. The field's value is not affected by the operation.
26-35	Operation code	**Operation Code** The name of operation to be done using Factor 1, Factor 2, and the Result field entries. Operation code extender
		Blank No operation code extender is specified
		H Half adjust, or rounding, will be applied to the result of the operation
		N For input operations, the record will be read but not locked. For disk files defined as UPDATE, the N operation code extender is allowed with READ, READE, READP, READPE, and CHAIN
		P Useful in data type character operations, where the result will be padded with blanks
		D Signifies an operational descriptor or field of data type date. The compiler will assume that the D operation code extender signifies that operational descriptors have been used whenever this extender appears with a CALLB operation code. Otherwise, the D will signify a data type date field and can be specified with the TEST operation code
		T Signifies a field of data type time and can be specified with a TEST operation code
		Z Signifies a field of data type timestamp and can be specified with a TEST
36-49	Factor 2	**Field name** The value of the specified field (which you must declare on a D-spec in the same program) can provide a value for an operation. The field's value is not affected by the operation.
50-63	Result field	**Field Name** The specified field is usually the target of an operation, or the field in which an operation's result is stored. This field's content usually changes as a result of the operation. For this reason, the Result field cannot be a figurative constant, literal, or named constant, as these

CONTINUED

Position	Description	Entries
		are all read-only. As with Factors 1 and 2, the Result field's type and value depend on the operation code requiring it. The field name you specify in the Result field must begin in position 50.
64-68	Field Length	**Field Length** You can use positions 64 through 68 and 69 through 70 to define a field on the fly within your RPG program. Note that you cannot define Factors 1 and 2 on a C-spec. That is, the field length and decimal positions fields can define only a result field. For data type numeric definition, the field length is required and must be between 1 and 30, and the field must be as long as or longer than the decimal positions specified in positions 69 and 70.
69-70	Decimal positions	**Dec. Positions** When the decimal positions are blank and you supply a field length, the compiler will assume the data type is character. In this case, the field length may range from 1 to 32,767.
71-76	Resulting	**Blank** No resulting indicator is required or provided.
		01 - 99 General RPG IV program indicators.
		KA - KN and KP - KY Function key indicators for files of type WORKSTN or DEVICE.
		H1 - H9 Halt indicators can be specified as resulting indicators and, once set on, will terminate the program.
		L1 - L9 Control level indicators, usually used with an input or output operation or a level break.
		LR Stops iteration of the RPG program cycle.
		RT Can be used as a resulting indicator and, if set on by the operation, will return program execution to the calling program. (Note that the RT indicator will be set off when the RPG program is called again.)
		U1 - U8 CL programs and other RPG IV programs can access the external indicators.
		OA-OG, OV Used with output operations and are set on to indicate that the last line on a page of output has been printed or passed via line feed. Overflow indicators are defined by the OFLIND keyword on a File-specification.

The fixed-form C-spec has nine parts: control-level indicators, conditioning indicators, Factor 1, Factor 2, the Result field, the operation code, the operation code extender, field definition (field length and decimal positions), and resulting indicators. The free-form C-spec has only four basic parts: control-level and conditioning indicators, operation codes, and operation code extenders. Free-form C-specs require fewer parts because you specify the necessary entries in the free-form Factor 2. The following table lists and explains the positional entries for free-form C-specs.

Free-Form C-Spec Positional Entries

Position	Description	Entries
6	Spec. definition	**C**
7-8	Control-level indicators	**blank** The specification will execute at detail calculation time for every program cycle if the condition specified in positions 9 through 11 is satisfied, or if this specification is part of a subroutine.
		L0 The specification will be performed at total calculation time for every program cycle.
		L1 - L9 When an indicator L1 through L9 is specified, the operation code in the same specification will execute at total calculation time if the specified indicator is on. A level break or an input or output operation sets on the L1 through L9 indicators.
		LR When the LR indicator is a control-level indicator, the C-spec will execute during the last calculation time of the RPG program cycle.
		SR Only for documentation within a subroutine. Subroutine specifications must follow total calculation specifications.
		And/or Creates complex indicator test conditions in conjunction with positions 9 through 11. Positions 7 and 8 of a specification that precedes an AND/OR specification applies to all the AND/OR specifications that follow.
9-11	Conditioning indicators	**Blank** The C-spec will be processed unconditionally.
		01 - 99 Useful in simulating IF-THEN-ELSE structures.
		KA - KN and KP - KY Function key indicators that you can use as condition indicators for display and workstation files.
		L1 - L9 Control-level indicators that you can set on via an input or output operation or, a level break.
		LR The last-record indicator can cause the C-spec to be performed at total calculation time.
		MR Allowed if one or more of the M1 through M9 indicators are defined for the primary, and at least one secondary, file in the program.
		H1 - H9 Halt indicators cause the particular C-spec to be executed, if it will be encountered by the compiler's runtime before the *GETIN step of the program cycle.
		RT The return indicator can condition C-specs and will signal to the compiler's runtime that program execution needs to return to the calling program. This test for the RT indicator occurs after the check for the LR indicator but before the program cycle processing the next record. Note that the RT indicator will be set off when the RPG program is called again.
		U1 - U8 The external indicators are accessible in CL programs and RPG IV programs.

CONTINUED

Position	Description	Entries
		OA-OG, OV The overflow indicators are defined by the OFLIND keyword on an F-spec and are set on whenever the last line on a page of output has been printed or passed via line feed.
12-25	Reserved	Factor 1 is not used in free-form C-specs
26-35	Operation code	**Operation Code** Free-form operations are limited to the DOU, DOW, EVAL, IF, and WHEN operation codes, which do not require Factor 1, and which have an extended Factor 2 field containing an expression. All these operation codes require a true/false or indicator expression, except EVAL, which requires a left side followed by an assignment operator, followed by a right side. EVAL accepts both indicator expressions and those that return other data types valid in RPG.
	Operation code extender	**Blank** No operation code extender is specified **H** Half adjust, or rounding, will be applied to the result of the operation
36-80	Extended Factor 2	Free-form expressions, assignments

C-Spec Coding Examples

To illustrate the difference between fixed-form C-specs with positional entries and free-form C-specs using expressions, let's look at two examples of code. The first clears the contents of a field, adds the contents of field B to the contents of field C, stores the result in field A, and then adds the value of field D to the result. To perform this calculation with fixed-form, positional C-specs, you need three operations: a Z-ADD (Zero and Add) and two ADDs.

```
*...1....+....2....+....3....+....4....+....5....+....6....+....7....+
C                   Z-ADD     *ZEROS        A
C        B          ADD       C             A
C                   ADD       D             A
```

The free-form construct to accomplish the same task uses the EVAL (Evaluate) operation code, which signals the compiler that Factor 2 contains a free-form expression. You specify EVAL in positions in positions 26 to 36 of the C-specs. The EVAL operation code lets you specify one expression to add the values of fields B, C, and D, and store the Result in field A.

```
*...1....+....2....+....3....+....4....+....5....+....6....+....7....+
C                   EVAL      A = B + C + D
```

The Output Specification

RPG IV Output specifications (O-specs) are where you specify the layout of reports you want to print and records you want to write. The most frequent use of O-specs is to specify and describe the record and the format of fields in a program-described print file. This use of the O-specs controls line spacing, placement of printed data, and formatting of numeric data.

Although the best way to define a printed report is to externally define it just as you externally define a database file, many AS/400 programmers still use less efficient and less flexible program-described printer files, so this book will discuss how O-specs work with program-described printed output. Nevertheless, we strongly urge you to stick with externally described printer files, which you output by means of the WRITE operation.

Each set of O-specs describes a single line of output. A set of O-specs is composed of one record-level O-spec with one or more subordinate field-level O-specs. For example, lines 40 through 44 are one output set. The record-level O-spec is where you identify the file to which the output belongs (that is, the printer file you named in the program's F-specs), the type of output (e.g., exception), any skipping and spacing information for that line, and the exception name. You can also use conditioning indicators to condition whether to print the record. On the field-level O-spec, you identify the field or literal you want to print. When you print a field, you can also apply formatting to numeric fields by entering either edit codes or edit words at the field level.

To identify an O-spec, you must enter an O in position 6. Positions 7 through 80 are the noncommentary portion of this specification. The commentary portion is from position 81 through 100.

O-Specs for Program-Described Output

Position	Description
Record-level positional entries	
6	O
7-16	File name
16-18	Logical relationship
17	Type
18-20	Record addition/deletion
18	Fetch overflow/release
21-29	Output conditioning indicators
30-39	Except name
40-42	Space before
43-45	Space after
46-48	Skip before
49-51	Skip after
52-80	Reserved

CONTINUED

Position	Description
Field-level positional entries	
6	O
7-20	Reserved
21-29	Output indicators
30-43	Field name
44	Edit code
45	Blank after
47-51	End position
52	Data format
59-80	Constant, edit word, date/time format, format name

Each field-level O-spec belongs to the last record-level O-spec. All field-level O-specs are in the same set until you start a new one by entering a new record-level O-spec or until processing reaches the end of the O-specs.

O-Spec Coding Example

Here is a sample O-spec set, showing both record-level and field-level O-specs for a program-described printer file.

The record-level specification defines this as an EXCEPT line that will be printed when the EXCEPT name HEADER is specified. The file name is QPRINT and the program will cause the printer to skip to line 3 before printing and space 2 lines after printing. The next three lines specify specific data that will be printed. The first two lines specify constant information to be printed. The third field-level line specifies the system date with a date edit code (Y).

```
*...1....+....2....+....3....+....4....+....5....+....6....+....7....+
OQPRINT     E           HEADER           1  3
O                                              17 'Program: ITEMLIST'
O                                              46 'Item Inventory'
O                       UDATE            Y     70
```

Several edit codes are available on the O-specs to control the format of the data. Chapter 12 will discuss all these codes and how to use them to create printer file output.

LOOKING AHEAD

This overview of RPG IV specifications prepares the way for examining all the features of this new version of the language. The following chapters will introduce and explore RPG IV. The topics will be data definition; database programming; arithmetic operation codes; move operation codes; indicators; structured operation codes; arrays and tables; string operation codes; date, time, and timestamp coding; workstation file processing; printing ILE; CALLS; and pointers.

CHAPTER 2

Indicators

Indicators are a special 1-byte, fixed-length, character data-type construct. An indicator can take a value of 0 or 1; they are switches that are *on* or *off*. Or, in computer science terminology, they are logical, or Boolean, variables that can take a value of true (on, or 1) or false (off, or 0).

Although indicators were once an indispensable way to control program flow, condition groups of calculations, define record types, control output, and check for errors, efficient programmers seldom use indicators any more. You can replace indicators with good structured programming techniques and constructs. However, indicators are unavoidable in some situations, so you need to know what types are available for what purposes, how to set indicators on and off, and what situations call for indicators. The prevalent ways to use an indicator are as a resulting indicator (positions 71 through 76 on the C-specs) for certain opcodes (Table 2.1 lists the opcodes that allow resulting indicators), as a conditioning indicator (in positions 10 and 11) to switch a process (such as displaying or printing a field) on or off in different situations, as a field-notation indicator (in positions 36 through 40) to condition some structured opcodes (such as IF), in DDS for communication with RPG programs, as exception indicators (in positions 73 through 74) to signal an error, as printer indicators to signal overflow, and as function key indicators.

TABLE 2.1

Operation Code	71-72	73-74	75-76	Operation Code	71-72	73-74	75-76
ACQ	N/A	Error	N/A	DIV	Plus	Minus	Zero
ADD	Plus	Minus	Zero	DSPLY	N/A	Error	N/A
ADDDUR	N/A	Error	N/A	EXFMT	N/A	Error	N/A
CABxx	High	Low	Equal	EXTRCT	N/A	Error	N/A
CALL	N/A	Error	LR	FEOD	N/A	Error	N/A
CALLB	N/A	Error	LR	IN	N/A	Error	N/A
CASxx	High	Low	Equal	LOOKUP	High	Low	Equal
CHAIN	No Rcd	Error	N/A	MOVE	Plus	Minus	Zero/Blank
CHECK	N/A	Error	Found	MOVEA	Plus	Minus	Zero/Blank
CHECKR	N/A	Error	Found	MOVEL	Plus	Minus	Zero/Blank
CLOSE	N/A	Error	N/A	MULT	Plus	Minus	Zero/Blank
COMMIT	N/A	Error	N/A	MVR	Plus	Minus	Zero
COMP	High	Low	Equal	NEXT	N/A	Error	N/A
DELETE	No Rcd	Error	N/A				

CONTINUED

TABLE 2.1 *CONTINUED*

Operation Code	71-72	73-74	75-76	Operation Code	71-72	73-74	75-76
OCCUR	N/A	Error	N/A	SETON	On	On	On
OPEN	N/A	Error	N/A	SHTDN	On	N/A	N/A
OUT	N/A	Error	N/A	SUB	Plus	Minus	Zero
POST	N/A	Error	N/A	SUBDUR	N/A	Error	N/A
READC	N/A	Error	End of File	SUBST	N/A	Error	N/A
READ	N/A	Error	End of File	TEST	N/A	Error	N/A
READE	N/A	Error	End of File	TESTB	Off	On	Equal
READP	N/A	Error	Beg of File	TESTN	Numeric	Blnk/Num	Blank
READPE	N/A	Error	Beg of File	UNLOCK	N/A	Error	N/A
REL	N/A	Error	N/A	UPDATE	N/A	Error	N/A
RESET	N/A	Error	N/A	WRITE	N/A	Error	N/A
ROLBK	N/A	Error	N/A	XFOOT	Plus	Minus	Zero
SCAN	N/A	Error	Found	XLATE	N/A	Error	N/A
SETGT	No Rcd	Error	N/A	Z-ADD	Plus	Minus	Zero
SETLL	No Rcd	Error	Equal	Z-SUB	Plus	Minus	Zero
SETOFF	Off	Off	Off				

RESULTING AND CONDITIONING INDICATORS

Resulting indicators signal the result of an operation that accepts such indicators. For example, on an ADD operation, the resulting indicator in positions 71 to 72 signals that a positive number resulted from the ADD; the indicator in position 73 to 74 signals a negative number; and the indicator in 75 to 76 signals a zero result. Conditioning indicators determine what action will occur, if a particular condition is true. For example, a conditioning-indicator can cause an EXCEPT operation to print a total if the end-of-file condition is true.

To specify resulting and conditioning indicators, you enter an indicator number on the C-specs. RPG IV allows one conditioning indicator (in positions 10 to 11) and up to three resulting indicators (in positions 71 through 76) on a C-spec. Here's an example of this type of indicator notation.

```
*....1....+....2....+....3....+....4....+....5....+....6....+....7....+.
C                   READ      ARTrns                                 90
C    90              EXCEPT    Totals
```

The resulting indicator 90 in positions 75 to 76 will turn on when an end-of-file condition occurs on a READ operation. Because indicator 90 is also in positions 10 and 11, it then conditions an EXCEPT operation to determine when to print report totals.

With conditioning indicators on the C-specs, you can enter OR and AN(D) in positions 7 through 8 to specify multiple conditions. Never use this method because it is extremely difficult to understand and maintain.

Field Notation Conditioning Indicators

To condition structured opcodes such as IF and free-form expressions with the EVAL (Evaluate) opcode, you can specify indicators in field-notation form. You enter *INxx in positions 36 through 40 on C-specs, where xx is a valid indicator number.

```
*...1....+....2....+....3....+....4....+....5....+....6....+....7....+
C                 IF        *IN90
C                 EXCEPT    Error
C                 ENDIF
```

Above is an example of such an indicator with an IF statement. This example tests the status of indicator 90 and executes the code in the IF construct when indicator 90 is on.

You can specify the modern notation, *INxx, with free-form expressions and structured opcodes. If, for example, you are using indicator 90 to signal that at least one error occurred during an edit, the code below will set on indicator 90 when either one or both errors in the edit occur.

```
*...1....+....2....+....3....+....4....+....5....+....6....+....7....+.
  *
  * Check that name was entered — if not, set on *IN91
C                 IF        Name = *Blank
C                 EVAL      *IN91 = *ON
C                 ENDIF
  *
  * Check that address was entered — if not, set on *IN92
C                 IF        Addr = *Blank
C                 EVAL      *IN92 = *ON
C                 ENDIF
  *
  *  Set on indicator *IN90 if any error occurred
C                 IF        *IN91 or *IN92
C                 EVAL      *IN90 = *ON
C                 ENDIF
```

COMMUNICATING WITH DDS FILES

An important use for indicators is to communicate with files you define in DDS, which has indicators to condition how to display fields. The DDS indicators correspond directly to indicators you specify in an RPG program. So if you want to condition a field that you have defined with a given indicator number in DDS, you set on the corresponding indicator in the program to control the field's display attributes.

Let's look at an example of an application that gets input from users through a display file. The user enters information, and then the RPG program processes it. If an entry into a field is in error, the program redisplays the screen with the field in error highlighted in reverse image. The user can easily see where the error occurred and correct it.

The DDS code fragment below defines fields that will display in reverse image for an error. This example shows two fields, each conditioned by a different indicator. When indicator 91 is on, the field Rate will appear in reverse image; otherwise, it will display with whatever attributes you define for the format. When indicator 92 is on, the field Freq will display in reverse image. The DDS DSPATR (Display Attributes) keyword's RI parameter sets the reverse image attribute for these fields.

```
*...1....+....2....+....3....+....4....+....5....+....6....+....7....+
A              Rate                    20
A         91                               DSPATR(RI)
A              Freq                    27
A         92                               DSPATR(RI)

*...1....+....2....+....3....+....4....+....5....+....6....+....7....+
 *
 * Validate rate — must not equal 0 and be positive
C                   IF        Rate<=0
C                   EVAL      *IN91=*ON
C                   ENDIF
 *
 * Validate frequency — must be M, Q, or A
C                   IF        Freq<>'M' and Freq<>'Q' and Freq<>'A'
C                   EVAL      *IN92=*ON
C                   ENDIF
```

The RPG program controls the display-attribute indicators. When this RPG code turns on indicator 91 or 92 and writes the format to the screen, the attributes that those indicators condition are in effect. As a result, the fields in error appear in reverse image.

EXCEPTION INDICATORS

Another use for indicators is as error, or exception, indicators on opcodes that accept them (Table 2.1 lists these opcodes). You specify these indicators in positions 73 through 74 on the C-specs. These indicators signal an error condition so that, for example, your program can check for a divide by zero on the DIV (Divide) operation and communicate an end-of-file condition on the READ operation.

The following example shows exception indicators with file processing. This code reads through two files, an order header and an order detail file. The program begins by setting a lower limit of *LOVAL to the header file to begin processing at the beginning of the file. The first READ operation retrieves the first record in the file. Resulting indicator 90 will turn on if the READ encounters an end-of-file condition — if no records are in the file. The indicator will turn off if the READ is successful.

```
*...1....+....2....+....3....+....4....+....5....+....6....+....7....+.
 * Set pointer to beginning of file — then loop to read each header
 * Ind 90 to signal end of file
C      *LOVAL         SETLL     ORDHDR
C                     READ      ORDHDR                              90
C                     DOW       *IN90
C                     EXSR      PRTHDR
 * Retrieve first detail record for header — then loop to get all
 * Ind 91 on CHAIN to signal no detail records
C      ORDER#         CHAIN     ORDDTL                            91
C                     DOW       *IN91
C                     EXSR      PRTDTL
 * Read all detail records that match header — then loop for next hdr
 * Ind 91 on READE to signal end of matching detail records
C      ORDER#         READE     ORDDTL                            91
C                     ENDDO
C                     READ      ORDHDR                              90
C                     ENDDO
```

The exception indicator is 91 on the CHAIN operation, which tries to retrieve a specific record. If that record does not exist, indicator 91 will turn on. Unlike READ, CHAIN requires a resulting indicator in positions 71 and 72. If CHAIN finds a record with key fields that match the key value in CHAIN's Factor 1, the exception indicator is set off. Otherwise, it is set on.

The third indicator is a resulting indicator on the READE (Read Equal) operation. Indicator 91 will remain off as long as the record retrieved matches the key specified in Factor 1. When the retrieved record does not match the key in Factor 1, indicator 91 will be turned on to signal that no more records have the specified key.

The example ends with another READ to the header file. Again, the program specifies a resulting indicator (90), which governs the DOW (Do While) loop and turns on at an end-of-file condition.

Some opcodes, such as CHAIN, allow an exception indicator and a resulting indicator. CHAIN allows one indicator to specify record not found and another to specify an error in the attempted retrieval.

PRINTER INDICATORS

Indicators you cannot avoid include printer-related indicators such as 1P, overflow indicators, and indicators to condition output. If you avoid the RPG cycle and write structured code, you will never need the 1P indicator. You specify it only when the cycle controls print output, printing headings on the first page of a report. Because we do not recommend using the cycle, we will not discuss 1P.

Overflow indicators are important for all print output. These indicators let a program print headings on each page on a report.

On O-specs, you can specify up to three indicators to condition the output of a record (line of printing) or a field. With conditioning indicators, you can code OR and AND in O-spec positions 16 through 18 to output a line under multiple conditions. This capability increases the number of indicators you can specify to condition output. For example, you can have six indicators on two different O-spec lines to condition the printing of a line only when all six are set on. You connect the code lines with the logical AND operation. Although this form is possible in RPG IV, it is hard to debug, so we recommend that you avoid it.

FUNCTION KEY INDICATORS

Function key indicators correspond to function keys (command keys) to signal that a user has pressed a function key and to identify which one. You can use function key indicators in a program if you specify corresponding function keys in display-file DDS by means of the CFxx (Command Function Key) or CAxx (Command Attention Key) keyword, where *xx* stands for the function key number. The function key indicators correspond to function keys 1 through 24.

Traditionally, RPG programmers have specified function keys with RPG's special indicator notation, Kx. The K signifies a function key indicator. The x is the alpha representation of the specific function key: The letters A through N represent Function keys 1 through 14. The letters P through Y represent function keys 15 through 24. The letter O is not assigned because, supposedly, you can confuse it with a zero. This notation is a very awkward and difficult way to program function keys. Indicator KA corresponds to Function key 1, KB to Function key 2 . . . KY to Function key 24.

You can use these indicators like the general 01 through 99 indicators. For example, you can condition code to execute when a user presses a function key. The code below uses field notation indicator form to condition the execution of a block of code to execute only when a user presses Function key 03 (indicator KC).

```
*...1....+....2....+....3....+....4....+....5....+....6....+....7....+
C                   IF        *INKC
C       TRANS       CHAIN     RECORD                              9091
C                   EVAL      PQUANTY=PQUANTY-TQUANTY
C                   UPDATE    MASTREC
C                   EXCEPT    ERROR
C                   ENDIF
```

The first line of code checks for indicator KC (Function key 03) being on. When it is, the IF construct is executed.

The code fragment below specifies Function key 03, which usually means the user has requested end of job. Because this form of function key indicators is awkward and not self-documenting, we do not recommend it.

```
*...1....+....2....+....3....+....4....+....5....+....6....+....7....+
C                   IF        *INKC
C                   EVAL      *INLR=*ON
C                   ENDIF
```

DDS Function Key Specification

To avoid having to count on your fingers to determine which function key KS (for example) maps to, you can use DDS to assign numbered indicators to the function keys. With the CFxx and CAxx DDS keywords, you can specify an indicator of the same number as the function key you're defining. This indicator is the parameter of the DDS keyword. An RPG program can then use this indicator instead of the KA through KY notation.

```
*...1....+....2....+....3....+....4....+....5....+....6....+....7....+
A           R SCREEN1
  *
A                                 CF03(03 'Exit Program')
A                                 CF12(12 'Prior Screen')
A                            5  28'Order:'
A                            8  28'Customer:'
A                           11  28'FOB Terms:'
A                           20  28'F3=Exit'
A                           20  45'F12=Return'
A             ORDER       10  00  5  36TEXT( Order Number')
A             CUST        20   0  8  39TEXT( Customer Name')
A             FOBTRM       3   0 11  40TEXT( FOB Terms')
```

The previous example is a portion of DDS that lets an RPG IV program evaluate indicators that correspond directly to particular function keys. The display file record Screen1 displays order information for the users and gives them two choices for response: They can press either Function key 3 to exit the program or Function key 12 to return to the previous screen. The first two detail lines in this DDS fragment demonstrate how to assign indicators to the function keys. The DDS keywords CF03 and CF12 map indicators 03 and 12 to the corresponding function keys. When a user presses Function key 3, indicator 03 will be set on and passed to the RPG program. Keyword CF12 sets on indicator 12 and passes it to the RPG program.

The RPG IV code that processes this display file record format is as follows.

```
*...1....+....2....+....3....+....4....+....5....+....6....+....7....+
 *Retrieve order from header file and loop if found
C       ORDER#        CHAIN     ORDHDR                              30
C                     IF        NOT *IN30
 *
 * Initialize indicators then write/read screen
C                     MOVE      *OFF         *IN12
C                     MOVE      *OFF         *IN03
C                     DOW       NOT *IN12
C                     EXFMT     SCREEN1
 *
 * Check for cancel or previous request
C                     IF        *IN03 or *IN12
C                     RETURN
C                     ENDIF
 *
C                     ENDDO
C                     ENDIF
```

If you set up all your function keys to map to contiguous indicators (01 through 24), you can use an indicator array — specified in the form *IN(xx) — to check whether any function keys are pressed. The code below shows how.

```
*...1....+....2....+....3....+....4....+....5....+....6....+....7....+
C                     Z-ADD     0            X
C                     DOW       X NE 24 AND *IN(X)=*OFF
C                     EVAL      X=X+1
C                     IF        *IN(X)=*ON
C                     EXSR      KeyPressed
C                     ENDIF
C                     ENDDO
```

This example goes through a loop from indicator 01 to indicator 24 until it finds an indicator that has been set on or until you run out of indicators. If the user has pressed a function key, the program executes a subroutine to process function keys.

Attention Indicator Byte

Another way to specify function-key indicators is with the Attention Indicator Byte (AIB). The AIB is a one-character field in a file information data structure for a workstation file. This field contains the hexadecimal representation of the key that a user last pressed.

You can set up named constants in a program's D-specs to represent each function key and then use the constant name instead of an indicator. Here is the RPG IV code to define the constants for the AIB fields. To reference a Function key in the C-specs, you compare the named constant with the field in the AIB. When the AIB contains the hexadecimal equivalent of the named constant, that key was pressed.

```
*...1....+....2....+....3....+....4....+....5....+....6....+....7....+
D AIB                     369     369
DFK01             C                       CONST(X'31')
DFK02             C                       CONST(X'32')
DFK03             C                       CONST(X'33')
DFK04             C                       CONST(X'34')
DFK05             C                       CONST(X'35')
DFK06             C                       CONST(X'36')
DFK07             C                       CONST(X'37')
DFK08             C                       CONST(X'38')
DFK09             C                       CONST(X'39')
DFK10             C                       CONST(X'3A')
DFK11             C                       CONST(X'3B')
DFK12             C                       CONST(X'3C')
DFK13             C                       CONST(X'B1')
DFK14             C                       CONST(X'B2')
DFK15             C                       CONST(X'B3')
DFK16             C                       CONST(X'B4')
DFK17             C                       CONST(X'B5')
DFK18             C                       CONST(X'B6')
DFK19             C                       CONST(X'B7')
DFK20             C                       CONST(X'B8')
DFK21             C                       CONST(X'B9')
DFK22             C                       CONST(X'BA')
DFK23             C                       CONST(X'BB')
DFK24             C                       CONST(X'BC')
```

The code below checks for Function key 03. When the user presses Function key 03, the value of the AIB will be hex '33'. By using the AIB to define and reference the function keys, you avoid the awkward Kx representation and save indicators that you would have to reserve for function keys if you use the CFxx keywords in DDS.

```
*...1....+....2....+....3....+....4....+....5....+....6....+....7....+.
C      FK03          IFEQ      AIB
```

SETTING INDICATORS

RPG gives you several ways to turn indicators on and off. The traditional method of setting on or off indicators is to specify the SETON or SETOFF opcode. You can use these opcodes only with numbered indicators in the indicator positions on the C-specs. This example shows how to code them.

```
*...1....+....2....+....3....+....4....+....5....+....6....+....7....+.
C                    SETON                              909192
C                    SETOFF                             151617
```

CHAPTER 3

Data Definition

RPG III provides many ways to define various types of data. You define data internal to the program, as needed, in the C-specs. You define data structures and data coming from data files in the I-specs. Arrays require an E-spec.

Now, with RPG IV, all these ways to define data are obsolete. RPG IV introduces D-specs to define fields, data structures, arrays, and tables all on one specification. This innovation improves the structure of RPG IV code and makes the E-spec obsolete, so IBM has dropped it from the language definition.

RPG IV D-specs organize data definition in a program. This chapter will explain how to define data in the new D-specs. The first topic is data types and classes, a new distinction that comes with RPG IV data definition. A discussion of how to define standalone fields illustrates the use of data types and classes. Next comes an explanation of named constants and literals and how to define them. The next type of definition is the data structure. Finally, you will see how to define arrays and tables.

DATA TYPES AND CLASSES

With D-specs, RPG IV introduces a distinction that is new for RPG but has been around for a long time in other languages: The distinction between *data types* and *classes* is important for understanding how to define data in RPG IV. This section examines this innovation and shows what classes and data types are valid in RPG IV. The following sections illustrate the basic data types and classes in the definition of standalone fields.

Data types, or types, specify the data formats that are valid in a program. You define each data item as a specific type (such as character or numeric), which determines what operations are possible on that data. For example, a mathematical operation is not possible for character data. The data type determines how the system will initialize the storage space associated with the data.

Data types fall into categories. For instance, data types zoned decimal, packed decimal, and binary fit the category of the numeric data type. All the data types in one such category form a *class*. A class is a group of data types, and the class determines which data types can interact with each other. For example, a numeric field defined as packed can interact with a field defined as zoned or binary in an arithmetic operation such as ADD or SUB (Subtract). However, a field defined as character cannot interact with a zoned field on an arithmetic operation.

The RPG IV classes are character, numeric, pointer, graphic, date, time, and timestamp.

The following table summarizes the RPG IV classes and their data types.

Class	Data Types
Character	Fixed Length
	Variable Length[1]
	Indicators
Numeric	Packed Decimal
	Zoned
	Binary
Pointer	Basing Pointer
	Procedure Pointer
Graphic	Graphic
Date and Time	Date
	Time
	Timestamp

[1]RPG does not directly support variable-length fields. DDS variable-length fields are either treated as fixed-length fields or are unavailable.

This table illustrates the relationships among the various data types that RPG IV supports. For example, you can see all the class numeric data types. Because they are in the same class, they can interact with each other in arithmetic operations.

RPG IV classes and data types determine how data types affect data definition. The basic element of data definition is a standalone field, so the discussion begins with how to define such a field as fixed-length character; class numeric with data type packed decimal, zoned decimal, or binary; and the new graphic class.

STANDALONE FIELDS

When you begin defining data, you start with fields. Fields are references to memory positions where a program can store values. You give each field a name that is a unique identifier in the program. When the program references a field name, the name is a shorthand reference to the content of the field. When a field is not part of a data structure or a named constant, it is a *standalone field*.

Fixed-Length Character Fields

A field can be any valid RPG IV data type. To begin the discussion of the D-spec, let's consider a fixed-length character field. An RPG IV fixed-length character type field can contain character data with a maximum length of up to 32K. You specify a field's length in positions 33 through 39 in the D-specs.

Before RPG IV, programmers often defined this type of field in the C-specs, either with a DEFN (Define) operation code or by specifying the field name in the Result field and defining its length and decimal positions (if the field was numeric) the first time it occurred. Although you can still use the old method, the D-specs are now the better way to define data fields.

```
*...1....+....2....+....3....+....4....+....5....+....6....+....7....+
D PgmName          S              10A   INZ('CUSTINQA')
D*
```

This D-spec shows a character field definition. When you define a fixed-length character field, the specification in positions 7 through 21 names the field you're defining. Here, the field's name is PgmName. Perhaps this field's purpose is to print or display the name of the program or to write the name to a log. The S in position 24 defines the field as a standalone field. The number in positions 33 through 39 determines that field PgmName's length is 10. The A (alphanumeric) in position 40 means that the field is a character field, though this specification is redundant because the default type is A if you enter no decimal positions for a field. The keyword INZ (Initialize) in positions 44 through 80 specifies that this field contains an initial value of 'CUSTINQ', so the program doesn't have to set it. INZ initializes the field before the first C-spec is executed.

Class Numeric Fields

You can represent numeric data in different formats in a program. On the AS/400, packed decimal is the most efficient form for numeric data, so packed decimal is the default representation.

To understand why this form is the default, you can think of a byte as one memory cell in the computer. The more information the system can store in one byte, the more efficient is the representation. For packed decimal fields, the AS/400 stores more than one digit in each byte of memory. And, although the AS/400 accepts other formats, it must first convert them into the internal format of packed decimal before any computation can occur. Because of this conversion, the packed decimal data type is generally more efficient on the AS/400 than other numeric data types.

System efficiencies aside, sometimes you need to work with numeric values in other formats. Many system APIs require you to receive or send data in binary format rather than packed decimal, although this requirement seems to contradict system efficiency. Also, you sometimes manipulate data from another system that stores data in, say, a zoned decimal format. For instance, you may have offices or sites that still have a System/36, which uses zoned as its native format.

To meet the need to work with various numeric formats, RPG supports several numeric data types: packed decimal, binary, and zoned. The program segment in Figure 2.1 defines three numeric fields, one of each of these data types.

FIGURE 2.1
Defining Numeric Fields with D-specs

```
*...1....+....2....+....3....+....4....+....5....+....6....+....7....+
D DeptAcct        S              5P 0
D SSNumber        S              9S 0
D DataLength      S              5B 0
```

Field DeptAcct is packed decimal, SSNumber is zoned decimal and DataLength is binary. In column 40, the P, S, and B, respectively, specify each of these formats. Let's examine each of these examples.

The Packed Decimal Numeric Data Type

In Figure 2.1, field DeptAcct is packed numeric. You define the field name in positions 7 through 21. To define this field as a standalone field, you put an S in position 24. The length specification, in this case, is in positions 33 through 39. The data type (P for packed decimal) is in position 40, followed by the number of decimal positions (positions 41 through 42).

Each byte of a packed decimal field can contain two decimal digits. The exception is the low-order byte, which contains one digit and a positive or negative sign. A hexadecimal 'F' value in the rightmost position of the low-order byte identifies a positive packed decimal value in the field, whereas a hexadecimal 'D' identifies a negative value. All remaining bytes are divided into 4-bit digit portions. Here, you see the layout of a packed decimal field with the value of +708 in hex (x'70 8F').

<----- Byte ----->		<----- Byte ----->	
Digit 1	Digit 2	Digit 3	+/– sign
0111	0000	1000	1111
77	0	8	F

Because packed decimal format is the default data type for RPG IV and is the format in which the AS/400 performs all calculations, all numeric data is first converted to this format before computation and then converted back again to its original format after computation. Of course, all these conversions occur internally and automatically.

The Zoned Decimal Data Type

In Figure 2.1, SSNumber is zoned decimal. As with all standalone fields, you enter the field name in positions 7 through 21. Because this field is a standalone field, an S must be in position 24. The length specification comes next, followed by the data type (S in position 40), followed by the number of decimal positions.

Zoned decimal format dictates that each byte of storage for the field contain one digit or one character and a zone. For each byte, the low-order 4 bits represent the digit. The zone, which is in the high-order 4 bits, determines the sign of the zoned decimal number. The diagram below shows a two-digit, zoned decimal number with a value of +08.

<----- Byte ----->		<----- Byte ----->	
Zone 1	Digit 1	Zone 2	Digit 2
1111	0000	1111	1000
F	0	F	8

Although each digit has its own zone, only the zone in the low-order byte provides the sign of the entire decimal number. As with packed decimal format, the system uses the standard sign values: hexadecimal 'F' for positive numbers and hexadecimal 'D' for negative. Another characteristic of zoned-decimal format is that it accepts the contents of any character or numeric field. So you can use a MOVE operation to place numeric data from a character field into a numeric field. This operation is sometimes necessary if you are reading data files from another shop or system and a field is in character format but contains numeric data. Just be sure all the characters you move represent valid numeric digits (0 through 9).

The Binary Numeric Data Type

In Figure 2.1, DataLength is a binary field. The field name is in positions 7 through 21, and because this field is a standalone field, an S is in position 24. In addition, you specify the length, the data type (B in position 40), and the decimal position.

In binary format, the sign of the number is in the leftmost bit of the sequence, and the digits are in the remaining bits. Negative numbers are stored in twos-complement form: Any field in binary format must be 2 or 4 bytes long. The RPG IV compiler assigns a length to every binary format input field for storage purposes, but you will always define your field by specifying the number of integer positions you want, not the number of bytes necessary to store the number. The highest decimal value that you can store in a 2-byte binary field is 9999; likewise, 999,999,999 is the largest value that you can store in a 4-byte binary field. The diagram on the following page represents the number 6,192 in binary form.

	<----- Byte ----->						<----- Byte ----->							
S	4	2	1													
I		0	0	0	5	2	1									
G		9	4	2	1	5	2	6	3	1						
N		6	8	4	2	6	8	4	2	6	8	4	2	1		
0	0	0	1	1	0	0	0	0	0	1	1	0	0	0	0	

The Graphic Class

The graphic data type, which is new for OS/400 Version 3 Release 1 (V3R1), is for representing double-byte character set (DBCS) data. You need this data type for national-language character sets (such as written Chinese) that require 2 bytes to represent any one character, because the characters are graphically too complex for the system to represent in 1 byte. For languages such as English, single-byte character sets suffice.

Unless you must deal with a DBCS language, you will not need this data type. If you are already working with such a language, you will recognize the improvement RPG IV brings by letting you declare fields as graphic fields.

You use the graphic data type in the same way as the character data type, but with DBCS character data. This sample code shows the definition of a graphic field in RPG IV. Note that the length you specify is the number of characters you are defining, not the number of bytes the character will use.

```
*....1....+....2....+....3....+....4....+....5....+....6....+....7....+
D PrevName        S              25G
*
```

Other Standalone Data Types

Besides character, numeric, and graphic, RPG IV supports several other data types. The date, time, and timestamp data types are specialized classes and have specialized uses. Chapter 10 will explain these. Pointers are also a new class of data, although not as widely used as the date, time, and timestamp. Chapter 13 covers pointers. Finally, indicators are a special data type within class character. Chapter 6 explains this data type.

NAMED CONSTANTS AND LITERALS

In addition to defining fields, you can define named constants and numeric, character, and hexadecimal literals in RPG IV D-specs. Unlike a field, a constant or literal has a value that you specify explicitly and that a program cannot change. The RPG IV compiler lets you give a name to constants. When you need to reference such a named constant, you specify its name. Using the name helps you avoid typographical errors and makes specification quicker and easier than keying the entire constant value every time you need it.

Each of the following sample D-specs defines a constant named MaxRcd. You can tell it is a named constant in two ways. First, the C in position 24 identifies the name as a constant (rather than a data structure or standalone field) name. The keyword CONST (Constant) provides the value for the named constant. The explicit specification of this keyword is optional. You can just specify the constant value (in this case, 500) without the keyword. Alternatively, INZ can provide the value for a named constant.

```
*...1....+....2....+....3....+....4....+....5....+....6....+....7....+
D MaxRcd          C                   CONST(500)
D MaxRcd          C                   INZ(500)
D MaxRcd          C                   500
```

Because CONST is valid only when column 24 contains a C, specifying CONST is pretty pointless except to illustrate the keyword's availability. We prefer either INZ or no keyword. Note that you specify no explicit precision (no length or number of decimal positions) for a named constant. The compiler will implement a named constant as necessary in each situation.

Literals

Literals are fields with an explicit, specified, unchanging value that can control processing such as loops, be compared against user-supplied data to validate a field's value, generate output to a program-described printer file, and define the number of elements in an array. Named constants have literals as their value. For example, the literal in the previous example is the value 500 that is the value of the named constant MaxRcd. Programs treat constants and literals as data, in that you can compare the values of each and assign these values to variables.

RPG IV supports three types of literal: numeric, character, and hexadecimal. Several rules govern how to specify a literal, and the next sections will discuss the rules for each type.

Numeric Literals

Figure 2.2 shows examples of valid and invalid numeric literals. The following rules govern the specification and use of numeric literals in RPG IV.

- Numeric literals consist of members from the set [0..9, ., +, −].
- If you specify a positive or negative sign, it must be in the leftmost position of the literal.
- Numeric literals with no positive or negative sign are treated as a positive value.

- Blanks cannot occur in numeric literals.

- Numeric literals can be anywhere that numeric fields appear, but you can't assign new values to literals.

- Depending on the print option you specify for the program, a period or comma represents a decimal.

You can specify numeric literals throughout a program. If you repeatedly use the same literal and it has a specific meaning to your application (such as a limit of some sort or a rate for something like calculation of overtime pay), consider making it a named constant. A named constant is more descriptive to maintenance programmers who might not immediately see that the literal 1.1 is an overtime pay factor but will readily identify the named constant OvrTimFctr. You specify the literal in the definition of the named constant, and you specify the named constant when you want to use the literal.

FIGURE 2.2
Valid and Invalid Literals

Valid Numeric Literals	Invalid Numeric Literals
12345	12+45
9	..7
−1	1−1

Character and Hexadecimal Literals

RPG IV supports two types of single-byte character-set literals: character and hexadecimal. Such literals are not so common as numeric literals. If you use program-described printer files, you will need character literals for placing constant data (not variables) on the O-specs. Most other character data will be in character fields, but character literals are useful in some other situations, including validating user input. For instance, the character literal strings 'Y' and 'N' are often in code if you validate user input. Also, you can specify error messages as character literals. You move the literals into a field and display it. As with numeric literals, character literals will be second-nature to most programmers.

Hexadecimal literals, on the other hand, are not nearly so common. You usually specify them for a literal that you cannot express as a character literal. For instance, you cannot key any characters below x'40' (a space) on a standard terminal. However, you sometimes need a character string that includes such non-keyable characters. To use these characters in a string, you need to specify them as hexadecimal literals.

The availability of hexadecimal literals means you can specify any available character by keying its hexadecimal equivalent. Examples of situations requiring hexadecimal literals include working with special equipment that requires control codes, or including control codes in printer streams to access printer capabilities that ordinary procedures do not specifically support (via DDS or printer device description). Suppose that to use superscripted characters, a printer requires a character stream consisting of a control code that signals a special command followed by that command, both in hex. If the printer needs a hexadecimal 04, followed by a 27, followed by the data, you can specify the hexadecimal control characters by entering the hexadecimal literal x'0427'. You can concatenate this value to the regular data or output it separately, followed by regular data. Probably more than any other type of literal, the hexadecimal literal is a good candidate for replacement with a named constant. In that case, you specify the literal when defining the named constant.

When you work with class character data, you need to be aware of some rules for their specification and use.

- All characters, including embedded blanks, are valid.
- Character literals must be enclosed in apostrophes (').
- When you need an apostrophe as part of the character literal, you specify two apostrophes (''). For example, you code the string, Dhavita's new bike, as 'Dhavita''s new bike'.
- Character literals are not valid in class numeric operations.
- Class character fields can contain character literal values.

Hexadecimal literals represent character strings. The following rules apply for their specification and use.

- Hexadecimal literals have the form x'x1x2x3...xn', where 'x1x2x3...xn' are characters from the set [A-F, a-f, 0-9].
- Hexadecimal literals must be enclosed in apostrophes (').
- Hexadecimal literals must be of an even length, with every two characters (e.g., xi) defining a single byte of the character string.
- A hexadecimal literal can appear anywhere a character literal can, except with the ENDSR (End Subroutine) operation code or as an edit word.
- Except for bit operations, a hexadecimal literal has the same meaning as its corresponding character literal.
- Hexadecimal literals can contain the hexadecimal equivalent of the apostrophe (x'7D') but do not require you to specify two apostrophes, as you must with character literals (there is no interpretive conflict with delimiters).

Each byte of a character literal corresponds to 1 byte of stored information, whereas every 2 bytes of a hexadecimal literal correspond to 1 byte of stored information. As long as you think of the hexadecimal literal as providing the two halves (the zone and digit) of each byte of a character string, you won't have problems understanding hexadecimal literals.

When you need any type of literal (other than in the D-specs), stop and ask whether you want to make the literal a named constant instead. A literal that you use only in one place in a program and whose value is self-explanatory is probably not a candidate to become a named constant. But a literal you use in many places and whose value does not express its purpose (as is the case with the overtime rate example in the discussion of numeric literals) is a good candidate for being a named constant. One benefit of named constants over literals is that you cannot accidentally specify a different value at different places in the program (either by forgetting to change one or mistyping a value). Also, you do not need to worry about the value once you define it, so you can think conceptually about the program as you code, without worrying about the values involved in the process.

DATA STRUCTURES

Another type of data you can define in D-specs is a data structure and its subfields. With the definitions of various types of data structures, you can specify the LIKE keyword, the OVERLAY keyword, the data area data structure, the DTAARA (Data Area) keyword, the DEFINE operation for data areas, the *LIKE DEFINE operation, the OCCURS keyword and OCCUR operation for defining multiple-occurrence data structures, the file information data structure (INFDS), and the program status data structure (PSDS).

A data structure is a single, contiguous area of storage that you can reference as a whole by naming it in an operation. Or, you can divide a data structure into smaller units, or *subfields*. When you address part of the data structure and define that part as a subfield, the data structure contains the subfield's value. Each subfield can address any part of the data structure and even readdress the same parts of the structure to let you view the data in a different format. For instance, you can define the first four positions of a data structure as both a binary subfield and as a character subfield. This dual approach lets you store a character string that contains numeric data and then use the binary definition to extract the numeric data as a binary field. Subfields can (but do not have to) overlap each other in a data structure, or different subfields can even define the same storage location in the data structure. The main difference between a data structure's subfields and standalone fields is that you cannot address a standalone field's data except by referencing the standalone field.

Data structures let you group related program data. Consider the data you need about a customer: name, address, and birthdate. Name and address can both be subfields of type character, implying that their data must be of type character, and they cannot be further reduced. Birthdate, however, can be an aggregate, reducible to three numeric elements: month, day, and year.

A data structure can partition one large field into smaller fields to access and manipulate the data in the large field. In addition, a data structure lets you apply different data formats to the same storage area. Also, data structures let you group noncontiguous data into contiguous internal storage locations and create multiple occurrences of a given data set.

Defining a Data Structure

Defining a data structure involves two main steps. First, you define the structure to reserve an area in storage. Second, you subdivide it by defining subfields.

You enter DS in positions 24 and 25 of the D-spec. You can name the data structure by placing a valid RPG name in positions 7 through 21.

Name your data structure only if you need the name for documentation (a recommended use) or intend to reference the entire data structure, perhaps to move a large field into it so you can subdivide the fields. In this case, naming your data structure will let you move your large field directly into the data structure and then access the parts by addressing the defined subfields. You can specify only the subfields and their sizes.

One reason not to name a data structure is that if you name a data structure, its size is limited to 32K (32,767) bytes. If you leave a data structure unnamed, it can be as large as 9,999,999 bytes. Of course, either length will be sufficient for most needs.

You can specify a length for the entire data structure by entering a number in positions 33 through 39. A length is not necessary, and you will probably not explicitly specify one for a data structure because the compiler will implicitly define the length, based on the last position occupied by the subfields you specify. This flexibility is an improvement over previous versions of RPG, where the structure requires an explicit size declaration.

Unless you need to specifically control the size of the entire data structure (perhaps to pass it to another program that expects a particular size structure), you can rely on the compiler's implicit size declaration. Ordinarily, you will be more concerned with the size of the each subfield than with the size of the data structure.

To explicitly define subfields, you must name them in positions 7 through 21. Then, in contrast to how you define other field types, for a subfield, you leave position 24 blank. An entry in this position means that the previous data structure definition is complete, and you're now defining a new standalone field, named constant, or data structure (the only types of allowed entries for position 24 through 25). Next, you designate a data type or accept the default of character if you specify no decimal positions, or packed if you specify decimal positions.

Specifying Subfield Size

The next requirement for defining data structure subfields is to specify the sub-field's starting and ending position (i.e., its length). Specifying the starting and ending positions of the subfield is the difficult way to define length. This method requires you to calculate the size of the subfield's storage (which means you have to understand how various data types are stored), and you have to remember to change the specification if any part of the data structure changes. Specifying the start and end positions, however, is necessary when you are using the data structure to divide a large field into subfields.

Specifying the subfield's size is the convenient length definition because you can ignore the size of the storage required. You need to know only that the subfield is a seven-digit field, but not that it requires 4 or 7 bytes of storage to implement, depending on data type. Specifying the subfield's size is best when you are using the data structure to group a set of fields, in contrast to using the structure to divide a larger field into smaller pieces.

Data Structure Subfield Keywords

You can specify keywords when you're defining a subfield. The LIKE keyword, lets you define the subfield to have the same characteristics as another field or subfield. OVERLAY lets the field you're defining use some or all of the storage of another field that you name as the parameter value on the OVERLAY keyword. Some special-purpose keywords, such as EXTFLD (External Field) and DTAARA (Data Area), are also available for data area definitions. The array definition keywords are also valid.

The LIKE Keyword

The LIKE keyword on a D-spec lets you reference a field definition as the model for defining the attributes of the field or data structure subfield you're defining. LIKE's one required parameter names the field that is the model. The field you are defining will have the same data type and size as the model field. If you reference a table or array, the newly created field will have the attributes of a single element or entry in the array or table. The new field will not be automatically defined as an array; you must also use the DIM (Dimension) keyword to make the new field an array. (If you need to make a duplicate array, the LIKE keyword will let you duplicate the element attributes, and the DIM keyword can use the built-in function %ELEM (Elements) to set the dimension of the array to the same number elements as the referenced array.)

When you specify LIKE to define a standalone field or subfield, you can make the new field the same size as, or longer or shorter than, the model field. You can't specify a length for the new field, but you can determine its size relative to the LIKE field's. For a same-sized new field, leave the *from* and *to* positions (26 through 39) blank and the decimal positions (41 and 42) blank — you can't change the decimal positions. To make the new field longer or shorter than the LIKE field, specify a positive or negative number in the *to* positions (33 to 39) to determine how much longer or shorter the new field will be.

LIKE is useful because programs need to save fields for comparison, build structures such as key lists or parameter lists that use fields, or make copies of data to use in multiple ways. With LIKE, when a field that you need to copy changes in length, you can just change the size of the referenced field and then recompile the program. You do not need to hunt down the fields that store copies of the changed field because, with the LIKE keyword, the system automatically resizes fields based on the referenced (changed) field. This capability is handy when you are working with externally described display, printer, and data files. With the LIKE keyword, you can reference the field definitions that are copied from the external files, effectively making the definition of any work fields in your program externally described, as well.

When you're working with a display file and you need to compare the values just read from the screen with the values originally written to the screen, you can take advantage of LIKE. This comparison, of course, requires that you save the originally written values into separate fields, so you have the original value to perform the comparison.

Consider an inquiry program where the users see a list of transactions and can position the cursor within that list by specifying the company and contract to display. Additionally, they can provide selection criteria based on the value of one or more displayed fields. Your task is to detect any changes in the selection criteria and then reload the screen based on users' selections. Because you cannot just reload the screen every time they press Enter, you must store the values last written to the screen and compare them to the current value to determine whether you need to reload the screen. LIKE comes into this scenario because it lets you define all the save fields based on the definitions of selected fields associated with the display file. The code below shows five field definitions based on fields defined elsewhere (in this case, the referenced fields are defined implicitly through the externally described display file).

```
*...1....+....2....+....3....+....4....+....5....+....6....+....7....+.
FCntInqD   CF   E              WORKSTN

*...1....+....2....+....3....+....4....+....5....+....6....+....7....+.
D SavComp         S                     LIKE(InqComp)
D SavCntrct       S                     LIKE(InqCnt)
D SavSts          S                     LIKE(InqSts)
D SavMinVal       S                     LIKE(InqMinVal)
D SavCntTyp       S                     LIKE(InqCntTyp)
```

```
*...1....+....2....+....3....+....4....+....5....+....6....+....7....+.
 *
 ... prepare screen and start loop to display it
 *
 * Store screen fields in save fields for later comparison
C                    EVAL      SavComp=InqComp
C                    EVAL      SavCntrct=InqCnt
C                    EVAL      SavSts=InqSts
C                    EVAL      SavMinVal=InqMinVal
C                    EVAL      SavCntTyp=InqCntTyp
 *
 * Display and read the screen
C                    EXFMT     InqFmt
 *
 * Handle any request that overrides a reload (such as an exit request)
 ... handle any immediate requests
 *
 * Check for change in selection criteria, and reload if needed
C                    IF        InqComp<>SavComp or InqCnt<>SavCntrct or
C                              InqSts<>SavSts or InqMinVal<>SavMinVal or
C                              InqCntTyp<>SavCntTyp
C                    EXSR      LoadScreen
 *
C                    ELSE
 * Process requests that are not overridden by reload
 ... handle any request by user
 *
 ... loop back to redisplay the screen
```

As reference fields to define the fields that will store the original values from the screen, this example uses some fields defined in the externally described file CntInqD. Storing the original values lets you compare them when the program reads the screen. If the size of any of these fields changes on the display file, you just recompile the program to continue working.

Consider what happens if you explicitly define the save fields instead of referencing the screen fields. If you enlarge a screen field and the save field becomes smaller than the screen field, the program might detect a change that doesn't exist. If the user keys a value that is larger than the save field value, the save field recognizes only part of the data on the next iteration and reports that the field has changed when it hasn't. That situation can result in seemingly random reloads of data.

*LIKE DEFINE

The DEFINE operation with *LIKE in Factor 1 lets you define a field's attributes as being the same as another field. The new field's length can be equivalent to or larger or smaller than the other field's. This operation is similar to the LIKE keyword in the D-specs but lets you define a field by referring to the field while you're working in the C-specs. Because defining all data in a central, standard location in code is good programming practice, the LIKE keyword in the D-specs is better than the *LIKE DEFINE operation.

You code *LIKE in Factor 1, DEFINE in the operation field, the referenced field in Factor 2, and the field you want to define in the Result field. As with the LIKE keyword, you can also specify that the new field have more or fewer characters or digits than the field it's based on.

The same restrictions that apply to the LIKE keyword apply to *LIKE DEFINE. You cannot specify a named constant or a literal in Factor 2. They have no explicitly stated size to reference. If you refer to a table, an array, or an array element in Factor 2, the newly created field will *not* be an array; it will be one (standalone) field with the attributes of one entry in the table or array. Note that you cannot, therefore, create an array whose elements match some other field. The LIKE keyword gives you more flexibility in this regard because you can mix LIKE with the DIM keyword to create an array whose element size is based on an existing field, table, or array. You cannot use conditioning or resulting indicators with *LIKE DEFINE.

The code below is similar to the example for the LIKE keyword. However, this example replaces LIKE's function with *LIKE DEFINE. This code shows the similarities and the differences between the techniques.

```
*...1....+....2....+....3....+....4....+....5....+....6....+....7....+.
FCntInqD   CF    E           WORKSTN

*...1....+....2....+....3....+....4....+....5....+....6....+....7....+.
   ... prepare screen and start loop to display it
 * Define the fields to be used to save previous values
C       *LIKE         DEFINE    InqComp        SavComp
C       *LIKE         DEFINE    InqCnt         SavCntrct
C       *LIKE         DEFINE    InqSts         SavSts
C       *LIKE         DEFINE    InqMinVal      SavMinVal
C       *LIKE         DEFINE    InqCntTyp      SavCntTyp
 * Store screen fields in save fields for later comparison
C                     EVAL      SavComp=InqComp
C                     EVAL      SavCntrct=InqCnt
C                     EVAL      SavSts=InqSts
C                     EVAL      SavMinVal=InqMinVal
C                     EVAL      SavCntTyp=InqCntTyp              CONTINUED
```

```
*...1....+....2....+....3....+....4....+....5....+....6....+....7....+.
 * Display and read the screen
C                   EXFMT     InqFmt
 *
 * Handle any request that overrides a reload (such as an exit request)
 ... handle any immediate requests
 *
 * Check for change in selection criteria, and reload if needed
C                   IF        InqComp<>SavComp or InqCnt<>SavCntrct or
C                             InqSts<>SavSts or InqMinVal<>SavMinVal
or
C                             InqCntTyp<>SavCntTyp
C                   EXSR      LoadScreen
 *
C                   ELSE
 * Process requests that are not overridden by reload
 ... handle any request by user
 *
 ... loop back to redisplay the screen
```

Because *LIKE DEFINE provides the same functionality as the LIKE keyword, for most of the explanation of this example, you can refer to the description of the example there. The difference between the LIKE and *LIKE DEFINE methods is that the data definition moves from the D-specs to the C-specs. You cannot condition the execution of the *LIKE DEFINE operation because the operation is not executed. It is processed at compile time to define the field you are creating, though this fact is not as obvious as it is when you specify the LIKE keyword instead. We recommend the LIKE keyword over the *LIKE DEFINE operation for data definition.

The OVERLAY Keyword

The OVERLAY keyword lets you define a new data structure subfield that overlaps the storage location allocated to a previously defined subfield in the same data structure as the subfield you're defining. Both the new subfield and the overlapped subfield remain valid, and you can access either one.

The new subfield with OVERLAY on its D-spec does not take on the attributes of the overlapped subfield. Instead, the new field occupies all or part of the overlapped subfield's storage. You determine the attributes of the newly defined subfield by defining its size in positions 33 through 39, the data type in position 40, and the number of decimal positions (if any) in positions 41 and 42. Note that, when using OVERLAY, you must use size notation for the new subfield; *from-to* notation is not allowed.

The OVERLAY keyword has two parameters, the second of which is optional. You specify the parameters in parentheses after the keyword and separate them with a colon (when you specify both). The first parameter is the name of the data structure subfield that you want to overlay with the new field. The second parameter specifies the position (in bytes) in the storage of the overlapped subfield where the new subfield is to start. If you do not specify the second parameter, the start position defaults to 1. A combination of the size definition of the new field and its data type determine the length of the overlapped storage.

Why do you need the OVERLAY keyword to redefine part of a data structure when you can simply redefine parts of a data structure using *from-to* notation? OVERLAY lets you define a subfield's location relative to the position of the overlapped subfield rather than requiring you to specify the location. This capability is important when you have externally described data structures. OVERLAY lets you redefine fields created from an external description without requiring you to know the location of the field in the data structure. Unfortunately, you still must have some knowledge of the attributes of the subfield you are referencing to make certain that the size of the new subfield does not exceed the size of the storage that the overlapped subfield uses. However, just the ability to redefine without regard to position is a big benefit.

Of course, OVERLAY is not restricted to externally described subfields. Because the D-spec lets you define subfields by specifying their size and data type instead of supplying *from* and *to* positions, the OVERLAY keyword is necessary to successfully define subfields that you will then further subdivide. Specifying size rather than position notation is much easier when you're defining the subfields of a data structure, so OVERLAY extends the redefinition process to make it independent of position.

The following code redefines the positions required for a six-digit, zoned numeric field that stores a date. This redefinition lets you individually access the year, month, and day parts of the field.

The example below defines an unnamed data structure to house the field TmpDate. Though an *unnamed* data structure is not required, you cannot simply name the data structure TmpDate because TmpDate needs to be a numeric field, and all data structures are character (though their subfields can be any data type). Naturally, you can give the data structure any name you please, but why name the data structure unless you intend to address it by name?

```
*...1....+....2....+....3....+....4....+....5....+....6....+....7....+
D                         DS
D TmpDate                       6S Ø
D   TmpMonth                    2S Ø OVERLAY(TmpDate)
D   TmpDay                      2S Ø OVERLAY(TmpDate:3)
D   TmpYear                     2S Ø OVERLAY(TmpDate:5)
```

The first subfield is TmpDate, which is a six-digit zoned decimal field with zero decimal positions. The data type is important here. A zoned decimal field means that each digit takes up 1 byte. Also, you can reference each digit or any contiguous subset of the digits as a zoned decimal field because the format of any such subset is also a valid zoned decimal. That point is important because it means you can look at each part of the date as a two-digit zoned decimal number. To allow that capability, you define the subfield TmpMonth as a two-digit zoned decimal subfield and then specify the OVERLAY keyword to make the new subfield overlay the subfield TmpDate, starting at the the default position, 1. The default is necessary if you do not explicitly state the starting position as the second parameter on the OVERLAY keyword.

The next two subfields have the same data type and size, providing three two-digit zoned decimal subfields. One will access the month, one the day, and one the year portion of the date that goes into the TmpDate subfield. The only difference in the definitions of the three new subfields is the starting position in the TmpDate subfield. The first subfield starts in position 1 of the TmpDate subfield by default. The second subfield starts in position 3 of the TmpDate subfield, to access the day. The third subfield starts in position 5 of the TmpDate subfield, to access the year. All three subfields are two digits long. Of course, the assumption here is that the date you put in the TmpDate field is in MMDDYY format.

This section has explained the concepts of data structures and how to specify a data structure and its subfields. Now let's look at some example data structures to see how you can use them.

Named Data Structures by Example

When you have a large field containing data you need to subdivide so you can access discrete pieces of data, you need to name the data structure. Then you can define subfields that let you address each portion of the data as you need it. Occasionally, you need to handle data that you receive as a string of characters but that has some internal structure. For example, system APIs sometimes have a general-purpose parameter that returns a character string that you must interpret based on a predefined format. Or, you sometimes implement an application's interface at an API level. You can request data from the application, and it returns data in one of several formats. In such cases (and many more that you can imagine), the data will have a predefined format, so you can write a program to let you easily divide the data the parameter returns into meaningful fields.

Let's say you are working with a software package that manages your bulk mailings. One facility this package provides is an API (a callable program). You can feed the program parts of an address, and it returns the data in one of several standardized formats. Suppose these formats apply different rules for which information to include, depending on the size of the format you're using. For instance, say you need to provide the title, first, middle, and last names; a suffix; honorifics (MD, Ph.D., etc.); and up to three lines of address for city, state or province, county, postal code, etc. You can specify whether to return a long or a short address format, a domestic or foreign format, and carrier route information. When you call the package's API, it will respond with any of these formats by returning a single field that holds the information in a pre-defined format. You then have a data structure divide that large field to handle each format you request. For example, if you request a short address (for mailing labels), the mailing software will follow rules for dropping parts of a name (such as title, suffix, middle name).

Figure 2.3 shows how a program can receive and interpret two formats if you specify a data structure to divide a large field into several smaller fields, arranging the large field's data in several ways. The D-specs define a named data structure, StdzdAddr (Standardized Address). The API that the program will call (pseudocoded in the example) has a defined parameter that is 500 bytes long. Through this parameter, the API will format the data as you want it and then return the address.

As you can see in the D-specs, StdzdAddr is a 500-byte data structure. At the end of the D-specs is the standalone field, Address, which is also 500 bytes long. You can specify the field Address on a call to the API program to receive the formatted string from the called program. Then, with the EVAL (Evaluate) operation in the C-specs, you can set the named data structure StdzdAddr equal to the value of Address. Now you can look at the data in the StdzdAddr data structure through its subfields.

FIGURE 2.3
Example of Defining and Using a Named Data Structure

```
*...1....+....2....+....3....+....4....+....5....+....6....+....7....+
D StdzdAddr       DS            500
 * short form (max 30 characters per line; max 4 lines)
D   SFLine1                1       30
D   SFLine2               31       60
D   SFLine3               61       90
D   SFLine4               91      120
 *
 * long form (max 45 characters per line; max 6 lines)
D   LFLine1                1       45
D   LFLine2               46       90
D   LFLine3               91      135
D   LFLine4              136      180
D   LFLine5              181      225
```
CONTINUED

FIGURE 2.3 CONTINUED

```
*...1....+....2....+....3....+....4....+....5....+....6....+....7....+
 *
D Address          S              500

*...1....+....2....+....3....+....4....+....5....+....6....+....7....+
 *
 * Get requested format
   ... read mailing request record to see what format is required
 * Get address to format
   ... read database address record
 *
 * Construct address by calling xxxxx package API; then break down
   ... call program, passing in address fields, requested format;
       receive 500-byte address field 'Address'
C                  EVAL      StdzdAddr=Address
 *
 * Print mailing label
   ... print mailing label using format requested
       (Either print SFLine1-SFLine4 or LFLine1-LFLine6)
 *
 * Get next database records and loop back to construct address
   ... read next database address record
```

This example uses *from-to* notation to define the length of subfields SFLine1-4 and LFLine1-6, which means the definition specifies an explicit starting and ending position for each field. Because you will be looking at the contents of the entire data structure in multiple ways (two are shown here), *from-to* notation is the most straightforward method. Length notation does not work because each view of the data area starts at the first byte. If you define all the fields with length notation, the second set of fields (the LFLinex fields) is defined in positions after the first set of fields (the SFLinex fields), and they do not occupy the same area in storage. If you specify OVERLAY-style definition, you calculate the starting and ending positions anyway, so it is no better than the method here. No data type is specified. Because no decimal positions are defined on any subfields, the default is data type character.

At this point, the program has loaded the value of the data structure. So, the program can now use either set of fields, the SFLine fields or the LFLine fields, to access the various lines of the formatted, printable address.

Data Structures with OVERLAY by Example

Sometimes, if you don't know the location of the data you need, you have to define a data structure subfield relative to the position of another subfield. In such situations, you can specify the OVERLAY keyword. Consider a third-party product you purchase to handle data collection by means of handheld devices. These devices automatically transmit data to the AS/400 in real time. When your system receives this data, a vendor-supplied program calls your program to update your database and process the received information. The vendor-supplied program's communications subsystem handles all the complexities of the data reception. The vendor-supplied program calls your program and passes one parameter, a formatted string containing the latest transaction received. Because the handheld devices are programmable, the data's format can vary, depending on what you are having them send. The vendor's program passes the record along after handling the data transmission aspects unique to the vendor's transmission protocols.

Although the handhelds are programmable, they always transmit a 200-byte record that the vendor's program receives and passes along, whether your application needs all 200 bytes or not. Your program must subdivide that data record and process it. Because you program the handhelds, you know what format to use to subdivide the data record.

This situation calls for a data structure. You do not need multiple views of the data structure. The program is concerned with interpreting the data string received. When you define your data structure, you will find length notation much more convenient than *from-to* notation.

As it happens, you must define one part of the data record for multiple purposes: The transaction ID that the handheld generates uses several pieces of information. When you load this transaction to the database, you will store the transaction ID as one field. However, as you process each transaction, you must also print a report for that transaction. On this report, you have to break out the information that goes into the construction of the transaction ID. This information includes the date and time of the transaction, the operator ID of the handheld's user, and a task ID that identifies what type of operation the user is performing. Because you need to subdivide only part of the data, you need the OVERLAY keyword to let you redefine a part of the data structure's storage. The following code fragment shows the data structure coding for this application.

```
*...1....+....2....+....3....+....4....+....5....+....6....+....7....+
D TrxnRcd          DS
  * Data record received from handheld
D   TrxnID                   28
D     TrxnDate               6S 0 OVERLAY(TrxnID:1)
D     TrxnTime               6S 0 OVERLAY(TrxnID:7)
```
CONTINUED

```
*...1....+....2....+....3....+....4....+....5....+....6....+....7....+
D     TrxnUser               10     OVERLAY(TrxnID:13)
D      TrxnTask               6     OVERLAY(TrxnID:23)
D    TrxnQty                 5P 0
D    TrxnSize                 2
D    TrxnColor                8
D    TrxnPrice                7  2
D    TrxnPrdCd               10
 *
D TrxnDta          S        200
 *

*...1....+....2....+....3....+....4....+....5....+....6....+....7....+
 *
 * Received parameter list
C      *ENTRY        PLIST
C                    PARM                    TrxnDta
 *
 * Break down transaction data via data structure
C                    EVAL      TrxnRcd=TrxnDta
 *
 * Process transaction received
 ... additional processing
```

The definition of data structure TrxnRcd does not include a length specification. This program is not concerned about the size of the data structure, but about its contents. Because the handheld device is creating a record that you have designed, you can be more casual about defining the location of each piece of data and be more concerned with the size and type of the data. Therefore, this definition uses the length notation for the subfields and ignores the overall size of the data structure. The compiler will implicitly define the data structure's size to be as big as necessary to accommodate the defined subfields.

The subfields, in contrast, have a size specification. In fact, you can see that the types and sizes differ from field to field (unlike in the previous example). The compiler will implicitly determine each subfield's start and end position in the data area.

Of course, this situation leads to a question: If you aren't concerned with the location of each subfield, how can you redefine positions in the data structure to allow multiple views of the data? The answer is in the OVERLAY keyword, which appears on the definitions of four fields, TrxnDate, TrxnTime, TrxnUser, and TrxnTask. For each field, the keyword references the TrxnID field and specifies a starting position. The size and data type for the subfields give them access to the same storage locations as the TrxnID field.

OVERLAY provides two benefits here. First, it bases the definition of the subfields TrxnDate, TrxnTime, TrxnUser, and TrxnTask on the definition of the subfield TrxnID. This method is an improvement over using multiple definitions via *from-to* notation because the relationship among the subfields is now explicit by reference rather than implicit by shared location. A programmer cannot introduce an error by forgetting to change the positions of the TrxnDate, TrxnTime, TrxnUser, and TrxnTask fields when the positions of the TrxnID field change. Second, the structure of the data is easy to see and follow. By creating the explicit relationship between TrxnID and its parts, you can readily see the large field as consisting of the smaller ones. The indentation in the definition of the subfields clearly shows that the named data structure starts in position 8, the first-level subfields start in position 9, and the second-level subfields start in position 11. Nothing is special about the indentation. The names can just as easily all start in position 7. However, the ability to indent this way makes demonstrating the structure of the data very easy.

The data is received into a field that is the appropriate size for the entire data string the other program provides. The field TrxnDta is received as a parameter when this program is called. The TrxnDta field is then immediately assigned to the TrxnRcd data structure. In this example, the data structure is not the same size as the original record. It is only as big as the part of the data you need. This approach is perfectly acceptable because you are interested only in the data for which you define subfields, anyway.

Types of Data Structures

This discussion of data structures began with user-defined data structures. In addition to letting you create such data structures, RPG IV provides several types of predefined data structures for specific uses. These types are data area data structures, file status data structures, and program status data structures.

Data Area Data Structures

Data areas (OS/400 object type *DTAARA) are system storage locations for small, single-occurrence pieces of data. You can think of data areas as single-record, program-described files, but data areas usually store one value.

RPG IV lets you create a special type of data structure that will automatically retrieve the information in a data area at program initialization, place and hold a lock on the data area object, and then update the data area when the program terminates, releasing the lock. You take advantage of this RPG facility by identifying a data structure as being a data area data structure: You place a U in position 23 of the D-spec when you define the data structure.

To specify which data area the data area data structure will access, you can choose among three ways: using the DTAARA (Data Area) keyword with an unnamed data structure, a named data structure, or either of these.

The DTAARA Keyword

The DTAARA keyword lets you associate a data structure, a data area data structure, a data structure subfield, or a standalone field with a data area (OS/400 object type *DTAARA) so your program can access that data area by referring to the name of the data structure or field that you associate with it (the program has to read and update the data areas by means of the special operations IN and OUT). Subfield and standalone field definitions can include this keyword if you do not also define these fields as arrays or tables. The field or data structure must be the same size and type as the data area you want to access (except when the data area is the local data area (LDA), in which case, the field or data structure can be any length up to 1024, but must be character).

DTAARA has a second role that is optional. As DTAARA's single parameter value, you can specify the name of the data area to access. You can name any valid, existing data area on the system, or you can enter one of two special values, *LDA or *PDA (for the program initialization parameter data area), to access these data areas. If you do not specify the optional parameter to name the data area, the name of the field or structure you are defining will be the name of the data area with which the field or structure is associated.

Ordinarily, you will use the DTAARA keyword on a data structure, a data area data structure, or a standalone field. You can specify DTAARA on a data structure subfield, unless the data structure is already associated with a data area, or the subfield is the subfield of a data area data structure, multi-occurrence data structure, program status data structure, or file information data structure. However, DTAARA on a data structure subfield can be very confusing to later maintenance programmers.

You usually specify DTAARA with a standalone field if the data area you want to access holds a single value you want to use or update, especially with numeric data areas. Some shops like to store such data as the next available number in a sequence in a numeric data area, but this is not a recommended practice. In a highly audited shop, you cannot journal data area changes or hold them under commitment control. Some shops will use a character data area to hold the name of the company or branch, because this is usually pretty static information, but it does change occasionally. Rather than storing the company name in a literal in the program and then updating all the programs when a company name changes, you can store the name in a data area. You then retrieve it into a character field in your program by associating the data area with a standalone field.

The sample code on page 63 associates numeric and character data areas with standalone fields. You can associate a data structure subfield with a data area in the same way, except the field must, of course, be a subfield of a data structure.

```
*...1....+....2....+....3....+....4....+....5....+....6....+....7....+
D NxtOrdNbr      S            7  0 DTAARA
D CompName       S            25   DTAARA(TXCOMP)
```

The first field, NxtOrdNbr, is associated with data area NxtOrdNbr. Because no parameter is on the DTAARA keyword, the default is the name of the field you are defining. The second field, CompName, is associated with data area TXCOMP. Here, the name of the data area is not very clear, but by entering the name CompName in the program, you can clarify the meaning of the field, and a maintenance programmer will see that the field holds the company name instead of the company ID or code.

The DTAARA keyword can appear on either data structures or data area data structures. The only difference is that the data area data structure (U in position 23) will automatically read the data area at the beginning of the program and automatically update the data area when the program ends with LR on. With a data structure, in contrast, you must load and write it using the IN and OUT operations, respectively. In either case, you will usually associate a data structure (of either type) with a data area when the contents of the data area include several pieces of information in some format. This practice is similar to accessing one data record. The data area you want to associate with the data structure must be a character data area. If it is numeric, you need to associate it with either a standalone field or a data structure subfield.

```
*...1....+....2....+....3....+....4....+....5....+....6....+....7....+
D CompCtl       DS                  DTAARA
D  CompCode              6
D  CompName              25
D  ARInst                1
D  APInst                1
D  PRInst                1
 *
D Recovery      DS                  DTAARA(BLLCHKPNT)
D  RcvPgm                10
D  EcvStep               10
D  RcvCntrct             8
```

The code above defines two data structures for accessing a pair of data areas, but the two data structures are not data area data structures. The first data structure, CompCtl, refers to a data area of the same name. The lack of a parameter on the DTAARA keyword means that the referenced data area will have the same name as the data structure. (No U is in position 23 because of the DTAARA keyword.) This example shows access to a data area that is probably read-only. The data area contains five pieces of information that remains static, such as information in software that is part of a suite. The first field in the data structure, CompCode, holds the code or identifier for the company. The second, CompName, holds the text name of the company. The third through fifth fields, ARInst through PRInst, hold flags that signal whether these parts of the software suite are installed. These flags can control whether the program will attempt to access or attempt to create records for communication among the components of the suite.

The second data structure is an example of one that the program needs to update periodically throughout a run. The data area this data structure points to holds information about which step the program last completed. The referenced data area, BLLCHKPNT, holds data to identify the last successfully executed program, logical step, and contract being processed. You specify the OUT operation and assume that only one job uses the data area. This program will record the last successfully executed point in the program each time it completes a step. You can write the program so that when it starts, it will use the data structure to interrogate this data area so the program can branch to the correct point to resume processing in case of a failure, such as a power outage or a premature ending of the job for other reasons.

You need to remember two things about data area data structures. First, the data area is locked once the program starts and is not released until the program ends. This situation makes access to a shared data area (multiple programs accessing it) difficult to manage when you use data area data structures. Second, though you can change the value of the subfields in the data area data structure, the data area is not updated until the program terminates *with the last record (LR) indicator on*. Note an exception to that second point: If you specify the DTAARA keyword to identify the data area to access, you can use the special operations IN, OUT, and UNLOCK to control the reading, writing, and releasing of the lock on the data area.

*DTAARA DEFINE

The *DTAARA DEFINE operation on the C-specs associates a data area data structure, data area subfield, or standalone field with a data area. With *DTAARA DEFINE, the name of the data area to access can go in Factor 2, and the name of the field or structure to use in the program must be in the Result field. You can define the field at the same time by specifying the size of the field in positions 64 through 68 and the decimal positions (if the data area is numeric) in positions 69 through 70. The operation allows no conditioning or resulting indicators.

If you do not specify Factor 2, the name in the Result field is the name of the data area to access. If you compare this approach to DTAARA on the D-specs, you see that *DTAARA DEFINE uses the Result field entry as DTAARA uses the field or structure name (positions 7 through 21) on the D-specs. Factor 2 is used the same way as the parameter of the DTAARA keyword: This operation is equivalent to the DTAARA keyword.

Because a data structure or data structure subfield requires you to create the data structure or subfield on the D-specs, the DTAARA keyword makes more sense than *DTAARA DEFINE. The same point holds for working with standalone fields, which you don't have to define on the D-specs: The D-specs are the preferred way to define them. The following two code segments re-create the definitions of the data structures and fields from the discussion of the DTAARA keyword.

```
*...1....+....2....+....3....+....4....+....5....+....6....+....7....+
C     *DTAARA      DEFINE                    NxtOrdNbr        7 0
C     *DTAARA      DEFINE   TXCOMP           CompName         25
```

The first example defines two fields and associates them with data areas. The first field, NxtOrdNbr, will be associated with a data area of the same name. The field is seven digits long and has zero decimal positions. This definition must match the definition of the data area. Leaving the Factor 2 entry blank means that the name of the data area is the same as that of the field defined in the Result field. The second field, CompName, will be associated with the data area TXCOMP. Here, specifying a different name in the program clarifies the meaning of the data area name. The field created for use in the program is 25 characters long, which must match the definition of the data area.

```
*...1....+....2....+....3....+....4....+....5....+....6....+....7....+
D CompCtl         DS
D  CompCode                    6
D  CompName                   25
D  ARInst                      1
D  APInst                      1
D  PRInst                      1
 *
D Recovery        DS
D  RcvPgm                     10
D  EcvStep                    10
D  RcvCntrct                   8
 *

*...1....+....2....+....3....+....4....+....5....+....6....+....7....+
C     *DTAARA      DEFINE                    CompCtl
C     *DTAARA      DEFINE   BLLCHKPNT        Recovery
```

The second example associates two data structures, which are defined in the D-specs, with two data areas. Both data structures are defined as usual for a data area. Both are named, which is a requirement when you associate them with a data area via the DEFINE operation. The first data structure, CompCtl, is associated with a data area of the same name because Factor 2 of the DEFINE operation is blank. The second data structure, Recovery, is associated with a data area called BLLCHKPNT, as named in Factor 2 of the DEFINE operation.

Assigning a Data Area to a Data Area Data Structure
Programmers usually specify data area data structures to access the LDA, though even that use is becoming increasingly uncommon. To access the LDA with a data area data structure, you can use any of the three methods shown below.

```
*...1....+....2....+....3....+....4....+....5....+....6....+....7....+
D                  UDS
D ... subfields
```

The first example is the traditional method for accessing the LDA: an unnamed data area data structure. The DS in positions 24 and 25 identify a data structure, and the U in position 23 identifies it as a data area data structure. Because the data structure has no name and no specific data area is nominated, the LDA is the default data area to access. This data structure's subfields will be used to read and change the LDA. The data area will be read at program initialization. Because the data area has no name, it will be updated only when the program ends with LR on.

```
*...1....+....2....+....3....+....4....+....5....+....6....+....7....+
D                  UDS                *DTAARA(*LDA)
D ... subfields
```

The technique in the second example is new to RPG IV. The D-spec defines a named data structure and associates it with the LDA by means of the DTAARA keyword on the data structure definition. This definition shares the characteristics of the previous example, but you can now name the data structure on the OUT operation to update the LDA before the program ends.

```
*...1....+....2....+....3....+....4....+....5....+....6....+....7....+
D                  UDS
D ... subfields

*...1....+....2....+....3....+....4....+....5....+....6....+....7....+
 *
C      *DTAARA      DEFINE      *LDA          LocalData
```

The method in the third example is also new to RPG IV. The D-spec defines the data structure as in the first example. Here, you can reread the data structure via the IN operation and update it by means of the OUT operation because the definition associates a name with the LDA on the *DTAARA DEFINE operation.

In summary, as is the case for all data area data structures, the LDA will be automatically read at program initialization, locked throughout the program's execution, and then automatically updated when the program ends with LR on. The second and third techniques let you reread the LDA via the IN operation and update it before program termination via the OUT operation.

Data area data structures are not limited to the LDA. It is just the default when you don't provide a data area's name. You can also access the PDA. This special data structure is for a prestart job — see a work management manual for more information on the PDA. For this alternative, you specify either the second or third technique above, entering *PDA rather than *LDA.

Finally, you can access any named data area on the system by specifying the name of an existing data area, in one of four ways. The following examples show each of these four ways to access the data area NXTINVNBR.

```
*...1....+....2....+....3....+....4....+....5....+....6....+....7....+
D NxtInvNbr      UDS
D ... subfields
```

In the first example, the data structure name and the data area name are the same, so you need only the U to identify the data structure as a data area data structure. The only difference between the first example here and the first LDA example is the naming of the data structure. Using UDS without naming a structure is just a special case (defaulting to the LDA) of the first example here. Note that although you name the data structure in this example, you still cannot use the IN operation to reload it or the OUT operation to update it because you do not reference it by specifying the DTAARA keyword or the *DTAARA DEFINE operation.

```
*...1....+....2....+....3....+....4....+....5....+....6....+....7....+
D NxtInvNbr      UDS                DTAARA
D ... subfields
```

The second example is similar to the first. The difference is that the DTAARA keyword without any parameter lets the program use the IN and OUT operations on the data structure to read and update the data area NXTINVNBR.

```
*...1....+....2....+....3....+....4....+....5....+....6....+....7....+
D NextInv        UDS                DTAARA(NxtInvNbr)
D ... subfields
```

The third example lets you associate a data area data structure with a particular data area, yet enter a different name from the name of the data area. You can choose this technique if your data area's name is cryptic (perhaps because you have to follow strict naming standards) and you want a meaningful name in your program. This approach has the added benefit of allowing the use of IN and OUT operations.

```
*...1....+....2....+....3....+....4....+....5....+....6....+....7....+
D NextInv        UDS
D ... subfields
```

```
*...1....+....2....+....3....+....4....+....5....+....6....+....7....+
 *
C     *DTAARA      DEFINE    NxtInvNbr    NextInv
```

The fourth example is similar to the third. The difference is that the *DTAARA DEFINE operation, instead of the DTAARA keyword on the data area data structure definition, achieves the same effect as in the third example.

Multiple-Occurrence Data Structures

One special type of data structure is the multiple-occurrence data structure, which is like a regular data structure, with two exceptions. First, you have multiple copies (*occurrences*) of the entire data structure, and each copy can contain different data. An occurrence is a given copy of the data structure, and you can access only one occurrence at a time. Second, you must specify the OCCUR operation to identify which copy of the data structure is the current one (the one you are working with).

The OCCURS Keyword and OCCUR Operation

To create a multiple-occurrence data structure, you specify the OCCURS keyword on the D-spec where you define the data structure (the D-spec that has the DS on it). The OCCURS keyword has one parameter, the number of occurrences that the data structure will have. You specify this number in parentheses immediately following the keyword name. The entry for the parameter can be a numeric literal, a named constant specified earlier in the program, or the result of a built-in function. The parameter value can be any one of these if it returns a non-zero integer value. Note that this number is set at compile time and is not dynamic; you cannot change it at runtime.

What you can and must change at runtime is which occurrence you are working with. You enter the OCCUR operation in the C-specs to determine which occurrence of the data structure is currently active. You specify OCCUR as the operation, and you cannot specify an operation code extender. You must specify either Factor 1 or the Result field. Factor 2, which is required, is always the name of a multiple-occurrence data structure, the one whose occurrence you are setting.

If you specify the Result field, it must be a numeric field. After the OCCUR operation, this field will contain the number of the currently active occurrence.

Although Factor 1 is optional, you will use it often to set a particular occurrence. The value you specify in Factor 1 becomes the occurrence that is currently active. You can specify a zero-decimal numeric field, a literal, or a named constant in Factor 1 to directly set the occurrence to a specific value.

You can specify an error indicator in positions 73 and 74. It will be set on if you attempt to set the occurrence of the data structure outside its allowable range. That can happen only if you attempt to set the occurrence to a negative number or zero or attempt to set it to a number larger than the number of occurrences you specify on the OCCURS keyword. Let's look at an example.

```
*...1....+....2....+....3....+....4....+....5....+....6....+....7....+
DLvlTotals         DS                  OCCURS(5)
D GrsSlsTot                      9 2
D NetSlsTot                      9 2
D SlsCommTot                     7 2
D CostTot                        9 2

*...1....+....2....+....3....+....4....+....5....+....6....+....7....+
 *
 * Loop through data file reading records sequentially by key
 * For each record
 *   If a level break occurs, print the totals; clear the accumulators
 *   Print the current record
 *   Accumulate current record to all levels
 ... read first records and start loop to read all records
 *
 * If company, division, department, or salesperson changes —
 *   Set accumulator data structure to occurrence for salesperson
 *   Print totals for salesperson
C    1              OCCUR     LvlTotals
 ... call routine to print salesperson totals
 *
 * Clear the salesperson level accumulators
C                   EVAL      GrsSlsTot=0
C                   EVAL      NetSlsTot=0
C                   EVAL      SlsCommTot=0
C                   EVAL      CostTot=0
 *
```

CONTINUED

```
*...1....+....2....+....3....+....4....+....5....+....6....+....7....+
 * If company, division, or department changes —
 *   Set accumulator data structure to occurrence for department
 *   Print totals for department
C     2              OCCUR     LvlTotals
  ... call routine to print department totals
 *
 * Clear the department level accumulators
C                    EVAL      GrsSlsTot=0
C                    EVAL      NetSlsTot=0
C                    EVAL      SlsCommTot=0
C                    EVAL      CostTot=0
 *
  ... handle division and company levels in similar manner using
      level 3 for division and level 4 for company
 *
 * Print the current record
  ... handle the printing of the current record
 *
 * Accumulate the current record to the salesperson level
C     1              OCCUR     LvlTotals
C                    EVAL      GrsSlsTot=GrsSlsTot + GrsSls
C                    EVAL      NetSlsTot=NetSlsTot + NetSls
C                    EVAL      SlsCommTot=SlsCommTot + SlsComm
C                    EVAL      CostTot=CostTot + Cost
 *
 * Accumulate the current record to the department level
C     2              OCCUR     LvlTotals
C                    EVAL      GrsSlsTot=GrsSlsTot + GrsSls
C                    EVAL      NetSlsTot=NetSlsTot + NetSls
C                    EVAL      SlsCommTot=SlsCommTot + SlsComm
C                    EVAL      CostTot=CostTot + Cost
 *
  ... handle accumulation to division and company in similar manner
      using level 3 for division and level 4 for company
 *
 * Read the next record and loop back to process it
  ... handle read of next record and loop
 *
 * Process final level breaks after processing entire file.
```

This code shows how a multiple-occurrence data structure can record a set of totals for each level in a report. Because a report typically requires totals of several columns, you will probably have several fields at each level for accumulating those totals. The accumulating fields at each level are usually identical, so a multiple-occurrence data structure provides just the type of structure to track each total. (Note that arrays are also appropriate for this type of task, and depending on your coding method, you may prefer to use several arrays — one for each field to be accumulated — instead of a multiple-occurrence data structure.) This example report has four level breaks, one each for salesperson, department, division, and company. The first-level break is salesperson, the second department, etc. Naturally, when a high-level break is triggered (the data changes from one record to the next), all lower-level breaks are also triggered.

This example creates a multiple-occurrence data structure that contains accumulator fields for four different fields that you need to total while generating the report. The data structure defined in line 01 is called LvlTotals. The DS in positions 24 and 25 determines that it is a data structure.

The OCCURS keyword in the D-specs makes the data structure a multiple-occurrence data structure. The only parameter of the OCCURS keyword, specified in parentheses after the keyword, determines how many occurrences the data structure will have. So, this example has four occurrences to correspond with the four levels for salesperson, department, division, and company.

The next four D-specs identify the fields that will be on each occurrence of the data structure. The four externally defined fields, GrsSlsTot, NetSlsTot, SlsCommTot, and CostTot, will track the totals accumulated at each level for each of the four fields on the report. When you're ready to work with the accumulators, you will need to set the data structure to the appropriate occurrence.

The C-specs perform some basic level-break processing to enable the accumulation and printing of the total and detail lines for the report. The example includes pseudocode for portions of the program not directly relevant to the use of multiple-occurrence data structures.

When the program detects a level-one change (a change in salesperson, or any higher level), you need to print the totals for that level and then clear them. Because each occurrence of the data structure LvlTotals contains one level's totals, you need to set the data structure to the appropriate level. Level 1 is for the salesperson totals, so the OCCUR operation specifies a 1 in Factor 1 to inform the program that it needs to activate the first occurrence of the data structure. You can then call a routine (or execute inline code) to print the salesperson totals and perform any other processing necessary at that time. Once the print is complete, you can clear the accumulators in preparation for accumulating the next salesperson. Because the data structure is already set to the proper occurrence, you just need to reference the names of the fields in the data structure in the calculations. Lines 21 through 24 set the values of the accumulators to zero.

The following code repeats the same process but sets a different occurrence of the data structure, 2 instead of 1. You can print the fields from occurrence 2 and then clear them, as with the salesperson totals (level 1, or occurrence 1). The program can then perform the same tasks for the next two levels, which print and then clear the accumulators for the division and company levels. When all the level-break total printing and clearing is complete, the program moves on to process the detail record. Part of that detail processing entails accumulating to the total accumulators.

This example demonstrates accumulating to all the levels from the detail level. You may prefer to accumulate from one level's totals to another level's. The method here is slower because each detail record is accumulated to every total level. However, this approach lets you see the totals as they grow. Select the processing method that makes the most sense for your application from a performance and maintainability standpoint.

The program again sets the occurrence of the data structure and then add the appropriate fields from the record you read into the corresponding accumulator field in the current occurrence of the LvlTotals data structure. The program then repeats the process to handle the department. The process continues to handle division and company. Finally the program processes final level breaks when it reaches end of file (this processing is pseudocoded here).

File Status Data Structure

Another data structure you can define in your program's D-specs is a file status data structure. You include this data structure to get information about the files the program will use. With this information, the program can handle errors without users' knowledge.

A file status data structure is a special data structure. It is not a special *type* of data structure because you define it just as you do any ordinary data structure. Any named data structure can become a *file status* data structure if you associate it with a file that your program opens. Then, the compiled program will place information about the associated file in the data structure you create.

You associate a named data structure with a file (making it a file status data structure) by entering the INFDS (Information Data Structure) keyword on the F-spec when you declare that file to the program. The value of the one parameter of INFDS is the name of the data structure in which you want to put information about the file. The name you specify in this parameter must be the name of a standard data structure: Data area data structures, multiple-occurrence data structures, and program status data structures are not allowed. Each file in the program can have an INFDS keyword to associate a data structure with it, but each file's data structure must be different.

Because you define this data structure on the D-specs in the same way you define any named data structure, because this data structure serves a very specialized purpose (file error handling), and because this structure's use is a more advanced topic than this chapter on D-specs can cover, this chapter only introduces you to the concept of the file status data structure. Appendix C, "Error Handling Data Structures," explains them in detail.

Program Status Data Structure

Another data structure that you define in the program's D-specs is the program status data structure. This error-handling data structure is similar to a file status data structure but is simpler to use and understand. Whereas a file status data structure contains information about a specific file, the program status data structure contains information about the entire program or the job in which the program is running.

The program status data structure gives you quite a bit of information and several values that can help you determine what errors occurred in your programs. With this data structure, you can do something as simple as log the error to an error file when you have a failure in your programs. Or, you can have your program automatically handle certain errors.

The program status data structure is a special *type* of data structure because you have to define it in a specific way. The program status data structure has a predefined format, consisting of certain subfields whose positions you define either by *from-to* notation or via special keywords. You create a program status data structure as you do any data structure, but you must include a special entry on the D-spec: S in position 23. This entry identifies the data structure as a program status data structure. That entry is the only requirement for defining a program status data structure.

The program status data structure is an advanced topic, and this chapter covers only how to define data in the program's D-specs. For details about this data structure, see Appendix B, "Error-Handling Data Structures."

ARRAYS AND TABLES IN RPG IV

The other definition you can enter in your program's D-specs is for arrays and tables. Arrays are contiguous lists that let you access list items by indexes, or subscripts, that point to a particular place in the list. Each item in the list is called an *element*. RPG IV supports three types of arrays: runtime arrays, compile-time arrays, and pre-runtime arrays. Like arrays, RPG IV tables are ordered, contiguous lists containing multiple copies of identically formatted data items. However, tables are different from arrays in that, rather than using indexes, you access them by means of the C-spec LOOKUP operation.

Because the topic of this chapter is data definition, this section will tell you only how to define arrays and tables in your program's D-specs. For details about arrays and tables and how to use them, see Chapter 8, "Arrays and tables."

Defining an Array

To define an array, in the D-specs you enter the name of the array, the size and type of its elements, a keyword to specify the number of elements the array has, and, optionally, a keyword to determine the method and time of loading the array (which determines the type of array you want). Valid keywords with arrays are DIM (Dimension), ASCEND, DESCEND, FROMFILE, TOFILE, ALT (Alternating loading), CTDATA (Compile-time Data), and PERRCD (Per Record). Here is a sample D-spec that defines a compile-time array called Invoice.

```
*...1....+....2....+....3....+....4....+....5....+....6....+....7....+
D Invoice         S              5A   DIM(10) CTDATA
  *
```

You enter the array's name (in this case, Invoice) in positions 7 through 21. The name of the array is not distinguishable from any field name in RPG.

In position 24, you place an S to specify that each element is a standalone field. This required specification may seem confusing, but array elements are like standalone fields.

The number of elements you define for your array is called the array's *dimension* value. In positions 44 through 80, you see this term reflected in the DIM keyword. This keyword's parameter is where you specify the number of elements in the array and, in fact, this keyword defines this entry as an array. The DIM keyword in this example associates 10 memory cells with the array Invoice. Positions 33 through 39 define each element's length as 5 and its type is character (position 40). The CTDATA keyword (also in positions 44 through 80) is an optional keyword that establishes that the array is a compile-time array and tells the compiler to load this array's data, which is at the bottom of the source member, at compile time.

Defining a Table

To define a table, in the D-specs you enter the name of the table, beginning with the letters TAB, specify the number of elements it has, and specify the type and size of the elements. For example, here are the definitions of two tables, TABCTY and TABDIF.

```
*...1....+....2....+....3....+....4....+....5....+....6....+....7....+
DTABCTY          S             10A   DIM(6) CTDATA PERRCD(1)
DTABDIF          S              1S 0 DIM(6) CTDATA PERRCD(1) ASCEND
```

As with array definitions, you specify the table name, but you prefix it with the obligatory TAB, in positions 7 through 21. The name of the table is distinguishable from any field or array name in RPG because of the initial three characters, TAB. In position 24, you place an S for standalone field (as you do with an array definition — again, like array elements, table elements are similar to standalone fields). In positions 33 through 39, you specify each element's length, and the data type is in position 40. All array keywords are also valid for tables. You specify the number of elements for a table by means of the DIM keyword.

CHAPTER 4

Database Programming

An important characteristic of the AS/400 is its robust database management system. Like RPG III, RPG IV continues to give you access to AS/400 database functions through native language syntax. This chapter covers RPG IV database programming, explaining database files and how to define them externally by means of Data Description Specifications (DDS). This discussion will lead to explanations of how to read data from and write data to database files, and to the operation codes that let you process the records. Discussion of commitment control and then the file information data structure and subroutine concludes this topic.

DESCRIBING DATABASE FILES

Before creating a data file on the AS/400, you need to decide what its layout will be. You need to know the fields you want in the file, their order, length, and data type. With this information, you can derive the file's record length, which is the combined lengths of the record's fields; an AS/400 database does not contain unused or undefined sections in a data record.

By entering DDS code in a source file, you record the file layout information. You then compile the source by issuing CL create commands such as CRTPF (Create Physical File) and CRTLF (Create Logical File). Compiling the DDS source creates a file object in a library.

The file object contains a description of itself: It records the size, location, and data type of each field it includes. As a result, when you compile an RPG program that uses a file object, the compiler can extract that information from the file, so you don't have to record the information in the program's source. You only have to address a field by its name. The compiler determines where to get the data out of a record you read or where to put the data in a record you write. A file object that you compile from DDS source is an *externally described* file because the file's description is stored externally (within the file object) from the programs that use it.

Old RPG programs sometimes have the data files defined in the program. Such files are *program described* because someone created them by defining the record's layout and the data attributes in the RPG program's I-specs.

RPG IV allows either external or program description of database files, but you will want to always describe your files externally. Here is a list of some reasons why externally described files are preferable to program-described files.

1. Externally described files improve maintainability when you need to change the layout of any record format. When a record format layout changes, all you have to do is adjust the external DDS source for the file and recompile it. You don't need any code change in the RPG program. You just recompile a program that uses the file, so that the program can learn about the new record layout and re-extract it.

2. You perform less coding in the program, which improves its readability.

3. You can reuse fields and record format definitions. If many programs use a file, you can define the fields once and let all your programs use them.

4. You can ensure consistency and, consequently, fewer errors across all programs that use the same external descriptions.

Never use program-described files for new programs. Following this rule, this chapter will concentrate on externally described files. It will explain how to define files in DDS and how to use them in an RPG program.

DDS File Definition

The two types of externally described data files are physical files and logical files. A physical file contains data and your description of the layout and attributes of that data. A logical file does not contain data. It is a description, or view, of one or more physical files.

To define and then create physical and logical files, you use DDS to specify all the details about the layout of the file's record format, which consists of fields. For example, you can have a file containing a customer information record format, consisting of such fields as name, address, zip, and phone number.

Describing a Physical File

To design a physical file, you decide what fields to include, what the attributes of those field are, and how to order the data. You enter DDS to describe those fields, which comprise that physical file's record format. You enter all the DDS in a source member and then issue the CRTPF command to produce the physical file object. (This chapter will cover the basic DDS file description, but DDS includes many more features and facilities than you'll learn about here. For more information about DDS, see IBM's reference manual, *Programming: Data Description Specifications Reference.*)

The sample DDS on page 79 defines several fields for physical file CLUBMBRP (Club Member Physical). Let's quickly tour the code. The first line specifies that the index built on this file will enforce unique key values. This UNIQUE keyword specification is an example of a DDS file-level keyword — it establishes an attribute for the entire file.

```
*...1....+....2....+....3....+....4....+....5....+....6....+....7....+
A                                         UNIQUE
A           R CLUBMBRPR
A             CMID          7  0         TEXT('Member ID')
A             CMFSTNAM     10            TEXT('First Name')
A             CMLSTNAM     10            TEXT('Last Name')
A             CMADRS       30            TEXT('Address')
A             CMCITY       20            TEXT('City')
A             CMSTATE       2            TEXT('State')
A             CMZIP         5            TEXT('ZIP Code')
A             CMBTHDTE      L            TEXT('Birth Date') DATFMT(*ISO)
A *
A           K CMID
```

The second line defines a record format. The R in position 17 signals the start of a record format definition. In DDS, each record format receives a name. This record format's name is CLUBMBRPR (Club Member Physical Record). An RPG program can reference this format name to access the record layout.

After you name the format, you can start describing the fields in the record. CMID (Club Member ID) is the name of a field that is a seven-digit, packed-decimal number, with zero decimal positions. Because position 35 (data type) is blank *and* the number of decimal positions is specified in positions 36 and 37, the data type defaults to packed decimal. The next line defines field CMFSTNAM (Club Member First Name) as length 10, no data type, and no decimal positions. The data type for this field defaults to character because no decimal positions are specified. The next five fields (CMLSTNAM, CMADRS, CMCITY, CMSTATE, and CMZIP) are also character fields with a length of 10, 30, 20, 2, and 5, respectively.

The AS/400 supports seven other data types, one of which you see on the last field definition. The last field, CMBTHDTE, has no length specified. However, it has a data type of L (in position 35), defining it as a date field. The system will automatically define the field's size because date fields have a predefined size.

All the field definitions use documentation in the form of the TEXT keyword, which assigns descriptive text to each field in the format. The last field, the date field, also uses the DATFMT (Date Format) keyword to format the date when a program reads this field from the database.

The end of the fields in the record format comes with the K in position 17, which serves two purposes: It signals the end of the record format, and it identifies which fields will make up this file's key. In this case, CMID is the key field to identify each record. Recall the UNIQUE keyword at the file level; it makes the system require that every record have a unique value in CMID.

By defining the file and then compiling it, you make the record format definition available to all programs. The length, type, order, name, and location of the fields in the record are stored outside the programs, so the definition remains consistent each time you access the fields. Additionally, RPG will automatically extract the key field definition, and the compiler will help ensure that you use fields of the correct size and type when you access records in this file. You never specify the location of each field, nor do you specify the record length in the program. Those values are derived from the size and order of the fields, which you do specify.

Describing a Logical File

Physical files make logical files possible. Logical files let you create various views of a physical file to change the order of the data, include a subset of the fields in the file, include a subset of the records in the files, and even combine fields from multiple files. As with physical files, you define logical files in DDS, compile them with a CL command (CRTLF), and then reference them in an RPG IV program.

```
*...1....+....2....+....3....+....4....+....5....+....6....+....7....+
A          R CLUBMBRPR              PFILE(CLUBMBRP)
  *
A          K CMLSTNAM
A          K CMFSTNAM
```

The previous example explains the DDS for the physical file CLUBMBRP. Now, let's look at some specifications for a logical file to view the physical file's records in a different order (different key sequence). This DDS for a logical file lets you view the physical file's data in name order.

This logical file description specifies the physical file's format name. When you compile the file by issuing the CRTLF command, you can name this file CLUBMBRL1 (Club Member Logical 1).

The first line, which starts the format CLUBMBPR, includes the keyword PFILE (Physical File) to identify the physical file over which you want to build the logical file. This logical specifies the same format name as is on the physical file, so you do not need to name any fields explicitly. All fields in the physical file's format are automatically available in the logical file's format. You have to add only the list of key fields.

The K in position 17 starts a key definition. CMLSTNAM is the first key, and the second is CMFSTNAM. This key specification lets you access the data in the underlying physical file in name order, which can be useful for printing invitations to club events.

Alternatively, you can specify the names of the fields to include in the logical file's format if you do not want all fields to be available through the logical file. For instance, to let users access a file that lets them see only the names of club members and the state they live in, you can specify the following DDS. This code prevents users from seeing other fields on the physical file.

```
*...1....+....2....+....3....+....4....+....5....+....6....+....7....+
A             R CLUBMBRL2R                PFILE(CLUBMBRP)
A               CMLSTNAM
A               CMFSTNAM
A               CMSTATE
 *
A             K CMLSTNAM
A             K CMFSTNAM
```

This logical file includes a new format, CLUBMBRL2R, that uses fields from the format in the underlying physical file, CLUBMBRP. This logical file (CLUBMBRL2) lets users see only the three fields in the logical file's DDS. You do not have to assign sizes or types to the fields; they pick up that information from the underlying physical file (identified in the PFILE keyword).

The fields appear in a different order from the order in the physical file. With a logical file, you can rearrange fields, select which fields you see, reorder records, select specific records, and more.

The most important component of this scenario is, of course, the physical file CLUBMBRP, which provides the data for the two logical files, CLUBMBRL1 and CLUBMBRL2. The physical file is essential because logical files are only views that let you see the physical file's data — that is, logical files do not contain any data.

DECLARING AND PROCESSING FILES

Once you externally define data files, to declare and process them in an RPG program, you use both the F-specs and the C-specs. The F-specs are where you declare the file and name it. The F-specs also define how to process the file and how to handle special circumstances.

Because you use the F-specs and C-specs together to define and process the files in an RPG program, let's examine them together. First, let's consider the simplest method of processing a file — processing an indexed file sequentially by its key — and then move on to random processing by key, sequential processing with a SETLL (Set Lower Limits) operation (which lets you dynamically position the record pointer in the file), and random processing by relative record number.

Sequential Processing by Key

The reason for building an index on a file is usually to ensure unique keys in the file. Another reason for indexing a file lies in a basic requirement of database design: the ability to process records in a particular order. For example, the key field in the sample logical file CLUBMBRL2 is the name of each club member. To print a list of members, you need an alphabetical list. You process the file's records sequentially based on their position in the index, or sequentially by key. Here is the F-spec to declare the file and specify that you want to process it for input by its key.

```
*...1....+....2....+....3....+....4....+....5....+....6....+....7....+.
FCLUBMBRL2 IF   E          K DISK
*
```

You begin by declaring the database file's name, starting in position 7. Here, the file name is CLUBMBRL2. In position 17, you specify how you will be using the file. The I (input) means the program will only read the information in the file. Position 18 is the file designation. An F here describes this file as full procedural. This designation lets you access data in a file without using RPG's built-in file-processing cycle (an outdated method of data access). Database files are usually fully procedural.

Position 22 is for the file format, and two values are permitted here: E and F. An E specifies that this F-spec is declaring an externally described file. During program compilation, the RPG compiler will search the current library or the library list to find this file and extract its record format descriptions. Alternately, an F in position 22 means that this F-spec is declaring a file containing records described in the RPG IV program's input/output specifications — an F in the file format position specifies a program-described file.

In position 34, you can enter a K to tell the compiler to use key values to process the file instead of processing it by relative record number (RRN). That RRN method gives you the records in the order in which they are stored in the file, rather than the alphabetical list you want here.

Finally, you need to tell the compiler that the file you are defining is a data file. Because RPG knows data files by the term disk file, you enter DISK as the device (positions 37 through 42).

Processing Sequentially with READ

The previous F-spec declares file CLUBMBRL2 to the program. When you want to read the next record in this file, you use a READ operation in the C-specs, as you see here.

```
*...1....+....2....+....3....+....4....+....5....+....6....+....7....+.
C                   READ      CLUBMBRL2                              9890
```

When you specify a READ operation with an externally described file, READ requires a file or format name in Factor 2. READ also requires a resulting indicator in positions 75 to 76. The resulting indicator is turned on when the operation encounters end of file. You can enter an indicator in positions 73 to 74 to signal an error on the READ.

The READ operation supports the N (No record locking) operation code extender. If you open a file for update, you can specify the N extender with READ to retrieve the record without locking it for update. READ(N) reads the record without locking it, but READ locks it, preventing anyone from reading it for update. Here is the syntax for READ.

Factor 1	Opcode	Extender	Factor 2	Result	Indicators		
Not allowed	READ	(N)	Required *file- or record-name*	Not allowed	N/A	Error	EOF

Processing a File with READ by Example

Using READ to print out a quick alphabetical list of club members will require a loop to read multiple records in the database file. The READ operation reads the next record relative to where the file's cursor is pointing. When a program first opens a file, the cursor is at the beginning of the file (unless the ODP — Open Data Path — is shared, in which case, the cursor will be set wherever previous processes left it).

Knowing that the cursor is at the beginning of the file when you start, you can read the records and continue until you hit end of file. (You will have to print each record you read and consider page headings and such; these details are pseudocoded in the example for this situation.)

Here, you see that using RPG IV to get a quick list of data out of an externally described file does not involve much work. Most of the coding for this program involves formatting the data, but the data access is quick and easy.

```
*...1....+....2....+....3....+....4....+....5....+....6....+....7....+.
FCLUBMBRL2 IF   E           K DISK
F ... printer file definition ...
```

The example below declares the CLUBMBRL2 file as an externally described, full-procedural, input file. Then, a DOW (Do While) operation loops through all the records in the file, as long as the condition expressed is true. The ENDDO statement at the end of the code defines the boundary of the DOW loop. You read the first record and then start a loop that continues as long as the indicator for the end of file is not turned on. At the bottom of the loop, you read the next record in the file.

```
*...1....+....2....+....3....+....4....+....5....+....6....+....7....+.
*
* ... Print page headings
*
* Read the first record to verify that records exist in file
```

CONTINUED

```
*...1....+....2....+....3....+....4....+....5....+....6....+....7....+.
C                    READ      CLUBMBRL2                              LR
C                    DOW       NOT *INLR
 *
 *  ... Process if not end of file
 *
 *  ... Write club member list entry to printer
 . . .
 * Get next record and loop back
 *
C                    READ      CLUBMBRL2                              LR
C                    ENDDO
```

Processing Sequentially by Key with READP

Usually, you want to read the *next* record in a file in key order, but some situations call for reading the *previous* record in the key order. RPG IV offers the READP (Read Previous) operation code for this purpose. READP reads the record that is before the position in the file's index where the cursor is pointing.

A frequent mistake is to assume that a READP will automatically start at the end of the index and work toward the beginning. However, when you first open the file, the file cursor is at the beginning of the index. Issuing a READP immediately will set on an indicator to inform you that you have reached the beginning of the file. You will usually issue READP when some other operation (such as a SETxx operation or a CHAIN) has already positioned the file cursor.

With READP, you begin by declaring the file in the same manner as with the READ operation code. You specify the file as full procedural, keyed, and externally described.

The difference between READ and READP is in the C-specs. The READP operation, like READ, requires a file name in Factor 2, allows an error indicator, and requires a beginning-of-file indicator. An indicator in position 73 to 74 will turn on if an error occurs when the system tries to read the record. An indicator in position 75 to 76 will turn on, in this case, when the beginning of file is reached. Here is a sample C-spec for READP.

```
*...1....+....2....+....3....+....4....+....5....+....6....+....7....+.
C                    READP     CLUBMBRL2                            9890
```

The READP operation supports the N (No record locking) operation code extender. If you open a file for update, you can specify the N extender with READP to retrieve the record without locking it for update. READP(N) reads the record without locking it, but READP locks it, preventing others from reading it for update. Here is the syntax for READP.

Factor 1	Opcode	Extender	Factor 2	Result	Indicators		
Not allowed	READP	(N)	Required *file- or record- name*	Not allowed	N/A	Error	EOF

Processing a File with READP by Example

Occasionally, you need a listing in reverse order to the index you are working with. For instance, say you need a club member listing in reverse alphabetical order. With the following change to the program that produced the original alphabetical listing, you can use the same access path as before but traverse it in reverse order.

```
*...1....+....2....+....3....+....4....+....5....+....6....+....7....+.
FCLUBMBRL2 IF   E          K DISK
F ... printer file definition ...

*...1....+....2....+....3....+....4....+....5....+....6....+....7....+.
 * Print page headings
    . . .
 * Set cursor to end of index and then read the last record.
 *
C      *HIVAL       SETLL     CLUBMBRL2
C                   READP     CLUBMBRL2                               LR
C                   DOW       NOT *INLR
 *
 * Process if not end of file
 *
    . . . write list entry to printer
 *
 * Get next record (previous in index) and loop back
 *
C                   READP     CLUBMBRL2                               LR
C                   ENDDO
```

Some operation usually positions against the file before a READP. In this case, SETLL (Set Lower Limit) positions to the end of the file before you begin reading it. SETLL lets you begin processing at the next record with a key greater than or equal to the key you specify in Factor 1. In SETLL's Factor 2, you enter the name of the file or record containing the data you want.

Once SETLL positions the file cursor to the end of the file, you can issue READP to read the last record. Because the file's cursor is pointing at the end of the file, reading the previous record gives you the last record in the alphabetical sequence. Now, you use a loop to continue reading backward through the index until you hit beginning of file (BOF). As in the previous example, LR is the indicator for BOF because this program will be reading the records only once through and then terminating.

One nice feature of READP is that you don't have to create a new index on a file that is keyed with the names in descending alphabetical order. DDS will certainly let you build such an index (via another logical file), but why add the burden of maintaining that new index when the need for the descending data order is rare? READP gives you the flexibility of controlling the direction of reading through an existing index.

Optional F-Spec Keywords for Externally Described Files

When you're working with externally described data files, some keywords are available to help you avoid some confusion about the way RPG IV handles format names and field names. Three of these keywords — INCLUDE, IGNORE, and RENAME — let you select and rename formats that your program uses in handling a file. The fourth keyword, PREFIX, lets you rename the fields in a format so that if you have identical external field names in multiple files, you can have RPG automatically create new field names by prefixing each field with characters you specify.

One capability RPG IV lacks is referencing a field within a context. In contrast, COBOL lets you have fields of identical names if you can uniquely address them through qualification. That qualification lets you access the same file multiple times or lets you access multiple files that include the same format or field name but still address the fields within the context of which file's data you want. RPG IV has no such facilities for addressing a field.

In addition, RPG IV does not let you use the same record format name twice in the files you are accessing. However, no such restriction exists for *fields*. They can have the same name on as many records as you want. The drawback is that if you read records from multiple files and each file has the same field name associated with it, the last record you read provides the data for the named field — each file does not have separate data in the field. Additionally, if two files have fields with the same name but different sizes or data types, the compiler fails to create your program because of multiple definitions of the same field. To get around these inconveniences, RPG IV provides two file-level keywords, RENAME and PREFIX. RENAME lets you give a format a new name so that you can get around the problem of having duplicate format names. PREFIX lets you create new field names. You can use these keywords together or separately, depending on your needs.

The RENAME Keyword

The RENAME keyword lets you provide an alias for an externally described record format name. This keyword helps prevent confusion when you're using multiple files and multiple record formats, some of which have similar or identical names. Of course, having numerous record formats with the same or very similar names isn't the best programming practice, but it happens. For example, a physical and logical file may use the same format name, or you may use the same file in a program multiple times, which means you must rename the format on all but the first use of the file. In such a case, RENAME lets you give one format a new name. RENAME has one parameter, where you give a record format's DDS-specified name followed by a colon and the new name you want for this format.

RENAME by Example

Physical file CLUBMBRP and logical file CLUBMBRL1 both use the same format name, CLUBMBRPR. If you need both files in a program, you need to have RPG IV rename one format. Needing both files is very likely if you are constructing a program to display the names of the club members in alphabetical order and then let users take some action on one of the records.

One drawback to using the CLUBMBRL1 logical file for processing this type of request is that multiple club members can have the same name. So your program cannot guarantee that it will access the record you want to process. For instance, if you let users delete a record and you just display the name on the screen to delete the record through the CLUBMBRL1 file, users can accidentally delete the wrong record if two members have the same name. To avoid this situation, you perform the update through a file that has a unique key. You then also include the CLUBMBRP file in the program. To unambiguously access the member's record through CLUBMBRP, you can use the club member's ID that you access when you read the original record.

Here are the F-specs for declaring both CLUBMBRL1 and CLUBMBRP in the same RPG program. The F-spec for CLUBMBRL1 contains the RENAME keyword to rename the format CLUBMBRPR to CLUBMBRL1R. This prevents compiler errors. The first parameter of the RENAME keyword specifies the DDS record format name, followed by a colon and the new name.

```
*...1....+....2....+....3....+....4....+....5....+....6....+....7....+
FCLUBMBRP   IF   E           K DISK
FCLUBMBRL1 IF   E           K DISK    RENAME(CLUBMBRPR:CLUBMBRL1R)
```

The PREFIX Keyword

Occasionally, you need to work with two or more files, each containing a field with the same name. But having the same field defined for multiple files gives you only one copy of the field, so the file that was last read will populate the field. This situation makes working simultaneously with two files that have identically named fields impractical, especially if you intend to read a record from each and then compare entries: They will always match.

RPG IV introduces the file-level PREFIX keyword to help solve this problem. Its format is PREFIX(string). When you declare the field to the RPG program, the value of the 'string' parameter will prefix every field name from the external description.

Two simple rules apply to PREFIX. First, if you explicitly rename a field on the I-specs for this file, the prefixing will not occur for that field. Second, the field name resulting from prefixing the external name with your string must not be greater than the maximum field name size of 10 characters. Naturally, you have to make certain that the new field names do not conflict with any existing names.

PREFIX by Example

The example for the RENAME keyword solved the problem of having multiple files with identical format names. However, you still cannot simultaneously work with a record from each file. The names of the fields on both files are CMID, CMFSTNAM, CMLSTNAM, CMADRS, CMCITY, CMSTATE, CMZIP, and CMBTHDTE. Reading a record from either file and then reading a record from the other file will wipe out the data from the file you first read unless you save the data in some other fields first or rename each field on an I-spec.

Prefixing lets you handle the process a little more generically than the I-spec renaming method but sacrifices some flexibility. The generic handling comes from the fact that PREFIX applies to all fields in a file. If you recompile a program after adding new fields to a file, the PREFIX keyword's prefix string will automatically rename the new fields. The loss of flexibility comes from the limitation that prefixing creates longer field names instead of replacing a field name with a name whose length you can control (which is the case with individual field replacement on the I-specs).

This example specifies PREFIX for the CLUBMBRL1 file. This keyword will rename the fields and ensure unique field names between the two files.

```
*...1....+....2....+....3....+....4....+....5....+....6....+....7....+
FCLUBMBRP  IF   E       K DISK
FCLUBMBRL1 IF   E       K DISK      RENAME(CLUBMBRPR:CLUBMBRL1R)
F                                   PREFIX(L1)
```

The specification continues onto the next line. No continuation characters are necessary, but the specification line must be blank except for the specification type, F, and the keyword area. The compiler automatically handles the line as a continuation of the last F-spec line that has a file identified. Notice, also, that PREFIX applies to the file with the renamed format. This prefixing keeps names consistent and helps you remember which file has this special treatment.

The field names that PREFIX will create when a program reads the definition of the CLUBMBRL1 from the externally described file are L1CMID,

L1CMFSTNAM, L1CMLSTNAM, L1CMADRS, L1CMCITY, L1CMSTATE, L1CMZIP, and L1CMBTHDTE. Now you can safely read a record from each file and know that the data will be in separate fields for each file.

Some of these field names reach the RPG IV maximum size for a field name. DDS allows field names of up to 10 characters, just as RPG IV does. This limitation means that you can't always use the PREFIX keyword for renaming your fields. If field names you create by prefixing exceed the allowed 10 characters, your compile will fail. In such cases, you have to fall back to the less generic, but more flexible, I-spec field-level renaming.

The INCLUDE and IGNORE Keywords

Two other keywords for handling externally described record formats are INCLUDE and IGNORE. These keywords let the program use or exclude specific record formats from a file's external description. Of course, because a physical file can include only one record format, these keywords do not apply to physical files. Logical, display, and printer files, on the other hand, can all include multiple record formats, so these keywords are useful with such files.

The INCLUDE keyword lets a program access only specific record format names. As INCLUDE's parameter value, in parentheses immediately following the keyword name, you can specify one or more record formats, separating format names with a colon.

The IGNORE keyword is the opposite. It lets a program exclude specified record formats in an externally described file. IGNORE's parameter works like INCLUDE's: In parentheses immediately following the keyword name, you list the names of the formats you do not need, and you separate the format names with colons. Obviously, you cannot have both keywords on the same file.

Don't include formats you can ignore. You may see no harm in letting a program access all record formats in a particular file, but this is not always the best programming practice. Suppose a program references two separate external descriptions, each containing a record format called RITEFMT. If you need only one, you must explicitly include one and ignore the other. Otherwise, your program can't tell which format named RITEFMT you want. (Of course, an alternative solution is to use the RENAME keyword to give one format a different name.)

RANDOM PROCESSING BY KEY

The discussion of the DDS definition of file CLUBMBRP explained that the customer number is the key value for the physical file (recall the K before field CMID). Keys organize the information in a data file. Keys, or indexes, are search arguments that determine which parts of the record you intend to reference each time you search a given database file. Because the AS/400 database manager can organize the file's data in advance, search efficiency improves.

Composite Keys

Sometimes, one key field is not enough to get the information you need. Such times call for composite keys, which consist of multiple key fields.

Any well-designed database will have composite keys if one file has a record that multiple records in a subordinate file support. An example is an order file and order detail file. The order file will have an order ID as the key, and the order detail file will have the order ID and the order line field as its keys. Orders are often uniquely numbered only within a department or division. In this case, the department or division ID is also part of the key. In fact, except for basic reference files, you will probably encounter a lot of files that have composite keys, especially if they are transaction files.

The CHAIN Operation Code

The CHAIN (Random Retrieval from a File) operation code lets an RPG program retrieve or verify the existence of a specific record from a full procedural file. You enter CHAIN in the C-specs, as the operation code (positions 26 through 35). In Factor 1 (the search argument), you specify a data file's key field or an RRN. If the data file is keyed, you can enter a field name, a named constant, a figurative constant, or a literal in Factor 1. To retrieve a record by RRN, in Factor 1, you must specify an integer literal or a numeric field with zero decimal positions. In Factor 2, you enter the name of the file or record format that contains the key field.

CHAIN supports the N (No record locking) operation code extender. If you open a file for update, you can specify the N extender with CHAIN to retrieve the record without locking it for update. CHAIN(N) chains to the record without locking it, but CHAIN locks it, preventing others from reading it for update. Here is a summary of the entries for CHAIN.

Factor 1	Opcode	Extender	Factor 2	Result Field	Indicators		
Required search argument	CHAIN	(N)	Required file- or format-name	Not Allowed	Not found	Error	N/A

CHAIN by Example

CHAIN retrieves a specific record or verifies the existence of a record (though SETLL provides a less I/O-intensive record-existence check). In either case, the file will probably be uniquely keyed, and you will use the entire key. However, you can also specify CHAIN if the file is not uniquely keyed or if you are using a partial key. When you specify CHAIN with a nonunique key value, you usually just want to position the file or check whether any records are in a given set. That type of use is rare, so let's talk about a more practical example.

Ordinarily, you will specify CHAIN to read a single record when you receive a key value from some source other than the file to which you are chaining. Suppose you need to retrieve information about a club member. For instance, say you are working from a report that, for security and privacy reasons, lists club members only by their club member ID — perhaps a report showing payments of club dues. A more system-oriented situation is if you have a transaction file that contains only a club member's ID, and you need to get the club member data to display or print. In fact, this first situation can feed the second: Assume you are working from a list of data, entering club member IDs into a file that you then use to print notices to members who have not yet paid their dues. First, you verify the existence of the record and maybe show some nonsensitive data. Second, you use the verified information in a second process to produce a batch of letters for mailing. The code below demonstrates how to code this CHAIN.

```
*...1....+....2....+....3....+....4....+....5....+....6....+....7....+
C      ClbMbrID      CHAIN     CLUBMBRP                              90
```

In this example, the field ClbMbrID, specified in Factor 1, supplies the value to find a record in the file CLUBMBRP, specified in Factor 2. Indicator 90 lets you verify the result of the CHAIN. If the record is found, indicator 90 will be set off. If not, indicator 90 will be set on. The indicator can then condition an error message or control some other type of processing.

You can also specify CHAIN to access a composite key. In this case, you must name the composite key in the program by specifying the KLIST (Key List) operation. Then you must list the fields that comprise the composite key. The KFLD (Key Field) operation is the means for listing the fields that make up the KLIST.

The KLIST and KFLD Operation Codes

The KLIST operation identifies and gives a name to the list of fields that form a composite key. You specify KLIST as the operation code (positions 26 through 35) in the C-specs. Factor 1, the unique name you're giving the composite key, is the only entry allowed on the KLIST operation. Conditioning indicators are not allowed. Here is a summary of the entries for KLIST.

Factor 1	Opcode	Extender	Factor 2	Result Field	Indicators
Required KLIST name	KLIST		Not Allowed	Not Allowed	Not Allowed

KLIST begins a composite key's definition in a program. Following KLIST, you must immediately specify one KFLD operation to identify each field that is part of the composite key. The last KFLD specification signals the end of a KLIST.

You specify KFLD in the operation code field (positions 26 through 35), immediately after either a KLIST or another KFLD operation code. The Result field contains the only entry allowed for KFLD: the name of a key field. This name cannot be an array or table name. Conditioning indicators are not allowed. Here are the entries for KFLD.

Factor 1	Opcode	Extender	Factor 2	Result Field	Result Indicators
Not allowed	KFLD		Not Allowed	Required *key name*	Not allowed

Note that programmers often create a separate key list for each use of a file, but this approach is not necessary. You can use a single key list many times, even for multiple files, if the attributes of the fields in the key list match those of the key fields on the file.

The READE and READPE Operations

Two read operations are available for keyed files. These two input operations are READE (Read Equal Key) and READPE (Read Previous Equal Key). READE and READPE are similar to READ and READP, but you must have keyed files for READE and READPE. They will return a record only if it matches the key or partial key you supply, and the resulting indicator will signal EOF not only if the EOF or BOF is reached, but also if the next record does not have a key that matches the one you request.

The syntax for READE AND READPE is similar to that for their non-key-matching cousins, with one exception: You can specify Factor 1 with READE and READPE to supply a key or partial key value to test before the program returns a record. Without Factor 1, the operation will read the next or previous record *if it has the same key as the current record.* Odd, you may say. However, it is not uncommon to be using a logical file that is indexed over some field or fields that are not unique. In such cases, the logical file is usually defined with a nonunique access path, and you can have READE or READPE read through a group of records that have the same key value. For instance, you can get all duplicate last names from a customer list. By reading the first record in a group and then specifying READE with no Factor 1 to continue reading through that group, you can avoid any need to test the values read from the database. RPG IV will automatically limit the reading of records to those have the same full key value as the last read record. Here is a syntax summary for READE and READPE.

Factor 1	Opcode	Extender	Factor 2	Result Field	Indicators		
Optional _search argument_	READE	(N)	Required _file- or record-name_	Optional _data structure_	N/A	Error	EOF
Optional _search argument_	READPE	(N)	Required _file- or record-name_	Optional _data structure_	N/A	Error	BOF

Programmers usually specify these operations with files that have composite keys. A typical example is when you need to read all the detail records for an order, all the dependent records for an employee, or all the financial transactions for a given date. Because composite keys are usually involved, key lists (KLIST) are also frequently involved. Also, you usually position the file with a SETLL to start at the beginning of a key value group and then use READE, specifying a partial (high-order fields) key to read through the subset of records.

SEQUENTIAL PROCESSING WITH SETLL

You can process a file sequentially from the beginning of the file to the end, or you can process a file randomly. Another possibility is sequentially processing a group of records in the file, but being able to select this group randomly. For example, in an order entry application, you have to read all the transactions for a given order number. Perhaps you are processing the orders randomly, but when you want to look at the detail in an order, you need to process it sequentially. For this purpose, you specify the SETLL (Set Lower Limits) operation to initially position the file cursor.

Of course, you are not limited to working with a subset of data, such as an order's detail records. You sometimes want to position the cursor in the file and start reading all the remaining records to the end or beginning of the file. You usually specify the READ and READP operations to perform the subsequent sequential reads.

The SETLL Operation

The SETLL (Set Lower Limits) operation lets you begin processing a full-procedural file at the next record that has a key greater than or equal to the key you must specify in Factor 1. To specify a key, you can enter a field name, named constant, figurative constant, or literal in Factor 1. Or, Factor 1 can be a KLIST name if you're using an externally described file that is keyed.

In Factor 2, you enter the name of the file (or, if the file is externally described, the name of the record format) that contains the data record you want. Factor 2 , like Factor 1, is required.

Resulting indicators are allowed with SETLL to return the operation's status. You can specify a resulting indicator in positions 71 and 72 if you want the indicator set on when the value in Factor 1 is greater than the file's highest key or RRN. You can specify a resulting indicator in positions 73 and 74 to set on the indicator in case of an error during the operation. You can specify a resulting indicator in positions 75 and 76 to set on the indicator for a record with a key or RRN equal to the value in Factor 1. Here are the valid entries for SETLL.

Factor 1	Opcode	Extender	Factor 2	Result	Result Indicators		
Required search argument	SETLL		Required file- or record- name	Not allowed	No record	Error	Equal

Note that if SETLL finds no records that fit your search criteria, the operation positions the file cursor at the end of the file. The operation is positioning to the first record whose key value is the same as the value in Factor 1 or whose key value is next in order, relative to the value in Factor 1. So if no records match or have a key value that follows the value in Factor 1, the end of file is the next index entry. If the operation does not reach the end of the file, you can issue another SETLL or CHAIN to reposition the file cursor if necessary. Note that by specifying a resulting indicator in positions 71 to 72, you can check whether SETLL positions to the end of the file.

Besides positioning a file, SETLL has another function. Instead of a CHAIN to verify whether a key exists, you can issue SETLL and an equal indicator in position 75 to 76. In this case, SETLL is faster than CHAIN. The SETLL only accesses the index of the file and does not retrieve the data record, whereas the CHAIN operation accesses the index to find the record and then also accesses the data record. (You also have the overhead of moving the data from the input buffer into the fields defined in your program.) Because SETLL involves less I/O and activity, it makes an ideal candidate for validating the existence of a record *if* you do not also intend to access the data in that record.

A word of warning about SETLL: You sometimes do not get the record you want even though you set a resulting indicator in positions 75 and 76 to tell you the operation has found a matching record. This problem is because SETLL does not *access* the record, but only places processing at a point where the program can read the specified record. Of course, before the program reads the file, other processing can add or delete records. However, this action is no different from what you expect if you issue a READ operation and expect to get a particular record in the next read. Another application program can insert a record between where the file's cursor is now positioned and the next record you expect to read.

The catch is that using a resulting indicator in positions 75 and 76 gives you a false sense of security because you have verified that a record exists. Because another application program can delete that record before you issue a READ operation, you can get a different record from the one you expect.

You have three ways to get around this little pitfall. First, you can allocate the files you are using so that no one else can update them, but that solution is restrictive in a multiuser environment. The second alternative is to use CHAIN to verify a record's existence and also retrieve the data. The third alternative is to perform a subsequent read with either a READE or READPE operation. You want to use SETLL with an exact key only to check record existence and not retrieve the data from that specific record. A good technique is to use SETLL with either a full or partial key provided, if subsequent reads are not expecting a particular record.

Processing by Keys and SETLL

Two uses for SETLL are verifying a record's existence and then positioning the file to start reading records. Especially in a relational database system, you often need to verify a record's existence. If you let users enter codes that identify people, products, and such, you need existence checks against data files to verify that the entered data is valid. Consider the club member file. If the user is entering club member IDs to store in a mailing list (another file) for a fundraiser, you want to verify that each club member ID entered exists on the club member file, CLUBMBRP. If you only want to validate the member ID and do not want to retrieve the data, SETLL is the operation for this check. The code segment below shows how to perform this existence check.

```
*...1....+....2....+....3....+....4....+....5....+....6....+....7....+.
C     MLMbrId        SETLL     CLUBMBRP                                 80
*
C                    IF        NOT *IN80
... perform error handling such as setting flag for re-display
    ... and sending errror msg
C                    ENDIF
```

MLMbrId (Mailing List Member ID) is a display field into which the user has keyed a member ID to identify a club member to put on the mailing list. The task is to ensure that the member ID is valid. Because this is a simple application that performs only validation, you have no need to retrieve the data in the club member's record. Consequently, SETLL is the choice. You use MLMbrId to position the file's cursor to the index entry that has the member ID you are validating. The indicator in positions 75 to 76 will turn on if you get an exact hit on the key value. Then, if indicator 80 is not turned on, you can handle any errors. This technique is also good for validating data in batch if you need to process files that outside parties supply.

The next example is for a situation where the user can enter information to position an online display of the club members' names. To help the users quickly find the name they are searching for, you can issue SETLL to position the file's cursor based on possibly incomplete data from the user. The following code demonstrates how to use SETLL to position the file when you don't know the exact key to use to start reading the file.

```
*...1....+....2....+....3....+....4....+....5....+....6....+....7....+.
C        MbrNamKey      KFLD
C                       KLIST     LastName
C                       KLIST     FirstName
 *
C                       MOVEL     InLstNam    LastName
C                       MOVEL     InFstNam    FirstName
C        MbrNamKey      SETLL     CLUBMBRL1                       90
 *
C                       IF        *IN90
 ... special handling when there are no records to display
C                       ELSE
 *
 * Read the first record
C                       READ      CLUBMBRL1                            90
 *
 * Loop while a record is found to load the record to the screen and to
 * get the next record
C                       DOW       NOT *IN90
 ... move database fields to screen fields
C                       READ      CLUBMBRL1                            90
C                       ENDDO
C                       ENDIF
 ... proceed with display of screen
```

Let's focus on what happens with the SETLL operation and how it sets up conditions for sequential processing. This example shows how the sequential processing will occur once the SETLL operation is executed. Note that indicator 90 on the SETLL operation is in positions 71 to 72, so you can see whether the SETLL operation immediately places the file cursor at the end of the file.

The key list defined in the first three lines lets you access the correct index entries on the CLUBMBRL1 file. This file is keyed by last name and first name. The next lines load the search values that the user entered, into the key list fields. The SETLL operation uses the key list to position the file's cursor. Indicator 90, in positions 71 to 72, will be turned on if the SETLL positions to end of file. In that case, instead of just displaying an empty list, you want to let the user know that no records are available. If no records are available to display, you can show the user a message saying no records can be found.

Next, you read the first record, the one to which SETLL positioned processing. Because you are not necessarily positioning with an exact key, you are not expecting to retrieve any particular record. You just want the next record. For instance, suppose the user enters SM in the last name field and nothing in the first name search field. SETLL positions processing to the first record with a last name that starts with SM, and you can start reading forward from there. Most likely, you will get a SMITH.

After the initial read, a DO loop begins and will execute as long as indicator 90 is off. Because indicator 90 signifies end of file on the read statement, the loop will continue as long as you can read a record. Next, you handle the data just read (perhaps you move it to the screen fields), and then you READ the next record. Again, indicator 90 on the READ statement checks for end of file.

Relative Record Number Processing

So far, the discussion of file processing has focused on processing a file by keys, the usual way of processing a file. An alternative method of retrieving records is to access them by their position relative to the beginning of the file, or by RRN. For example, the RRNs of a file's first, third, and tenth records are 1, 3, and 10. Both the CHAIN and SETLL operations can accept either a key or an RRN. So, to use the RRN to access the third record in the file, you enter the value 3 in the Factor 1 field for a CHAIN operation code. After positioning the file with CHAIN or SETLL, you can READ or READP to process the file.

Note that you cannot choose between and RRN and keyed access on a whim. The F-spec for a file determines whether the CHAIN and SETLL operations will attempt RRN or keyed processing. All operations on the file will be one way or the other. You cannot mix them for a single file.

Relative record processing can be useful. First, you can process by RRN if you want to process every record in a file and are not concerned with the order of processing. This type of processing is in *arrival sequence:* You will process each record in the same sequence in which it was written to the file. Another reason for processing by RRN is that it can be very fast. The database management system doesn't have to consult an index to find the next record, but can just get the next physical record in the file. When a program is processing sequentially by key, data management may have to jump up and down the file looking for the next record to read.

With RRN processing, you can improve performance even more by controlling the blocking of records so that you can read more records in a single I/O to the disk. RPG will automatically block your data if it can, but you can control it yourself by means of CL commands.

Random processing by RRN is obsolete because it exactly contradicts the concept of a relational database. And, one big warning about RRN processing is that you can never reorganize your physical file if your application relies on RRNs. Reorganization can and probably will change the RRN of the records. If you can't reorganize a file, any records you delete from the file will continue to take up space because reorganization is necessary to remove deleted records. Additionally, copying the data from one file to another can be hazardous because copying can also change RRNs.

Let's look at how to specify RRN processing for a file. Here is the F-spec for a file ProdCmt to be processed by RRN. This F-spec declares file ProdCmt as an input, full-procedural file (positions 17 and 18). The E in position 22 declares that the file is externally described. DISK (starting in position 36) is the device type.

```
*...1....+....2....+....3....+....4....+....5....+....6....+....7....+
FCProdCmt  IF   E              DISK     RECNO(RECID)
 *
```

So far, this declaration looks like any other file declaration, but there are two important differences. The first difference is that the record address type, which you specify in position 34 of the F-spec, must be blank for RRN processing. The entry in this position determines whether RPG IV will use keyed access to the file or RRN access. When you process a file by key, position 34 will contain a K. To specify RRN processing, you leave position 34 blank. This entry is the only required difference when you are just going to read the file.

The second different specification is the keyword RECNO (Record Number). This keyword provides a field that will contain a retrieved RRN for operations that reposition the file.

The RECNO Keyword

The RECNO keyword names a field for the system to update with the current record's RRN each time you read a record from a file you are processing by RRN. The RECNO keyword is optional for an input file. Its purpose with an input file is to retrieve the number of the record to which the file's cursor is currently pointing. When you first open a file, or when RPG IV opens it for you, the named field will be set to 0. As you access records in the file, the field will be updated with the RRN of the current record.

RECNO is also optional for update files. Its purpose on update files is the same as for input files. It lets you know the RRN of the record you have most recently read.

For output files you are processing by RRN, input files that allow add, and update files that allow add, RECNO can play a more important role. Specifying RECNO in such cases means you want to control which record in the file to create. Suppose you write a record to a file that has been opened in one of these ways and is being processed by RRN. To identify which record to write, the program must set the RECNO value to the number of the record to be written. Additionally, the record you are writing must already exist as a deleted record in the file. Note that RECNO is not necessary if you want to write records to files opened in these ways; but if you specify this keyword, these restrictions apply.

Note that processing files by RRN is an old method, predating keyed files and the relational database model. Avoid RRN processing. The purpose for discussing it here is in case you need to maintain or convert old code. Although RRN processing can be extremely fast, the relational database model relies on index-based organization. Processing by RRN may be applicable if you want to process all the records in a particular file in the order of their arrival, but this is not often a requirement. Usually, you need to extract data or process it in an organized sequence.

FILE OUTPUT

This chapter has covered basic concepts including files, file keys, key lists, record formats, and reading data. It's time to discuss writing and updating records in a file. Let's examine the four operations (WRITE, UPDATE, DELETE, and EXCEPT) that let you add, change, or delete records in a file. This discussion will include a review of the F-spec entries that let you use each operation.

Output with WRITE

The WRITE operation creates a new record in a file. After you establish the values for all the fields in the record format you want to write, you issue a WRITE operation with that record format named, and the record is created. Note that if you have already read another record from the same file and the file is an update file, you can lock the record you read. That lock will be removed because WRITE moves the file cursor. You can specify WRITE when a file is open for output (O in position 17 of the F-spec), for input with add (I in position 17 and A in position 20 of the F-spec), or for update with add (U in position 17 and A in position 20 of the F-spec).

Factor 1 is not allowed with WRITE. Factor 2 must contain the name of a record format if you are writing to an externally described file. The Result field is not allowed when you are writing to an externally described file. A resulting indicator is optional in positions 73 and 74 to signal an error such as an attempt to write a duplicate key. Conditioning indicators are allowed. Here is the syntax of WRITE.

Factor 1	Opcode	Extender	Factor 2	Result	Result Indicators		
Not allowed	WRITE		Required file- or format- name	Optional data structure	N/A	Error	N/A

With WRITE, you code no O-specs. When creating the records, the compiler will provide a listing of the fields to output, but O-specs are not involved. The naming of the format identifies the fields you need and how to write them to the file, which is why you must specify a format name in Factor 2: When you're writing the record, that format defines the fields to use and their layout.

Output with UPDATE

The UPDATE operation changes an existing record in a file. Before you can issue an UPDATE operation, you must first read the record for update and lock it. You can do so by means of any database access operation, such as READ, READP, or CHAIN, if you don't use the no-lock operation extender on the operation you use to read the record. Once you read the record for update, you need to establish the new values (those that you are changing). Then you issue the UPDATE operation, naming the format, and the record will be updated. When the record is updated, the lock is removed. UPDATE is allowed only when you open a file for update (U in position 17 of the F-spec).

Factor 1 is not allowed with UPDATE. Factor 2 must contain the name of a record format when you are updating a record in an externally described file. The Result field is not allowed when you UPDATE an externally described file. You can specify a resulting indicator in positions 73 and 74 to signal an error such as an update that causes a duplicate key. You can specify conditioning indicators. Here is the syntax of the UPDATE operation code.

Factor 1	Opcode	Extender	Factor 2	Result	Result Indicators		
Not allowed	UPDATE		Required file- or format- name	Optional data structure	N/A	Error	N/A

UPDATE is the operation code you will want for updating records in a file. You must remember that all the fields in the named format will be updated with the current values in the program. If you need to update only a few fields on the file, you will probably use the EXCEPT operation. The only time you will be concerned about updating just some of the fields is if, between the last read and the current update, something changes the fields that are named on the format through which you are updating. You just need to avoid changing the values of fields that you do not want changed on the database, and UPDATE will serve you well.

As with the WRITE operation, when you use UPDATE, you code no O-specs. The compiler will provide a listing of the fields to change when you update the record, but O-specs are not involved. The naming of the format identifies the fields needed and determines how to write them to the file, which is why you must specify a format name in Factor 2: The format defines what fields to use and their layout.

The DELETE Operation

The DELETE operation removes an existing record from a file. Like the UPDATE operation, DELETE operates on the last record read for update by means of any database access operation, such as READ, READP, or CHAIN, if you don't use the no-lock operation extender on the read operation. Once you read the record for update, you can issue DELETE, naming the format. Note that you must also ensure that the record you previously read for update uses the same format name you specify in DELETE's Factor 2. When the record is deleted, the lock is removed. You can DELETE only when you open a file for update (U in position 17 of the F-spec).

Factor 1 is allowed with the DELETE operation. Factor 2 can contain either a file name or a record format name when you're deleting a record in an externally described file. The Result field is not allowed. You can specify a resulting indicator in positions 73 and 74 to signal an error on the delete, such as an attempt to delete a record in a file for which you do not have security rights to delete. Another resulting indicator in positions 71 and 72 is required when you are also using Factor 1; otherwise, this indicator is not allowed. You can also specify conditioning indicators. Here is the syntax of the DELETE operation code.

Factor 1	Opcode	Extender	Factor 2	Result	Result Indicators		
Optional search argument	DELETE		Required file- or format- name	Not allowed	No Record	Error	N/A

If you leave Factor 1 blank, the DELETE process requires you to perform some database access operation to identify the record to delete. The DELETE operation deletes only records currently locked for update. However, if you specify Factor 1, you can locate and delete a record in a single operation. By entering a key value using a field, named constant, literal, or (if a file has a composite key) the name of a key list, DELETE can find and lock the record you want to delete. In fact, if you do not need to access the values of the fields in the record you want to delete, DELETE is a little faster and more efficient than another operation to read the record for update. You do not have to move data into fields from the input buffers, and no fields in the program are affected.

If you use the Factor 1 method for locating the record, you must code a resulting indicator in positions 71 and 72, and this indicator will be set on if DELETE cannot find the record you want to delete. This indicator is similar to the not-found indicator when you CHAIN to the file first. As with the WRITE and UPDATE operations, with DELETE, you will code no O-specs.

WRITE, UPDATE, and DELETE by Example

Consider a corporation that has several branch offices, each of which maintains an individual client list. Periodically, each branch delivers its current customer lists to the main office for consolidation in the corporate database. Naturally, each branch will regularly gain new clients, update the information for existing clients and, occasionally, request that the corporate office purge an old client from the corporate database. The following program will let the corporate office process and consolidate a file received from one of the branch offices.

```
*...1....+....2....+....3....+....4....+....5....+....6....+....7....+.
FBrClient  IF   E          K DISK
FCoClient  UF A E          K DISK


*...1....+....2....+....3....+....4....+....5....+....6....+....7....+.
 **
 * Loop through all the branch client records
 *  For each, create, update, or delete the corresponding corporate
 *  record. A code on the branch record indicates a request for delete
 **
 * Read the first record
C                   READ      BrClientR                              LR
 *
 * Loop while we have a record
C                   DOW       Not *INLR
 *
 * If Delete requested, perform it
C                   IF        BrDltRqs = 'Y'
C     BrClientID    DELETE    CoClientR                           9091
 *
 * Else read the record, and if one is not found, create it;
 * otherwise update it
C                   ELSE
 *
 *  Get the record
C     BrClientID    CHAIN     CoClientR                           9091
 *
 *  Move the branch file fields into the corporate file fields
 ... move fields
 *
 *  Perform the create when the record wasn't found
C                   IF        *IN90
C                   WRITE     CoClientR
 *
 *  Perform the update when the record was found
C                   ELSE
```

CONTINUED

```
*...1....+....2....+....3....+....4....+....5....+....6....+....7....+.
C                    UPDATE    CoClientR
C                    ENDIF
 *
C                    ENDIF
 *
 * Read the next branch record and loop
C                    READ      BrClient                                LR
C                    ENDDO
C                    RETURN
```

This program updates the corporate client list from a branch client list. Three actions are possible. If the branch wants to delete a client, the branch record will contain a choice code to signal the request. If the client is new to corporate, the branch information will provide the information to create a record in the corporate list. If corporate is already aware of the client, the branch information will update the cooperate information.

The first line declares the file BrClient as an externally described, input, full-procedural data file that will be processed by key. This file contains the branch client records. The second line declares CoClient as an externally described, update, full-procedural data file that will be processed by key. CoClient also allows adds, as you can tell by the A in column 20, and allows deletes, updates, and creates.

A READ reads the first record from the branch client file. Notice that the file name BrClient is not specified on the READ; the format name BrClientR is there, instead. Though you can specify a file name, programmers usually specify record format names, instead of file names, to handle both reads and updates to database files. Because this example is demonstrating operations (UPDATE, WRITE, DELETE) that require format names, format names appear throughout. LR serves as the record-not-found indicator because this program will terminate after processing the last record in the branch file.

Next, a loop begins and will iterate as long as LR is not on. This loop and the READ at the end of the loop will provide the basis for processing each record in the branch file. Note that if no records are in the file, the first READ turns on LR, and the program skips the entire loop.

The loop first checks whether the record read contains a request for a delete from the corporate client file. If so, you enter the client ID field (BrClientID) with the DELETE operation to find and delete the corresponding corporate client record. Note that because Factor 1 identifies the record to delete, you do not need a record access operation to first read the corporate record for update. This method is more efficient than accessing the record and then deleting it. Indicator 90 signals whether the record you want to delete is in the database.

Indicator 91 signals whether the DELETE is successful (if the record is found). Possible cause of a failure to delete is if another program has the record locked already. No error-handling code is present here, but you can make a note in a log or take some such action when this condition occurs.

If no delete is requested, the program moves into the ELSE portion of the delete request test. Now you can CHAIN to the corporate client file, using the client ID from the branch file as the key to find. Again, you access the file by specifying the format name in Factor 2. As on the DELETE above, indicator 90 checks whether the record is not found. The value of this indicator will determine whether to create a new record or update an existing record. Indicator 91 checks for an error on the CHAIN. If another program has the record locked (you are attempting to lock it here), the CHAIN can fail. Again, no error checking code is in this example.

The program tests whether indicator 90 is on and uses the test result to conditionally create or update a corporate record. If indicator 90 is on, you did not find the requested record on the CHAIN, so you must create it. However, if indicator 90 is *not* on, you need to update the record. Either way, just before you start this block of code, you move the branch client information into the fields for the corporate client information. In this block of code, the WRITE or UPDATE statement creates or updates the corporate record. Note that no O-specs are in the program because WRITE and UPDATE do not allow O-specs.

Two ENDIFs close out the two logical tests (the inner one to see whether a corporate record already exists; the outer one to see whether a delete is requested). Following those operations, another READ attempts to get the next record. If no more are available, LR will be set on because it is the resulting indicator. If this program does other processing, LR is not an appropriate choice as the resulting indicator. After you attempt the read, the ENDDO sends processing back to the top of the DOW loop to test the LR indicator to see whether to repeat the loop. If you are finished with the records, the program will drop to the first statement after the ENDDO, and a RETURN operation will terminate the program.

The EXCEPT Operation

The EXCEPT operation can perform any of the three other output/update operations, UPDATE, WRITE, and DELETE. Unlike the other three, EXCEPT works with O-specs. EXCEPT's use of the O-spec has some interesting and attractive effects in the right situation.

Although this section will be discussing EXCEPT and database access, EXCEPT also lets you output for program-described printer files. Program-described database output can also use the EXCEPT operation, but that type of database output is obsolete, so this book does not cover it.

You specify EXCEPT as the operation code on a C-spec. The operation does not allow Factor 1, the Result field, or resulting indicators. You can use conditioning indicators. Factor 2 is optional. In Factor 2, you specify a name that will be matched up with O-specs to select which O-specs to execute for the output/update. The O-specs that an EXCEPT operation will consider are those belonging to a record-level O-spec that has an E (exception) in position 17. Each such O-spec is checked for the exception name you specify on the EXCEPT operation. If that name is present, EXCEPT considers the O-spec for output. You can leave Factor 2 blank, and EXCEPT will consider only exception output records that do not have exception names specified. Below is the syntax summary for the EXCEPT operation code.

Factor 1	Opcode	Extender	Factor 2	Result	Result Indicators
Not allowed	EXCEPT		Optional *except name*	Not allowed	Not allowed

You can specify conditioning indicators for each record and field that you output via O-specs, which can lead to some pretty interesting code. You can condition the EXCEPT operation, you can condition each record considered for output, and you can condition each field in an output record. That means a lot of layers of conditioning, and only indicators identify the conditions. If you decide to use EXCEPT for database output/update, avoid conditioning indicators in the O-specs used for exception output because these indicators make the code terribly difficulty to read and maintain. Instead, use different EXCEPT names, condition your EXCEPT operations, and have each EXCEPT operation name a unique set of O-specs.

EXCEPT will use O-specs that have an E in position 17 on the record-level O-spec. Additionally, an EXCEPT name must be in positions 30 to 39 of the record-level O-spec.

With this explanation of exception O-specs in mind, let's discuss the unique attributes of EXCEPT for database operations with an externally described file. First, you do not specify a file name on the record-level O-spec. Instead, you specify a format name. All output to externally described files occurs by format names. Second, EXCEPT can create, update, and delete records. The action depends on the entry in positions 18 through 20 of the record-level O-spec. If these positions are blank, the action is an update. If these positions contain ADD, the action is a create. If these positions contain DEL, the action is a delete.

The WRITE and UPDATE operations use all the fields for the format when placing data in the record. Because a DELETE operation is deleting a whole record, specific fields are unimportant. However, exception output is different in that you must specifically request which fields to update or write. Only the fields you specifically name in the field-level O-specs will be moved into the record buffer and written to the data file. For an ADD, any fields not specified will retain their default values defined on the external file. For an update, only the fields specified will be updated, and any others will remain unchanged. This situation can be useful to update a selected set of fields. But be warned: A common problem occurs with exception output to database files. You can forget to add a new field to the O-specs when you're working with a program that uses a file with an added field. Because fields that are not specifically named are not output, this problem will occur only when you run the program and examine the output. Of course, the compiler listing identifies the dropped fields, but you have to remember to look there before you get this information.

The lack of resulting indicators means that you cannot trap errors as easily as with the other I/O operations. You can detect failed WRITEs, UPDATEs, and DELETEs by specifying the error resulting indicator; no such convenience with EXCEPT. When you specify EXCEPT for output, you have to handle all file errors by supplying an INFSR, a file-specific error-handling subroutine.

Finally, because EXCEPT processes all exception O-specs whose record level O-spec exception name matches the name in Factor 2, EXCEPT can perform multiple output/update actions at once. You can use the same except name on multiple O-specs. Ordinarily, you will want a different EXCEPT name on each set of exception O-specs to ensure that the C-spec code has explicit control over what output occurs. However, you will sometimes want to include output to multiple files at the same time or print something at the same time you perform an action against a file. In those cases, specifying EXCEPT to handle multiple operations is an acceptable alternative to multiple I/O operations in the C-specs.

EXCEPT by Example

To illustrate the differences between EXCEPT and the other I/O operations, let's re-create the example that illustrated WRITE, UPDATE, and DELETE and modify it to use exception output. One important note is that O-specs are now necessary to identify which fields in the formats to include on the newly written records. The code shown on pages 107 and 108 uses EXCEPT to output to database files.

The structure of the program doesn't change much from the previous example. The major changes are that an EXCEPT replaces the DELETE, WRITE, and UPDATE statements. Each new EXCEPT specifies an exception name. As each EXCEPT is executed, the corresponding exception O-specs are interrogated to see what action to take (create, update, or delete), and the appropriate action occurs.

Another change is that resulting indicators are no longer on the lines with EXCEPT. Though no INFSR is included here, INFSRs are necessary to programmatically handle any I/O errors.

The last change is the O-spec for each EXCEPT name. Each set of O-specs identifies the record format to which it pertains; determines whether to update, create, or delete (positions 18 through 20); and then identifies which EXCEPT name will trigger the operation (positions 30 through 39). For the update and create operations, you have to include the name of each field you want to output. Note that the O-specs have no ending positions specified and, in fact, they are not allowed with exception output to externally described files. You supply only the list of field names, in any order.

The only other parts of the field-level O-spec that are valid when you're performing exception output for externally described files are the conditioning indicators and the blank-after (position 45). Neither is recommended because they make code hard to understand.

```
*...1....+....2....+....3....+....4....+....5....+....6....+....7....+.
FBrClient  IF   E           K DISK
FCoClient  UF A E           K DISK
```

```
*...1....+....2....+....3....+....4....+....5....+....6....+....7....+.
 **
 * Loop through all the branch client records
 *  For each, create, update, or delete the corresponding corporate
 *  record. A code on the branch record indicates a request for delete
 **
 * Read the first record
C                   READ      BrClientR                              LR
 *
 * Loop while we have a record
C                   DOW       Not *INLR
 *
 * If delete requested, perform it
C                   IF        BrDltRqs = 'Y'
C                   EXCEPT    DoDelete
 *
 * Else read the record and, if not found, create it; otherwise update
 * it
C                   ELSE
 *
 *  Get the record
C    BrClientID     CHAIN     CoClientR                           9091
 *
 *  Move the branch file fields into the corporate file fields
 ... move fields
 *
```

CONTINUED

```
*...1....+....2....+....3....+....4....+....5....+....6....+....7....+.
 *   Perform the create when the record wasn't found
C                    IF        *IN9Ø
C                    EXCEPT    DoCreate
   *
 *   Perform the update when the record was found
C                    ELSE
C                    EXCEPT    DoUpdate
C                    ENDIF
   *
C                    ENDIF
   *
 *  Read the next branch record and loop
C                    READ      BrClient                             LR
C                    ENDDO
C                    RETURN


*...1....+....2....+....3....+....4....+....5....+....6....+....7....+.
OCoClientR E            DoUpdate
O                       CoClientID
O                       CoClientNm
  ... other field names to be updated
  *
OCoClientR EDEL         DoDelete
  *
OCoClientR EADD         DoCreate
O                       CoClientID
O                       CoClientNm
  ...other field names to be included in write
```

THE FILE EXCEPTION/ERROR SUBROUTINE

Programs need to account for the possibility of I/O errors. Examples of input/output situations that demand an error-handling strategy are retrieving a record that does not exist, writing a record that results in duplicate keys, attempting to open a file that another application has locked, and trying to open a file that has no data members. Actions available in such situations include instantly ending the application, displaying an unable-to-continue message on the user's workstation, trying again if the database file is locked by another user's program running concurrently, and letting the user re-enter the search data in an interactive application.

The point here is to remind you of some considerations for developing an error-handling strategy. A strategy can be as simple as an IF-THEN-ELSE structure or a program loop, or you can harness the power of ILE if you implement a condition handler.

An important error-handling feature of RPG IV is the file exception/error subroutine, a user-written subroutine that takes control when a file-related operation fails during program execution. Although you must provide the content of the subroutine, at runtime the compiler will send program execution to the subroutine in the event of an error.

The INFSR Keyword

To enable this capability, you specify the INFSR (File Information Subroutine) keyword on the F-spec declaring a file, along with the name of the error-handling subroutine as a parameter. You also can specify *PSSR as the subroutine name parameter. The *PSSR is a specially named subroutine that is automatically executed when an unhandled error occurs in an RPG program.

You associate an exception/error subroutine with a particular file, and the subroutine will not be invoked for file operations against files that are not declared with the INFSR keyword. One INFSR can handle more than one file if you specify the same subroutine name as the INFSR keyword's parameter on more than one file's F-spec.

Specifying an Exception/Error Subroutine

When you create a file exception/error subroutine (or any other subroutine) in an RPG IV program, you start with a BEGSR (Begin Subroutine) operation on a C-spec. Factor 1 of BEGSR names the subroutine. (You can then enter this name as the name parameter on the INFSR keyword on a file's F-spec.) In an exception/error subroutine, you can specify any valid RPG operations. You end this subroutine with a ENDSR (End Subroutine) operation.

Positions 36 to 49 (Factor 2) can specify where program execution control will return on completion of the error/exception-handling subroutine. Possible values for return points are shown below. Note that you can supply such a return point as a figurative constant, literal with no leading blanks, or RPG program field or array element of class character.

Value	Return Point
*DETL	The start of detail line specifications
*GETIN	The get input record routine - part of the program cycle
*TOTC	The beginning of the total calculation specifications
*OFL	The beginning of the overflow line specifications
*DETC	The beginning of the detail calculation specifications
*CANCL	The cancellation of the program's execution.
blanks	The default error handler

If you specify the return point using a field or array element, the field or array element will be set to blanks on completion of the file exception/error-handling subroutine. If you specify a field or array element as the return point, but it contains blanks when the subroutine is called, the RPG IV default error handler will receive control on the subroutine's completion. One exception to this rule is when the EXSR (Execute Subroutine) operation invokes the error-handling subroutine. In this case, the return point is the next logical C-spec following the EXSR.

The INFDS Keyword and Other Feedback Data Structures

How do you find out what type of file error occurred? Each file has a special data structure, the INFDS (file information data structure), associated with it. You can access that data structure by specifying the INFDS keyword on the F-spec for a file.

The F-spec INFDS keyword identifies a file exception/error-handling data structure. This data structure belongs to a special class of data structures, feedback information data structures. These data structures map to an area of storage known as the feedback area, which the ILE RPG runtime compiler maintains.

The five types of feedback data structures are the file feedback, open feedback, input/output feedback, device-specific feedback, and get-attributes feedback data structures. The file feedback data structure is the file-related portion of the feedback area. Information that you can obtain from the file feedback data structure includes the file name for which the error/exception occurred, the record being processed when the error/exception occurred, the last operation code executed before the error/exception occurred, and status code information (specific information about, possibly, why the error/exception occurred; for example, an end-of-file on input — status code 00011 — and an error on implicit OPEN/CLOSE operation — status code 01216. A comprehensive list of the possible status codes is in the *ILE RPG IV Reference* manual). This data structure also contains the name of the RPG routine in which the error/exception occurred.

The INFDS keyword requires one parameter that names the data structure to use. In the same way that the INFSR keyword associates a file with a file error/exception handling subroutine, the INFDS keyword associates a file with a file information data structure. Your responsibility is to describe that data structure in the program.

All types of feedback data structure map to storage in the feedback area. The feedback area is like a superset of all the information necessary to accommodate the five specific feedback data structures. You can access information from the feedback area by providing *from* and *to* positions corresponding to the desired information, to describe a data structure with subfields. For example, the file feedback information is in the first 80 bytes of the feedback area. The open feedback information is in positions 81 through 240 in the feedback area. Positions 241 through to 366 provide information for the input/output feedback data structure. Device-specific and get-attributes feedback data structures depend on different areas of the overall feedback area.

Although you must specify the starting and ending positions of most information in the INFDS, special reserved words can give you access to parts of the data structure without your having to explicitly identify the starting and ending positions. These reserved words predefine the positions for you. You can use these reserved words instead of coding the positions, or you can specify the positions.

With efficiency in mind, the RPG compiler's developers decided not to let anything update this fairly large storage area without good cause. That is, unless a particular data structure is referencing information in the feedback area, the compiler will not update that portion of the feedback area, with one exception: The compiler always maintains positions 1 through 66 of the feedback area.

All five feedback areas are available for you to define with the INFDS. Each area can give you specific information about a file such as how it was opened and what type of file it is.

As you become familiar with the INFDS, you will find many uses for it. When you first start using the INFDS and INFSR, though, you will probably use the information to handle a basic error recovery option, ending your program gracefully while alerting someone responsible and giving some relevant information about the error.

COMMITMENT CONTROL

Commitment control lets you change a group of records all at once to ensure synchronization of record updates. For example, if you want to simultaneously adjust a group of records in a general-ledger database file, you use commitment control.

The general ledger is a good illustration because so many updates need to occur for a *transaction* to be complete. A transaction is a group of updates that you have to make at the same time; they are "atomic." At a minimum, you have to debit one account while crediting another. In an extreme situation, a single transaction will update the balances of 10 different debit accounts and 15 different credit accounts. Because a company's books must always be in balance, you must ensure that either the entire transaction (all updates) are complete or, in the event of a failure, that none are complete. Commitment control lets you wrap all your updates between two boundaries to create a transaction, and then the system treats the bounded transactions as an atomic unit. If your job gets canceled accidentally or the system loses power, AS/400 database management will automatically reverse any updates within the transaction boundary if the entire transaction is not yet committed to the database.

Commitment control sounds like an advanced topic in database processing. However, if you bear its purpose in mind, the concepts become easy to understand. Commitment control ensures one outcome of input/output file operations: Either all file operations are successful, or no file operations are successful.

To start using commitment control for files in an RPG program, you issue the CL STRCMTCTL (Start Commitment Control) command before you execute the program. You use RPG-specific keywords and operation codes to open the files under commitment control. You must specify the COMMIT keyword on the F-spec for each file you want to run under commitment control. The ROLBK opcode lets you reverse any changes. You can specify the USROPN (User Open) keyword to prevent RPG from opening your files automatically, especially if you take advantage of a new feature, the ability to decide at runtime whether to run a file under commitment control. Though the OPEN and CLOSE operations are not specific to commitment control, you will probably use them with USROPN to control opening and closing files under commitment control.

The COMMIT Keyword

The COMMIT keyword on an F-spec specifies that all input/output operations are under commitment control for the file you are declaring. To open a data file for commitment control, you enter the COMMIT keyword on the F-spec that declares the data file to your program.

One new RPG IV capability for commitment control is that you can determine at runtime whether to open a file under commitment control. In RPG III, you have to define a file for commitment control or not. So if you have code that several sites use and only some sites need commitment control, you have to maintain two versions of an RPG III program to have one that runs under commitment control and one that does not. An RPG IV program can decide at runtime, so you can support both environments from a single code base.

The COMMIT keyword supports an optional parameter that will accept any RPG variable name. If you specify this parameter, you do not need to declare the variable you name. It is automatically declared as a character field with a length of 1. You can set this parameter to a value of '0' or '1' (the "control flag") to determine whether to open the file under commitment control. When the value in this optional parameter is '1', the file will be opened under commitment control.

You must set the parameter before the file is opened. Because you must access this field before opening the file, you will want to specify USROPN with OPEN to keep RPG IV from opening the file before you set the field.

The USROPN Keyword

To control file opens, you need the USROPN (User Open) keyword. You specify USROPN on the F-spec that declares a database file. The file will *not* be opened during program initialization. If you do not specify USROPN, the program automatically (or *implicitly*) opens the file.

The OPEN Operation Code
The OPEN operation lets you explicitly open a file. As the required Factor 2 value, this operation code accepts the name of the file to open. Of course, the file cannot already be open.

Ordinarily, if you want to control the opening and closing of the file, you will also specify USROPN on the file. You can open a file with OPEN whether it has never been opened (USROPN specified), or it has been recently closed (USROPN specified or not).

You can optionally specify an error indicator in positions 73 and 74. This indicator will be set on if the open is not successful. If you do not specify this indicator, on an unsuccessful open, execution will go to the error-handling subroutine if you have one. If no subroutine is specified, the default error handler or exception handler will receive program execution control. Here is the syntax summary for the OPEN operation code.

Factor 1	Opcode	Extender	Factor 2	Result	Result Indicators		
Not allowed	OPEN		Required *file name*	Not allowed	N/A	Error	N/A

The COMMIT Operation Code
The COMMIT operation releases all record locks for files that are under commitment control and changes all files you have under commitment control no matter whether the program issuing the COMMIT operation or another program in the same activation group or job issues the changes. The program that executes COMMIT need not have files under commitment control.

To appreciate this operation code, you need to understand that all the records you update or create under commitment control retain record locks until the transaction is committed. Files that have records locked under commitment control include files opened for commitment control and files for which you've specified output operations since the previous COMMIT or ROLBK operation, or since you started commitment control if this is the first commit operation.

No other job can update locked records until they are committed. In fact, your job cannot update those records again unless the operation occurs while the file is open for commitment control. You cannot have one program perform an update under commitment control and then call another program to update the same record if the other program does not also use commitment control, unless you first commit the transaction by issuing the COMMIT operation.

The COMMIT operation code accepts a constant or variable as an optional Factor 1 field, the "boundary." The value of the Factor 1 field or constant is recorded in a journal entry that marks the COMMIT operation. This factor will help identify the committed, or grouped, input/output operations for each COMMIT operation executed. You can choose this capability to record information about the latest commit, such as the order number being worked on.

An optional error indicator is supported in positions 73 and 74. The RPG compiler sets on this indicator if an error (such as the job not being under commitment control if you forget to issue the STRCMTCTL command) occurs when you're trying to perform the commit. Here is the syntax summary for the COMMIT operation code.

Factor 1	Opcode	Extender	Factor 2	Result	Result Indicators		
Optional *boundary*	COMMIT		Not allowed	Not allowed	N/A	Error	N/A

In ILE, COMMIT is activation-group conscious: COMMIT is not restricted to the database files in the program executing the COMMIT operation. It encompasses all output operations for any database file under commitment control that is referenced by any program in the same activation group as the program executing COMMIT.

Assume you have three programs to perform a particular function. The first program presents a list of items for the user to select from. When the user selects an item and the action to perform against it, a second program is called to perform the action. This second program is the only one of the three that performs database updates. It opens the files under commitment control. Finally, after the database updates are complete, a third program is called to display the results of the action (new account balances, changes to schedules, etc.) and to ask the user to confirm the results of the action. Once they are confirmed, the third program issues a COMMIT. Although the third program has no files under commitment control, it issues the command to commit the updates done in the second program. If all three programs (or at least the second and third ones) are in the same activation group, COMMIT from the third program finalizes the transaction updates that the second program performed. The point is that COMMIT will commit all updates in the transaction in the same activation group, not just those in the program that issues the COMMIT.

From a performance standpoint, you need to be aware that changes you make to a file while it is open for commitment control are real changes and are recorded in the database. However, the record lock is retained after the update. If you COMMIT the transaction, beyond the overhead that journaling the physical files imposes, you have very little performance overhead for using commitment control. The same is not true when you choose not to COMMIT the transaction.

The ROLBK Operation Code

For files under commitment control, the ROLBK (Roll Back) operation code reverses all changes since the previous COMMIT or ROLBK operation. If you have no previous COMMIT or ROLBK operations, ROLBK reverses all output operations executed since commitment control started in the current activation group. Here is the syntax summary for the ROLBK operation code.

Factor 1	Opcode	Extender	Factor 2	Result	Indicators		
Not allowed	ROLBK		Not allowed	Not allowed	N/A	Error	N/A

To reverse the updates and restore the record to its condition before the change, the system uses a *before* image of each change that it records in journals. After the changes are reversed, all record locks are released.

ROLBK's reversing of updates initiates database updates to restore the records to their original values and to access the entries in the journals to get the original values for the records. So ROLBK can be an expensive operation in terms of overhead. Take care to design your applications to use ROLBK only for unforeseen errors, not as a standard method for reversing a transaction.

Building on the scenario in the previous section, assume that the user decides not to accept the results of a transaction that the third program presents. You can issue a ROLBK to reverse the transaction instead of committing it. Keeping in mind the recommendation about using ROLBK only for error recovery, you may want to avoid ROLBK and reverse the transaction in program code. The decision depends on the performance characteristics of the application and your system. Avoiding ROLBK means more coding for you but better performance for users.

As in the previous scenario, issuing the ROLBK in the third program will reverse all the updates in all the programs in the same activation group, not just those in the program that issues the ROLBK. ROLBK encompasses all output operations for any database file under commitment control that is referenced by any program in the same activation group as the program executing the ROLBK operation. The program executing ROLBK need not have any database files under commitment control.

The CLOSE Operation Code

The CLOSE operation lets you explicitly close a file. As Factor 2, this operation code accepts the name of the file to close. Alternatively, you can specify *ALL in Factor 2 to close all database files associated with the executing program. Note that you cannot specify an array or table as Factor 2. You can specify an error indicator in positions 73 and 74. This indicator will be set on if the close is not successful. Here is the syntax summary for the CLOSE operation.

Factor 1	Opcode Extender	Factor 2	Result	Result Indicators		
Not allowed	CLOSE	Required *file name*	Not allowed	N/A	Error	N/A

Ordinarily, you will not want to CLOSE files and reopen them because opening a file involves significant overhead. In most cases, a program will close the files only when it is finished with them or is about to terminate. Likewise, opens generally occur at program initiation, usually to let you handle some task, such as preparing for commitment control, before opening the file.

Commitment Control by Example

Obviously, unexpected failure is an important obstacle to maintaining database integrity. Such problems as having a job canceled at an inopportune moment, losing power to the system during execution of a job, and finding that you cannot lock a record for update can cause the system to partially complete a transaction and leave the data in an inconsistent state. Commitment control helps solve the problem.

Let's consider an application that uses one file. The program must write multiple records to complete a transaction. This situation frequently occurs in the processing of a payment to a company. When you receive a payment, you must record it. Standard accounting practices dictate that you record the information in at least two places: You probably need to update a cash account (or bank account) to record the increase in that asset, and you need to update an accounts receivable account to record the decrease in that asset. In a real business setting, many more updates are necessary, but these two will suffice for now.

Identifying a transaction is probably the most difficult part of designing an application to use commitment control. Always try to keep a transaction small, as in the example on pages 117 and 118. The maximum number of record locks that can be maintained at once under commitment control before they must be committed or rolled back is 131,072. However, if your transactions ever approach that number of updates, you need to rethink your design. Typically, a transaction needs to be closer to a maximum of 10 or 15 updates before you commit.

This simple program accepts a file that contains records for all the payments received today. For each record in that file, the program will write two records to another file that contains the general ledger transactions. Each record in the transaction file will cause multiple updates to the general ledger file. Additionally, as each transaction record is processed, the program marks it as being posted to the general ledger. So you have three updates to keep synchronized. The first two, the new records for the general ledger, must both make it to the database, or neither must make it. If only one record or the other is successfully updated, the accounts for the company will no longer balance. Likewise, when those records are updated, the transaction record must be marked to ensure that you do not try to post it again if you have to restart the process. So you simultaneously have to make three changes to the database. This situation illustrates the simplest form of a transaction under commitment control.

```
*...1....+....2....+....3....+....4....+....5....+....6....+....7....+.
FGenLdgr    UF A E            K DISK    COMMIT
FRcvdPmt    UF   E            K DISK    COMMIT

*...1....+....2....+....3....+....4....+....5....+....6....+....7....+.
 **
 * Read through all the received payments and —
 *   Write the debit record to the general ledger file
 *   Write the credit record to the general ledger file
 *   Mark the payment as having been posted to general ledger
 *   Close down
 **
 * Read the first payment record & loop while payment records
C                   READ      RcvdPmt                              90
C                   DOW       Not *IN90
 *
 * Write the debit record
   ...set up account number and amount for output
C                   WRITE     GenLdgrR                             91
C    91             GOTO      EndTrxn
 *
 * Write the credit record
   ...set up account number and amount for output
C                   WRITE     GenLdgrR                             91
C    91             GOTO      EndTrxn
 *
 * Update the payment transaction to indicate it has been posted
C                   UPDATE    RcvdPmtR                             91
 *
 * If error occurred, warn user and rollback transaction; else commit it
C    EndTrxn        TAG
C                   IF        *IN91
 ... issue warning message or record error in a log
C                   ROLBK
C                   ELSE
C                   COMMIT
C                   ENDIF                            CONTINUED
```

```
*...1....+....2....+....3....+....4....+....5....+....6....+....7....+.
 *
 * Read the next payment record and loop
C                     READ      RcvdPmt                           90
C                     ENDDO
 * Exit the program
C                     SETON                                       LR
C                     RETURN
```

Before the program begins, you need to execute the STRCMTCTL command. You usually issue this command in a CL program that then calls this program.

In the program's F-specs, you mark both files for open under commitment control. You do not need to open all files in a program for commitment control, but most programmers do. Some files, such as one that stores the next available order number, can be updated but do not need to be part of the atomic transaction.

A loop in the C-specs lets you read through the payment records. After setting up the appropriate account numbers and amounts (shown in pseudocode), the program writes a record for both the debit and the credit. Then the program updates the payment transaction to show that it has been posted. Next the program loops back to the next record.

On each WRITE and on the UPDATE, 91 is the error indicator. If an error occurs on any of these operations, a conditioned GOTO, with the tag EndTrxn as its target, immediately passes control to the end of the transaction. At the end-of-transaction point, which processing will also reach if no errors occur, you test indicator 91 to find out whether an error occurred. If it has, no matter which file caused it, you execute the ROLBK operation. If not, you COMMIT.

Consider what failures can occur. Suppose that after writing the first general ledger record, you cannot write the second because the write causes a duplicate key in a logical file built over the GenLdgr file. You have to remove the first record to prevent the books from being out of balance. Or suppose you write both general ledger records and then something prevents the update of the payment record. This situation keeps the books in balance, but the next iteration of the process can post the payment a second time. The general ledger will balance, but the adjustments will be overstated and will not balance back to the payments received.

No matter what the cause of the error, all the database changes use the same indicator to signal the error. The error indicator works for errors you can trap while the program is running. But what about errors the program can't trap? Suppose someone accidentally cancels the job, and the program gets terminated between file updates. Again, a partial update will result in an inconsistent database. And, if the program terminates, it has no way to ROLBK.

A great benefit of commitment control is that the system can perform automatic cleanup for you. If a job terminates and still has uncommitted updates, the operating system automatically rolls back those updates. If the system loses power, it doesn't have the chance to clean up because it isn't on. Again, OS/400's robustness saves the day. At IPL time, the system automatically rolls back any uncommitted updates made under commitment control.

Runtime Selective Commitment Control

The previous example demonstrates how to use commitment control in an RPG program. That example shows that you have to meet certain requirements before you can use commitment control. One important requirement is that you have to journal all files you open under commitment control. This requirement means that every change to the file results in the entire record being written to a journal at least once and maybe twice. During a commitment control cycle, the system always writes two images to the journal: the before image and the after image (unless you are creating or deleting, of course, in which case, only one image exists). All this data going to disk can eat up a lot of storage, so some shops prefer to run without journaling, commitment control, and all the hardware resources they eat up.

Some situations demand commitment control, and others don't. Sometimes, different sites using the same application have different commitment control needs. If you are writing code for multiple sites or a package to sell to multiple clients, you need to let your application control whether updates occur under commitment control. The optional parameter on the F-spec COMMIT keyword lets you decide whether to open a file under commitment control. Usually, you will also want to explicitly control the opening of the file.

To make commitment control optional, some basic changes to the previous program are necessary. These changes are in the following example (on pages 120 and 121). One change is the addition of file SysCtl to contain the operating parameters of the application. This file has a field, SysCmtCtl, that determines whether the application will run under commitment control. A field called CmtCtl is the parameter on the COMMIT keyword on the F-spec for the payment and general ledger files. USROPN lets you control the initial open of the files you will have under commitment control.

The first change in the calculations is to retrieve the SysCmtCtl code from the SysCtl file. If no record is in the SysCtl file, the commitment control code defaults to 0 to open this file without commitment control. After you load the CmtCtl field, you can open the files by means of the OPEN operation.

No more changes occur until you reach the end of the transaction, where the error checking happens. The previous example just checked whether an error was present and then either issued a message and rolled back, or committed. The situation is more complicated now, because the ROLBK and

```
*...1....+....2....+....3....+....4....+....5....+....6....+....7....+.
FSysCtl    IF   E           K DISK
FGenLdgr   UF A E           K DISK     COMMIT(CmtCtl) USROPN
FRcvdPmt   UF   E           K DISK     COMMIT(CmtCtl) USROPN

*...1....+....2....+....3....+....4....+....5....+....6....+....7....+.
 **
 * Read system control file to see if commit control is to be active
 *  (default is off)
 * Open the files
 * Read through all the received payments & —
 *   Write the debit record to the general ledger file
 *   Write the credit record to the general ledger file
 *   Mark the payment as having been posted to general ledger
 *   Close down
 **
 * Read system control file to get commit control active code,
 * SysCmtCtl and set the flag for opening the files
C                   READ      SysCtl                              90
C                   IF        *IN90
C                   EVAL      CmtCtl='0'
C                   ELSE
C                   EVAL      CmtCtl=SysCmtCtl
C                   ENDIF
 *
 * Open the payment and general ledger files for processing
C                   OPEN      GenLdgr
C                   OPEN      RcvdPmt
 *
 * Read the first payment record & loop while payment records
C                   READ      RcvdPmt                             90
C                   DOW       Not *IN90
 *
 * Write the debit record
 ... set up account number and amount for output
C                   WRITE     GenLdgrR                            91
C   91              GOTO      EndTrxn
 *
 * Write the credit record
 ... set up account number and amount for output
C                   WRITE     GenLdgrR                            91
C   91              GOTO      EndTrxn
```

Continued

```
*...1....+....2....+....3....+....4....+....5....+....6....+....7....+.
 *
 * Update the payment transaction to indicate it has been posted
C                   UPDATE    RcvdPmtR                              91
 *
 * If error occurred, warn user and roll back transaction; else commit
 *   it
C     EndTrxn       TAG
C                   IF        *IN91
 ... issue warning message or record error in a log
C                   IF        SysCmtCtl='1'
C                   ROLBK
C                   ENDIF
 *
C                   ELSE
 *
C                   IF        SysCmtCtl='1'
C                   COMMIT
C                   ENDIF
 *
C                   ENDIF
 *
 * Read the next payment record and loop
C                   READ      RcvdPmt                               90
C                   ENDDO
 *
C                   CLOSE     *ALL
 *
 * Exit the program
C                   SETON                                           LR
C                   RETURN
```

COMMIT operations will not necessarily be used. Here, the execution of the ROLBK and COMMIT operations is conditioned on whether the SysCmtCtl field is set to 1. The 1 value means that you are running under commitment control, so you need to perform either the ROLBK or the COMMIT. If the value is not 1, you just settle for a warning message and continue processing. Someone will have to come along later and correct the transaction to reconcile the database entries.

To illustrate the usefulness of the INFDS and INFSR for handling file errors, the code on pages 123–126 shows a reworking of this example, which slightly changes the method for handling file errors. The commitment control example has its error recovery mechanism in the main process. Error recovery isn't isolated, and the error recovery code has to provide a way to let a non-error situation go through it gracefully. In this example, the error handling is in a separate subroutine, so it does not intrude on the main logic, and you can maintain it separately.

Looking through the changes to this program, you first notice the addition of the INFSR and INFDS keywords for the GenLdgr and RcvdPmt files. The goal in this example is not only to shut down the program in an orderly manner if it fails, but also to record the details of the operation that caused the failure. To reach this goal, you specify INFDS on both files and a separate INFSR for each file, so each subroutine can handle unique data structure fields for each file. Because the goals of the subroutines are to log the file-specific error and close down the program, each subroutine must access a separate data structure.

The next changes are in the D-specs, which define two fields, GenLdgrExc and RcvdPmtExc, as the flag fields to check for recursive calls in the INFSR subroutines. When the flag field is blank, the error routine is running for the first time. If the flag field is not blank, the routine is already executing, and you have a more serious problem. Another change is the addition of two data structures in the D-specs, GenLdgrFDS and RcvdPmtFDS, the ones named in the INFDS keywords.

When you need to know what is happening with a file, you can check the defined subfields (GLFile, GLStatus, GLOper, RPRecord, RPMsgID, etc.). In particular, you want to record this information in a failure log so you can find out what caused a problem in a job run. This data in the data structure is updated as each file is accessed. Illustrating the two alternatives for specifying the data structure subfields, you can see the subfields defined both with the special words (*FILE for GLFile and RPFile) and positional notation (positions 46 to 52 for GLMsgID and RPMsgID).

As you get down into the body of the code, you see one improvement immediately. The error indicators are removed from the two WRITE statements and the one UPDATE statement. Also, the GOTO conditioned by the error indicator is gone from after each of those operations, so the TAG is no longer necessary. The previous code had a conditional ROLBK or COMMIT after the completion of the updates. Now, the code is much cleaner: You COMMIT as soon as you finish the updates.

The error checking is now in the subroutines you identify in the INFSR keywords in the F-specs. These two subroutines are similar. Their only differences are their names and the names of the fields they must use. Each has a separate recursion-check flag field, GenLdgrExc and RcvdPmtExc. And, as you read in the pseudocode, each subroutine passes a different set of data structure subfields to the function that is called to log the database I/O error. Each subroutine performs the prescribed check for recursion and logs recursion if it happens. If not, each logs the file error that has occurred and then does a ROLBK on the transaction. After the roll back, the program terminates.

To spiff up this code, you can set a return code using a program parameter to signal the calling program that an error has occurred. Enabling error checking this way makes the code longer, but the improvements are significant. The logic in the main program is cleaner. You can readily see that you expect to perform two writes and an update and then commit the transaction. You don't have error trapping processes mingled in with the business logic. These changes will make the function easier to read and maintain down the road.

Also, the error logging improves significantly. By accessing data in the INFDSs, you can pinpoint which statement has failed and why. This type of information will be invaluable to a maintenance programmer who must find out why a program has failed.

```
*...1....+....2....+....3....+....4....+....5....+....6....+....7....+....8
FGenLdgr   UF A E           K DISK     COMMIT INFSR(GenLdgrErr)
F                                             INFDS(GenLdgrFDS)
FRcvdPmt   UF   E           K DISK     COMMIT INFSR(RcvdPmtErr)
F                                             INFDS(RcvdPmtFDS)

*...1....+....2....+....3....+....4....+....5....+....6....+....7....+....8
 *
D AcctCredit       S              10A
D AcctDebit        S              10A
D GnlLdgrExc       S               1A   INZ(' ')
D RcvdPmtExc       S               1A   INZ(' ')
 *
DGenLdgrFDS        DS
D GLFile             *FILE
D GLStatus           *STATUS
D GLOper             *OPCODE
D GLRecord           *RECORD
D GLMsgID            46      52
 *
DRcvdPmtFDS        DS
D RPFile             *FILE
D RPStatus           *STATUS
D RPOper             *OPCODE
D RPRecord           *RECORD
D RPMsgID            46      52
```

Continued

```
*...1....+....2....+....3....+....4....+....5....+....6....+....7....+....8
 **
 * Read through all the received payments
 *  For each payment
 *   Construct account number of account to debit (some funds account)
 *   Construct account number of account to credit (a receivables account)
 *   Write the debit record to the general ledger file
 *   Write the credit record to the general ledger file
 *   Mark payment as having been posted to general ledger
 *  Close down
 **
 *
 * Read the first payment record
C                   READ      RcvdPmt                                  90
 *
 * Loop while we have a payment record
C                   DOW       Not *IN90
 *
 * Construct account number of account to debit
 ... call a function to create account number and place in AcctDebit
 *
 * Construct account number of account to credit
 ... call a function to create account number and place in AcctCredit
 *
 * Load and write the debit record
C                   MOVE      AcctDebit      GLAcctNbr
C                   Z-ADD     PmtAmt         GLTrxnAmt
C                   WRITE     GenLdgrR
 *
 * Load and write the credit record
C                   MOVE      AcctCredit     GLAcctNbr
C                   Z-SUB     PmtAmt         GLTrxnAmt
C                   WRITE     GenLdgrR
 *
 * Update the payment transaction to show it has been posted
C                   Z-ADD     *DATE          PmtPostDte
C                   UPDATE    RcvdPmtR
 *
 * Commit the transaction
C                   COMMIT
 *
```

Continued

```
*...1....+....2....+....3....+....4....+....5....+....6....+....7....+....8
 * Read the next payment record and loop
C                    READ      RcvdPmt                              90
C                    ENDDO
 * Exit the program
C                    SETON                                          LR
C                    RETURN
 *************************************************************************
 * If an error occurred on the GL file, warn user and roll back transaction
 *************************************************************************
C     GenLdgrErr     BEGSR
C                    IF        GenLdgrExc='Y'
 * If recursive call, note in log
  ... call program to log recursive call error
 *
 * Handle error
C                    ELSE
 *
 * Set recursive call control flag
C                    EVAL      GenLdgrExc='Y'
 *
 * Record error received in error log and notify operator
  ... call program to issue warning message and record error in a log
      recording the file, status, operation, rec name, and msg ID received
 *
 * Roll back any uncompleted transaction; then exit the program
C                    ROLBK
C                    RETURN
 *
C                    ENDIF
 *
C                    ENDSR
 *
 *************************************************************************
 * If an error occurred on the payment file, warn user and roll back trans
 *************************************************************************
C     RcvdPmtErr     BEGSR
C                    IF        RcvdPmtExc='Y'
 * If recursive call, note in log
  ... call program to log recursive call error
 *
 * Handle error
```

CONTINUED

```
*...1....+....2....+....3....+....4....+....5....+....6....+....7....+....8
C                   ELSE
 *
 * Set recursive call control flag
C                   EVAL      RcvdPmtExc='Y'
 *
 * Record error received in error log and notify operator
   ... call program to issue warning message and record error in a log
       recording the file, status, operation, rec name, and msg ID received
 *
 * Roll back any uncompleted transaction; then exit the program
C                   ROLBK
C                   RETURN
 *
C                   ENDIF
 *
C                   ENDSR
```

CHAPTER 5

Arithmetic Operation Codes

Because RPG has a history as a language oriented toward business applications, its set of arithmetic operation codes is relatively small and cumbersome to use. This situation has improved in the latest incarnation of the language, thanks to the EVAL (Evaluate) operation code. This chapter will examine the traditional arithmetic operation codes (listed below) and discuss the improvements EVAL brings to arithmetic operations.

Opcode	Description
ADD	Add
Z-ADD	Zero and Add
SUB	Subtract
Z-SUB	Zero and Subtract
MULT	Multiply
DIV	Divide
MVR	Move Remainder
SQRT	Square Root
XFOOT	Cross Foot (sum elements of an array)

As you read about RPG arithmetic operations, keep in mind that the system performs all arithmetic computation in packed-decimal format, and OS/400 will convert any data that is not already in this format into packed-decimal format before any computation can occur. Because OS/400 works with packed decimal, the RPG compiler uses this format for internal representation of numeric values.

Also note that an arithmetic operation code manipulates numbers as opposed to characters, so an arithmetic operation code is a numeric operation. Because numeric operations require numeric data, in any calculations with these operation codes, you can specify only a numeric subfield, numeric array, numeric array element, numeric table element, numeric named constant, numeric figurative constant, or numeric literal.

THE CALCULATION SPECIFICATIONS

Chapter 1 introduced all the RPG specifications. Now, because you specify arithmetic operations in the C-specs, let's look at these specs in detail. You specify all operation codes in positions 26 through 36 of a program's C-specs. With each opcode, you can specify a Factor 1 field (positions 12 through 25), a Factor 2 field (positions 36 through 50), a Result field (positions 50 through 63), or some combination of these elements. In addition, some opcodes allow conditioning and resulting indicators. Finally, some opcodes permit an operation code extender such as H for half adjust (rounding).

Factor 1 and Factor 2

All RPG arithmetic opcodes except EVAL allow Factor 1 and 2. You specify Factor 1 and Factor 2 to identify the fields whose values you want to use in a computation. The result of an arithmetic operation that you perform on the Factor 1 and Factor 2 fields will be in the field you specify as the Result field. For example, you can ADD the value in the Factor 1 field to the value in the Factor 2 field. The sum of this addition will be in the Result field.

With all arithmetic opcodes, Factor 1 and Factor 2 are read-only fields, so the operation does not affect the value of these fields. An operation will modify the value of the Factor 1 or Factor 2 field only if you specify the same field for one of these factors and for the Result field because the outcome of an operation appears in the Result field.

The ADD, SUB, MULT, or DIV operation codes do not require Factor 1. When you do not specify Factor 1, these operations use Factor 2 and the Result field. For example, if you do an ADD operation, specifying Factor 2 and the Result field, the value in the field you specify as Factor 2 will be added to the value in the field you specify as the Result field, and the sum will be in the field specified in the Result field. For operations accepting Factor 1, Factor 2, and the Result field, the following rules are true.

- Factor 1, Factor 2, and the Result field can be the same field.

- Factor 1, Factor 2, and the Result field can be different fields.

- Factor 1 and Factor 2 can be the same field.

- Factor 1 and the Result field can be the same field.

- Factor 2 and the Result field can be the same field.

The Result Field

The Result field will contain the result of an arithmetic operation. Naturally, because arithmetic operations create a new value that you need to store somewhere, you can specify only variables in the Result field positions on the C-spec; numeric constants and literals are not allowed.

RPG, unlike languages such as BASIC, Visual BASIC, C, and C++, requires you to give each variable you create a discrete size. RPG (in contrast to DDS) has no such thing as a variable-length field. These other languages provide for *types* of data but not for specific *sizes* of data. In these languages, the type of data implies maximum sizes, but you cannot request that a field have a size of, say, 2 digits that can hold all values from –99 to +99. RPG, on the other hand, requires you to specify the sizes of your fields. As in other languages, RPG has maximums for each type of data, but RPG's maximums apply to the definition you give the variable rather being maximums for the variables. For instance, an integer data type in many languages limits the allowed values to −32768 to +32767 but provides no facility to limit values to, for example, 3 digits.

Because RPG variables can have many different sizes, you must ensure that each calculation stores its result in a variable that is large enough to hold the final value. RPG will not ordinarily issue any type of error when a calculation results in a value that is too large for its intended variable. Nor does RPG provide any *simple* way to code a check for this occurrence. This situation means you must be aware of the sizes of the calculated values in relation to the size of the variable that has to hold it. If the variable is not large enough to hold all the calculated digits to the left of the decimal point, additional (and probably important) digits can be truncated.

The term *overflow* refers to this truncation. On the other hand, *underflow* is when the fractional portion of the result is too precise for the result field to accommodate it. If the result is truncated, the compiler respects the decimal position of the Result field and, depending on the position of the decimal separator and whether the situation is overflow or underflow, determines whether the truncation is left or right. RPG does not change the defined decimal positions of a field you use for the result in an arithmetic operation. To let you specify whether to allow truncation on the left or to issue a runtime error in case of truncation, RPG IV offers a new compile option, TRUNCNBR (Truncate Number), for both the CL CRTBNDRPG (Create Bound RPG Program) and CRTRPGMOD (Create RPG Module) commands.

Conditioning Indicators

With arithmetic operations, you can use conditioning indicators. Conditioning indicators let you specify the circumstances under which a calculation occurs. To condition calculations, you can put indicators on the same line as the operation code, in positions 7 and 8 and in positions 9 through 11. Positions 7 and 8 are for control-level indicators, the last record (LR) indicator, or continuing an indicator test from previous lines. Positions 9 through 11 are for testing the values of any indicators defined in RPG.

Although you can use indicators to condition the execution of a calculation, better form is to condition such statements by enclosing them in an IF statement or other similar structured operation. Indicators can be cryptic because the names of the indicators provide no way to know what they are supposed to condition.

Resulting Indicators

Except for SQRT and EVAL, arithmetic opcodes let you specify resulting indicators in positions 71 through 76 of the C-specs. Resulting indicators let you test the Result field for a positive, negative, or zero result after the arithmetic operation. For example, if you specify an indicator in position 73 to 74 on a SUB operation, the indicator will turn on if the resulting value is negative. For all the arithmetic operations, indicators specified in positions 71 through 72, 73 through 74, and 75 through 76 correspond to positive, negative, and zero, respectively.

Half Adjust

Half adjust is an RPG technique for performing a type of rounding. The name comes from the technique for the rounding. Ordinarily, results of RPG calculations are truncated after the last defined decimal position. Half adjust rounds the result before that truncation occurs. The unit value of the last defined decimal position is divided in half (hence, half adjust), and that halved value is then added to the calculated result. Half adjust affects the result only if the number of decimal positions in the calculated result is greater than the number of decimal positions in the Result field.

Here are some examples of how the system implements half adjust. ADD, DIV, SUB, and MULT all accept half adjust as an operation code extender. EVAL, MVR, and DIV (when followed by MVR) do not.

Initial Result	Defined Decimal Positions	Unit Value of Last Decimal Position	Adjustment Value (Added to Result)	Adjust Value	Final Result (Truncated)
45.28	1	.1	.05	45.33	45.3
45.23	1	.1	.05	45.28	45.2
45.5	0	1	.5	46.0	46
45.4	0	1	.5	45.9	45

To specify half adjust, you key the operation code, followed by an open parenthesis, followed by H (for half adjust), followed by a close parenthesis. For example, you enter ADD(H) and DIV(H).

THE ADD OPERATION CODE

The ADD operation code lets you add the value of Factor 1 and Factor 2 and store the sum in the Result field. Factor 1 is optional. If you do not specify Factor 1, ADD lets you add the value of Factor 2 and the initial value of the Result field and store the sum in the Result field (replacing the original value there).

As with other arithmetic operation codes, you can specify resulting indicators in positions 71 through 76. As you see in the following table, the elements of ADD are Factor 1, which is optional; Factor 2, which is required; and the Result field, which is required. Conditioning and resulting indicators are optional.

Factor 1	Opcode	Extender	Factor 2	Result	Indicators		
Optional addend	ADD	(H)	Required addend	Required sum	Positive	Negative	Zero

You can use two different combinations of these three elements: a three-field ADD (Factor 1, Factor 2, and the Result field) and a two-field ADD (Factor 2 and the Result field).

```
*...1....+....2....+....3....+....4....+....5....+....6....+....7....+
 * REG_TIME = 8.00   OVER_TIME = 2.25
 * The value of TOT_HOURS after the next operation will be (10.25).
 *
C       REG_TIME      ADD       OVER_TIME      TOT_HOURS
```

The example above is a simple, three-field ADD. It adds the value of Factor 1 (REG_TIME) and the value of Factor 2 (OVER_TIME). The sum is in the Result field, TOT_HOURS. This way, you can calculate the sum of the values in two fields, and each field retains its original value.

The second variation of ADD is a shorter form that does not use Factor 1. This two-field ADD operation adds the value of Factor 2 to the value of the Result field and then stores the sum in the Result field. An example of this variation is when you are accumulating a total of multiple items. The example below shows this form of ADD.

```
*...1....+....2....+....3....+....4....+....5....+....6....+....7....+
 * Calculate invoice total
C                     ADD       SALES_TOT      INV_TOTAL
C                     ADD       SALES_TAX      INV_TOTAL
C                     ADD       SHIPPING       INV_TOTAL
C                     ADD       HANDLING       INV_TOTAL
```

This ADD takes the current value of the Result field, adds the value in Factor 2, and then places the total back in the Result field. The value of the field in Factor 2 is *added to* the value in the Result field. The value in Factor 2 does *not* replace the value in the Result field. This approach contrasts to the three-field variation of the ADD operation, where the sum of the value in Factor 1 and 2 replaces the value in the Result field. In the example, the Result field (INV_TOTAL) value changes each time you add another field to it.

THE Z-ADD OPERATION CODE

Z-ADD (Zero and Add) clears the value of the Result field and then replaces that value with the value in Factor 2. Factor 1 is not allowed, Factor 2 is required, and the Result field is required. Indicators are optional. As in the previous opcode, indicators in positions 71 through 72, 73 through 74, and 75 through 76 correspond to positive, negative, and zero, respectively. Here are the elements you can use for Z-ADD.

Factor 1	Opcode	Extender	Factor 2	Result	Indicators		
Not allowed	Z-ADD	(H)	Required *addend*	Required *sum*	Positive	Negative	Zero

The following code illustrates a typical use of this operation. If the code in the previous example is in a program that calculates daily invoices, you have to clear the invoice total for each new customer. The code here sets the field INV_TOTAL to zero before it calculates the total.

```
*...1....+....2....+....3....+....4....+....5....+....6....+....7....+
C                   Z-ADD     0              INV_TOTAL
C                   ADD       SALES_TOT      INV_TOTAL
C                   ADD       SALES_TAX      INV_TOTAL
C                   ADD       SHIPPING       INV_TOTAL
C                   ADD       HANDLING       INV_TOTAL
```

Another variation of Z-ADD is shown below. This form of coding saves one operation by combining the Z-ADD with ADD operations. Z-ADD changes the value of the Result field INV_TOTAL to zero and then adds the value in Factor 2 (SALES_TAX) to the Result field. The Result field's value now is the value of SALES_TOT. You then continue with the operations to calculate the invoice total.

```
*...1....+....2....+....3....+....4....+....5....+....6....+....7....+
C* Calculate Invoice Total
C                   Z-ADD     SALES_TOT      INV_TOTAL
C                   ADD       SALES_TAX      INV_TOTAL
C                   ADD       SHIPPING       INV_TOTAL
C                   ADD       HANDLING       INV_TOTAL
```

With a Z-ADD operation, you can specify half adjust in the operation code extender field, for rounding. If you are carrying a value to a certain precision in, say, a 7.4 field and then need to round it to a 5.2 field, Z-ADD with half adjust lets you round the value when you use the 7.4 field in Factor 2 and the 5.2 field in the Result.

THE SUB OPERATION CODE

The SUB (Subtract) operation code places the difference between the value in Factor 1 and Factor 2 in the Result field. Factor 1 is optional. If you do not specify Factor 1, SUB subtracts the value of Factor 2 from the Result field's value and places the outcome in the Result field.

Factor 2 and the Result field are required. As with the previous two operation codes, you can specify resulting indicators with SUB. Positions 71 through 72, 73 through 74, and 75 through 76 correspond to positive, negative, and zero, respectively. Here's a summary of SUB's elements.

Factor 1	Opcode	Extender	Factor 2	Result	Indicators		
Optional *minuend*	SUB	(H)	Required *subtrahend*	Required *difference*	Positive	Negative	Zero

As a consequence of these optional and required elements, you have two possible variations of the SUB operation: the three-field SUB and the two-field SUB. This simple three-field SUB example subtracts the value of Factor 2 (TotalDeds) from the value of Factor 1 (GrossPay) and stores the result in the Result field (NetPay).

```
*...1....+....2....+....3....+....4....+....5....+....6....+....7....+
 *   GrossPay = 100.00   TotalDeds = 15.50
 *   NetPay   =  84.50   after operation
 *
C     GrossPay      SUB       TotalDeds      NetPay
```

The second variation of SUB is a two-field operation that deducts the value of Factor 2 directly from the Result field. This example calculates sales that do not fit in a specific category. To find such sales, you subtract over-the-counter sales, catalog sales, and telemarketing sales from total sales. The first line of the routine uses a three-field SUB operation to initialize the value of OTH_SALES. Then, you subtract CATALOG and TELEMKTG with two-field SUB operations. Each operation reduces OTH_SALES.

```
*...1....+....2....+....3....+....4....+....5....+....6....+....7....+
 * Calculate Other Sales
C     TOTAL_SLS     SUB       OTC_SALES      OTH_SALES
C                   SUB       CATALOG        OTH_SALES
C                   SUB       TELEMKTG       OTH_SALES
```

SUB brings up an interesting psychological phenomenon. Most people have a harder time conceptualizing the subtraction of a negative number than the addition of a negative number. This problem stems from the confusion implicit in a double negative. Programmers specify SUB to reduce a value, forgetting that they have already allowed for reduction by making the Factor 2 field's value a negative number. In that case, they need to be ADDing rather than SUBing. Just don't forget that SUBing a negative number is the same as ADDing the positive value of that same number.

```
*...1....+....2....+....3....+....4....+....5....+....6....+....7....+
*   VALUE1 = 9.50   VALUE2 = -20.875
*   RESULT = 30.78   after operation
*
C       VALUE1        SUB(H)    VALUE2        RESULT
```

This code illustrates the effect of a negative Factor 2 in a SUB operation. The operation subtracts VALUE2 (–20.875) from VALUE1 (9.50). The result of this operation (9.50 – (–20.875)) is 30.375. Because this example specifies half adjust (RESULT is defined as having 2 decimal positions), the value of RESULT at the end of this operation is 30.78.

THE Z-SUB OPERATION CODE

Z-SUB (Zero and Subtract) subtracts the Factor 2 field's value from zero and moves the difference into the Result field. A typical use of this operation is to change the sign of a numeric field.

Factor 1 is not allowed. Factor 2 and the Result field are required. With Z-SUB, you can put resulting indicators in positions 71 through 76 of the C-specs. This table summarizes the elements you can use for Z-SUB.

Factor 1	Opcode	Extender	Factor 2	Result	Indicators		
Not allowed	Z-SUB	(H)	Required subtrahend	Required difference	Positive	Negative	Zero

Let's look at two examples of Z-SUB. The first shows how to change the sign of a numeric field. The field CREDIT can be a negative number in your program, so if you want to print it as a positive number, you have to reverse the sign. This situation frequently arises if you are printing debits and credits in separate columns. Rather than printing a negative number for a credit, you want to print the positive value so you don't give the impression of a negative credit.

```
*...1....+....2....+....3....+....4....+....5....+....6....+....7....+
* Reverse the sign of the field CREDIT
*
C                       Z-SUB     CREDIT        CREDIT
```

Similar to Z-ADD, Z-SUB first zeroes the Result field value and subtracts the value in the Factor 2 field from 0. (Z-SUB is similar to and the unary minus in C or Pascal.)

A second example shows a slight variation of Z-SUB. To maintain the value of CREDIT for further operations in your program and still print it as a positive number, you can Z-SUB it into a different field. In this example, because you want to print the profit in whole dollars only, the code defines the field CRED_PRINT with zero decimal positions and specifies half adjust.

```
*...1....+....2....+....3....+....4....+....5....+....6....+....7....+
*   Change the sign of the field CREDIT
*     and store it in a field for printing
*
C                       Z-SUB(H)  CREDIT            CRED_PRINT
```

THE MULT OPERATION CODE

The MULT (Multiply) operation code, multiplies the value of Factor 1 and Factor 2 and stores the product in the Result field. Factor 1 is optional. If you do not specify Factor 1, MULT multiplies the value in Factor 2 by the value in the Result field and places the product in the Result field.

This table shows the elements you can use for Z-SUB. Factor 1 is optional. Factor 2 and the Result field are required. Indicators are optional.

Factor 1	Opcode	Extender	Factor 2	Result	Indicators		
Optional multiplicand	MULT	(H)	Required multiplier	Required product	Positive	Negative	Zero

The example below demonstrates a three-field variation of the MULT operation code. This variation lets you calculate a product (EXT_PRICE) by multiplying QUANTITY by UNIT_PRICE. The second line of code specifies half adjust.

```
*...1....+....2....+....3....+....4....+....5....+....6....+....7....+
* Multiply quantity by unit price to get extended price
C      QUANTITY       MULT      UNIT_PRICE    EXT_PRICE
*
* If unit price has more than 2 decimals defined, use half adjust
C      QUANTITY       MULT(H)   UNIT_PRICE    EXT_PRICC
```

The second variation of MULT is a two-field operation. In this example, the Result field serves as both the multiplicand and the product. If your customers can negotiate volume buying rates, you can store the negotiated rate as a percentage of the nondiscounted price, or a rate factor. In that case, once you calculate the regular extended price, you can apply the rate factor to adjust the extended price.

```
*...1....+....2....+....3....+....4....+....5....+....6....+....7....+
*   After calculating extended price,
*   adjust it by Rate Factor
C      QUANTITY       MULT      UNIT_PRICE    EXT_PRICE
C                     MULT(H)   RATE_FCTR     EXT_PRICE
```

THE DIV AND MVR OPERATION CODES

The DIV (Divide) operation code performs division. Factor 1 is optional. If you specify Factor 1, DIV lets you divide the value in Factor 1 by the value in Factor 2. If you don't use Factor 1, this operation divides the value in the Result field by the value in Factor 2. The result is then in the Result field.

This table shows the elements you can use for DIV. Factor 1 is optional. Factor 2 and the Result field are required. Indicators are optional. You can specify both conditioning and resulting indicators.

Factor 1	Opcode	Extender	Faction 2	Result	Indicators		
Optional *dividend*	DIV	(H)	Required *divisor*	Required *quotient*	Positive	Negative	Zero

The MVR Operation Code

The DIV operation is analogous to the DIVIDE operator in COBOL and DIV in Pascal. In all these operations, the remainder is lost. However, as COBOL provides the REMAINDER operation and Pascal has MOD, RPG lets you capture the remainder of a DIV operation with MVR (Move Remainder). Any remainder resulting from the divide operation is lost unless you specify MVR on the C-spec immediately after DIV. Otherwise, unpredictable remaining values can result.

If you use MVR, you must use the DIV and MVR operation codes sequentially together. After a division operation, MVR will store any remainder in the Result field.

Although the compiler will catch any attempt to use MVR when DIV does not precede it, you can accidentally condition DIV and MVR so that they won't execute together. Additionally, note that you cannot use MVR after a DIV that has requested rounding (half adjust).

This table gives the elements you can use for MVR. Factor 1 and Factor 2 are not allowed. The Result field is required. Indicators are optional.

Factor 1	Opcode	Extender	Faction 2	Result	Indicators		
Not allowed	MVR		Not allowed	Required *remainder*	Positive	Negative	Zero

Coding DIV and MVR

Let's look at how to use DIV. This example distributes costs for a training program evenly over the months that the training takes. This code shows how to round the result to get one figure for each month.

```
*...1....+....2....+....3....+....4....+....5....+....6....+....7....+
C* Calculate monthly cost of training program
C*
C       NET_COST        DIV(H)    PGM_MONTHS    MONTH_COST
```

You divide the value in Factor 1 (NET_COST) by the value in Factor 2 (PGM_MONTHS). The answer (MONTH_COST) is then in the Result field. This calculation gives you a cost for each month but might not total the cost exactly if the amount is not evenly divisible by the number of months. To calculate the exact amount, specify MVR and do not use rounding, as shown below.

```
*...1....+....2....+....3....+....4....+....5....+....6....+....7....+
C* Calculate monthly cost of training
C* and capture extra amount with MVR
C       NET_COST        DIV       PGM_MONTHS    MONTH_COST
C                       MVR                     COST_ADJ
```

You can also use a two-field variation of DIV. If you are having a half-price sale and want to divide each invoice total by 2 to calculate the discounted amount, you can use the code below. In this case, because you don't use Factor 1, the operation divides the Result field (INV_TOTAL) by Factor 2 (2). The quotient is then stored in the Result field.

```
*...1....+....2....+....3....+....4....+....5....+....6....+....7....+
 * Calculate discounted invoice total for half-price sale
 *
C                       DIV(H)    2             INV_TOTAL
```

To get every possible penny, you specify half-adjust on this operation. Remember that when you use MVR following DIV, you cannot use half adjust to round the result of the DIV.

THE SQRT OPERATION CODE

SQRT (Square Root) places the square root of the Factor 2 field in the Result field. The following table summarizes the elements you can use for the SQRT operation code. Factor 1 is not applicable. Factor 2 and the Result field are required. Resulting indicators are not allowed.

Factor 1	Opcode	Extender	Factor 2	Result	Indicators		
Not allowed	SQRT		Required *value*	Required *root*	Positive	Negative	Zero

The example below demonstrates the SQRT operation code to get the square root of numeric variable X. This operation code is not one you will use often.

```
*...1....+....2....+....3....+....4....+....5....+....6....+....7....+
 *   If the value of X is equal to 9 then
 *   the value of RI after the SQRT operation will be 3.
 C                       SQRT      X               SquareRoot
```

THE XFOOT OPERATION CODE

The XFOOT (Cross foot) operation sums the elements of an array. XFOOT accumulates the value of each element in the array you specify in Factor 2 and stores the sum in the Result field.

This table shows the elements you can use for XFOOT. Factor 1 is not applicable. Factor 2 and the Result field are required. Resulting indicators are optional. You can specify half adjust as the operation code extender.

Factor 1	Opcode	Extender	Factor 2	Result	Indicators		
Not allowed	XFOOT	(H)	Required array name	Required sum	Positive	Negative	Zero

XFOOT has advantages over simply using multiple fields and then summing them for a total. If you are accumulating values for each month within a year, you don't have to accumulate a total for the year at the same time. This approach saves the calculation of the annual total and speeds processing at the detail level. Of course, you can achieve that task without XFOOT. You just have to add up the various elements when you reach the proper point in your program. However, XFOOT is not concerned with the number of elements in an array. So, instead of having to include and maintain code to total each element of the array, you can use XFOOT to calculate a total of all the elements, no matter how many you have. If you later add additional array elements (you need to track 18 rather then 12 months), the XFOOT code does not change, and you don't risk forgetting to include the new months when you calculate the grand total for all the periods.

ARITHMETIC OPERATION CODES BY EXAMPLE

Because most RPG applications are for a business environment, let's discuss the arithmetic operations in action in a receipts program. Pseudocode will represent file I/O, so you can focus on the math operations.

As the program reads a payment from the database, the total payment is applied to the outstanding invoices. A single payment can apply to a single invoice, or it can cover several invoices. For each open invoice, the program calculates the remaining balance and then applies as much of the payment as possible to that balance. Once the program calculates the amount to apply, you update the invoice with the new amount applied and create a commission-payable record to record the sales commission.

The IFGT (If Greater Than), ELSE, and ENDIF (End If) operation codes set up conditional execution of the code on lines 26 and 28. If the value of Lft_2_Dist is greater than the value of Open_Amt, the Z_ADD on line 26 will be executed. If it is less than or equal to (ELSE), the Z-ADD on line 28 will be executed. This section of code demonstrates ADD, SUB, Z-ADD, and MULT.

```
*...1....+....2....+....3....+....4....+....5....+....6....+....7....+
 *
 *  ... Read the next unprocessed payment record getting:
 *  ...     - Account ID
 *  ...     - Amount Paid
 *
C                   Z-ADD     RPAmt_Paid    Lft_2_Dist
 *
 * While Lft_2_Dist remains non-zero, loop through all the
 * customer's open invoices to apply payment. For each open invoice,
 * calculate the open amount and the amount to be applied. Apply it.
 * Also calculate the standard 7% commission based on the amount
 * applied and write commission payable record.
 *
 *
 *  ... Read the next open invoice getting:
 *  ...     - Invoice Total
 *  ...     - Total Paid on Invoice to Date
 *  ...     - Selling Agent ID
 *
 * Calculate the open amount
C     IVInv_Tot     SUB       IVTtl_Paid    Open_Amt
 *
 * Amount to apply is either the entire open amount or however much
 * is left to distribute (whichever is smaller)
C     Lft_2_Dist    IFGT      Open_Amt
C                   Z-ADD     Open_Amt      Apply_Amt
C                   ELSE
C                   Z-ADD     Lft_2_Dist    Apply_Amt
C                   ENDIF
  *
  * Reduce the amount left to distribute
C                   SUB       Apply_Amt     Lft_2_Dist
```

CONTINUED

```
*...1....+....2....+....3....+....4....+....5....+....6....+....7....+
*
* Add the applied amount to the total paid on the invoice
C                     ADD       Apply_Amt      IVTtl_Paid
*
* ... Update the "Total Paid on Invoice to Date" with the amount
* ... applied by the current payment (update the invoice file).
*
* Calculate the standard commission and record it
C     Apply_Amt       MULT(H)   .07            CPComm_Amt
*
* ... Write a record to the commission payable file
*
* If money is still left to distribute, loop back to read
* next open invoice for the customer
*
```

FREE-FORM EXPRESSIONS WITH THE EVAL OPERATION CODE

An important enhancement to RPG IV is that in addition to the fixed-form arithmetic operations just discussed, you can now specify *free-form expressions*. A free-form expression is a collection of one or more subexpressions. *Subexpressions* consist of RPG field names, named constants, literals, parentheses, and zero or more *operators* such as add, subtract, and divide. The operators are not the fixed-form operations discussed so far; rather, their *function* is like that of the fixed-form operations, but free-form operators have different syntax.

Free-form expressions are available to perform many functions in RPG IV, but this chapter will cover just the arithmetic functions, add and concatenate, subtract and negate, multiply, exponentiate, and divide. This table shows the five free-form arithmetic operators in RPG IV.

Arithmetic Operators	
+	addition and concatenation
−	subtraction and negation
*	multiplication
**	exponentiation
/	division

You can specify all these operators with two *operands,* and you can use some operators with just one. Operands, like factors in fixed-form operations, provide the values to which you want to apply the operator.

Free-form expressions let you perform more than one operation on one C-spec: Free-form operations provide brevity in coding, so free-form specifications also improve the readability and maintainability of RPG programs.

The EVAL (Evaluate) operation code is the vehicle that lets you code free-form arithmetic expressions. This operation code tells the compiler that a particular C-spec contains a free-form expression. EVAL is new with RPG IV.

The EVAL Operation Code

EVAL signals the compiler that Factor 2 contains a free-form expression. You specify EVAL in the operation code field (positions 26 to 36) of the C-specs. Factor 1 is not permitted, and the Factor 2 field is *extended,* which means it uses all code positions from 36 to 80. So you cannot specify a Result field, field size, or resulting indicators on a line that uses EVAL; the extended Factor 2 takes over those positions.

Factor 1	Opcode	Extender	Factor 2	Result	Indicators
Not allowed	EVAL	(H)	Extended expression (pos 36-80)	Not applicable	Not applicable

Above is a summary of EVAL. You can specify conditioning indicators. You can also have an operation code extender for half adjust (H). Resulting indicators are not allowed.

The free-form expression following EVAL must contain an *assignment operator* (=). The assignment operator divides the expression into a *left side* and *right side.* The free-form expression syntax for EVAL is shown below.

```
EVAL        target field = expression
```

The left side is the expression's *result,* or *target,* which can be a field name, array name, array element, data structure, data structure subfield, or a built-in function such as %SUBST (Substring). The right side is an expression that will be resolved to a value that will be stored in the target field (the left side of the expression). The data type of the value on the right and left side must be the same. The operation code extender is valid only for class numeric expressions to achieve half-adjust.

The Difference Between Fixed- and Free-Form Expressions

To illustrate the difference between fixed-form operations and free-form expressions, let's look at some RPG IV code. Suppose you are working in a payroll program, and you must add the straight-time pay and overtime pay to get the total pay, add any holiday pay to the total pay, and then subtract the cost of purchasing stock via the company's employee stock purchase plan. RPG's old operations make coding this problem as convoluted as that last sentence. To perform this task with the old operations, you need three operations, as the code segment below shows.

```
*...1....+....2....+....3....+....4....+....5....+....6....+....7....+
C        StrTimePay      ADD       OvrTimePay    TotalPay
C                        ADD       HolidayPay    TotalPay
C                        SUB       EmpStckPrc    TotalPay
```

The first operation adds StrTimePay and OvrTimePay and puts the result in TotalPay. But this value isn't really the total pay. You must add in HolidayPay. Then, you subtract the EmpStckPrc. You need three steps to get one value.

Now, using EVAL and free-form expressions, you can perform that same calculation with one operation code. The new version of the calculation appears below.

```
*...1....+....2....+....3....+....4....+....5....+....6....+....7....+
C                        EVAL      TotalPay = StrTimePay + OvrTimePay
C                                            + HolidayPay - EmpStckPrc
```

Note that the four values in the equation are all necessary to calculate the final value. In the previous example, you can easily miss part of the equation, especially if that code segment is buried in a series of other math operations or moves.

Also note that the expression continues onto the next line. You can continue free-form expressions onto as many lines as you need. The only requirement is that the line onto which you are continuing must have positions 7 through 35 blank. Note that with numeric expressions, you need not enter a continuation character to continue onto the next line. The example shows the entire expression on the right of the equals sign, but the expression can just as easily continue under the TotalPay field.

When you specify EVAL with arithmetic expressions, you get several advantages over traditional RPG math operations. First, you can perform complex algorithms without having to resort to intermediate variables. RPG automatically tracks the intermediate results from free-form calculations and doesn't require you to store values temporarily. Every operator has a maximum of two operands, but now you can build expressions that rely on the system-maintained result of an operation rather than the programmer-maintained intermediate result.

The next advantage is that you now can specify parentheses to determine the order of calculations. No longer do you have to put several lines of code in just the right order to get your result, only to find that another programmer misinterprets your intentions and moves one or more lines of code around. If you have to force one part of an expression to calculate before another, you can show the order by specifying parentheses. Not only do the parentheses order the hierarchy of operations and remove logical ambiguity, but they also visually organize the operations, which can be invaluable to the next programmer.

Another advantage is that you can use free-form expressions for exponentiation so you don't have to write loops to perform calculations. Although the AS/400 has not traditionally been the choice for higher math functions, the machine's presence in insurance and banking means programmers often need to perform simple exponentiation. To use RPG IV's exponentiation capabilities, you must specify EVAL with a free-form expression.

Finally, with EVAL's ability to process expressions that continue on subsequent lines, you can express longer calculations with field names that don't have to be cramped down to just a few characters.

Let's take a common calculation in a system that calculates loan payments. Using this formula to calculate a simple interest loan payment is straightforward. But the same calculation with old RPG techniques is no simple matter.

$$1 - \frac{\text{Principal x Periodic Rate}}{\dfrac{1}{(1 + \textbf{Periodic Rate})^{\text{Number of Periods}}}}$$

To code this formula in RPG IV, the first task is to redesign the formula to use the available tools. The formula indicates the logical separations. To represent the formula in correct algebraic terms, you specify EVAL and follow the standard algebraic hierarchy for the sequence of operations. Parentheses let you describe the sequence for executing the operations.

Below, you see the formula in standard algebraic terms. The innermost parentheses first give you 1 + PerRate. Next, the outer parentheses cause processing of the second half of the equation. Within that part, exponentiation is the first operation. Next, is the division operation, and then its result is subtracted from 1. When two operations are on the same level in the hierarchy, processing is from left to right.

```
Principal x PerRate / ( 1 - 1 / ( 1 + PerRate) ** NumPer )
```

Although this version of the formula will work, you can specify some additional parentheses to remove any ambiguity for maintenance programmers. Adding parentheses around the top of the original equation clearly defines it. You already have parentheses around the lower half of the original equation. Adding parentheses around the entire value to be subtracted from 1 will further clarify that part. Now the equation looks like this:

```
(Principal x PerRate) / ( 1 - (1 / ( 1 + PerRate) ** NumPer ))
```

Once you insert parentheses to ensure the calculations occur in the correct order, you can put this equation into a free-form expression on an EVAL statement. The PerRate field is the periodic rate, so if you are calculating a monthly payment, PerRate is the monthly interest rate. If you start with an annual percentage rate, you divide by 12 to get the monthly rate. Also, the rate must be in decimal form, so you express a period rate of 1 percent as .01 rather than 1.

```
*...1....+....2....+....3....+....4....+....5....+....6....+....7....+
C                    EVAL (H)  Payment=(Principal * PerRate)/
C                              (1 - (1 / (1 + PerRate) ** NumPer))
```

EVAL makes this calculation easier than the code you have to write without it. The code below shows what's necessary without EVAL.

```
*...1....+....2....+....3....+....4....+....5....+....6....+....7....+
 *
 * Calc main numerator (Principal x PerRate)
C     Principal     MULT      PerRate         Numerator
 *
 * Calc temporary value for (1 + PerRate)
C     1             ADD       PerRate         Temp1
 *
 * Calc temporary value for raising previous value to NumPer power
C                   Z-ADD     Temp1           TotExp
C     NumPer        SUB       1               PwrCnt
C                   DO        PwrCnt
C                   MULT      TotExp          TotExp
C                   ENDDO
 *
 * Calc temporary value for division of previous value into 1
C     1             DIV       TotExp          Temp2
 *
```

```
*...1....+....2....+....3....+....4....+....5....+....6....+....7....+
 * Calc the main denominator by subtracting previous value from 1
C     1             SUB       Temp2           Denominatr
 *
 * Perform final calculation
C     Numerator     DIV (H)   Denominatr      Payment
 *
```

This code covers all four advantages of EVAL: You need no intermediate variables, you can specify parentheses to order the calculations, you can do exponentiation, and you can continue a long expression over multiple lines. In fact, you can make the RPG expression look similar to the original equation, with the expression in the numerator above the expression in the denominator.

CHAPTER 6

Move Operation Codes

The two basic RPG IV move operation codes are MOVE (Move right from source to target) and MOVEL (Move Left from source to target). The other move operation codes are MOVEA (Move Array) and MxxZO (Move Zone). Chapter 8, "Arrays and Tables," discusses MOVEA. The MxxZO operations are rare in any modern use of RPG, so this book will not discuss them.

The two basic RPG move operation codes, MOVE and MOVEL, let you copy data from a source field you specify in Factor 2 to a target you specify in the Result field. Because the MOVE operation codes *copy* the data, not *move* it, the data in the source of the MOVE operation remains intact.

MOVE and MOVEL can copy data across RPG's numeric, character, date, time, timestamp, and graphic data types, so these operations let you convert data from one type to another. For instance, a MOVE operation can copy (and thus translate) a numeric field into a character field and vice versa. In the same way, the move operations let you convert numeric and character data into dates and times, and vice versa. With some experience, you can use the move operation codes to convert from one numeric class data type to another.

Even if you have little programming experience, you know that the data you need to process is often not in the correct format. Because you need a way to convert that data to the format you need, these operation codes are vital for their conversion capabilities alone. Note that because the conversion capabilities are so important for the use of the move operation codes, a thorough understanding of RPG data types is essential. (See Chapter 3, "Defining Data," for details about classes and data types and how to specify them.)

USAGE GUIDELINES

The general usage guidelines for MOVE and MOVEL explain what these operation codes do and how to specify them. These rules also govern length, class compatibility for the source and target field (including rules for conversion and how zones and signs convert), resulting indicators, and decimal positions.

Specifying Move Operation Codes

Move operations copy the source field, Factor 2, to the target, the Result field. With a move operation, Factor 1 must be blank, unless you are moving date, time, or timestamp data type fields to numeric or character fields, or vice versa.

Factor 2, the source field for the move, can be a field, data structure, data structure subfield, literal, named constant, figurative constant, an array, or array element. The Result field, the field into which the MOVE copies the data from the Factor 2 field, can be a field, data structure, data structure subfield, array, or array element. Note that Factor 2 and the Result field cannot be overlapping data structure subfields.

Any field you specify as Factor 2 in a move remains unchanged after execution of that move operation. Only the Result field is altered.

Length

The length of the source and target fields is important with move operations because truncation can occur or you can have data left over from the original data in the target field. Here are the rules for length, where LENGTH is the length of the data field (including the shift-out and shift-in characters that mark the beginning and end of a double-byte character string).

1. If LENGTH (Result field) = LENGTH (Factor 2 field), the entire Result field will be overwritten.

2. If LENGTH (Result field) < LENGTH (Factor 2 field), the entire Result field will be overwritten, left truncation of the source value will occur on a MOVE, and right truncation will occur on a MOVEL.

3. If LENGTH (Result field) > LENGTH (Factor 2 field), the number of bytes overwritten in the Result field is given by LENGTH (Factor 2 field). You can specify padding by placing a P in the opcode extender field.

Class Compatibility for Source and Target

The class of source and target fields for RPG move operations can be numeric, character, date, time, timestamp, or RPG IV's new graphic class for use with double-byte character sets for languages such as Chinese and Hebrew. You can have source and target fields of different classes, which is what enables translation of one class to another. You have a great deal of flexibility in combinations of classes in the source and target fields that are compatible for move operations. For example, you can translate character data to numeric and numeric to character. You can also convert character or numeric data to date and time data. This table shows which data types are not compatible the move operations.

Class of Source	Class of Target	Compatible
Numeric	Graphic	NO
Graphic	Numeric	NO
Date	Time	NO
Time	Date	NO

Character and graphic class data are compatible: Either class can act as the source or the target of a move. You can move graphic class data to character class fields, and you can move character class data to graphic class Result fields. The graphic and numeric classes are not compatible for use with move operation codes. The graphic class is also not compatible with the date, time, and timestamp classes. Finally, the date and time classes are incompatible with each other.

Knowing what classes are compatible is the first step. Now let's look at how move operations work for compatible source and target fields.

Character and Numeric Class Move Operations

Character and numeric classes are compatible, and either class can serve as the source or target field. You can use RPG move operation codes to copy data from a character field to a numeric field. The significance of this capability is that you can extract numbers from character strings. Or you can copy data from a numeric field to a character field, so your program can map a numeric value to a character string. You often need to perform this type of conversion when you use a numeric variable to construct a sequential identifier but need to record that identifier as a character field.

To understand the implications of conversion of character and numeric data, you need to know how RPG performs such conversions. The table below shows some characters with their EBCDIC (Extended Binary Coded Decimal Interchange Code) representation.

Character / EBCDIC Representation

blank = x'40'		- = x'60'								0 = x'F0'
		/ = x'61'	a = x'81'	j = x'91'			A =x'C1'	J =x'D1'		1 = x'F1'
			b = x'82'	k = x'92'	s = x'A2'		B =x'C2'	K =x'D2'	S =x'E2'	2 = x'F2'
			c = x'83'	l = x'93'	t = x'A3'		C =x'C3'	L =x'D3'	T =x'E3'	3 = x'F3'
			d = 84	m = 94	u = x'A4'		D =x'C4'	M=x'D4'	U=x'E4x	4 = x'F4'
			e = 85	n = 95	v = x'A5'		E =x'C5'	N =x'D5'	V =x'E5'	5 =x'F5x
			f = 86	o = 96	w = x'A6'		F =x'C6'	O=x'D6'	W=x'E6'	6 = x'F6'
			g = 87	p = 97	x = x'A7'		G=x'C7'	P =x'D7'	X = x'E7'	7 = x'F7'
			h = 88	q = 98	y = x'A8'		H =x'C8'	Q =x'D8'	Y =x'E8'	8 = x'F8'
			i = 89	r = 99	z = x'A9'		I = x'C9'	R=x'D9'	Z =x'E9'	9 = x'F9'
. = x'4B'	$ =x'5B'									

Conversion of Character Data to Numeric

When the source data is class character, only a portion of each character participates in the move. To understand this concept, let's look at how each character is represented. The AS/400's character set for storing and processing all data is EBCDIC. Each character is stored as 8 bits. The first four (high-order) bits are called the zone, and the last four (low-order) bits are called the digit.

The previous table shows the uppercase and lowercase alphabet, the numbers 0 through 9, some miscellaneous characters, and the hex representation of each of their EBCDIC values. Each hex digit represents either the high-order or the low-order bits for the character. The alphabet uses values that make the digit portion of the character always correspond to one of the digits 1 through 9. The dash and the slash characters also have digits within the 1 to 9 range. The decimal point and dollar sign characters, however, have digits outside that range. They (and other non-alphabet characters) cannot be in a character string you're moving to a numeric field; they will cause decimal data errors (invalid numeric data).

When you convert character to numeric data, only the digit is used from each character. However, the zone of the rightmost character in the character string determines the sign of the resulting numeric value. The only time this character's zone is also ignored is with the MOVEL operation, when the string being moved (Factor 2) is shorter than the target (Result) field. In that case, the sign of the target field does not change unless you specify padding to set extra positions to the right to zero, which will set the field's sign to positive.

The use of the rightmost character's zone to determine the sign is most surprising if you attempt a MOVEL when the source is longer than the target. Although you probably expect the sign of the result to be based on one of the characters that is moved, it is based on a character that is truncated and does not participate in the move. Here are the rules.

1. The system will convert the digit portion of each character moved and place it in the corresponding position in the Result field; the zone of each character is ignored for this step.

2. Blanks correspond to zeros in this conversion (a blank in hex is x'40', so the digit portion is a zero).

3. The zone of the rightmost character in the source string determines the sign of the resulting numeric field, *except* with MOVEL when the source string is shorter than the target field. In this case, the move does not affect the sign of the target field.

Rule 1 has an important corollary: If the hexadecimal value of the digit portion of a character being moved *does not* have a value of 0 through 9, the move will result in a data-decimal error. None of the other hexadecimal values (A through F) have single-digit decimal equivalents, so they do not result in a runtime error. MOVE and MOVEL do not respect a decimal point in the source string. This situation is different from what you encounter in CL, where the same type of character-to-numeric conversion via the CHGVAR (Change Variable) command *does* handle decimal alignment. Consequently, a decimal point (x'B') in the character string will result in a runtime error.

Zones and Signs

The system consults the zone portion of the rightmost character of a string to determine, in most cases, the sign of the resulting numeric value. Once you get past the relative complexity of determining *where* the sign came from (as in the previous section), the rules for determining *what* the sign will be are pretty simple.

1. If the zone of the character is a D, the resulting value receives a negative sign.
2. If the zone is anything other than a D, the resulting value receives a positive sign.

For example, the EBCDIC table shows that any letter J through R has a zone of D. If any of these letters is in the rightmost position of a source string, the move will assign a negative sign to the resulting value. Another character that has this effect is the right brace (}). Six other rarely used characters also cause a negative sign. They are |, û, ü, ù, ú, ÿ (vertical bar, lowercase u with circumflex, lowercase u with dieresis, lowercase u with grave accent, lowercase u with acute accent, and lowercase y with dieresis).

Beware when you specify a MOVEL with a source string smaller than the target field. In this case, the sign of the target field is unaffected; the rules for determining the sign do not apply.

Conversion of Numeric Data to Character

You can convert any numeric value to a character literal by specifying a valid numeric class field for Factor 2 and a character class field as the Result field. Each digit (numerical digit, not the 4-bit kind of digit) of the number will go into a separate character in the target character field. Any defined decimal positions will be ignored, and *no* decimal position is placed in the character string.

When you are moving negative numbers to character strings., RPG will *not* put a negative sign in the resulting field; instead, one of the digits moved indicates the sign. If the move includes the last digit (rightmost, regardless of decimal point position), the sign of the numeric source value will be incorporated in the character placed in the target character field. The move won't include this digit if you are using MOVEL and have a number that has more defined digits than you have character positions in the target field. In that case, the sign of the number has no effect.

When placing each digit in the character field, the system uses the character representation of each digit (0 through 9). In hex, these representations are F0, F1, . . . F9. However, when the last digit of a negative number is in the move, the zone will be replaced by the number's sign. So if you move the number –17 into a 2-byte character field, it will show as 1P. When you put the character 7 (x'F7') into the target field, its zone is replaced with a D, which indicates the source field is a negative number. The resulting character is a P (x'D7'). If the last digit moved is a non-zero digit, the resulting character will be x'D1' through x'D9', which translates to J through R. If the last digit is a zero, the resulting character will be a right brace (x'D0').

Graphic and Character Class Move Operations

Graphic characters are class graphic and represent characters in languages such as Chinese. When the source field is class graphic and the target is class character, MOVE and MOVEL move the graphic data into the character field, and each graphic character takes up two characters (bytes) in the target field (a double-byte character set). The data in the target character field will contain a shift-out (SO) character at the beginning and a shift-in (SI) character at the end of the moved data. Additionally, the target field must be at least 4 bytes long to contain the SO/SI characters, and at least one of the graphic characters (1 byte each for the SO/SI, and 2 bytes for the graphic — double byte — character). The target field can be longer than 4 bytes, but it must always be an even-length field to ensure that each graphic character moved has 2 bytes to occupy and that the SO/SI pairs have a place.

Important note: If the target field is more than 2 bytes longer than twice the number of graphic characters in the graphic field (>2* (graphic field length) + 2), the move will not affect some of the characters in the target field. In the case of a MOVE, some characters in the field's leftmost positions will remain. In the case of a MOVEL, some residual characters will remain in the rightmost positions. In either case, the SO/SI characters that are added at the beginning and end of the moved data will enclose only the data that was moved, and not the unchanged characters already in the field. This character field may no longer be valid for moving to another graphic field. You must ensure that the SO/SI characters are still balanced after such a move.

Resulting Indicators

Another general set of usage guidelines for move operations concern resulting indicators. RPG move operation codes support high, low, and equal resulting indicators except when the MOVE or MOVEL operation code has an array as the Result field. These indicators can signify the sign of the Result field after the operation or, for a class character Result field, whether the Result field is blank.

The rules for indicator usage with character and numeric class Result fields apply to all move operation codes. When the Result field is class character, you can specify only the equal indicator. In this case, when the Result field is blank after the move operation, the equal indicator will be set on during program execution. When the Result field is numeric, you can specify all three indicators. The high indicator will be set during program execution if the resulting value is greater than zero. Similarly, the low indicator is set on when the resulting value is less than zero. Otherwise, if specified, the equal indicator is set on when the resulting value is zero.

We do not recommend indicators if you can use comparisons instead. A comparison using IF is much clearer and makes maintenance easier than indicators.

Decimal Position

The next general guideline for move operations applies when both Factor 2 and the Result field are class numeric. In this case, the operation is called a *numeric move*. With numeric moves, RPG ignores the decimal position. For example, when you move a value (8.33) to a Result field defined as 3.1, the new value will be (83.3).

This is an interesting point. For calculations where you need to move the decimal point of a value, to improve performance, you can use the move operations instead of multiply and divide operations. For instance, if you let the user enter a tax rate of 5.25% into a 5.2 field, the value in the field is 005.25. To easily convert that value for use in calculations, you can MOVE it into a 5.4 field, where it will then have the value 0.0525. This technique is easy and faster than dividing by 100. Conversely, you can perform the same move in the other direction to display the tax rate for the user while storing it as a field that can be used directly in calculations where you want to apply the tax rate.

Padding

The move operation codes support padding. You can pad the Result field by specifying a P in the opcode extender position. Padding is from the left with MOVE and from the right with MOVEL. The pad value depends on the class of the Result field: For a character Result field, the padding character is a blank; for a numeric Result field, the padding character is 0; for an indicator Result field, the padding character is 0; and for a graphic Result field, the padding character is a graphic blank.

Padding occurs only *after* the operation is complete because the movement of the data from source to target fields takes precedence over padding. So if after a move the number of bytes moved exactly matches the length of the result, padding will not occur.

If you specify a non-array as the source (field, literal, constant, etc.) and an array as the target, the system will pad each array element when you specify the MOVE or MOVEL operation code with the P operation code descriptor. When you use these move operations on an array, they cause a separate move of the source value for each element of the array. The padding occurs independently for each element.

If both the source and target for a MOVE or MOVEL are arrays, the elements are paired between the two arrays, and a separate move occurs for each pairing. The first element of the source array moves to the first element of the target array, the second to the second, and so on. Padding occurs independently for each of these moves. If the source array has the same number of elements as the target array, or has more elements than the target array, a move will occur for each element in the target array (due to pairings with elements from the source array). So padding will occur, if needed, for each element of the target array. However, if the source array has fewer elements than the target array, only as many moves will occur as there are elements in the source array (because of the pairings with elements in the target array). Again, padding occurs on each independent move. Because the additional elements in the target array (the ones not paired with an element in the source array) do not participate in a move, they also do not participate in the padding; the move does not affect them in any way.

Figurative Constants with Move Operations

MOVE and MOVEL usually copy data from one field to another or put a literal into a field. You will also occasionally need RPG figurative constants (*BLANKS, *ZEROS, *HIVAL, *LOVAL) to initialize a field. The greatest convenience with figurative constants is that they adapt themselves to the size of the target field: If the target field's size changes, you don't need to touch the code that sets its value because the figurative constant is always the same length as the target field. The following code demonstrates this capability.

```
*...1....+....2....+....3....+....4....+....5....+....6....+....7....+
*
* Clear Company level totals
*
C                   MOVE      *Zeros         CoSalesTot
C                   MOVE      *Zeros         CoCommTot
C                   MOVE      *Zeros         CoQtyTot
*
* Conditionally include the company's account number
*   in the heading for the company
```

CONTINUED

```
*...1....+....2....+....3....+....4....+....5....+....6....+....7....+
 *   1. Print when creating report for management
 *   2. Do not print when creating report for sales force
 *
C                   IF        MgmtOrSls *EQ 'M'
C                   MOVE      AcctNbr        PrAcctNbr
C                   ELSE
C                   MOVE      *BLANKS        PrAcctNbr
C
```

The two most commonly used figurative constants, *BLANK(S) and *ZERO(S), let you clear a field. A frequent use of *ZERO(S) is to set an accumulator to zero at the beginning of a routine to calculate a running total. This routine can read a set of records and calculate their total, or it can be a routine for calculating totals for level breaks on a report. *BLANK(S) will let you clear a character field, possibly to conditionally avoid printing some data.

Another use of MOVE with figurative constants is to set a field to its highest or lowest possible value. The figurative constants *HIVAL and *LOVAL provide different values for character and numeric fields. For character fields, these constants provide a value of all hex FF (all bits on) and all hex 00 (all bits off), respectively. For numeric fields, the constants provide a value of all 9s with a positive sign and all 9s with a negative sign, respectively. These figurative constants let you initialize a field to find the highest or lowest value in a set of data. If you are looking for the highest value, set the field to *LOVAL before beginning the comparisons. If you are looking for the lowest value, set the field to *HIVAL before beginning. The code below demonstrates these principles.

```
*...1....+....2....+....3....+....4....+....5....+....6....+....7....+
 *
 * Initialize fields that hold lowest Sales and highest Sales
 *
C                   MOVE      *HIVAL         LowSales
C                   MOVE      *LOVAL         TopSales
C                   MOVE      'N'            DataFound
 *
 * Loop through data. For each data item see if it is
 * the highest or lowest value so far
 *
   ... access next set of data
 *
```

CONTINUED

```
*...1....+....2....+....3....+....4....+....5....+....6....+....7....+
 * Set flag indicating a record was tested
C                   MOVE      'Y'           DataFound
 * Check for highest
C                   IF        CurSales *GT TopSales
C                   MOVE      CurSales      TopSales
C                   ENDIF
 * Check for lowest
C                   IF        CurSales *LT LowSales
C                   MOVE      CurSales      LowSales
C                   ENDIF
    ... loop to get next set of data
```

Although this code uses *HIVAL and *LOVAL to initialize comparison fields, the most useful (and practical) aspect of the example is setting LowSales to *HIVAL. If you set LowSales to zero when you start, odds are that you will find no CurSales values that are lower, and the lowest of the CurSales figures will never be reported. The same reasoning holds true for the TopSales, and you need to follow the same practice — though, you can probably initialize Top-Sales to zeros. However, if you have only returns rather than sales and record those returns as negative sales or roll them into the CurSales field, you might not get an accurate number in the TopSales figure.

If these figurative constants don't meet your needs, you can create your own. Whereas *BLANK(S) and *ZERO(S) return the correct number of blanks and zeros to fill the target field, and *HIVAL and *LOVAL return the correct number of characters and digits to fill the target field, RPG gives you some specialized figurative constants to define filler characters. The *ALL'x..' figurative constant and *ALLG'iK1K2...' fill a field with graphic data. *ALLX'x1..' fills a field with hexadecimal data.

These figurative constants define a constant that is a repeating pattern of any literal you want. This capability is helpful to create a divider of some sort. Say you need an 80-byte string filled with equal signs to create a border. Or, for a more interesting border, you want a string of dashes and asterisks. The code below will create both these borders.

```
*...1....+....2....+....3....+....4....+....5....+....6....+....7....+
 *
 * Create visual separators for printing on report
 *  1. all = signs
 *  2. repeating pattern of -*-
 *
C                   MOVE      *ALL'='       Double          80
C                   MOVE      *ALL'-*-'     Fancy           81
```

Here is the appearance of these two separator fields after the above operation.

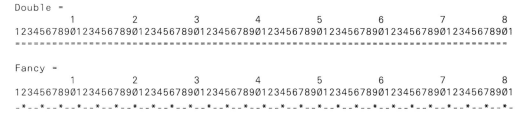

```
Double =
          1         2         3         4         5         6         7         8
1234567890123456789012345678901234567890123456789012345678901234567890123456789012345678901
===========================================================================================


Fancy =
          1         2         3         4         5         6         7         8
1234567890123456789012345678901234567890123456789012345678901234567890123456789012345678901
-*--*--*--*--*--*--*--*--*--*--*--*--*--*--*--*--*--*--*--*--*--*--*--*--*--*--*--*--*--*--*-
```

The string you specify in the *ALL'x..' figurative constant repeats until it fills the target field. If the target field's length is not a multiple of the string being repeated, the last occurrence of the repeated string will be truncated on the right when the length of the target field is reached. No matter whether you are using MOVE or MOVEL for the various forms of *ALL, the system first creates the string to move so it matches the target field's length, and then moves it. Because the moved string always equals the size of the target string, you get no difference in the result of the move.

The two other forms of *ALL, *ALLG, and *ALLX perform the same way, but the type of literal you provide with them is different. For *ALLG, you must specify a graphic literal with the shift-in and shift-out characters at either end. For *ALLX, you must specify a hexadecimal literal that must be even in length.

With the move operations, three more figurative constants are valid. You can use the first, *NULL, only to set the value of a pointer to *NULL, signifying that the pointer doesn't point to anything. You probably won't use this one too much, unless you are heavily using the system APIs that require pointers. The last two figurative constants are *ON and *OFF. These represent strings of 1s and 0s, respectively. They generally set an indicator's status, but you can also use them to load a character or numeric field with all 1s or 0s. This code shows how to specify *ON to set on the LR indicator to end your program.

```
*...1....+....2....+....3....+....4....+....5....+....6....+....7....+
 *
 * Set the LR indicator on
 *
C                   MOVE      *ON            *INLR
```

THE MOVE OPERATION CODE

MOVE is probably the most widely used RPG data manipulation operation. You will generally call on it to save values for later, copying data from the fields in one context to the fields in another (the fields from a database file to the fields from a display file). Or you will place data in a field you have reserved for a special purpose such as a key list (KLIST) entry, parameter list (PLIST) entry, or an array or multiple-occurrence data structure. Occasionally, you will need to convert data from one data type to another. (You might prefer to map multiple field definitions to the same location in memory by specifying OVERLAY in the D-specs. But, generally speaking, to perform such conversions, moving the data is easier and more straightforward than relying on an understanding of how the system can represent overlaid data in storage.)

The MOVE operation uses a method that you might not suspect at first. You ordinarily expect such an operation to function like the assignment operators in other languages. Assignment operators handle character fields on a left-to-right basis. In contrast to such operations, MOVE works on a right-aligned basis, which can cause truncation of characters at the left of the string. Without padding, the MOVE operation sometimes affects only a subset of the target character field. These considerations are of no consequence when the target and source values are the same length, but don't forget the padding and alignment characteristics of the MOVE operation. Most other languages will handle decimal alignment when you're dealing with numeric values or variables. MOVE ignores all that and performs on a right-aligned basis. For a more conventional operation that handles character data on a left-to-right basis, see the MOVEL operation. For a more conventional operation that handles numeric assignment with decimal alignment, see the Z-ADD operation.

Let's look at MOVE's syntax and briefly review the rules for what can go in each field. Factor 1 is not permitted for MOVEs except when a MOVE involves date, time, and timestamp data type fields and fields that are *not* of those data types. Factor 2 is required because it identifies the source of the data you want to copy. The Result field is required because it is where the data is headed. Factor 2 and the Result field need not be the same data type or class. RPG will automatically convert among the various numeric data types. Conditioning and resulting indicators are optional. The table below summarizes the valid elements for MOVE.

Factor 1	Opcode	(Extender)	Factor 2	Result	Indicators		
Optional for *Time/Date only*	MOVE	(P)	Required *source field*	Required *target field*	plus	minus	zero / blank

Of the resulting indicators, only EQ (positions 75 to 76) is allowed when the Result field is character; all are allowed when the Result field is numeric. No indicators are allowed if the Result field is an array (but they are allowed if the Result field is an array *element*).

MOVE Operation by Example

The code below shows how to move fields to a key list to retrieve a record that the user identifies. This MOVE demonstrates RPG's ability to convert from one data type to another.

```
*...1....+....2....+....3....+....4....+....5....+....6....+....7....+
 *
 * Build key list using fields entered by user
 *
C                   MOVE      DspCompany    KeyCompany        6
C                   MOVE      DspDivison    KeyDivision       6
C                   MOVE      DspAgtNbr     KeyAgtNbr         5 0
 *
C     AgentKey      KLIST
C                   KFLD                    KeyCompany
C                   KFLD                    KeyDivision
C                   KFLD                    KeyAgtNbr
```

The MOVE statement lets you copy the values for the company, division, and agent number from the fields on the screen to the fields that build the key list, AgentKey. This key list will let you access the agent file. Two types of MOVEs occur here. The company and division MOVEs are character-to-character MOVEs. The agent number move is a numeric-to-numeric move. Because the DspAgtNbr field is from a display file, it cannot have a packed-numeric data type; it must be zoned numeric. Also, because the KeyAgtNbr is defined in the code, the default data type is packed decimal.

The next code segment demonstrates how to change the decimal position. This method is quicker than the DIV (Divide) operation, but not necessarily better. This technique demonstrates the capability of the MOVE statement to move data without regard for decimal point position. Of course, this demonstration is also a warning that you must understand and be aware of how a MOVE works when you're dealing with numeric fields.

```
*...1....+....2....+....3....+....4....+....5....+....6....+....7....+
 *
 * Convert tax rate from internal 5.4 format to 5.2 format for display
 *
C                   MOVE      TaxRate       DspTaxRate
```

The fields in this example, TaxRate and DspTaxRate, represent the percentage rate for calculating taxes due. The TaxRate field comes from the database, and DspTaxRate comes from a display file. Their sizes are 5.4 and 5.2, respectively. TaxRate is suitable for calculations because you can directly calculate a tax amount in a multiplication operation. In contrast, DspTaxRate is suitable for display to the user because you can show it as a percentage (7.35%) rather than as the rate of .0735. The presentation as a percentage is easier for the end user to understand, and the rate is better suited to calculations.

When a program calls other programs, it must pass the data to the programs that you call in the format that the calling program expects. If the calling program expects a binary field (as so many system APIs do), you may have to convert the data in your program to binary before calling the other program. Fortunately, RPG's ability to MOVE data freely between different data types makes this conversion easy. The code below shows how. First, you define two fields, one as packed decimal and the other as binary.

```
*...1....+....2....+....3....+....4....+....5....+....6....+....7....+
D DataLen         S              5P 0
D DataLenB        S              5B 0
 * (5 and greater digit binary fields are stored as 4-byte binary)
 * (4 and fewer digit binary fields are stored as 2-byte binary)
```

Then you use MOVE code to convert the data.

```
*...1....+....2....+....3....+....4....+....5....+....6....+....7....+
 *
 * Convert data length from packed to 4-byte binary
 *
C                    MOVE      DataLen       DataLenB
```

This program is preparing to call an API that needs to know the length of a string that you are passing to it. The API requires the length in a 4-byte binary format. But for efficiency, and by default, the program has all numeric fields defined as packed. MOVE makes this task a snap. You define the field to pass to the API as a binary field in the D-specs and then move the packed field into it.

This example shows the definition of both fields on the D-spec. The original field can come from a database file, from the screen (in which case it is probably zoned, not packed), or it can be passed in as a parameter. Or the field can be a work field in the program. You need the data in binary form only when the program is communicating with the function that requires the field in that form. For all other purposes, you need it in packed format.

Let's look at some data manipulation uses for MOVE. The following code shows how MOVE can extract the last character of a string.

```
*...1....+....2....+....3....+....4....+....5....+....6....+....7....+
 *
 * Extract Season Code character
 *
C                    MOVE      ProdCode      ProdSsn                1
```

This example assumes that ProdCode is a field on a data file that has been read. The last character of the product code identifies the season in which it is ordinarily sold. Because MOVE works by aligning the source and target fields at the right and then copying, MOVE in this example will extract only the last character from the ProdCode field. Note that this technique is easier to code than RPG string-handling facilities, because you do not need to know the length of the ProdCode field. All RPG string-handling facilities require you to either derive or hardcode the starting position to access the last character, which means you have to know or derive the size of the ProdCode field. A MOVE extracts the rightmost positions from a character string by moving the string into a field whose length matches the length of string you want.

Padding occurs only after a move. If you specify a P in the opcode extender field, the Result field will be left padded if it is longer than Factor 2. If you do not specify padding on the opcode extender, the Result field's leftmost characters that exceed the length of the Factor 2 field remain unchanged. Left-truncation occurs if the Factor 2 field is longer than the Result field.

```
*...1....+....2....+....3....+....4....+....5....+....6....+....7....+
*
* Translate measurement units for printing
*
C                   SELECT
C                   WHEN      UnitOfMeas = 'CT'
C                   MOVE (P)  'Carton'       UOMDesc            6
C                   WHEN      UnitOfMeas = 'EA'
C                   MOVE (P)  'Each'         UOMDesc
C                   WHEN      UnitOfMeas = 'BG'
C                   MOVE (P)  'Bag''         UOMDesc
C                   WHEN      UnitOfMeas = 'PK'
C                   MOVE (P)  'Pack'
C                   ENDSL
```

Padding comes in handy when you conditionally move different values into a character field. Because you can move any one of several different-length fields or literals into a field, padding is a good idea to ensure that you don't leave extra characters in the target field.

To move varying-length strings to the Result field, you can use padding, as in the sample above. This example moves one of several descriptive units of measure into a field. The description must always be right adjusted. The padding on each move ensures that, if the previous iteration was dealing with cartons, you don't accidentally leave the "Ca" from "Carton" in the field when you move "Each" into the field. The same is true for "Bag" when you can accidentally wind up with "CarBag", "EBag", or "PBag" if you don't pad when moving in "Bag." Even worse, if you deal with *Cartons,* then *Each,* and then *Bag* in succession, the description on the *Each* iteration can contain "CaEach," and the *Bag* iteration can then contain "CaEBag." Each padded MOVE ensures that the UOMDesc field, which is 6 bytes, will always have blanks in the extra spaces not used by each of the literals you're moving.

THE MOVEL OPERATION CODE

The MOVEL (Move Left) operation code, which is not as widely used as MOVE, lets you copy data from the fields in one context to the fields in another. For example, you can copy the fields from a database file to the fields in a display file. Or you can copy data into a field you have reserved for a special purpose, such as as a KLIST entry, PLIST entry, or an array or multiple-occurrence data structure. You can also use MOVEL to convert data of one type to another.

MOVE and MOVEL differ in the alignment the system chooses when you copy data from the source field: MOVEL aligns the moved values on the left, whereas MOVE aligns them on the right. Similarly, when truncation is necessary, MOVE truncates from left to right, and MOVEL truncates from right to left.

This direction of truncation determines how MOVEL handles the sign of the target field when the target field is smaller than the source field. In this case, the system cannot assign a positive or negative sign for the target field. The reason is that the rightmost byte of the source string determines the sign, and MOVEL truncates the moved value from right to left if the target field is shorter than the source field. The position that determines the sign is the first position that gets truncated.

With character strings, the MOVEL operation performs like the assignment operator in other languages. MOVEL aligns from left to right. Although it behaves like an assignment operator when you have character values, MOVEL does not provide any type of decimal alignment for numeric values, although you expect this capability of an assignment operator. Instead, like MOVE, MOVEL aligns the data (albeit on the left) and then starts moving it. Also, in contrast to assignment operators in other languages, MOVEL sometimes affects only a portion of the field, up to the length of the source value. Of course, padding will fill the entire target field when it is longer than the source value.

Factor 1 is not permitted for MOVEL except when you have a date, time, or timestamp data type with fields that are *not* of those data types. Factor 2 is required, as it identifies the source of the data you want to copy. The Result field is required because it is where the data is going. Factor 2 and the Result field need not be the same data type or class. RPG will automatically convert among the various numeric data types. Conditioning and resulting indicators are optional. Of the resulting indicators, only EQ (positions 75 and 76) is allowed when the Result field is character; all indicators are allowed when the Result field is numeric. None are allowed if the Result field is an array (but they are allowed if the Result field is an array *element*). The following table summarizes these rules.

Factor 1	Opcode	(Extender)	Factor 2	Result	Indicators		
Optional for *Time/Date only*	MOVEL	(P)	Required *source field*	Required *target field*	plus	minus	zero/ blank

MOVEL by Example

Suppose you are working with a file that contains one 32-byte field holding both an inventory count and a description. Say each field contains the count in the first seven characters and a description in the last 25 characters. MOVEL can extract the count from the character string, truncating everything but the number you want. Suppose the first few records contain the data you see in the following illustration.

```
        1   1   2   2   3
....5....0....5....0....5....0..
0002586LARGE WIDGET
0000058SMALL WIDGET
0000155LARGE THINGAMABOB - BROWN
0000455LARGE THINGAMABOB - WHITE
```

This field is called InvData. You can extract the information you need by executing a MOVEL and a MOVE to separate the inventory count and description. Here's the code.

```
*...1....+....2....+....3....+....4....+....5....+....6....+....7....+
C                 MOVEL     InvData      InvCount        7 0
C                 MOVE      InvData      InvDesc        25
```

Here, you want MOVEL to convert character to numeric data. The 25-byte InvDesc field will receive the values you expect on each pass of this code, as shown below.

```
        1   1   2   2
....5....0....5....0....5
LARGE WIDGET
SMALL WIDGET
LARGE THINGAMABOB - BROWN
LARGE THINGAMABOB - WHITE
```

Because, with MOVEL, the source field's rightmost byte determines the target field's sign, the resulting numeric values hold a surprise. The first two and the last records will perform as you expect. Values of 2856, 585, and 45 will go into InvCount. But on the third record, which shows a count of 155, InvCount will receive a value of –155, a negative number. Because the rightmost character of the source string has a zone of D (the N in BROWN has a hexadecimal notation of x'D5'), the numeric value resulting from the move gets a negative sign. You and your company can be quite embarrassed when this seemingly random bug jumps out at you. The solution is to first move the numeric portion of the original string to a smaller string that will hold only the number, and then perform the character to numeric conversion, as in the code below.

```
*...1....+....2....+....3....+....4....+....5....+....6....+....7....+
C                   MOVEL     InvData        InvCountA          7
C                   MOVE      InvCountA      InvCount           7 0
C                   MOVE      InvData        InvDesc           25
```

This code corrects the sign problem by using MOVEL to perform a character-to-character move and then using MOVE to do a numeric-to-character move. Now when the character-to-numeric conversion is executed, the zone of the rightmost character in the source string (the 5 in 0000155) is an F (5 = x'F5'). Because it is not a D, the result is set to a positive sign.

You will probably find it easier to get the supplier of the data to always include a sign symbol in a separate character. That way, you can always convert to produce a positive result and then check the separate sign character to set the sign to a negative if necessary.

When the target field is longer than the source, with MOVEL, the rightmost byte won't influence the sign of a numeric target field. In this case, the numeric field will retain its original sign after the MOVEL.

The example on page 163 demonstrates the benefits of padding with MOVEL. This code constructs a 9-byte zip code field if you need to prepare and send data files to an offsite or third-party service to handle mass mailings. In this scenario, the external entity needs the zip in a 9-byte character field, but your system stores the zip code in two numeric fields, CustZIP and CustZIP4. The CustZIP field is for the basic zip code, and you've added the CustZIP4 field for the four-digit extension to the zip code. Not all your customers have provided four-digit extensions yet, and your mailing sizes have not yet justified getting them. Now you have to build a 9-byte field for the mass mailing. The catch is that the zip data you submit must have four blanks at the end if you don't yet have a customer's four-digit extension.

To handle this requirement, you can first MOVEL the CustZIP field into the ZIP9 field. That takes care of the first 5 bytes. You specify padding to force the last 4 bytes in the ZIP9 field to blanks. Without padding, the ZIP9 field still has whatever four digits were left there from the last customer with a four-digit extension. Next, you can check whether you have the four-digit extension for this customer. The last 4 bytes will be zero if you don't have it. If you have the extension, you MOVE it into the last 4 bytes of the ZIP9 field.

```
*...1....+....2....+....3....+....4....+....5....+....6....+....7....+
 *
 * Construct ZIP with optional +4
 *
C                   MOVEL (P) CustZIP        ZIP9
C                   IF        CustZIP4  Ø
C                   MOVE      CustZIP4      ZIP9
C                   ENDIF
```

CHAPTER 7

Structured Operation Codes

A problem confronting both new and experienced programmers is coding a program to be clear, effective, and bug free. One way to address this problem is to follow the concepts of *structured programming*. But those two words sometimes put midrange programmers on their guard, although structured programming is not difficult or mysterious. It only requires dividing a program into several small tasks, by identifying each step the program must go through and then writing a section of code to handle each step.

To identify each task and clearly code it, you need a programming language that supports structured programming methodology. Up to now, RPG has provided only limited support. Now RPG IV adds to that support, introducing new structured programming operations and facilities.

Although these new capabilities let you incorporate structured programming methodology in your programs, this methodology is not familiar to some programmers. So to ensure that everyone can understand and correctly implement RPG IV's new structured programming capabilities, the first section of this chapter will deal, briefly, with structured programming concepts. Then we will focus on the new operations and features listed and described below.

Structured Operation Codes

Operations	Description
COMP	Compares the values of two fields or literals (not used much any more; avoid it)
IFxx, IF ANDxx ORx, ELSE ENDIF, END	Conditionally executes a section of code depending on whether a condition is true or false
SELECT WHENxx, WHEN OTHER ENDSL, END	Conditionally executes one of several sections of code when one of multiple mutually exclusive conditions is true
CASxx, CAS ENDCS, END	Conditionally executes one of several subroutines when one of multiple mutually exclusive conditions is true
CABxx, CAB	Conditionally branches to a specified point in the program
GOTO	Unconditionally branches to a specified point in the program
DO, ITER LEAVE ENDDO, END	Unconditionally loops through a section of code and can force next iteration of the loop or exit the loop without executing all the code in the loop

CONTINUED

Operations	Description
DOWxx, DOW ITER LEAVE ENDDO, END	Conditionally loops through a section of code while a specified condition is true; can force next iteration of the loop or exit the loop without executing all the code in the loop; 0 or more iterations of loop
BEGSR ENDSR	Names and marks start or end of a section of code (a subroutine) that can be executed from other points in the program
EXSR	Executes a subroutine defined in the program

STRUCTURED PROGRAMMING: A BRIEF INTRODUCTION

One fundamental principle of efficient programming dictates the hierarchical subdivision of large, complicated problems into smaller, simpler subproblems. The subdivision process occurs repeatedly until the subproblem is no longer divisible. If you're correctly subdividing the large problem, at any time during this process, you can explain the solution for the original, large problem in terms of these small subdivisions. This process is *structured analysis.*

A key trait of software you develop according to structured analysis principles is *modularity*, meaning that each final subproblem you identify is a program *module.* In the strictest sense, a module is a program block, or a segment of code, that has one entry point and one exit point and is executed from top to bottom. At no point within the block can a branch go to a program instruction earlier in the code segment.

Note that, at this point, the discussion of a module is at the conceptual level, and you can't confuse the concept of a module in structured programming with the creation of a code module in ILE. An ILE code module is a specific implementation of the concept of a module.

So a *structured program* is a program you develop with the methods of structured analysis. The structured program consists of modules, each corresponding directly to a subproblem identified through analysis. In addition, as with the subdivision of the original problem, a structured program organizes the modules in a hierarchical fashion to provide a total solution to the problem, in the form an application.

You can learn much more about the interfacing that occurs among the various modules of a structured program. However, structured programming *per se* is not the topic here. The reason for explaining some concepts of structured programming is to clarify the use of the operation codes that are the topic of this chapter. These operation codes are necessary for any linear, structured, programming language and are most useful in the creation of structured programs. But without a basic notion of what structured, modular code is, you can use these operation codes to create highly inefficient and unmaintainable programs. So you need to know about the attributes of good programming practice: modularity and maintainability.

Modularity

A structured program consists of modules, each addressing a subproblem rather than the entire original problem. In a good structured program, each module is no larger than a page of code, and its intent and interface to the rest of the application are clear.

But when you're ready to implement this concept, what constitutes a module in RPG IV? You can create subroutines in your program that seem to meet the criteria for a module. A subroutine can be a module but, of course, not all subroutines are modules. Imagine writing an entire program in a single subroutine consisting of 5000 lines of code (excluding the code necessary to call the subroutine). Naturally, that subroutine does not qualify as a module because those 5000 lines of code probably do not handle a single action in the program.

The definition of a module says it's a program block, or segment of code, that has one entry point and one exit point and is executed from top to bottom. The word subroutine never appears in that definition. Of course, neither does anything in the definition preclude a subroutine or a 5000-line program block from being a module.

However, the definition does say that a module must handle a subproblem of a larger task. If the block of code isn't handling one subproblem, it isn't a module. Of course, you have to be pragmatic about your definition of a subproblem. You can't say that every MOVE statement is a subproblem just because one task is to *move the customer name from the database field to the screen field*. However, you can say that *move the customer database fields to the screen fields* is a subproblem, as are *move the invoice database fields to the screen fields* and *validate the invoice fields from the screen*.

Structured methodology requires a *hierarchy* of modules in programs. You can combine two of the identified subproblems, *move the customer database fields to the screen fields* and *move the invoice database fields to the screen fields*, to create a subproblem that is one level higher (superordinate): *move database fields to the screen fields*. The superordinate module you will create for this subproblem will execute the modules for the two subordinate subproblems. Thus, you get a hierarchy and each subproblem's module is executed by a higher-level module until you finally get to the uppermost module.

The higher-level modules are controlling modules. They don't perform actions directly; they call other modules that perform actions such as moves. Controlling modules execute the action modules. In addition to executing action modules, controlling modules make decisions. They must decide which action modules to execute. Often, a controlling module will execute several action modules unconditionally. Or a module can exist only to decide which subordinate modules, control or action, to call.

If you have a file maintenance program, you can break it down into tasks that will become modules. The following illustration is a simplified description of a file maintenance program with each module identified. The arrows and indentation illustrate the hierarchy of these modules.

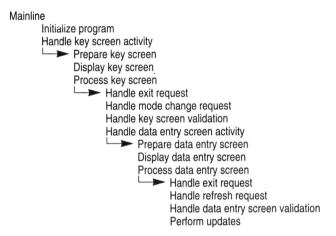

```
Mainline
        Initialize program
        Handle key screen activity
          └──► Prepare key screen
                Display key screen
                Process key screen
                  └──► Handle exit request
                        Handle mode change request
                        Handle key screen validation
                        Handle data entry screen activity
                          └──► Prepare data entry screen
                                Display data entry screen
                                Process data entry screen
                                  └──► Handle exit request
                                        Handle refresh request
                                        Handle data entry screen validation
                                        Perform updates
```

Each separate step (and all are not listed here) is a distinct module in the program. Each can have other subordinate modules not shown above. For instance, *Handle data entry screen validation* can have other subordinate modules: one for checking for required fields, one for checking that foreign key values are valid, one for verifying user calculations, one for validating that the values that users key into various fields are valid combinations, and so on.

Maintainability

To ensure maintainability, a good structured program has appropriately named variables, well-documented code, an efficient design, and clearly defined modules. Let's examine each of these elements.

- **Appropriately named variables:** The variable name clearly describes the variable's purpose and use. The new expanded field names in RPG IV help make variable names understandable.

- **Well-documented code:** A guide for documentation is to provide one line of documentation for every four lines of source code. The best time to document is during the coding process, and maintenance of the documentation occurs with the source maintenance.

- **Efficient design:** Program design needs to minimize execution steps. Generally, the more concise the algorithm, the more efficient. An example of a concise sorting algorithm is Donald Knuth's well-known *Quicksort* (see Robert L. Kruse, Bruce P. Leung, Clovis L. Tondo, Data *Structures and Program Design in C*, Prentice Hall, 1991; Brian W.

Kernighan, Denis M. Ritchie, *The C Programming Language*, Prentice Hall, 1988).

- **Clearly defined modules:** The root of good structured programs is the clear definition of each module or task the program handles. The two most important rules for a clearly defined module is that it perform a specific task or function and that it be relatively small. If you have to read through your code to find a problem or change a program, clearly defined modules will help you find the appropriate section of code quickly. Clearly defined modules also help you ensure that when you change or correct the code, the rest of the program will remain unaffected.

STRUCTURED OPERATION CODES

With this quick overview of structured programming in mind, let's talk about the language requirements necessary to implement it and how RPG IV addresses these requirements. The most important requirements for a language that supports structured programming are the ability to perform sequential execution and branching, conditional execution, and iteration.

Sequential Execution and Branching

Sequential execution is a top-to-bottom order of execution: The code executes in the order in which it appears in the source. Like most linear programming languages, RPG IV allows sequential execution. In RPG, sequential execution occurs in the C-specs.

In structured programs, the order of execution deviates from being sequential only if you issue a branching operation. Branching is the transfer of execution control from one point in the program to another. The GOTO and LEAVE (exit a loop) operations, which most linear programming languages support, enable branching. RPG IV supports the conditional branching operation codes CABxx (Compare and Branch), GOTO, ITER (Iterate), LEAVE, and TAG. Let's discuss the basic branching operations, GOTO and its required TAG. Then we can examine condition testing and the conditional branching operations.

Branching: GOTO and TAG

The GOTO operation code immediately transfers execution to a particular specification. You can code a GOTO operation anywhere in the C-specs. You specify a label in Factor 2 of GOTO to identify the *branch point* (the point where you want execution to continue).

You mark the branch point by specifying a TAG operation. In TAG's Factor 1, you enter the same label name that you specified on the GOTO operation's Factor 2. The following code shows how to specify GOTO with a label.

```
*...1....+....2....+....3....+....4....+....5....+....6....+....7....+
C*                      :
C*                      :
C*                      :
C                       GOTO       Label_1
C*                      :
C*                      :
C*                      :
C       Label_1         TAG
C*                      :
C*                      :
C*                      :
```

The label must be a unique symbolic name in the RPG program. Only Factor 2 is required. Resulting indicators, Factor 1, and the Result field are not permitted with GOTO. This table summarizes valid entries for GOTO.

Factor 1	Opcode	Factor 2	Result	Indicators
Not allowed	GOTO	Required *Target TAG or ENDSR*	Not allowed	Not allowed

You can branch from a detail C-spec to another detail C-spec, a total C-spec to another total C-spec, a detail C-spec to a total C-spec, in a subroutine to a TAG or ENDSR in the same subroutine, in a subroutine to a detail C-spec, or in a subroutine to a total C-spec. By taking advantage of some of these options, you can cause a real mess. Imagine branching out of a subroutine to a TAG back in your mainline code. Any reasonable programmer will expect control to return to the statement after a subroutine call when that subroutine terminates. This possibility is the reason for the term "spaghetti code" (with apologies to the pasta). We highly recommend that you use GOTO sparingly if you use it at all. Even if you use the operation correctly, branching only to ends of logical blocks of code, how much trust will the next programmer have in the code when GOTO carries such a stigma?

TAG

The TAG operation identifies the branch point that is the target of a GOTO. TAG's Factor 1 contains the name of the label you specified as Factor 2 on the GOTO. The label the TAG operation code defines must be a unique symbolic name in the RPG program. Processing can reach the label by means of a GOTO or CABxx operation code. You can specify TAG anywhere in the C-specs. Conditioning indicators are not permitted. More than one CABxx or GOTO operation can refer to the label the TAG operation defines. This table shows the entries for TAG.

Factor 1	Opcode	Factor 2	Result	Indicators
Required	TAG *label name*	Not allowed	Not allowed	Not allowed

Structured programmers consider the GOTO operation code poor programming because it can send execution jumping around a program haphazardly. This use of GOTO leads to programs that are difficult to understand and maintain. But GOTO need not be all that bad. After all, before RPG received the structured programming operations, GOTO was the only way to program a loop in RPG. In fact, RPG's structured programming operations are nothing more than IFs and GOTOs disguised as more palatable alternatives. Of course, these operations are more controlled because the tops and bottoms of the structures define their implicit branch targets. GOTO gets its bad reputation from programmers' incorrect use of it.

Any branch is supposed to terminate a basic block. Programs heavily relying on the GOTO operation code for control are often (justifiably) referred to as spaghetti programs. We do not present this operation code so that you will include it in your programs, but you need to know about GOTO to understand the concept of unconditional branching.

CONDITION TESTING: FIXED FORM AND FREE FORM

Condition testing is a concept familiar from constructs such as IF and WHILE in programming languages such as Pascal and C. Logical and relational expressions test the content of control variables in a program. RPG provides fixed- and free-form condition testing. The IFxx operation code lets you implement a fixed-form test condition. Alternatively, you can state the same test condition using the IF free-form operation code.

The following section will briefly discuss fixed-form condition testing. The text will explain operation codes that use fixed-form condition testing but will not provide examples. We recommend free-form condition testing when possible because it creates more readable code and is not as cumbersome when you're working with complex conditions.

Fixed-Form Conditions

Several operation codes support fixed-form condition testing. These operation codes are IFxx, ANDxx, ORxx, DOWxx (Do While), DOUxx (Do Until), WHENxx, CASxx (Compare and Invoke Subroutine), CABxx (Compare and Branch), and COMP (Compare).

Except for COMP, these operation code names all end in xx. The xx stands for the condition test to perform. You can replace the xx with any value in the following table. COMP does not have this feature, but COMP is a special case of fixed-form condition testing that dates back to the earliest days of RPG, before all the structured operation codes were available.

Test Code for Fixed-Form Condition Operations

Code	Description
GT	Greater than
LT	Less than
EQ	Equal to
NE	Not equal to
GE	Greater than or equal to
LE	Less than or equal to
blank	Unconditional processing (CABxx and CASxx only)

Fixed-form condition testing involves one of these comparisons against a value in Factor 1 and a value in Factor 2. If the result of a comparison is *true*, the process the operation conditions is executed. For example, a subroutine is called, a branch is executed, or a section of code is executed. If the result of the comparison is *false*, the conditioned process does not occur. The values in Factors 1 and 2 can be any field, constant, or literal. Note that array elements are allowed, but arrays (with no subscript specified) are not.

Rules for Comparing

The free-form comparison opcodes all follow some basic rules. These are the rules that the RPG manuals list for comparands.

- If you compare numeric fields, fields of unequal length are aligned at the implied decimal point. The fields are filled with zeros to the left and/or right of the decimal point to make the field lengths and number of decimal positions equal for comparison.

- All numeric comparisons are algebraic. A plus (+) value is always greater than a minus (–) value.

- Blanks in zoned numeric fields are assumed to be zeros if you specify the FIXNBR(*ZONED) compiler option when you compile the program.

- All graphic comparisons use the hexadecimal representation of the graphic characters. The alternate sequence is not used.

- If you compare character or graphic fields, fields of unequal length are aligned to their leftmost character. The shorter field is filled with blanks to equal the length of the longer field so that the field lengths are equal for comparison.

- If you specify an alternate collating sequence (via the ALTSEQ{(*NONE *SRC *EXT)} keyword on the H-spec) for the comparison of character fields, the comparands are converted to the alternate sequence and then compared. If you enter *HIVAL and *LOVAL to set up the comparison, the alternate collating sequence may alter the value before the compare operation.

- When you compare date fields, they are converted to a common format.

- When you compare time fields, they are converted to a common format.

- When you compare basing pointer fields for anything except equality or inequality, the results will be unpredictable unless the pointers point to addresses within contiguous storage (for example, all point to positions within the same data structure, array, or standalone field).

- When you compare procedure pointer fields for anything except equality or inequality, the results will be unpredictable.

- You cannot specify an array name in a compare operation, but you can specify an array element.

The example below illustrates how to specify fixed-form condition testing; in this case, on the IFxx operation. This example tests whether the user has entered the character Y on a confirmation prompt. If so, the code that the IF conditions is executed; if not, the code is not executed.

```
*...1....+....2....+....3....+....4....+....5....+....6....+....7....+
 ... other code
C     Confirm        IFEQ       'Y'
 ... conditioned code
C                    ENDIF
```

The EQ specification replaces the xx in this operation code. All the other operations that end with xx handle fixed-form comparison in the same way.

Unlike these operations, the COMP operation does not directly condition any processing. Instead, COMP is a pure comparison operation. COMP compares the values in Factor 1 and Factor 2. You must record the result of the comparison by entering indicators in the resulting indicator positions (71 through 76). Before the comparison occurs, all the indicators in positions 71 through 76 are turned off. Then if Factor 1 is greater than Factor 2, the indicator in 71 and 72 is turned on. If Factor 1 is less than Factor 2, the indicator in 73 and 74 is turned on. If Factor 1 is equal to Factor 2, the indicator in 75 and 76 is turned on. Once you record the results by means of indicators, you can use those indicators to condition other operations. As you can see, this operation is not exactly intuitive or clean. Because much more advanced operations, such as IF, are available, you will not have much call for COMP. We recommend you avoid it, so this chapter will not discuss COMP separately.

Fixed-Form Compound Conditions: ANDxx and ORxx

You can use fixed-form conditions to compare the value in Factor 1 to the value in Factor 2. But often, you need to compare several fields at the same time, or you need to compare the same field to several values. You sometimes need to compare a transaction date to the starting and ending dates of a contract, for instance.

To handle this type of comparison when you have only two comparands (Factor 1 and Factor 2) in a fixed-form operation, you must combine several operations in the proper sequence. To achieve this feat, you can extend the condition by following the operation immediately with ANDxx and ORxx operations. ANDxx and ORxx perform two-factor comparisons. All ANDs are performed from top to bottom, and then all ORs are performed from top to bottom.

You can follow IFxx, WHENxx, DOWxx, and DOUxx with a series of ANDxx and ORxx operations to construct rudimentary compound conditions — rudimentary because building a very complex condition using ANDxx and ORxx is extremely difficult. Because you must stack up several operations, you have no support for controlling the grouping of the comparisons. Also, if you start combining several ANDxx and ORxx operations, reading the condition becomes difficult. Logical expressions and free-form conditions provide much more robust support for compound conditions. (Note that CASxx and CABxx do *not* support ANDxx or ORxx to build compound conditions.)

Here are some compound conditions with the IFxx operation and ANDxx and Orxx. The conditioned code will execute if the transaction date is greater than or equal to the contract's effective date and less than the contract's expiration date. If you have open-ended contracts, you will not know a contract's expiration date until you and the customer agree to terminate it, so the expiration date can be zero. The code below shows just how complicated this kind of logic can get. (Assume you have numeric variables instead of date data type fields to hold the dates. Date fields do not allow zero in the field).

```
*...1....+....2....+....3....+....4....+....5....+....6....+....7....+
... Verify transaction date within contract effective dates
C         TrxnDate      IFGE      CntEffDate
C         TrxnDate      ANDLT     CntExpDate
 ... conditioned code
C                       ENDIF
```

CONTINUED

```
*...1....+....2....+....3....+....4....+....5....+....6....+....7....+
... Verify transaction date within contract effective dates
C         CntExpDate    IFEQ     *Zero
C         TrxnDate      ANDGE    CntEffDate
C         CntExpDate    ORNE     *Zero
C         TrxnDate      ANDGE    CntEffDate
C         TrxnDate      ANDLT    CntExpDate
 ... conditioned code
C                       ENDIF
```

This code will compare the transaction date to the effective date only when the expiration date is zero, but it will compare the transaction date to both the effective and expiration dates when the expiration date is *not* zero. This code is hard to read. Imagine a comparison that is even more complex. This kind of logic can become a maintenance programmer's nightmare.

ANDs take precedence over ORs. Probably the biggest problem with reading fixed-form AND/OR logic in this example is that the OR separates the first two comparisons from the last three comparisons. Setting the OR in the middle of the third comparison makes this situation hard to see.

To understand the precedence, start at the beginning of the operation, the IFEQ. If that condition is true *and* the next operation is true, the entire condition is true. But if either condition is false, you proceed to the other side of the OR to see whether it is true. On the other side of the OR, you find three comparisons ANDed together. If all three are true, the entire expression is true.

Free-Form Conditions

The discussion so far has been about fixed-form conditions and the operations that use them. Several operations in this discussion have free-form counterparts that do not use the xx notation or Factor 1 and Factor 2. Instead, an extended Factor 2 lets you code an expression.

Free-form expressions eliminate the need for ANDxx and ORxx to create compound conditions, so they are not allowed after the free-form operations. The free-form conditional operations are IF, DOW (Do While), DOU (Do Until), and WHEN.

To specify these operations, you enter the operation on a C-spec and then include an expression in the extended Factor 2. This expression must evaluate to *true* or *false*.

Relational Expressions and Logical Operators

A relational expression lets you specify a logical operator, such as "not" or "greater than" or "equal to," and evaluate whether that logical condition is true or false. Relational expressions can be simple or complex. A simple relational expression has one logical operator and at least one comparand. A complex expression supports relational expressions and mathematical expressions.

Logical Operators for Expressions

Operator	Description
>	Greater than
>	Less than
=	Equal to
<>	Not equal to
>=	Greater than or equal to
>=	Less than or equal to
NOT	Reverses the true/false result of an expression
AND	Both comparands must be true
OR	Either comparand can be true
(and)	Parentheses control order of evaluation of other operators

This table lists the logical operators and describes them. The first seven logical operators are for a simple expression. The first six operators are *binary* operators that require two values, or comparands, one on each side of the operator. The comparands can be fields, literals, or constants. They can also be expressions, in which case you have a complex expression. The eighth operator, NOT, is a unary operator: It requires only one comparand.

```
*...1....+....2....+....3....+....4....+....5....+....6....+....7....+
C                    IF        RentalRate > MaxRate
```

This example of an IF operation involves a relational expression with a binary operator to evaluate whether a rental rate that a user enters is greater than the maximum rate. When you compare the entered rate to the maximum allowed rate, the expression is true if the value in RentalRate is greater than the value in MaxRate. Any other relationship (e.g., RentalRate is less than MaxRate or RentalRate equals MaxRate) is false.

This is the type of simple relational expression you will see most often, but RPG has a simpler version of a relational expression: You can specify an indicator (*IN25, for instance) as a relational expression. Because a relational expression evaluates to an indicator value in RPG, you can specify any indicator as an expression. Because indicators appear so often in communication with display files in RPG, you will no doubt need to check the values of indicators. Once you begin using free-form expressions, you will want to test your indicator values this way. Here is a test for *IN25 being on.

```
*...1....+....2....+....3....+....4....+....5....+....6....+....7....+
C                    IF        *IN25
```

Slightly more complicated are expressions that incorporate the NOT operator, which requires only one operand. That operand is either an indicator or the
result of an expression (the result of an expression is really an indicator). The
operand expression can be either simple or complex.

We highly recommend that you take great caution in implementing expressions that contain the NOT operator. It is not a complicated operator, but it
introduces an exercise in negative logic, and human beings tend to have a
mental lockup when it comes to understanding the negation of an expression.
From a standpoint of readability, NOTs are not usually a good idea in expressions. You are better off expressing simple expressions by changing the operator instead of using NOT.

Still, some expressions can benefit from NOT. Take the example of the simplest form of relational expression, an indicator. In that case, you have little
problem comprehending NOT.

```
*...1....+....2....+....3....+....4....+....5....+....6....+....7....+
C                   IF        NOT *IN25
  ...
C                   IF        NOT (Action = 'D')
```

As the first example shows, NOT with an indicator is easy to understand, so it
is an acceptable coding practice. However, you can see that NOT on the result
of the expression comparing Action to 'D' is not as clear. The expression
Action <>'D' is better than NOT to negate the entire expression.

You can specify parentheses to determine the order for evaluating expressions. Because NOT usually is performed before the = operator, parentheses are
necessary around the Action = 'D' expression to force it to evaluate first. The list
below shows the order for handling all operators in RPG expressions. Note that
a set of parentheses is the first item to be processed. NOT (with the other unary
operators) comes in third in the order of precedence.

Order of Precedence List

1	( )
2	built-in functions
3	unary +, unary –, NOT
4	**
5	*,/
6	binary +, binary –
7	=, >=, <=, <, <>
8	AND
9	OR

In a relational expression, the AND and OR operator let you compare the results of other relational expressions. Those other relational expressions can be simple expressions (including the simplest, an indicator), or they can be complex relational expressions. What makes an expression relational is that it eventually evaluates to a true or false value, so a relational expression must contain relational operators to perform that evaluation. Like all relational operators, AND and OR both evaluate to either true or false. Both are binary operators requiring two operands. As with the NOT operator, the operands must be indicators or the results of expressions. AND evaluates to true if the expressions on both sides of the AND are true. If either expression is false, the entire expression is false. OR evaluates to true if the expression on either side of the OR is true. If both are true, OR still returns a true. If both are false, OR returns a false.

Unlike the NOT operator, the expressions that AND and OR use as operands do not have to be in parentheses. The order-of-precedence list shows why. The expressions on either side of the AND and OR operators are evaluated before the AND or OR operator is executed because all other operators are executed before AND and OR. NOT doesn't have that luxury because it is one of the first operators processed.

The following code shows seven examples of complex relational expressions. The first example specifies AND to see whether indicator 15 is on *and* the action that the user requested is 'D' (for Delete). This example shows how an application can require a two-step process to delete a transaction. A 'D' is required in the Action field, and the user must press a function key (to which you must attach indicator 15) to delete.

```
*...1....+....2....+....3....+....4....+....5....+....6....+....7....+
C                   IF        *IN15 and Action = 'D'
  ...
C                   IF        Action = 'A' or Action = 'U'
  ...
C                   IF        RentRate >= MinRate and
C                             RentRate <= MaxRate
  ...
C                   IF        NOT (RentRate >= MinRate and
C                                   RentRate <= MaxRate
  ...
C                   IF        RentRate < MinRate or RentRate > MaxRate
  ...
C                   IF        CustSrc = 'T' or
C                             CustSrc = 'M' or
C                             CustSrc = 'N' or
C                             CustSrc = 'P'                    CONTINUED
```

```
*...1....+....2....+....3....+....4....+....5....+....6....+....7....+
 ...
C                   IF        RentRate < MinRate and RentRate <> Ø or
C                             RentRate > MaxRate and MaxRate <> Ø
```

The second example uses OR to verify that the user has requested either an 'A' (Add) action or a 'U' (Update) action. Such a technique can condition execution of a validation routine (which is required only if the user wants to add a record or update an existing record). OR requires that just one of the two expressions evaluate to true.

The third example uses the AND operator again. Here, the two operand expressions must both be true before the entire expression is true; RentRate's value must be between the value of MinRate and MaxRate. This technique can condition the calculation of an invoice item extension because the rate that the user entered is within the prescribed rental rate bounds for the product being rented.

The fourth and fifth examples verify that the RentRate is not outside the bounds of the MinRate and MaxRate field values. This example illustrates how NOT can negate an entire expression but makes the expression difficult to read. If you do not specify NOT, as in the fifth example, you can restructure the expression to help a maintenance programmer understand. Example four requires that the rental rate not be between the minimum and maximum (which means the rate must be less than the minimum or greater than the maximum). Example five states the situation more simply: The expression is true if the rental rate is less than the minimum or greater than the maximum — funny how the explanatory restatement of the first expression exactly matches the description of the second expression. Again, when determining the truthfulness of a situation or expression, humans think in positive terms instead of negative. You can use either of these approaches to trigger an error message to let the users know they have entered an invalid rental rate.

Example six shows how a series of ORs can let you validate a user-supplied value against an allowed set of values. CustSrc is compared to several literals, and because OR is the operator, if one of the simple expressions is true, the entire complex expression is true.

Example seven shows how you can combine ANDs and ORs to create even more complex conditions. This code takes care of two nagging possibilities that example five does not consider. If a rental rate is optional, a zero rate will always be lower than any established minimum. If a particular item has no maximum rate and you store the maximum as a zero, any rate entered will exceed the maximum. This code checks whether the rental rate is less than the minimum and whether the rental rate is not zero. It also checks whether the rental rate is greater than the maximum rate and whether the maximum rate is not zero.

You can see the precedence order for AND and OR at work here. Logically, the four simple expressions will be evaluated first, followed by the two AND operations. Last, the OR operation will handle the results of the two AND operations. Understanding the precedence helps you understand that the OR can't be evaluated until the second AND is evaluated.

You can override this order by specifying parentheses. In addition, parentheses can also make the order of processing clear to read if they emphasize the existing order of operations. For instance, placing parentheses around the two AND expressions in this example can make the operation of the entire expression easy to comprehend quickly.

Expression Continuation

RPG IV lets you continue an expression to the next line of code. Below is an example of a free-form expression that is continued to a second line.

```
*...1....+....2....+....3....+....4....+....5....+....6....+....7....+
... Verify transaction date within contract effective dates
C                    IF        TrxnDate >= CntEffDate and
C                              TrxnDate < CntExpDate
... conditioned code
C                    ENDIF
```

Note that no continuation character is necessary. You can continue expressions over as many lines as you need. This capability makes the expression easily readable. In this example, the conditioned code will execute if the transaction date is greater than or equal to the effective date and less than the expiration date.

CONDITIONAL EXECUTION: **IF-ELSE-ENDIF** STRUCTURES

The traditional logical construct to conditionally execute code in many programming languages is IF-THEN-ELSE. RPG supports this capability with the IF, ELSE, and ENDIF (or END) operations. (END is functionally equivalent to ENDIF when you specify END with an IF statement.) The flowchart on page 181 illustrates execution flow of the IF-THEN-ELSE structure.

The logical expression you specify as the condition of the IF statement is evaluated. If the expression is true, the *if-body* (or "body of the IF") executes. When the condition structure contains an ELSE operation code, the if-body is the segment of source between the IF and ELSE operation codes. When the branch-on-condition structure does not contain an ELSE operation code, the if-body is the source segment between the IF and ENDIF (or END) operation codes.

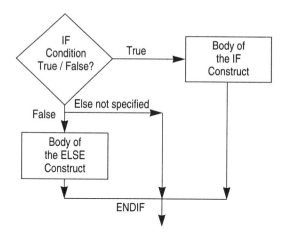

When the IF condition is false and an ELSE operation is present, the else-body is executed. The *else-body* is the code between the ELSE operation and the ENDIF (END) operation that terminates the entire IF. Another term for the group of specifications delimited by an ELSE and END is "the body of the else." If no ELSE operation is present, when the IF's condition is false, execution passes to the first instruction after the END or ENDIF operation code.

IF and IFxx

The IF (IFxx) operation tests for a condition (e.g., equals, greater than, or less than) and, depending on the outcome, causes a body of C-specs to execute. The IF operation code and a corresponding ENDIF operation code delimit these C-specs. The test condition (e.g., IFEQ) can be fixed-form, where it is a relation between Factors 1 and 2, or free-form (IF) with an expression (IF x=y) in the extended Factor 2 field. Only if the condition is satisfied will the C-specs following the IF operation code execute.

RPG IV lets you nest IF/ENDIF operations so that one IF/ENDIF structure can be inside another one. In this case, you pair the outermost IF and ENDIF, followed by the next-to-the outermost pair, continuing until you get to the inner-most pair of operations. Up to 100 levels of nesting are allowed. An IF/ENDIF structure can appear inside the conditioned code of an ELSE operation (part of the overall IF/ENDIF structure) or a WHEN operation (part of a SELECT/ENDSL structure). As you can imagine, you can get interesting looking (read "ugly and unmaintainable") code by nesting conditional operations inside other conditional operations. We suggest that you keep nesting to a minimum.

The IF/ENDIF structure supports only two paths of execution, the *true path* and the *false path*. You can use nested IFs to build multiple paths. However, before you do, we urge you to look at the SELECT/ENDSL structure to handle multiple-path decision points.

The following table summarizes the valid entries for IF and IFxx. Resulting indicators are not permitted with either variation of the IF operation code.

Factor 1	Opcode	Factor 2	Result	Indicators
Required *comparand 1*	IFxx	Required *comparand 2*	Not allowed	Not allowed
Not allowed	IF	Extended *logical expression*		

ANDxx and ORxx

If you use the fixed-form IFxx operation, you can specify the ANDxx and ORxx operations to build compound conditions. However, we do not recommend fixed-form operations or ANDxx and ORxx.

ELSE

The ELSE operation defines an *otherwise-clause* for an IF group. That is, ELSE defines the group of C-specs that will execute if the test condition on the corresponding IF operation is not satisfied.

Factor 1	Opcode	Factor 2	Result	Indicators
Not allowed	ELSE	Not allowed	Not allowed	Not allowed

This table lists the valid entries for ELSE. The ELSE operation code accepts no factors or indicators.

ENDIF and END

The ENDIF or END operation code terminates an IF group. The IF group includes all C-specs that the IF and optional ELSE operations condition. The IF operation controls the execution of all code between it and the corresponding ENDIF operation. If the structure contains an ELSE operation between IF and ENDIF, the value of the expression on the IF operation will control whether the code between IF and ELSE or the code between the ELSE and ENDIF will execute. A true value executes the former code, and a false value executes the latter code. If no ELSE is present, all code between the IF and ENDIF executes when the IF expression's value is true.

Factor 1	Opcode	Factor 2	Result	Indicators
Not allowed	ENDIF	Not allowed	Not allowed	Not allowed

The END/ENDIF operation code accepts no factors or indicators with the C-spec. The table above summarizes the valid entries for ENDIF.

Nested IF Structures

You can nest IF structures: A particular if-body can contain other IF structures. The maximum nesting level for RPG IV is 100. However, keep in mind two important caveats when you consider nested structures. First, the 100-level maximum applies not just to nested IFs, but to all structures that support nesting (IF, DOx, SELECT). If you have an IF structure in a DO loop, that combination counts as two levels of nesting. Second, nesting is very difficult to read if it gets too deep. If you have more than three levels of nesting, consider placing the code inside subroutines and conditionally executing those subroutines instead of building large nested blocks of inline code.

IF, ELSE, ENDIF by Example

The IF/ENDIF structure is a basic necessity that lets programs handle different conditions that can arise within the application's business rules. IFs let you condition code to meet the needs of different types of data and transactions you will encounter. Let's consider, for example, the calculation of a transaction total. Assume that you have already accumulated the total cost of the items to be purchased in the transaction, and you now need to calculate the taxes and fees to apply to the purchase.

To demonstrate IF, ELSE, and ENDIF and nesting, let's impose some rules for this program. First, you will apply a general tax that amounts to a certain percentage of the total purchase price, but only if the purchaser is not exempted from the taxes. Additionally, you will charge a flat fee for the purchase. This fee is a per-transaction fee that the seller imposes as a type of dues that the purchaser pays to be a member of a buying group. However, you will charge the fee to the transaction only if some money is changing hands and only if the purchaser does not have a special exemption. As the seller provides some products that are free to any purchaser, you need to be sure *not* to apply that fee if the transaction involves only those products and, therefore, has a zero total purchase price. Finally, for transactions where you apply the transaction fee, you will have to reduce the fee by 50 percent when the total purchase price is under $100.00. The code fragment on page 184 processes these rules.

First you check the customer's tax-exempt status. If the customer is not exempt, a TaxExempt status flag is set to N and you calculate a tax amount (pseudocoded in the example). The calculation is in the IF/ENDIF construct.

```
*...1....+....2....+....3....+....4....+....5....+....6....+....7....+
 *
 * Calculate sales tax for non-exempt purchasers
C                   IF        TaxExempt = 'N'
 ... Calculate the amount of the tax
C                   ENDIF
 *
 * Apply fee for trans if trans is non zero and customer is not exempt
C                   IF        TrxnTot > 0 and FeeExempt = 'N'
 *
 * Apply partial or full fee
C                   IF        TrxnTot <= DscFeeMax
 ... calculate fee as 1/2 of standard fee
C                   ELSE
 ... calculate fee as full standard fee
C                   ENDIF
 *
C                   ENDIF
```

The next step calculates the transaction fee. Recall that you apply it only if the transaction is not zero and the customer is not exempt from the fee. By comparing the transaction total to 0 and testing the flag that signals exemption from the fee, the next IF tests whether to apply the fee. If the transaction is not zero *and* the customer is nonexempt, all the code inside the IF/ENDIF construct is executed. That IF/ENDIF construct has another IF construct nested inside it. Here you check whether to reduce the fee or charge the full fee. The next IF compares the transaction total to a field that contains the maximum transaction total that still qualifies for a discounted fee. If the the transaction total falls below this maximum or equals the maximum, the code between the IF and ELSE is executed. However, if the condition is *not* true (the transaction exceeds the maximum), the code between the ELSE and the ENDIF is executed.

Note the relationship between the ELSE and the IF. The ELSE in this example is paired, as an ELSE always must be, with the most recent, unended IF. In this small example, you can easily see which IF. However, imagine multiple IFs and ELSEs and several levels of nesting. The situation can get nasty quickly. We highly recommend that IF/ENDIF structures be as short as possible, that you nest them as little as possible, and that when you violate either of those rules, you move the inline code into a subroutine to be executed as a separate module. In this case, the IF/ENDIF will condition the execution of the subroutine.

Multi-Condition Selective Execution: **SELECT, WHEN, OTHER**

The IF/ENDIF structure takes a binary view of the world. When working with an IF/ENDIF, you get to check a condition and then take one of two directions. If no ELSE is involved, you either perform the conditioned code or you don't. If an ELSE is involved, you perform either the code between the IF and ELSE or the code between the ELSE and ENDIF. However, life and business rules are not always binary. Often, you have to take one of several roads. Although you can code for multiple possibilities with nested IF structures, they can get really messy and very difficult to read. Fortunately, RPG IV offers another structure, SELECT/ENDSL, that lets you select from one of several conditions and execute a section of code based on the first of those conditions that is true.

The performance of a SELECT/ENDSL structure is roughly the same as that of a set of nested IF/ENDIF structures. The SELECT/ENDSL structure's benefits come in the area of readability and maintainability. Nested IF/ENDIFs can be very difficult to read because of all the structures inside each other, but the SELECT/ENDSL has a single starting and ending point. Additionally, another programmer can clearly see that you intend to execute only one of several sections of code. With nested IF/ENDIFs, you always have the nagging question of whether you accidentally misplaced an ENDIF in all the nesting.

The old CASxx/ENDCS structure is similar to the SELECT/ENDSL in that it also supports multiple branches and executes the first branch whose condition is true. However, the CASxx/ENDCS structure supports only the conditional execution of subroutines, and the SELECT/ENDSL structure supports conditional execution of inline code (which, of course can execute a subroutine). If you are used to the CASxx/ENDCS structure and you execute fairly small subroutines, you may find a small performance gain by using a SELECT/ENDSL structure instead and moving the subroutine code into the SELECT/ENDSL structure as inline code. However, the gain is probably small enough that you will not want to switch if it means you are reducing the code's readability.

As with the IF/ENDIF and DOx/ENDDO structures, the SELECT/ENDSL structure supports nesting of conditional structures. The WHEN clause of the structure can contain IF/ENDIF structures, DOx/ENDDO structures, and even other SELECT/ENDSL structures. This nesting is limited to a maximum of 100 levels.

SELECT

The SELECT operation marks the beginning of a code segment called a *select-group*, which you terminate by coding an ENDSL (End Select) or END operation. SELECT and ENDSL define a select-group. This structure lets you check multiple conditions to find the one condition you want to execute.

You specify SELECT in the operation field. Factor 1, Factor 2, and the Result field are not allowed. You cannot specify any resulting indicators. You can use conditioning indicators on the SELECT operations. If you do, the indicator conditions the entire select-group and control passes to the first statement following the ENDSL operation when the conditioning indicator is not on. We do not recommend conditioning indicators at all, much less to condition groups of code such as this. This table summarizes the syntax for the SELECT operation code.

Factor 1	Opcode	Factor 2	Result	Indicators
Not allowed	SELECT	Not allowed	Not allowed	Not allowed

A select-group can have zero or more WHENxx operations and an OTHER operation associated with it. Each operation conditions a block of code that is executed conditionally.

Although we do not necessarily recommend nesting, you need to understand how a nested SELECT/ENDSL structure works inside another SELECT/ENDSL structure: Because each structure can have WHEN and OTHER operations, which SELECT/ENDSL structure does each WHEN and OTHER belong to? A WHEN or OTHER operation is always associated with the most recent SELECT operation that has not yet ended with an ENDSL or END operation.

ENDSL

The ENDSL (End Select) operation marks the end of a SELECT-group. No fields are permitted with the ENDSL operation. Conditioning and resulting indicators are not permitted. This table summarizes the entries for ENDSL.

Factor 1	Opcode	Factor 2	Result	Indicators
Not allowed	ENDSL	Not allowed	Not allowed	Not allowed

WHEN

The WHEN operation, which can be fixed form or free form, is similar to the IF operation. WHEN specifies a condition using either fixed- or free-form condition rules. The fixed-form version lets you extend the condition by entering the ANDxx and ORxx operations. The free-form version lets you specify a free-form relational expression in the extended Factor 2. The table below shows the syntax summary for WHEN.

Factor 1	Opcode	Factor 2	Result	Indicators
Required *comparand 1*	WHENxx	Required *comparand 2*	Not allowed	Not allowed
Not allowed	WHEN	Extended *relational expression*		

Like the IF operation, WHEN conditions the execution of a section of code. This section includes all the code between the WHEN operation and the next WHEN, OTHER, or ENDSL (or END) operation. This section is the *when-body*. Keep the when-body small. If it is getting very large, consider moving the code into a subroutine and executing the subroutine from within the when-body.

Although you can specify a CASxx/ENDCS structure to execute subroutines, WHENs within SELECT/ENDSL structures are much more flexible. Sometimes you will have when-bodies in the structure to execute subroutines, other when-bodies may process only inline code. You can also use when-bodies to mix the two approaches so that you can call the same routine from several when-bodies but include inline code in each when-body that performs some unique setup work for that particular condition.

Within the SELECT/ENDSL structure, each of the WHENs' conditions is evaluated from top to bottom. The when-body of the first WHEN with a true condition is executed. Once that code is complete, control passes to the first operation following the ENDSL operation of the SELECT/ENDSL structure. So only one when-body is ever executed. This fact makes the conditions you specify on each WHEN operation mutually exclusive: Only one can be true and cause its when-body to be executed. Of course, the conditions need not be mutually exclusive, but even if two or more WHEN conditions are true, only the first one will be executed.

A when-body can be empty. This is useful if the WHEN conditioning the empty when-body is a more restrictive condition than on subsequent WHENs or if the condition needs to override all the conditions on subsequent WHENs.

OTHER

The OTHER operation conditions the execution of a block of code within a SELECT/ENDSL structure. This block of code is the *other-body*, and it includes all code between the OTHER operation and the ENDSL in the SELECT/ENDSL structure. OTHER does not use Factor 1, Factor 2, or the Result field. The OTHER operation does not support resulting indicators, and conditioning indicators are not allowed. This table shows the valid entries for OTHER.

Factor 1	Opcode	Factor 2	Result	Indicators
Not allowed	OTHER	Not allowed	Not allowed	Not allowed

The OTHER operation code is a catch-all in a SELECT group. That is, if all WHENxx conditions in the group evaluate to false, the other-body is executed. The OTHER operation is optional to the SELECT group. If you omit OTHER and all the WHEN conditions are false, execution flow passes to the specification immediately following the ENDSL operation.

The OTHER operation's catch-all role makes it the ideal place to handle unexpected conditions. Unless you know that one of the conditions on the WHEN operations in the SELECT/ENDSL structure will always be true, you can use the other-body to trigger an error message or recovery processing when an unknown or unexpected condition arises. For instance, if each WHEN in the SELECT/ENDSL structure tests for a particular value in a transaction-type field, the other-body can alert you or the user when an unknown transaction type is encountered. Of course, you can use WHENs and OTHER to handle situations where most transactions require the same processing, but certain transactions require unique processing. In that case, you can code each exception condition on a WHEN operation, and the when-bodies can handle them while the standard processing is in the other-body of the SELECT/ENDSL structure. The flowchart below illustrates the execution flow of a SELECT-WHEN-OTHER construct in RPG IV.

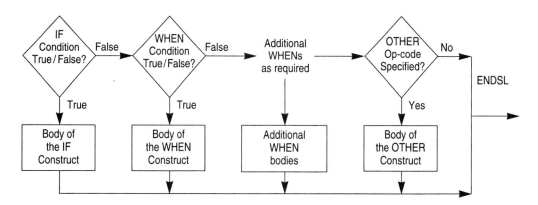

As the code below shows, a SELECT-group can contain several WHENxx segments, each being an alternative test condition. Each WHENxx condition is tested in sequence. If all WHENxx conditions evaluate to false, the OTHER segment executes.

```
*...1....+....2....+....3....+....4....+....5....+....6....+....7....+
C                   SELECT
C                   WHEN      expression-1
  ...                 when-body-1 code
C                   WHEN      expression-2
  ...                 when-body-2 code
                      .
                      .
                      .
```

CONTINUED

```
*...1....+....2....+....3....+....4....+....5....+....6....+....7....+
C                     WHEN        expression-n
   ...                      when-body-n code
C                     OTHER
   ...                      other-body code
C                     ENDSL
```

SELECT, WHEN, OTHER by Example

Remember, you will frequently specify a SELECT/ENDSL structure when you have multiple conditions to check for but want to act on only one of those conditions. This makes the SELECT/ENDSL structure a way to work down through a hierarchy, selecting the first applicable level in the hierarchy or selecting one item out of a set.

The program below is part of a human resources planning application. The code segment is responsible for handling employee performance analysis. The program lets you classify each employee into a group based on total output for a given month. This function works down through a hierarchy.

The rules for this application are that you have four tiers of performance: outstanding, above average, average, and below average. A SELECT/ENDSL structure will let you work your way down through the tiers so that each employee is counted in the correct group.

```
*...1....+....2....+....3....+....4....+....5....+....6....+....7....+
C                     SELECT
   *
C                     WHEN        ProdUnits > OutStdLvl
C                     ADD         1               OutStdCnt
   *
C                     WHEN        ProdUnits > AbvAvgLvl
C                     ADD         1               AbvAvgCnt
   *
C                     WHEN        ProdUnits > AvgLvl
C                     ADD         1               AvgCnt
   *
C                     OTHER
C                     ADD         1               BlwAvgCnt
   *
C                     ENDSL
```

This code processes the number of units, ProdUnits, an employee produces in the evaluation period. The program compares the employee's units to each of the performance tier thresholds in descending order. The OutStdLvl, AbvAvgLvl, and AvgLvl fields, which hold the number of units necessary to achieve an outstanding, above average, or average rating, represent the thresholds. Anything below the lowest threshold is below average.

The program maintains a count of employees in each category. These numbers are stored in OutStdCnt, AbvAvgCnt, AvgCnt, and BlwAvgCnt. If you assign the values 300, 200, and 100 to the three thresholds, you can see how an employee who produces 150 parts is in the average category, so the ADD operation increments the AvgCnt field by 1. The program evaluates the expression in the first WHEN, comparing 150 to 300. Because 150 is less than 300, the next WHEN's condition is tested. There, 150 is compared to 200 and found to be less than 200. The next WHEN finds that 150 is greater than 100, so that expression is true. The code in the when-body executes and increments the AvgCnt counter field. Because the code in the when-body is finished, execution branches out of the SELECT/ENDSL structure, bypassing the OTHER operation.

If you follow the same logic, an employee who produces 250 parts is in the above-average category. An employee who produces 350 parts is outstanding.

```
*...1....+....2....+....3....+....4....+....5....+....6....+....7....+
C                   SELECT
     *
C                   WHEN      TrxnCde = 'PO '
C                   EXSR      ProcPurORd
     *
C                   WHEN      TrxnCde = 'MSG'
C                   EXSR      VldtUser
C                   EXSR      SndUsrMsg
     *
C                   WHEN      TrxnCde = 'INQ'
C                   CALL      'ELECINQ'
     *
C                   OTHER
C                   WRITE     ErrFmt
     *
C                   ENDSL
     *
```

Another strength of the SELECT/ENDSL structure is the ability to determine how to process based on one of a set of values. The example above demonstrates that type of processing. Here, a transaction processing program receives business transactions electronically and then routes them to the appropriate department. That routing can mean that the transaction received is written to a data file, as in the case of a purchase order. Or, sometimes, a message goes to a user, as is the case if customers can send electronic messages. Or, sometimes, a set of data is prepared to be returned to the person who sent the transaction if you provide electronic inquiry facilities. Of course, the content of the received transaction will vary, depending on what type of transaction it is, and your responses to these transactions will vary.

As with any such application, eventually an invalid transaction type will creep into the process, and you will have to alert someone or log the incident in an error file. Again, the SELECT/ENDSL structure provides an ideal method for handling the initial routing of the transaction.

This example's SELECT/ENDSL structure handles the three different transaction types. The TrxnCde field has a defined set of three possible values: PO for receipt of a purchase order, MSG for receipt of a message, and INQ to initiate an electronic inquiry. The WHEN operations of the SELECT/ENDSL structure let you select an action based on which transaction type you receive.

CONDITIONAL BRANCHING (CABXX) AND CONDITIONAL SUBROUTINE EXECUTION (CAS)

CABxx (Compare and Branch) and CASxx (Compare and Invoke Subroutine), let you compare Factor 1 with Factor 2 and, depending on the comparison's result, branch to a label or execute a subroutine. The Result field specifies the destination of the branch or the name of the subroutine to execute. The *xx* in these operation codes can be GT, LT, EQ, NE, GE, or LE. The section on fixed-form conditions earlier in this chapter gives you the rules for the comparison between Factor 1 and Factor 2. Note that neither of these operations supports ANDxx and ORxx to extend the relation. You can specify only the two factors of the operation in the relational test.

Both these operations are obsolete, and CABxx shares a bad reputation with GOTO because it can lead to spaghetti code. CASxx does not have quite such a bad reputation, but you will probably prefer SELECT/ENDSL to provide the same type of processing.

CABxx

The CABxx (Compare and Branch) operation code compares Factor 1 to Factor 2. Success of the tested relation immediately transfers control to the label you specify in the Result field. As with the IFxx operation, Factors 1 and 2 are the comparands. You must define the label on the CABxx operation code with a TAG that occurs in the same program. This table describes the syntax of the CABxx operation code.

Factor 1	Opcode	Factor 2	Result	Indicators		
Required *comparand 1*	CABxx	Required *comparand 2*	Required *target TAG or ENDSR*	GT	LT	EQ

CABxx is a standalone operation, like GOTO. In fact, CABxx really is a GOTO with the ability to make a comparison before branching. CABxx's available targets are the same as for the GOTO operation. Consequently, CABxx shares some of GOTO's bad reputation.

CABxx supports fixed-form condition testing only and does *not* allow extension via the ANDxx and ORxx operations. You can specify a CABxx operation without the relation test (the xx), but the two comparands are always required. If you do not specify a relation test, the branch is unconditional, even though Factors 1 and 2 must be tested. A CABxx with no relation test and a label in the Result field is simply a GOTO in disguise. This operation has no free-form version.

If you specify resulting indicators, CABxx operates like a COMP operation. In fact, if you leave the Result field blank (providing no tag to branch to), the operation is nothing more than a COMP in disguise. Resulting indicators are set just like they are for COMP, based on a comparison between the values in Factor 1 and Factor 2. Oddly, the comparison occurs without regard for any relational test you specify on the CABxx operation. This can be a really confusing process, though, and we recommend that you not use the COMP-like capabilities of the CABxx operation (if you choose to use the operation at all, which is *not* something we recommend).

Factor 1 and 2 can be a literal, named constant, a figurative constant, a table name, an array element, a data structure name, or a field name. Factor 1 and 2 must be of the same type. Conditioning indicators are permitted with CABxx.

Branching into a subroutine is not permitted. That is, you cannot specify CABxx to branch to a label in a subroutine if the program is not already executing within that subroutine. You can branch to a label on a preceding or subsequent C-spec, from a detail C-spec to another detail C-spec, from a total C-spec to another total C-spec, from a detail C-spec to a total C-spec, from within a subroutine to a TAG or ENDSR specification within the same subroutine, from within a subroutine to a detail C-spec, or from within a subroutine to a total C-spec.

CAB by Example

The example of the GOTO operation demonstrated a conditioned GOTO by wrapping it inside an IF/ENDIF structure. You can accomplish that same operation with the CABxx operation. The code below re-creates the example from the GOTO operation and changes it to include a CABxx operation instead of an IF/ENDIF structure. Of course, this approach is backward to the way you probably want your coding career to progress: Moving toward structured operations is better than moving away from them.

```
*...1....+....2....+....3....+....4....+....5....+....6....+....7....+
C    FLAG           CABEQ     'DONE'         END
... other code
C    END            TAG
C                   SETON                                             LR
```

CASxx

The CASxx (Compare and Invoke Subroutine) operation performs a comparison using the comparands in Factors 1 and 2. If the comparison succeeds, program execution will call the subroutine you specify as the Result field of the CASxx operation. Like CABxx, CASxx applies a test condition against the comparands in Factors 1 and 2. The difference is that if the CASxx test is successful, execution control passes to the subroutine specified on the Result field. This table summarizes the valid entries for CASxx.

Factor 1	Opcode	Factor 1	Result	Indicators		
Optional comparand 1	CASxx	Optional comparand 2	Required subroutine name	GT	LT	EQ

The relational test the CASxx operation performs follows the rules for fixed-form conditions. However, you cannot specify ANDxx and ORxx to extend that relational test. Like the CABxx operation, CASxx lets you specify resulting indicators that will be set as they are for the COMP operation. The setting of the resulting indicators follows the COMP rules, and the relational test you specify on CASxx has no effect on the resulting indicators. Evaluation of the relational test and the setting of the resulting indicators are independent processes.

CASxx marks the beginning of a CAS group. The group, which is very similar to a SELECT-group, terminates when the compiler encounters an ENDCS operation. Whereas SELECT/ENDSL structures can perform any action in response to a true WHEN condition, a CAS group can execute only one subroutine when a true condition is found. The only operations allowed between a CASxx operation and ENDCS (or END) are other CASxx operations. A CAS group is just a series of CASxx operations terminated by ENDCS. Each CASxx operation's relational test is evaluated in order until the first one that has a true condition. That CASxx's subroutine is executed. After that subroutine, execution returns to the first C-spec following the ENDCS operation code.

With CASxx, you can also execute a subroutine unconditionally to provide a catch-all similar to the OTHER operation in a select-group. You leave Factor 1 and Factor 2 blank. This use of CASxx is equivalent to an EXSR (Execute Subroutine) operation code.

You must observe the following guidelines when you code a CAS group. Only valid subroutine names can be in the Result field of any CASxx operation. User-defined subroutines, *PSSR, and *INZSR are all permitted, and if the test condition is satisfied, the subroutine will be executed. The CASxx operation is part of the CAS group. On success of a test condition within a CAS group, the associated subroutine is executed. After the subroutine, execution will continue with the first C-spec following the ENDCS operation code.

The comparands can be a literal, named constant, figurative constant, field name, table name, array element, or data structure name. Both factors must be of the same data type. Blanks are permitted for Factor 1 and 2 if the test condition (xx) is also blank and no resulting indicators are specified with the CASxx operation. In this case, note that CASxx is identical to EXSR, which can only invoke a subroutine. Note that if you specify resulting indicators in positions 71 through 76, you must also specify Factors 1 and 2.

The test condition (xx) is optional. It can be GT, LT, EQ, NE, GE, or LE. If your goal is to unconditionally call the subroutine specified in the Result field, you can specify blanks for the test condition and Factors 1 and 2 of CASxx. Note that once the program encounters an unconditional CASxx, the RPG runtime compiler will not execute any other subsequent CASxx operation in the CAS group.

ENDCS

The ENDCS (End Compare and Invoke Subroutine) operation marks the end of a CAS group. No fields are permitted with the ENDCS operation. Conditioning and resulting indicators are not permitted. This table shows the valid entries for ENDCS.

Factor 1	Opcode	Factor 2	Result	Indicators
Not allowed	ENDCS	Not allowed	Not allowed	Not allowed

CASxx by Example

The CASxx operation is a popular way to handle the sequential testing of a group of conditions when you know that a subroutine will be executed to handle each situation. One example is processing a screen after the user presses a function key. The example below assumes that the indicators are assigned to the same-numbered function keys, so 25 is assigned to Page down and 26 is assigned to Page up.

```
*...1....+....2....+....3....+....4....+....5....+....6....+....7....+
C                     EXFMT     DtlFmt
 *
 * Handle user response/requests
C         *IN03       CASEQ     *ON             ExitPgmSr
C         *IN05       CASEQ     *ON             RfrshDsp
C         *IN09       CASEQ     *ON             ChgMode
C         *IN25       CASEQ     *ON             PageDown
C         *IN26       CASEQ     *ON             PageUp
C                     CAS                       ProcDtlFmt
C                     ENDCS
    ... other code
```

In this example, the CASxx operation handles a series of exceptions followed by a general process. When the EXFMT (Execute Format) operations display a screen to the users, they have several choices. Usually, they will key some data and then press Enter. In that case, no indicators that correspond to function keys will be on. The program will enter the top of the CAS group and test each condition in turn. Because no indicator is on, none of the first five CASEQ operations will evaluate to true. Processing will drop to the unconditional CAS operation, which will then execute the ProcDtlFmt subroutine. It will process the detail format, the data the user just entered on the screen. However, if the user presses a function key to take any other defined action (F3 to exit the program, F5 to refresh the display, F9 to switch from add to change mode and vice versa, or Page down or up to scroll to the next or previous records), the corresponding indicator will turn on, and the appropriate CASEQ operation will trigger the desired subroutine. Once the subroutine executes, control will return to the line of code following ENDCS.

ITERATION: USING LOOPING CONSTRUCTS

Another important feature of structured programming languages is iteration, or repeating a process. RPG IV allows iteration through the program cycle or looping constructs. RPG's built-in program cycle causes the iteration of a program's C-specs. Only the SETON LR (Set On Last Record) operation terminates cycle-based iteration *at the end of the current cycle (iteration)*, ending the program. RETURN lets you explicitly exit the cycle at any time.

This book pays little attention to the RPG program cycle, a built-in looping mechanism that processes records in primary and secondary files that you define for the program. The program cycle has many other complexities, but a detailed explanation is not pertinent to the point here.

The point is that *the RPG program cycle is not a conventional construct* and can become a hindrance. It can hinder readability and it makes source translation into other languages difficult, and such translation is becoming increasingly important on the AS/400. Because of these drawbacks, programmers are unwise to use coding practices that take advantage of the cycle and result in constructs that conventional languages cannot easily accommodate.

Instead of relying on the cycle, you can explicitly create iterative structures by specifying looping operation codes. RPG IV has four basic ways to code iterative structures: You can code combinations of TAG and GOTO to manually build such a structure, or you can code the three built-in looping operations, DO, DOW (Do While), and DOU (Do Until). These operations also have fixed-form versions, DOWxx and DOUxx.

You must pair each loop-beginning operation with another operation that marks the end of the loop. The terminating operation can be either ENDDO or END; the two are equivalent when working with a DOx loop. END is a general terminator that you can pair with other operations besides DOx operations. ENDDO, on the other hand, lets you specifically end a DOx loop. ENDDO will let the compiler catch an error and will let a maintenance programmer see the top and bottom of the DOx structure quickly.

DO, DOW, and DOU
Most programs have some reason to perform a series of calculations or actions repetitively. Of course, if you follow the strict guidelines of structured, modular programming, you can write any loop you need simply by specifying the necessary branching operations, such as GOTO and CABxx, and providing the necessary targets for those branches with the TAG operation. But that approach leads to errors. Instead, RPG provides the DO loop. A DO operation marks the start of a block of code that will be processed repeatedly. The ENDDO or END operation terminates the block.

The three types of DO loop are one that iterates a fixed number of times (DO), one that iterates *until* a condition is true (DOU), and one that iterates *while* a condition is true (DOW). The fixed iteration DO is really a special case of the DOW, but DO is easier to code and figure out when you're reading code.

All code between the DO/DOW/DOU and the ENDDO/END is the *loop-body*. The loop-body can contain any operation, including other DO loops, but cannot contain the start or end of a subroutine.

A simple DO loop performs a block of code a specified number of times. DO is a fixed-form operation, but it has a different form of fixed-form condition testing. This operation has no free-form version.

A DO-until loop performs a block of code *until* the loop test condition is true. DOU is the free-form operation. You enter a condition in the extended Factor 2. DOUxx is the fixed-form version, and you can extend it with ANDxx and ORxx. This structure is a *post-test loop* because the loop is always executed at least once, and the test condition is executed after the loop-body.

A DO-while loop performs a block of code *while* a specified test condition is true. The DOW operation code is the free-form version. You enter the condition you want in the extended Factor 2. The DOWxx operation is the fixed-form version, which you can extend by issuing ANDxx and ORxx.

This type of loop is a *pretest loop*, which means that the loop will not be executed, not once, unless the loop test condition is satisfied. In a pretest loop, an IFxx operation code will not let execution control pass through to the loop-body unless the IFxx condition is satisfied. The *xx* part of the operation code represents the test condition, which can be GT, LT, EQ, NE, GE, or LE.

The DO Operation Code

The DO operation code is a looping construct that marks the beginning of a section of code that will repeat a specified number of times. DO is analogous to the FOR loop constructs in other HLLs, such as Pascal, BASIC, and C.

You specify DO with Factor 1, Factor 2, and the Result field. Factor 1 contains the starting value to track how many times the loop will repeat. This value is a class numeric value with zero decimal positions. The operation increments this initial index value each time the loop repeats. When this value matches the total number of times to repeat the loop (i.e., the value in Factor 2), the loop terminates. You can specify a named constant, field name, or class numeric literal as the starting value. If you do not specify Factor 1, the compiler assumes that the initial value for the loop index is 1. This value is moved to the index field (Result field) when the loop begins.

Factor 2 contains the limit value, which, like the start value, is class numeric, with zero decimal positions. This value determines how many times the loop-body will execute. If you do not provide Factor 2, the compiler will assume that the limit value is 1.

The Result field identifies a field that will hold the index value. The index value is initialized to the starting value. As the DO mechanism is iteratively processed, the index value is incremented with each iteration. Factor 2 of the corresponding END or ENDDO provides the increment value. This arrangement lets the program perform the loop while the index value is less than or equal to the limit value. When the index value is greater than the limit value, execution control will pass to the C-spec after the END or ENDDO operation associated with the DO loop. You can see now why DO is really a special case of DOW. Both execute the loop-body only while a condition is true.

If you do not specify a Result field, the compiler will generate an internal, temporary one for you. However, if you need access to the value of the index for the current loop, you must specify a field in the Result field. The table below shows the syntax for DO.

Factor 1	Opcode	Factor 2	Result	Indicators
Optional *starting value*	DO	Optional *limit value*	Optional *current index value*	Not allowed

A common problem with coding a DO loop is to accidentally make the field that holds the index value too small. You must always make certain that the field can contain a number that is equal to the limit value plus the increment value. If you do not, you can accidentally create an infinite loop. For instance, if you want to perform a DO loop nine times and code the value 9 as the limit value, you will probably feel comfortable using a 1-digit field to hold the index value. However, at the end of the ninth iteration of the loop, when the increment value is added to the index value, the new index value will be 0, not 10, because of truncation of the high-order digit. The test that determines whether the loop will iterate uses the value 0 to compare to the limit value. Because the value in the index variable will never be greater than 9, the loop will continue indefinitely. You usually specify this type of construct when you know the number of required iterations. The flowchart below illustrates the execution of a DO looping structure.

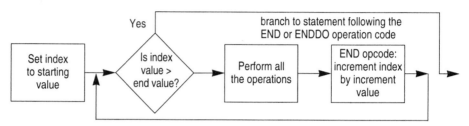

The ENDDO Operation Code

Every DO operation must have a matching ENDDO operation code to signal the end of the DO loop. When, and only when, paired with a DO, ENDDO accepts a Factor 2 field. Factor 2 provides the increment value for the corresponding DO. If you specify a negative value, the DO loop will be a never-ending loop. If you omit Factor 2, the system assumes a value of 1. The following table summarizes the entries for ENDDO.

Factor 1	Opcode	Factor 2	Result	Indicators
Not allowed	ENDDO	Optional *increment-value*	Not allowed	Not allowed

The ENDDO operation supports conditioning indicators. Unlike the conditioning indicators that DO supports, these indicators are checked on each iteration of the loop. If the conditioning indicators are not satisfied on any iteration, the loop terminates immediately. We highly discourage the use of conditioning indicators on the ENDDO operation. They make your code hard to understand.

The system checks any conditioning indicators you specify with the DO operation first. If the conditions are satisfied, only then will the loop processing begin. This check occurs only once, and the value of any conditioning indicators with the DO will not have any effect on subsequent iterations of the DO loop. Conditioning indicators on a DO operation control whether the DO group executes at all. We do not recommend conditioning indicators on DO groups.

Before the loop begins, the value of ENDDO's Factor 2, the starting value, is moved to the index field specified as the Result field. If you do not provide an index field, the compiler-generated index field will be used.

At the top of the loop, a check determines whether the current index value is greater than the limit value (Factor 2). If it is, the looping is complete and execution passes to the first operation after the ENDDO operation that terminates the DO loop. While the index value is less than or equal to the limit value, the code in the loop-body will be executed. Note that if the starting value is greater than the limit value when the operation begins, the loop will not be executed at all.

We highly recommend that you *do not* change the current index value within the loop-body. You will be much better off to let only the DO operation change the field containing the index value, when the index is automatically incremented. You can, however, reference the current index value while processing is in the loop-body.

At the end of each loop iteration, the ENDDO operation is processed. Then the increment value is added to the current index value.

Usually, you will leave the Factor 2 on the ENDDO operation blank, so the default value of 1 will be the increment value for the index. Sometimes, however, you need to increment by a different number. You do so by specifying the increment value on the ENDDO operation.

DO by Example

DO lets you repeat a process or series of processes a certain number of times. Usually, you specify DO with no Factor 1 and the corresponding ENDDO with no Factor 2. This approach makes very clean syntax for a fixed number of iterations. For instance, consider an application uses a 12-element array to store the current sales figures for each month. Because this book has not yet covered arrays, this example will pseudocode the array references and focus on RPG's ability to handle the looping this application requires.

The code below can perform 12 iterations of a process. On each iteration, you can use the loop's current index value to index the array that holds the 12 months' sales figures.

```
*...1....+....2....+....3....+....4....+....5....+....6....+....7....+
D Mon `            S              3 0
   *
```

```
*...1....+....2....+....3....+....4....+....5....+....6....+....7....+
C                   DO        12           Mon
 ... process current month entry of array
C                   ENDDO
```

That solution is quick and easy. Because no Factor 1 is on the DO operation, the loop will start with an index of 1, the default. The field Mon will contain the value 1 on the first pass through the loop, 2 on the second pass, and so on. At the end of each loop iteration, Mon will be incremented by 1, again the default, because no Factor 2 is on the ENDDO operation.

Your programs will have more complex needs. For instance, a user will want to process a range of months in the current year. Fortunately, the DO operation can accommodate that need. By entering variables for Factor 1 and Factor 2 on DO, you can work through any range you need. Below is an example of how to code a DO loop that can process any range in this 12-element array.

```
*...1....+....2....+....3....+....4....+....5....+....6....+....7....+
D StrMon          S              3 0
D EndMon          S              3 0
D CurMon          S              3 0

*...1....+....2....+....3....+....4....+....5....+....6....+....7....+
C     StrMon         DO        EndMon        CurMon
 ... process current month entry of array
C                    ENDDO
```

The user can provide any range of months. The starting month is in the StrMon field, and the ending month is stored in the EndMon field. When the DO operation starts, CurMon will be set equal to the StrMon. If CurMon is not greater than or equal to EndMon, the loop will be processed one time. At the end of the loop, CurMon will be incremented by 1, and execution will return to the top, where the field will again be compared to EndMon to determine whether another iteration is necessary. Of course, you have to assume that somewhere else the same program validates the values of StrMon and EndMon to ensure that the user did not request numbers outside the allowed range of 1 to 12, and that StrMon is less than or equal to EndMon. The former test is required to ensure that you don't attempt to access array elements that don't exist. The latter test, though not required, ensures that the user has made a reasonable request.

The DOW and DOWxx Operation Codes

Like DO, DOW and DOWxx begin a pre-test loop. DOW is the free-form version and supports free-form relational expressions with the extended Factor 2. DOWxx is the fixed-form version and supports fixed-form conditions. Because DOWxx uses fixed-form condition specification, you can specify the ANDxx and ORxx operations to provide extended fixed-form condition tests. The following table shows the syntax for the DOWxx operation code.

Factor 1	Opcode	Factor 2	Result	Indicators
Required *comparand 1*	DOWxx	Required *comparand 2*	Not allowed	Not allowed
Not allowed	DOW	Extended *relational expression*		

DO uses a simple test to determine whether the loop will execute. In contrast, DOW gives you freedom to control the looping process. DO checks whether a current loop index is greater than a maximum value that you supply with the DO operation. DOW lets you execute a loop any number of times, as long as the conditioning expression or comparison is true.

DOW lets you perform an action repeatedly, when you need to perform that action only under certain circumstances. Because the operation will continue to loop until the controlling condition is no longer true, you must change the conditions somewhere inside the loop-body. This code shows how to specify the fixed-form DOWxx operation.

```
*...1....+....2....+....3....+....4....+....5....+....6....+....7....+
C     Comparand     DOWxx     Comparand
C                     :
C                     : DOWxx Body
C                     :
C                   ENDDO
```

This code shows how to specify DOW in its free-form style.

```
*...1....+....2....+....3....+....4....+....5....+....6....+....7....+
C                   DOW         <relational expression>
C                     :
C                     : DOW body
C                     :
C                   ENDDO
```

DOW and DOWxx support conditioning indicators, but we recommend against them. Conditioning indicators on such structures are even more confusing than conditioning indicators in general. If DOW or DOWxx is conditioned, the entire DO loop is conditioned.

The loop-body is executed *only* when the condition (not conditioning indicators) that you specify on the DOW or DOWxx operation is true. The condition is retested before each iteration of the loop-body. On failure, execution passes to the specification immediately following the END or ENDDO operation code.

Note that, as with DO, the DOWxx loop-body sometimes is not executed if the condition you specify on the DOW or DOWxx is not true when the operation is first encountered. In this case, execution passes to the specification immediately following END or ENDDO. This is the natural behavior of a pre-test loop, as the flow chart below illustrates.

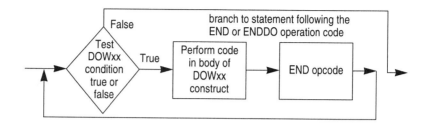

The system checks any conditioning indicators you specify on the DOW or DOWxx first. If the conditioning indicators are satisfied, only then will the loop processing begin. This check occurs only once, and the value of any conditioning indicators you specify with the DOW or DOWxx operation code will not have any effect on subsequent iterations of the DOW or DOWxx loop.

At the top of each loop iteration, the condition you specify on the DOW or DOWxx is tested. If the condition is true, the body of the DOW loop is executed one time. If it is false, execution transfers to the first operation after the ENDDO that terminates the DOW loop. Again, keep in mind that this means the loop will not execute at all if the conditioning expression or comparison is false when the DOW or DOWxx operation is first processed.

The ENDDO operation supports conditioning indicators. Unlike the conditioning indicators for DOW or DOWxx, these indicators are checked on each iteration of the loop. If the conditioning indicators are not satisfied on any iteration, the loop terminates immediately. Obviously, we highly discourage conditioning indicators on the ENDDO operation. They make code hard to understand. You can terminate a DOW loop by changing the values in the condition on the DOW or DOWxx operation so that the condition is no longer true. You can also use the LEAVE operation to exit the DOW loop.

DOW by Example

The DOW loop works best when a program must perform a series of actions only if a condition remains true and only while that condition continues to be true. Such a situation is when a loop reads through a file and processes the records read. Because you want to process a record only if you find a record, the actions must occur only while you have a record to process. With DOW and DOWxx, you have to set up the initial conditions before you enter the DOW loop. Inside the loop, you can process the record you just read and then read the next record. The processing of the record on every iteration of the DOW loop is valid because you know that, even on the first iteration of the loop, you have a record to process. Remember, you cannot enter the loop unless the condition you are testing is initially true.

```
*...1....+....2....+....3....+....4....+....5....+....6....+....7....+....8
 *
 * Perform initial read of file
C                     READ      DataRcd                          30
 *
 * Loop through all records in file, processing each one found until EOF
C                     DOW       Not *IN30
 ... process record
 *
 * Read the next record
C                     READ      DataRcd                          30
C                     ENDDO
```

The example above illustrates the need to establish the initial conditions before attempting to process the DOW loop and how to change the conditioning expression to a false value from within the DOW loop. You establish the initial conditions by performing an initializing read of the database file. Indicator 30 lets you detect the end of the file. At this point you know, from the value of *IN30, whether you have read a record or hit the end of the file. Sometimes no records are in the file. If not, *IN30 is immediately turned on. When the DOW is executed, the expression Not *IN30 is evaluated. Because *IN30 detects and signals the EOF condition, the expression is saying, "Do while not at end of file," or, more important, "Do while a record has been retrieved." If you do not hit end of file on the initial read, you can proceed into the body of the DOW loop, confident that you *do*, indeed, have a record to process.

The DOW loop can process the record, an action that the example code presents as pseudocode. The last step on each iteration of the DOW loop is to reset the conditions of the loop control to determine whether to execute the loop again. You do this step by reading the next record from the data file. Again, indicator 30 detects and signals an EOF condition. If you get another record, 30 will remain off. If you hit EOF, 30 will turn on. Regardless of the outcome, you will return to the top of the loop to re-evaluate the conditioning expression. The code will continue to loop as long as you read a record. When the condition is no longer true, execution will move to the first operation after the ENDDO.

Because an indicator is in the DOW relational expression, to clear any misconceptions we need to point out that this is not a *conditioning indicator*, but an indicator for a relational expression. The relational expression will be evaluated on each iteration of the DOW loop. If you code the indicator as a conditioning indicator (positions 9 through 11), it will be evaluated only once, and the logic will fail. Syntactic rules still require some relational expression in the extended Factor 2, even if a conditioning indicator is present.

DOU and DOUxx

Unlike DO and DOW, DOU and DOUxx begin looping constructs that use a *post-test* loop. So the evaluation and testing of the condition that controls loop iteration occurs at the *end* of each iteration. Because the test does not occur until the end of an iteration, a DOU loop will always execute the code in the body of the loop at least once.

DOU is the free-form version and supports free-form relational expressions in the extended Factor 2. DOUxx is the fixed-form version and supports fixed-form conditions, so you can extend it by specifying ANDxx and ORxx. The example below shows how to specify the free-form DOU.

```
*...1....+....2....+....3....+....4....+....5....+....6....+....7....+
C                   DOU           <relational expression>
C                    :
C                    : DOU body
C                    :
C                   ENDDO
```

The flowchart below depicts the behavior of the DOU looping structure. The loop-body executes before the program tests the relation specified in the DOUxx operation. Iteration of the loop-body continues until the relation is satisfied. Then, execution passes to the specification immediately following the ENDDO that delimits the loop-body.

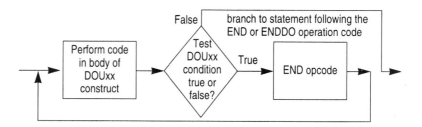

The syntax of DOUxx is similar to DOWxx's syntax. However, although the DOUxx operation code precedes the loop-body in the code, the condition is tested after execution of the loop-body. The following table shows the syntax for DOU and DOUxx.

Factor 1	Opcode	Factor 2	Result	Resulting Indicators
Required *comparand 1*	DOUxx	Required *comparand 2*	Not allowed	Not allowed
Not allowed	DOU	Extended *relational expression*		

Below is the structure of a DOUxx looping construct on the C-specs. The DOU loop is a post-test loop, so the loop-body will execute at least once. Note however, that if any conditioning indicators specified with DOUxx are not satisfied, the loop will not execute once.

```
*...1....+....2....+....3....+....4....+....5....+....6....+....7....+
C       Comparand    DOUxx      Comparand
C                      :
C                      : DOUxx Body
C                      :
C                    ENDDO
```

Although these operations support conditioning indicators, we strongly recommend against them, especially on a structure such as DOU. They can introduce confusion because they are not really part of the DOU looping process.

Every DOUxx operation must have an associated ENDDO. As with ENDDO with DOWxx, ENDDO with DOUxx does not accept a Factor 2 entry.

ENDDO supports conditioning indicators. Unlike the conditioning indicators that DOU or DOUxx supports, these indicators are checked on each loop iteration. If the conditioning indicators are not satisfied on any iteration, the loop terminates immediately. Obviously, we highly discourage the use of conditioning indicators on ENDDO. They make code hard to understand. The way to terminate a DOU loop is by changing the values in the condition on the DOU or DOUxx so that the condition is no longer true. You can also use LEAVE to exit a DOU loop.

At the *end* of each loop iteration, the condition you specify on DOU or DOUxx is tested. If the condition is true, execution returns to the top of the loop for another iteration. If the condition is false, execution transfers to the first operation after the ENDDO that terminates the DOU loop. Remember that because the conditioning expression or comparison is checked only at the end of the iteration, the loop will always be processed at least once. This means the loop will always be executed, even if the conditioning expression or comparison is false when the DOU or DOUxx operation is first processed.

DOU by Example

DOU is most useful when you have a process that must execute repeatedly and the condition that terminates the loop is always created inside the loop.

This situation occurs in a present-and-respond process such as you find in an interactive program, where you ordinarily display a screen to the user and then act on the user's response. Generally, an interactive program will redisplay its screen after each transaction until the users signal that they are finished with the program and request the end, which typically means that the user has pressed F3.

Of course, users can do many things before they press F3. After each non-terminating action, the program will redisplay the screen for the next transaction. Here, you definitely need a loop. And because the user can't press F3 on the screen until the screen appears, you need a looping construct that always processes at least one iteration of the loop. This kind of application makes good use of DOW.

```
*...1....+....2....+....3....+....4....+....5....+....6....+....7....+
 *
 * Loop to display and process screen until user presses F3
C                   DOU       *IN03
 *
 ... prepare detail screen
 *
 * Display the screen and accept input
C                   EXFMT     DetailFmt
 *
 * Handle responses other than termination request
C                   SELECT
C                   WHEN      *IN03
 ... handle exit request (pre-exit housekeeping)
C                   WHEN      *IN05
 ... handle refresh request
C                   WHEN      *IN26
 ... handle Page down request
C                   OTHER
 ... handle Enter key
C                   ENDSL
 *
C                   ENDDO
 *
```

The example above demonstrates present-and-respond processing. The program enters a loop that will always execute at least once because it is a DOU loop. Note that subsequent iterations of this loop will depend on the relational expression on the DOU operation. In this case, turning on the indicator for the F3 key will be the signal that the loop needs to end.

Inside the loop, the program prepares the screen for display (the example shows pseudocode for that part) and then displays the screen to the users and awaits their input. Here is the "present" part of present-and-respond.

When the user responds, the program checks which key was pressed. A SELECT/ENDSL structure lets you check for each possible response from the user. Now the program will select an action based on which key the user pressed. This is the "respond" part of present-and-respond.

One possible response is F3, represented by indicator 03. When the condition that terminates the loop is set early in the loop, you should make certain that you condition the code that comes between the setting of the condition and the bottom of the loop. In this example, the SELECT/ENDSL structure conditions the execution of all code in the loop. When the user presses F3, the cleanup code, which is pseudocoded here, will execute. Execution will fall to the bottom of the DOU loop, the conditioning expression on the DOU loop will be evaluated, and because *IN03 is now on, the loop will terminate and execution will continue with the first operation following ENDDO.

The LEAVE and ITER Operations

Infrequently, you need to exit a loop or return to the top of the loop structure unconditionally. The LEAVE and ITER (Iterate) operation codes are for these situations. The LEAVE operation code lets execution control exit a loop-body. LEAVE causes immediate transfer of execution control. This operation is useful if your loop-body is very large and complex, and you want to exit immediately when you encounter a particular condition. An example is a serious application error. ITER transfers control to the bottom of the current loop so that the next iteration can begin immediately (if the loop's conditioning allows it).

From a performance perspective, LEAVE, ITER, and GOTO are equivalent. Although more structured than the GOTO operation, LEAVE and ITER can also be bad programming practice because the resulting code can be difficult to read and maintain.

LEAVE

The LEAVE operation code transfers execution from a point in a loop-body to the first operation following the ENDDO or END that terminates the most recently initiated DO loop. If the loop-body you are exiting is a nested loop, execution control leaves only the innermost loop.

You can specify LEAVE with DO, DOU, DOUxx, DOW, and DOWxx. Factors 1 and 2 and the Result field are not permitted with LEAVE, nor are resulting indicators. Conditioning indicators are allowed, but we discourage you from using them. This table summarizes the valid entries for LEAVE.

Factor 1	Opcode	Factor 2	Result	Indicators
Not allowed	LEAVE	Not allowed	Not allowed	Not allowed

ITER

The ITER (Iterate) operation immediately transfers execution to the ENDDO or END associated with the most recently initiated DO loop. ITER lets you skip all the code in the loop between the ITER operation and the end of the loop-body. Once execution arrives at the ENDDO or END, loop processing proceeds as usual, with the code returning to the top of the loop to test the condition to see whether to execute the loop-body again. Remember that although the operation is called ITER, it does not guarantee that another iteration of the loop-body will occur — only that the current iteration is terminated immediately and the next iteration is tested for.

This operation helps when your code determines at an early point in the loop-body that the remainder of the loop-body is meaningless in the current iteration, and processing needs to proceed to the next possible iteration. This use of ITER will become clear in the next example.

You can specify ITER in a DO loop initiated with a DO, DOW, DOWxx, DOU, or DOUxx operation. ITER does not use Factor 1, Factor 2, or the Result field. You cannot specify resulting indicators. Conditioning indicators are allowed, but they are not recommended. This table summarizes the syntax for ITER.

Factor 1	Opcode	Factor 2	Result	Indicators
Not allowed	ITER	Not allowed	Not allowed	Not allowed

LEAVE and ITER by Example

LEAVE and ITER are useful when you have a DO loop. Because DO/ENDDO constructs usually execute a fixed number of times, breaking out of these loops prematurely can be difficult. In fact, you want a DO loop to execute without interruption because you don't want to alter the index value that conditions the iterations of the loop. LEAVE can help you exit cleanly. ITER, on the other hand, can be beneficial in such a loop when the remainder of the logic in the loop becomes meaningless. Instead of conditioning all the rest of the loop-body in an IF/END construct, passing processing immediately to the next iteration of the loop-body can be a clean and easy-to-understand solution.

The following example demonstrates both ITER and LEAVE in nested DO loops. The situation is a sales analysis project. You must find the first day in each month on which the monthly total sales objectives are met or exceeded. The sales manager wants to know whether the goals are too high or too low. If all goals are met within, say, the first two weeks of the month, the goals are probably a little low. Each day's monthly sales to date are in a file that is keyed

by date (because some other analysis processes also use the file). The monthly
goals are in a file that is keyed by year and month. The program must loop
through the months of the year to analyze each in turn. Within each month, the
program must loop through the days to find the first date on which the monthly
sales-to-date exceeded that month's goal.

```
*...1....+....2....+....3....+....4....+....5....+....6....+....7....+....8
D CurMon          S              2  0
D CurDay          S              2  0
D SlsYr           S              2  0
D SlsYrMon        S              4  0
D SlsDate         S              6  0
D DaysInMon       S              2  0
 *


*...1....+....2....+....3....+....4....+....5....+....6....+....7....+....8
 *
 * Loop through months in year
C                 DO        12            CurMon
 *
 * Retrieve monthly goal
C                 EVAL      SlsYrMon = SlsYr * 100 + CurMon
C     SlsYrMon    CHAIN     SlsGoalFmt                      30
 *
 * If there was no goal record or it was zero, do not process this month
C                 IF        *IN30 or SGSlsGoal <= 0
C                 ITER
C                 ENDIF
 *
 * Call routine to get days in month
 ... call to day-in-month routine returning DaysInMon
 *
 * Set GoalDate to 0 until we find one
C                 EVAL      GoalDate = 0
 *
 * Loop through days in month checking each for attainment of sales goal
C                 DO        DaysInMon     CurDay
 *
 * Retrieve month-to-date sales (MTDSls) for current month and day
C                 EVAL      SlsDate =
C                           SlsYear * 10000 + CurMon * 100 + CurDay
C     SlsDate     CHAIN     SlsDataFmt                      30
```

CONTINUED

```
*...1....+....2....+....3....+....4....+....5....+....6....+....7....+....8
 * If day not found (we aren't there yet) or we achieve the goal, set the
 * date, stop looping in current month, and proceed to next month
C                     SELECT
C                     WHEN      *IN30
C                     LEAVE
C                     WHEN      SDMTDSls >= SGSlsGoal
C                     EVAL      GoalDate = SlsDate
C                     LEAVE
C                     ENDSL
 *
C                     ENDDO
 *
 * If GoalDate determined for month, print it
C                     IF        GoalDate <>0
... print data for achieved goal
C                     ENDIF
 *
C                     ENDDO
```

This example demonstrates the LEAVE operation from two levels in a pair of nested DO loops. After the definition of the working variables, whose meanings are apparent, the code segment starts a loop through the 12 months of the year.

You can assume that the routine receives the year to be analyzed in the field SlsYr. The second DO operation initiates a loop that will repeat 12 times, once for each month in the year. Inside this loop, the program constructs a YYMM field called SlsYrMon, using the year that was passed to the routine and the month from the current iteration of the loop. This year/month field lets you retrieve the sales goal for the month by issuing the CHAIN operation.

If you do not find a record in the file giving a goal for the month, or if the goal for the month (in SGSlsGoal) is less than or equal to zero, you do not want to process the daily sales records for the month. If you continue executing code in the current iteration, it will process those records. Instead, under either of those conditions (record not found or goal not greater than zero), you can issue ITER to transfer control to the ENDDO for the current loop. Processing will return to the top of the loop for another iteration. If you find a record and the sales goal is specified, you continue to look through the daily records to find the goal-meeting date.

The pseudocoded process of getting the number of days in the current month provides the control for the next DO loop (the nested one). Having the number of days in the month of the current iteration, you can now start a DO loop that will execute that number of times. The next DO operation starts a loop that will execute DaysInMon times (28, 29, 30, or 31 times) to process each day in the month. Inside this inner loop, you construct a current date and retrieve the month-to-date sales (SDMTDSls) for the current date.

You have three possibilities after you retrieve the month-to-date sales. Two require the processing for the month to stop immediately. If you find no record for the current date, assume that you have not yet processed data for that date (or any subsequent dates, because they occur in order). In that case, you have no reason to continue looking at other dates in the month, so you can LEAVE the DO loop immediately. Execution transfers to the first operation *after* the ENDDO associated with the most recent DO. This step takes you to the ENDDO.

The second possibility is that the month-to-date sales will have met or exceeded the goals for the month. Now, you must set the GoalDate field to the SlsDate field to record the date when the goal was met. Again, you no longer need to continue with the loop, so you can LEAVE immediately. Control again passes to the ENDDO.

The third option, which does not require the loop to terminate immediately, is that you find a record, but the sales goal is not yet met. In that case, you just fall through to the end of the current iteration and loop back to try the next date.

This example uses both LEAVE and ITER to simplify exiting a loop and to clarify the intent of the code. The alternative is to code DOW or DOU loops and include the conditions that terminate the loops in the expressions that control iteration. Imagine the confusion of a programmer who has to figure out why the record-not-found indicator (*IN30, in this case) and the retrieved month-to-date sales figures are such a set of expressions. The code in this example makes the necessary decisions about immediately skipping to the next iteration or exiting a loop when the conditions occur.

SUBROUTINES

This chapter has discussed only inline coding constructs. With inline constructs, nothing but a construct's top and bottom separates the construct from other code in the program. Additionally, the only way to execute the constructs is to have the logical flow of the program enter the top of the construct and then drop out of the bottom (unless you involve those nasty branching functions, GOTO and CABxx). You can consider each inline construct a module of code: The construct generally does one thing or a compact series of things.

A problem with inline constructs, though, is that if you need the same logic in more than one place in the program, you must include all the logic in each place. Clearly, this repetition is not a good practice. From a maintenance standpoint, it creates a nightmare. Imagine how easily a programmer can change the logic in one place in the program, while being completely unaware that the same change is necessary in other places in the code.

To handle this dilemma, RPG provides subroutines. A subroutine is a section of code that has a name. By referencing that name, you can execute this code from multiple places in the program, but the subroutine remains in only one place. Now when someone modifies the code, you can be confident that the change will be in effect every time you use this code.

Anything you can put on a C-spec can go into a subroutine, including standalone operations such as EVAL and ADD and complete constructs such as IF/ENDIF, DO/ENDDO, and any combination of the two. You cannot have a subroutine inside another subroutine.

Beyond the subroutine name, a subroutine does *not* have formal interfaces with the rest of the program. Subroutines do not support local variables or parameters at this point in the life of RPG, but you can expect such support in the near future. Although the code that comprises a subroutine is segregated from the rest of the program, the data that the subroutine uses and modifies is global; changing data from within a subroutine changes that data for all processes in the program. Of course, this fact also means that a subroutine can access all variables defined in the program and can act on any of them.

You can execute a subroutine by referencing it in the program. Two operations, CASxx and EXSR (Execute Subroutine), let you execute a subroutine. CASxx accepts the name of a subroutine in the Result field. This subroutine will be executed if the conditioning relation on the CASxx operation evaluates to true.

The EXSR Operation

EXSR (Execute Subroutine) unconditionally calls a subroutine. EXSR uses Factor 2 to name the subroutine to execute. Factor 1 and the Result field are not allowed, nor are any resulting indicators. As usual, you can specify conditioning indicators, but we still caution against them, preferring structured operations. The table below shows the valid entries for EXSR.

Factor 1	Opcode	Factor 2	Result	Indicators
Not allowed	EXSR	Required *subroutine name*	Not allowed	Not allowed

When EXSR is processed, control passes to the called subroutine. Processing will then proceed from the top to bottom of the subroutine until the subroutine ends. Then control will return to the operation following the EXSR operation that invoked the subroutine.

The BEGSR and ENDSR Operations

You define a subroutine by specifying the BEGSR (Begin Subroutine) operation at the beginning of the subroutine code. You identify the end of a subroutine by specifying ENDSR (End Subroutine). BEGSR uses Factor 1 to name the subroutine you're creating. You can enter any valid RPG name if it is not already the name of another subroutine in the program; subroutine names must be unique in a program. Factor 2, the Result field, and resulting indicators are not supported. Conditioning indicators are not valid. The table below summarizes the entries for BEGSR and ENDSR.

Factor 1	Opcode	Factor 2	Result	Indicators
Required subroutine name	BEGSR	Not allowed	Not allowed	Not allowed
Optional tag name	ENDSR	Not allowed except in *PSSR	Not allowed	Not allowed

You can specify two subroutine names to create subroutines that special RPG processes use. A subroutine named *PSSR defines a program status subroutine, otherwise known as an error/exception routine. This subroutine will automatically execute when the program encounters an error, such as a divide by zero or a subscript out of range. (For more information on error handling, see Appendix B.)

Another special subroutine name is *INZSR. This name defines an initialization subroutine. RPG automatically executes this subroutine during program initialization when the program is first called. This subroutine establishes initial field values and performs any one-time setup processing that the program needs. Other than the special execution of these two subroutines, nothing else about them is different from other subroutines.

You can specify ENDSR alone, or you can specify Factor 1 to define a TAG name. Placing a valid RPG name in Factor 1 lets you use a GOTO or CABxx operation to immediately branch to the end of the subroutine from anywhere within the subroutine. If you specify *PSSR, ENDSR can have Factor 2 specified as a field, literal, or named constant that evaluates to one of several special values: *DETL, *GETIN, *TOTC, *TOTL, *OFL, *DETC, and *CANCL. These values correspond to specific points in the built-in cycle of an RPG program. Alternatively, you can leave Factor 2 blank. If you do and the subroutine is invoked for an error, processing will pass to the default internal error handling routine. Because we do not advocate using the built-in cycle and because the most effective use of the *PSSR involves logging the error in some way and then shutting down the program, we recommend that you specify *CANCL to terminate your program after you take care of error reporting and logging.

Subroutines in an RPG program must come after any non-subroutine C-specs. Once you start defining subroutines, you can specify only subroutines on the C-specs after that first subroutine. The non-subroutine part of the program is the *mainline code*. Often, mainline code consists of little more than subroutine calls. Those subroutines can then call other subroutines, and so forth. Take care not to code yourself into a loop so that the chain of executed subroutines comes back around on itself. RPG does not support recursive subroutine calls, directly or indirectly.

Subroutines by Example

Subroutines in RPG provide a basic building block for programs. As you identify individual processes and modules, you will want to use subroutines to implement both control and action modules. Because the only role of the subroutine definition operations is to define the start and end of subroutines, this chapter includes a small example of how to code those operations. The content of each subroutine is completely pseudocoded because the processing in a subroutine can be almost anything.

```
*...1....+....2....+....3....+....4....+....5....+....6....+....7....+....8
C                   SELECT
 *
C                   WHEN      TrxnCde = 'PO '
C                   EXSR      ProcPurORd
 *
C                   WHEN      TrxnCde = 'MSG'
C                   EXSR      VldtUser
C                   EXSR      SndUsrMsg
 *
C                   WHEN      TrxnCde = 'INQ'
C                   CALL      'ELECINQ'
 *
C                   OTHER
C                   WRITE     ErrFmt
 *
C                   ENDSL
 *
 *****************************
 * ProcPurOrd - Process Purchase Order
 *   Handles the processing of a new purchase order received
 *   electronically
 *****************************
 *
```

Continued

```
*...1....+....2....+....3....+....4....+....5....+....6....+....7....+....8
C     ProcPurOrd    BEGSR
 ... code to process purchase order
C                   ENDSR
 *
 *****************************
 * VldtUser - Validate User ID
 *  Makes sure that user ID received is a valid ID and exists on the system
 *****************************
C     VldtUser      BEGSR
 ... code to validate user ID
C                   ENDSR
 *
 *****************************
 * SndUsrMsg - Send User Message
 *  Calls necessary programs to send a message to a user on the system
 *****************************
 *
C     SndUsrMsg     BEGSR
 ... code to validate user ID
C                   ENDSR
```

Comments are generally at the head of each subroutine. This placement lets you explain the function of the subroutine and visually set the code apart from other code in the program.

CHAPTER 8

Arrays and Tables

Many applications require storing and manipulating data in memory. Using standalone fields, data structures, and constants is one way of storing and manipulating program data. However, when a solution involves many repetitions of program data, you can find better approaches.

Consider a program that verifies a state code. The United States includes 50 states plus the Virgin Islands, Puerto Rico, and Washington, D.C. Each has a two-character abbreviation that the application can use as a code. Many data entry applications require the operator to key this code into a record that the program must verify. Obviously, standalone fields, data structures, or constants are not the ideal way to store the valid codes for the editing process.

Arrays are contiguous memory cells that you access by providing an index value that points to a particular memory cell location. In an RPG program, an array is a list of information. An array is a more appropriate choice for storing state codes because it saves steps in processing repetitive information. If you supply an array of the valid codes, the application can edit the users' entries into the state code field.

Arrays give you flexibility in your applications that require repetitive manipulation of similar pieces of data. Unlike languages such as C, Pascal, and COBOL, RPG has three types of arrays: compile-time arrays, pre-runtime arrays, and runtime arrays. This chapter will explain the three types of arrays and the keywords and operations that support them.

While you're thinking about arrays and the processing they facilitate, you also need to consider tables. An old RPG implementation of a concept similar to arrays, tables are still available in RPG IV, although they do not provide the functionality or ease of use of arrays. For example, in contrast to arrays, tables must be loaded at compile time or pre-runtime; runtime tables are not available. And RPG tables cannot have an index. Although arrays have supplanted the purpose tables once served (and you'll want to avoid tables and take advantage of arrays), you still need to maintain old programs, and many old programs will have tables. Because tables are still around, this chapter will explain them.

RPG's Three Types of Arrays

All three RPG array types — compile-time, pre-runtime, and runtime — follow the same rules governing how a program can use and reference the individual pieces of information, or *elements*, in the array. The differences among the three types of arrays lie in *when* each type is loaded with data: at compile time, at pre-execution time, or at runtime. This chart summarizes the differences among the three types of arrays.

Time Line

Program Compiled	Program Called	Program Executing
Compile-time arrays	Pre-runtime arrays	Runtime arrays
Data loaded at compilation time	Data loaded at pre-execution time (when program is called)	Data loaded at runtime (during program execution)

Compile-Time Arrays

The system loads compile-time arrays during compilation of the RPG program source. You enter the data for a compile-time array at the bottom of an RPG program.

Pre-Runtime Arrays

The system loads pre-runtime arrays when you've called the program and before it is totally loaded into memory. Pre-runtime arrays are loaded as soon as you execute the CALL command but before any RPG operations execute. You specify the information for this array type in a disk, or data, file.

Runtime Arrays

The system loads runtime arrays from files, other fields, or user input at execution time. Your program controls the loading of runtime arrays.

Defining an Array

To understand array definition, you first need to know about array elements. The basic unit of an array is an element. In an array, each piece of information, such as product order number, is an element. Because an element is similar to a field, you must give each element a size and data type. An array of one element of type character will have the same memory size allocated to it as a character standalone field; an array with 10 elements of type binary will have the same memory size as 10 standalone fields of type binary.

Although you define array elements like fields, you do not refer to array elements in the same way you refer to fields. Whereas each standalone field has a unique name, an array has one name that identifies all its elements at once. An index points to an element you need to reference at any given time.

To define an array, in a program's D-specs, you enter the name of the array, the size and type of its elements, the number of elements the array has, and the method and time of loading the array (which determines the type of array you want). For example, these D-specs define a compile-time array called St_Codes.

```
*...1....+....2....+....3....+....4....+....5....+....6....+....7....+
D*
D St_Codes       S             2A   DIM(52) CTDATA
```

You enter the array's name (in this case, St_Codes) in positions 7 through 21. The name of the array is not distinguishable from any field name in RPG. Because RPG IV lets you float the name anywhere in the field-name specification area, this example begins the array name in position 8 for readability.

In position 24, you place an S, the entry for a standalone field. This required specification may seem confusing, but when you think that array elements are like standalone fields, the requirement is easier to understand.

The number of elements you define for an array is called the array's *dimension*. In the D-spec keyword section (positions 44 through 80), the DIM keyword reflects this term. This keyword's parameter is where you specify the number of elements in the array. In the example, the DIM keyword instructs the compiler to associate 52 memory cells with the array St_Codes. The length specification (positions 33 through 39) defines each element's length as 2, and its type is character (position 40). The CTDATA (Compile-Time Data) keyword (on the same line in the D-spec keyword section) establishes that the array is a compile-time array and tells the compiler to load the array's data, which is at the bottom of the source member, at compile time.

Other keywords for arrays are FROMFILE, TOFILE, PERRCD (Per Record), ALT (Alternate Loading Sequence), ASCEND, and DESCEND. The table below summarizes the positional entries you need to define an array.

Array Name	Standalone Field	Elements' Length	Elements' Type	Keywords
7 - 21	24	33 - 39	40	44 - 80

Array Indexes

Once you define an array, you can manipulate its data in your C-specs. When you specify only the name of an array, that specification refers to the entire array with all its associated elements. For certain operations, the ability to refer to an entire array can be extremely useful. For example, you can use the array name St_Codes in Factor 2 on the MOVEA (Move Array) operation code to move the entire array to another array that you specify in the Result field.

Although accessing an entire array is useful, you also need to access each element of an array. An *index*, or subscript, allows such access. An index is a numeric-class reference that identifies a particular element of an array by giving the element's ordinal position in that array. For example, you can refer to the fifth element of array St_Codes by entering St_Codes(5). If you use a variable to specify an index value, the variable must be class numeric and have zero decimal positions. If you use an expression, the result must be a numeric value with zero decimal positions.

Again, the array name can be any valid name that follows the rules for defining field names in RPG. The index can be any valid numeric field or constant, or the result of an expression if the value has zero decimal positions.

Because arrays contain repeating groups of data and you have to give an array a predetermined number of elements, arrays work best when the number of items you need to track or store is relatively stable. For instance, names of months, number of days in a week, and names of days will probably not change, and the number of elements will stay the same.

Suppose you need to store the totals on a report for each level break, and at each level break, you need each month's total. If you have a report that is sorted on company and department, you can create the arrays in the code below to accumulate company and department totals for every month.

```
*...1....+....2....+....3....+....4....+....5....+....6....+....7....+
 * Arrays for monthly totals by department
D DpSls           S              11P 2 DIM(12)
D DpCom           S              11P 2 DIM(12)
D CoSls           S              11P 2 DIM(12)
D CoCom           S              11P 2 DIM(12)


*...1....+....2....+....3....+....4....+....5....+....6....+....7....+
*

   ... other processing
 *
 * Detail processing:
 *  For each transaction, accumulate the sales and commissions
 * to the department
 *  totals and the company totals for the month of the transaction.
 *
C                 ADD       TxnSls        DpSls(TxnMo)
C                 ADD       TxnCom        DpCom(TxnMo)
C                 ADD       TxnSls        CoSls(TxnMo)
C                 ADD       TxnCom        CoCom(TxnMo)
   ... other processing
```

This example creates four arrays: DpSls for department-level sales totals, DpCom for department-level commission totals, and CoSls and CoCom for company-level sales and commission totals. Each array definition specifies elements that are packed numeric, 11-digit values with two decimal positions. The DIM(12) keyword gives each array 12 elements, one for each month in the year. Finally, you see the index at work when you use the transaction month field, TxnMo, from each detail record as an index to each total-holding array to record the transaction's sales and commission amounts in the appropriate month for the department and company levels.

Indexes and Array Programming Errors

A word of warning is in order about indexes and the most common programming errors with arrays. From the discussion of indexes, you can infer that you can easily make the mistake of coding an index that refers to an element that is beyond the range of elements for a particular array. Another common mistake is to code your program so that the index can have a value of zero. A less typical mistake is to accidentally get a negative number in the field you use as an index. Any of these three mistakes will cause a runtime error.

You need to ensure that the index is valid. You can either test the value before using it or you can ensure that you can always trust the source of the index value.

Unlike languages such as C, RPG will try to validate any index values at compile time. If you reference an array element by specifying a constant as the index, the compiler will try to validate that index against the defined size (dimension) of the array. Of course, the compiler has no way of knowing what value will be in a variable that you use as an index, so verifying valid indexes is up to you if you use variables. If an invalid index gets through, the system will issue a runtime error, and the users will see an unfriendly inquiry message that they must respond to.

With this overview of RPG arrays and indexes, you have the basic knowledge to begin exploring the specifics. Each array type has particular considerations that you need to beware of, so let's look at each type individually.

COMPILE-TIME ARRAYS

A compile-time array contains data that the compiler loads while compiling the program in which you specify the array. If you know at compile time what data you want to store in array, a compile-time array is what you need. You define a compile-time array and its elements on the D-specs. Then you list the array's elements at the end of the source program.

Compile-Time Array Keywords

In addition to specifying the array's name, data type, and length, you need a few keywords on the D-specs to declare a compile-time array. They are DIM(x) to specify the number of elements in the array, CTDATA (Compile-Time Data) to tell the compiler that you are defining a compile-time array and where to find the array elements, PERRCD(x) (Per Record) to specify the number of array entries per record, and EXTFMT (External Format) to specify the data format for compile-time and pre-runtime arrays. Another keyword for compile-time arrays is ALT (Alternate) to alternate the loading of two arrays. In addition, you can use the ASCEND and DESCEND keywords with the SORTA (Sort Array) operation code to determine the order of loading; these keywords are discussed with SORTA, in the section on array operation codes.

The DIM Keyword

The DIM keyword tells the compiler the dimension, or number of elements, to allocate for the array you are defining. You enter DIM in positions 44 through 80 of the D-spec where you specify the array's name, data type, length, etc. Immediately following the keyword, within parentheses, you specify the number of elements. You are limited to 32,767 elements in an array — more than enough for most applications.

The CTDATA Keyword

The CTDATA keyword makes an array a compile-time array. This keyword tells the compiler to load the array elements as part of the program compilation process. You specify CTDATA in the keyword section (positions 44 through 80) on the same D-spec where you define the array.

You specify a compile-time array's data elements by entering a **CTDATA record at the end of the source. Or you can omit CTDATA and enter ** at the bottom of the source member. The compiler knows that when you specify the CTDATA keyword on the D-specs, the data you want in this array will appear after the **CTDATA or ** record at the end of the source.

To insert compile-time data, you have two choices that are especially important if you have more than one compile-time array in a program. To identify which array data goes with which array, at the end of the source and before you begin listing the data, you can either specify **CTDATA *array-name*, or you can enter only **. The **CTDATA *array-name* technique lets you specify the name of the array to which you want to apply the data and then enter the data immediately following that specification. The ** technique tells the compiler that the data for each array in the source file is listed under a ** record, and the ** records are in the same order as the order in which you specify the arrays on the D-specs.

You cannot mix these two techniques in a program. The first method is recommended because it frees you from having to keep D-specs and sets of array data in a synchronized order. The program segment below has two compile-time array definitions and the corresponding **CTDATA records at the end of the source.

```
*...1....+....2....+....3....+....4....+....5....+....6....+....7....+
D*  Compile-time arrays of state abbreviation and name
D St_Code           S              2A    DIM(53) CTDATA PERRCD(1)
D St_Name           S             14A    DIM(53) CTDATA PERRCD(1)

*...+....1....+....2....+....3....+....4....+....5....+....6....+....7....+
**CTDATA St_Name
Alabama
Alaska
Arizona
 .  .  .
Wyoming
**CTDATA St_Code
AL
AK
AZ
 .  .  .
WY
```

Each defined array, St_Code and St_Name, has a separate set of data in the source. Each set of data starts with **CTDATA *array-name.* Notice here that the data sets are in a different order from the order in which the arrays appear in the D-specs. If you use the ** technique here, the data loaded in each array will be incorrect.

You must follow a few rules when entering array elements.

1 The first array entry for each **CTDATA record must begin in position 1.

2. All elements must be the same length and follow each other with no intervening spaces.

3. You need not fill an entire **CTDATA record with entries. You can include blanks or comments after the entries.

4. If the number of array elements on the D-specs is greater than the number of entries in the **CTDATA record, the remaining elements are filled with the default values for the data type specified.

5. Each **CTDATA record, except the last, must contain the number of entries specified on the PERRCD keyword. In the last record, unused entries must be blank.

6. Each entry must fit entirely on one **CTDATA record. You cannot split an entry between two records; therefore, the length of a single entry is limited to a maximum of 100 bytes (characters).

7. You can load arrays in ascending or descending order, or in no sequence.

As rule 5 implies, each line of code following the **CTDATA specification is one record. On each record, you can specify one array element or multiple elements. To let the compiler know how many elements you're putting in each record, you need to specify the PERRCD keyword.

The PERRCD Keyword

The PERRCD (number of array entries Per Record) keyword determines how many array elements you will specify on each data line, or record, following the ** CTDATA *array-name* or ** specification. If you do not specify the PERRCD keyword, the number of elements per line defaults to one.

In the state code and state name example, it is easier (although more difficult to read) to enter multiple states on one **CTDATA *array-name* or ** record than to enter one state per record. The example below shows how to code it.

Rule 5 applies to the St_Code entries. The first **CTDATA *array-name* record has 32 entries, but because the example has only 53 entries (50 states plus the District of Columbia, Puerto Rico, and the Virgin Islands), only 21 entries are in the second record.

```
*...1....+....2....+....3....+....4....+....5....+....6....+....7....+
D* Compile-time arrays of state abbreviation and name
D St_Code         S              2A   DIM(53) CTDATA PERRCD(32)
D St_Name         S             14A   DIM(53) CTDATA PERRCD(1)

*...+....1....+....2....+....3....+....4....+....5....+....6....+....7....+
**CTDATA St_Code
ALAKAZARCACOCNDCDEFLGAHIIDILINIAKSKYLAMEMDMAMIMNMSMOMTNENVNHNJNM
NYNCNDOHOKORPAPRRISCSDTNTXUTMTMAVIWAWVWIWY
WY
**CTDATA St_Name
Alabama
Alaska
Arizona
Arkansas
. . .
Wyoming
```

The EXTFMT Keyword

The EXTFMT(x) (External Format) keyword lets you specify the format of the elements for both compile-time and pre-runtime numeric arrays. The allowed values are in the table below. For compile-time arrays, only S, L, and R are valid. All values are valid for pre-runtime arrays. Data in a compile-time array is usually in the S format, and because S is the default, you will not ordinarily need to specify this value. However, because packed is the default data format for numeric fields in files you've created, you will probably need to use the P value when you load data from a data file for a pre-runtime array. Finally, if a separate character provides the element's sign (in which case, your data cannot be packed) and you use either the L or R code to place the sign, you must allow for one extra character per entry in the data you load to the array. Whereas the length of the data records is usually calculated as *element-length* * PERRCD-value, if you use data with the L or R code, it must have a length of (*element-length* + *1*) * PERRCD-value.

Value	Meaning
S	Data is in signed numeric format
P	Data is in packed numeric format
B	Data is in binary format
L	Data is in character format with leading sign
R	Data is in character format with trailing sign

The ALT Keyword

The ALT (Alternating Sequence) keyword tells the compiler to load each element of the compile-time array (or pre-runtime array or table) that you are defining in alternating sequence with each element of another array. The array definition on which you specify the ALT keyword is the alternating array, and the array name you specify as ALT's parameter is the main array. The alternating array definition may precede or follow the main array definition. The keywords on the main array define the loading order for both arrays. The data is loaded in alternating order, beginning with the main array: main . . . alt. . . main . . . alt. . . main. . . The code below shows how to load a state code and state name array in alternating sequence. This method of loading compile-time arrays makes reading the entries easy when the two arrays are closely related.

```
*...1....+....2....+....3....+....4....+....5....+....6....+....7....+
D* Compile-time arrays of state abbreviation and name
D St_Code        S             2A    DIM(53) CTDATA PERRCD(1)
D St_Name        S            14A    DIM(53) ALT(St_Code)
```

```
*...+....1....+....2....+....3....+....4....+....5....+....6....+....7....+
**CTDATA St_Code
ALAlabama
AKAlaska
AZArizona
Arkansas
 .  .  .
WYWyoming
```

Compile-Time Arrays by Example

Because you store compile-time array data in a program and these arrays are loaded when you compile the program, they are most useful when you have information that does not change over time. In the past, before RPG let you define and use named constants, compile-time arrays were a means to store any string longer than 8 bytes. This use increased the length of a string to the maximum length of a compile-time array. With that need a thing of the past, compile-time arrays have fewer uses. Their use is limited to non-changing sets of data, unless you prefer arrays to named constants.

Let's see how a compile-time array can extract the name of a day of the week when you have a particular date. The example below takes advantage of some RPG IV date manipulation capabilities to numerically identify the day of the week. You can convert that numeric representation to a character representation of Monday, Tuesday, Wednesday, etc. Knowing that the date January 1, 1904, was a Friday, you can calculate the number of days that have elapsed since that date, calculate the number of full weeks that have passed, and then use the number of days in the remaining partial week (if any) to determine which day a particular date falls on. The code fragment below identifies all the elements to perform this task. Note that the result of the calculation is a number between one and seven, which you can use to look up the day of the week in the compile-time array.

```
*...1....+....2....+....3....+....4....+....5....+....6....+....7....+
D DayNames        S              9A    DIM(7) PERRCD(1) CTDATA
D*
D DayName         S              9A
D KnownDate       S               D    INZ(D'1904-01-01')
D DateToCvt       S               D
D NumDays         S              5P 0
D NumWeeks        S              5P 0
D DayOfWeek       S              1P 0
```

```
*...1....+....2....+....3....+....4....+....5....+....6....+....7....+
 *
 * Subtract known Friday from current data to get number of days
 *  elapsed
 *
C       DateToCvt      SUBDUR     KnownDate      NumDays:*D
 *
 * Determine number of whole weeks elapsed by dividing by 7 and number
 *  of days in partial week by storing remainder from division
 *
C       NumDays        DIV        7              NumWeeks
C                      MVR                       DayOfWeek
 *
 * Adjust day of week by 1 to convert 0 to 6 result to 1 to 7 index
 * and thenplace name of day in variable
 *
C                      EVAL       DayName = DayNames(DayOfWeek+1)

*...1....+....2....+....3....+....4....+....5....+....6....+....7....+
**CTDATA DayNames
Friday
Saturday
Sunday
Monday
Tuesday
Wednesday
Thursday
```

Because the names of the days will not change, they illustrate the ideal type of data for compile-time arrays. The first D-spec defines the array, DayNames, which has elements, each defined as a nine-character standalone field. Keywords identify it as an array and determine the type of array that it is. The DIM(7) keyword defines a seven-element array. The CTDATA keyword identifies the array as a compile-time array, meaning that the data will be loaded from the end of the source code. The PERRCD(1) keyword indicates that the data at the end of the source has one array element on each record. At the end of the source, the lines starting at **CTDATA DayNames define the elements. The first of these lines identifies the start of the data for compile-time arrays, and the DayNames entry on the **CTDATA line means that the immediately following lines are data for the DayNames array.

Field DayName holds the result of the process, the name of the day. KnownDate is a base date for determining the number of days since that known date. DateToCvt is the date for which you want to know the name of the day of the week. NumDays and NumWeeks are work fields to hold the number of days and weeks elapsed since the base date. DayOfWeek holds the number of days in a partially elapsed week so you can calculate the index to the DayNames array to get the name of the day of the week.

The first step is to determine the number of days since a known date. This example uses a field called KnownDate to hold the value January 1, 1904. That date fell on a Friday. You calculate the number of days, NumDays, between the date you want to convert, DateToCvt, and the known date, KnownDate.

Once you know how many days have elapsed, the DIV and MVR operations find out how many complete weeks and how many days (if any) are in the remaining partial week. Dividing by seven gives you the number of complete weeks, and MVR retains the remainder from the division, the number of days in the partial week. Because the base date falls on Friday, the remainder of the division will tell how many days from Friday the current date is — a zero means the day is also a Friday, a 1 indicates Saturday, and so on.

Given the day of the week, you can look up the character name of the day in the compile-time array. Because RPG arrays are one-based (they start at element 1, in contrast with C, where arrays are zero-based), you cannot use the calculated values 0 through 6 to get the day name. Instead, you increment the day number by one to get a value of 1 through 7, which you can then use as an index to the DayNames array.

Compile-Time Arrays in Alternating Format

Suppose you've got an array that lists all the food items you need to track for a grocery store management system. To handle the pricing information for these items, you can create two compile-time arrays and load both at compile time. Or you can have the compiler alternate between loading one element of each array. That is, if you declare arrays Product and Price and specify them as alternating arrays, the compiler will load the first element of Product and then the first element of Price, the second element of Product and then the second of Price, and so on. You accomplish this alternating loading by using the ALT keyword when you define the arrays that you want loaded in alternating sequence. The example below illustrates this approach.

```
*...1....+....2....+....3....+....4....+....5....+....6....+....7....+
DProduct          S             10A   DIM(10) CTDATA PERRCD(1)
DPrice            S              5S 2 DIM(10) ALT(Product)
DTempDS           DS            36
```

```
*...1....+....2....+....3....+....4....+....5....+....6....+....7....+
  .  .  .
C     1              DO        10              I              3 0
C     'ITEM is --> 'CAT        Product(I)    Temp            30
C                   MOVE       '  PRICE --->'Temp
C                   MOVEL      Temp          TempDS
C                   MOVE       Price(I)      TempDS
C                   ENDDO
```

```
*...1....+....2....+....3....+....4....+....5....+....6....+....7....+
 **CTDATA Product
BANANA      00035
APPLE       00089
LEMON       00123
TOMATO      00149
CUCUMBER    00073
ONION       00053
PEPPER      00115
BREAD       00149
GARLIC      00015
EGGS        00125
```

You declare the Product array to contain the product names, and the Price array to contain the prices. The definition of Price has the ALT keyword to tell the compiler to alternate loading Price with loading Product, which you specify as the parameter of the ALT keyword. The PERRCD(1) keyword on the definition of array Product specifies that each **CTDATA record contains only one element for this array. Because these are alternating compile-time arrays, each record contains two entries per line, or one per array. So when you specify array data at the bottom of the source, you must make sure to allocate enough space. In other words, because the Product array's size is 10 characters and Price's size is five digits, you must pad the items with blanks and the prices leading zeros. Below, you see the output if the program writes each iteration of TempDS as it is created.

```
ITEM is --> BANANA      PRICE --> 00035
ITEM is --> APPLE       PRICE --> 00089
ITEM is --> LEMON       PRICE --> 00123
ITEM is --> TOMATO      PRICE --> 00149
ITEM is --> CUCUMBER    PRICE --> 00073
ITEM is --> ONION       PRICE --> 00053
ITEM is --> PEPPER      PRICE --> 00115
ITEM is --> BREAD       PRICE --> 00149
ITEM is --> GARLIC      PRICE --> 00015
ITEM is --> EGGS        PRICE --> 00125
```

The alternating format capability available with the ALT keyword lets you load the two arrays to produce output that combines the two arrays' information. The result is a list of each item with its price.

PRE-RUNTIME ARRAYS

If you know at compile time what data you want stored in arrays, compile-time arrays are all you need. However, you don't always know in advance what values will be available. Sometimes, array data is available only during runtime, so runtime arrays are required. Between these two situations lies the circumstance in which data is available at runtime but resides in a disk file. This situation calls for pre-runtime arrays.

A pre-runtime array lets you load an array with data from a disk file before the program executes and then write the data back to a disk file after the program terminates. For example, an order entry program checks for products that are out of stock before producing an invoice. The application can include a file that contains all products that are out of stock. The order entry program loads this file as a pre-runtime array and uses it to check for out-of-stock items. The program updates the array if the daily orders produce new out-of-stock products. At the end of the program, the array is automatically written out to disk. Then a stock ordering and receiving application can use the data.

You define a pre-runtime array by entering the array name, the element length, the data type, and the array's dimension (DIM keyword). To signal the compiler that the array is a pre-runtime array and to identify the file(s) from and to which you want to load array data, you specify the FROMFILE (and optionally, the TOFILE) keyword.

The FROMFILE Keyword

The FROMFILE keyword lets you specify the disk (data) file from which you want to load the data for the array you are defining. The loading occurs before the program executes. In parentheses immediately following FROMFILE, you specify the name of the file that contains the data. Here is an example of how to load an array from a disk file.

```
*...1....+....2....+....3....+....4....+....5....+....6....+....7....+
FBackOrdrsIT    F   8Ø          DISK

*...1....+....2....+....3....+....4....+....5....+....6....+....7....+
DB_O_Prts          S              5A   DIM(5ØØ) FROMFILE(BackOrdrs)
D                                       PERRCD(1Ø)
```

The FROMFILE keyword tells the compiler that array B_O_Prts is a pre-runtime array that will get its elements from disk file BackOrdrs. The array's dimension is 500. The PERRCD keyword specifies that 10 array elements will be on each database record. The BackOrdrs disk file is defined with an I in position 17 of the F-spec to define this file as input capable. To specify that the disk file data is a table/array file, a T is in position 18 (file designation). The F in column 22 defines the file as fixed format with a length of 80 characters. The data in the disk file contains the records shown below.

```
....5....Ø....5....Ø....5....Ø....5....Ø....5....Ø....5....Ø....5....Ø....5....Ø

AØØ10AØØ11B7827N2837B7373C2312J7273F23Ø8V7361X4Ø15
A1234A5678A5543A5785A5567A8675A2234A1122A7657A9987
B7666B7785B5573B7884B8567B9988B3456B6533B7276B5544
CØ987C9876C8765C7654C6543C5432C4321C1223C5577C4456
D3462D7755D9532D8689D3357D3764D3356D8765
```

The content of the disk file is important to understanding how FROMFILE works and how the pre-runtime array is loaded. The rules for storing this information are the same as for array data stored in a source file for a compile-time array. Any type of data can be on each record. You can have fewer entries (overall) than defined on the array; entries that don't get a value from the file will be set to their default values. Note that each record except the last one contains 50 characters of data. The additional 30 characters (80 minus 50) in each record can contain any data you want. The RPG source code specifies that each record has 10 entries with 5 bytes for each entry, which is how you get the 50-character data length for each record. The last record contains only the number of entries necessary to fill out the number of backordered products. All remaining array entries will be set to blanks in this example, because the array is defined as character. If you define the array as numeric (binary, zoned decimal, or packed), the remaining entries will be set to zero. The table below shows the data from this example.

Element Number	Value	Element Number	Value	Element Number	Value	Element Number	Value	Element Number	Value
1	A0010	2	A0011	3	B7827	4	N2837	5	B7373
6	C2312	7	J7273	8	F2308	9	V7361	10	X4015
11	A1234	12	A5678	13	A5543	14	A5785	15	A5567
16	A8675	17	A2234	18	A1122	19	A7657	20	A9987
21	B7666	22	B7785	23	B5573	24	B7884	25	B8567
26	B9988	27	B3456	28	B6533	29	B7276	30	B5544
31	C0987	32	C9876	33	C8765	34	C7654	35	C6543
36	C5432	37	C4321	38	C1223	39	C5577	40	C4456
41	D3462	42	D7755	43	D9532	44	D8689	45	D3357
46	D3764	47	D3356	48	D8765	49	*blank	50	*blank
...	...	...	...	...	...	...	...	...	...
496	*blank	497	*blank	498	*blank	499	*blank	500	*blank

The TOFILE Keyword

The TOFILE keyword lets you specify the disk (data) file to which you want to write the array's data after the program terminates. In parentheses immediately following TOFILE, you specify the name of the file you want to write the data to. Here's an example of how to code TOFILE.

```
*...1....+....2....+....3....+....4....+....5....+....6....+....7....+
FBackOrdrs IT   F   80        DISK
FNew_BOs   O    F   80        DISK
```

```
*...1....+....2....+....3....+....4....+....5....+....6....+....7....+
DB_O_Prts            S              5A   DIM(10) FROMFILE(BackOrdrs)
D                                        PERRCD(10) TOFILE(New_BOs)
```

Line 1 defines disk file BackOrdrs, the file from which to get the array's contents. The I in position 17 defines BackOrdrs as input only. Line 2 defines disk file New_BOs. At termination time, the program will write the array B_O_Prts out to the disk file New_BOs. The O in position 17 defines file New_BOs as output only.

A C in position 17 of the F-spec where you define the disk file for this array's data means the file from which you are loading the array is a combined file. In this case, the *file-name* parameter for the FROMFILE and TOFILE keywords must be the same. The system reads the file that contains the data for the array before the program is executed. The program can then manipulate the data in the array during the execution. Then, at the close of the program, the system writes the data back out to the same data file. The example below shows this use of FROMFILE and TOFILE.

```
*...1....+....2....+....3....+....4....+....5....+....6....+....7....+
FBackOrdrs CT   F   80        DISK
```

```
*...1....+....2....+....3....+....4....+....5....+....6....+....7....+
DB_O_Prts            S              5A   DIM(500) FROMFILE(BackOrdrs)
D                                        PERRCD(10) TOFILE(BackOrdrs)
```

Pre-Runtime Arrays by Example

Pre-runtime arrays are useful when you have a repeating group of information that can change over time but has a finite number of entries and is a relatively simple set. Pre-runtime arrays let programs use a caching technique: The data is loaded into the program once and then accessed in the array, rather than from disk, each time an entry is needed. A program can just as easily read the file each time it needs information, but by loading the data into the program at the start, you can save the overhead involved with a read to the database for each access to a record.

Using pre-runtime arrays with the ALT keyword can give you limited access to the array by key. Take, for example, a company with discounts that are always percentage based according to the quantity of a product ordered. If you load a pair of pre-runtime arrays using the ALT keyword, you can keep the discount schedule in a data file where other programs can access it. But when the program runs, the data is loaded into the pair of arrays immediately to increase the speed of accessing the data at runtime.

```
....5....Ø....5....Ø....5
ØØ1ØØØØ2ØØ
ØØ5ØØØØ5ØØ
Ø1ØØØØ1ØØØ
Ø5ØØØØ2ØØØ
```

Here are the current contents of a file that contains the discount threshold quantity and the discount percentage. This data represents a 2 percent discount for quantities of 100 or more, 5 percent for 500 or more, 10 percent for 1000 or more, and 20 percent for 5000 or more. If you can allow a finite number of discount thresholds, you can load this data into a pre-runtime array and have it handle all discount calculations. Naturally, you need a procedure to prevent modification of the discount schedule in the file while the program using the discount table is executing. The code below loads this discount table into a pair of arrays.

```
*...1....+....2....+....3....+....4....+....5....+....6....+....7....+....8
FDiscSched IT   F   1Ø         DISK

*...1....+....2....+....3....+....4....+....5....+....6....+....7....+....8
DDscLevel          S             5  Ø DIM(5Ø) PERRCD(1) FROMFILE(DiscSched)
DDscPct            S             5  4 DIM(5Ø) ALT(DscLevel)
```

The F-spec identifies file DiscSched as an input-capable file that will be opened and loaded into an array. The T means the program will load an array with this file's contents. The F specifies that the file has a fixed-length record. The 10 determines each record's length. DISK means that this is a data file on the system's disks.

Once you declare the file, you can describe the arrays to load with the file's data. The first D-spec defines the array DscLevel, which will contain a list of the quantities necessary to trigger a given discount. Each element is five digits long with zero decimal positions. The DIM keyword specifies 50 elements. PERRCD determines that only one entry is on each record in the data file. The FROMFILE keyword specifies that the array will be loaded when the program is called but before it starts running, and identifies the file (from the F-spec) from which to load the data.

The next D-spec defines the DscPct array. Each of its elements is five digits long with four decimal positions. Like the DscLevel array, DscPct has the number of elements specified on the DIM keyword. The ALT (DscLevel) keyword specifies that this array is in the same file as the DscLevel array and that each record in that file contains an element of the DscLevel array, followed by an element of the DscPct array.

The program can now find the appropriate discount level in the DscLevel array. Once the program knows the index of the DscLevel array entry, the program can access the same entry in the DscPct array to get the corresponding discount percentage (or rate).

RUNTIME ARRAYS

If you have ever used arrays in a language other than RPG, you already know what runtime arrays are. As the name implies, runtime arrays are loaded during program execution. Your program can initialize them, manipulate the data in them, and perform operations on them.

To recognize a runtime array in an RPG IV program, examine the array's D-specs. From the discussions of compile-time and pre-runtime arrays, you can infer that runtime arrays cannot include the CTDATA, PERRCD, FROMFILE, TOFILE, EXTFMT, or ALT keyword because these are specific to other types of arrays. You can recognize runtime arrays by the lack of these keywords in the D-specs. The D-specs will look like the specs below.

```
*...1....+....2....+....3....+....4....+....5....+....6....+....7....+
D RunArry        S             5A   DIM(10)
```

Here, as with all array definitions, the runtime array name is in positions 7 through 21, and an S is in position 24. The length is in positions 33 through 39, and the data type is in position 40. The DIM keyword specifies how many elements are in the array.

Runtime Array Values

Runtime arrays get the value of their elements from a program while it runs. The values in these arrays will change frequently during program execution. If the values are static during program execution, a compile-time or pre-runtime array is easier to use than a runtime array.

Like the value of other standalone fields in a program, the initial value of an array's elements is zero for numeric arrays and blanks for character arrays. During execution, a program can set an array element's value in several ways. For example, the INZ keyword can specify an initial value for the elements, but INZ is necessary only to initialize to a value other than the default.

Or you can load an array or array element by coding it directly on a file's I-specs, if the file is program described. When loading an array, if the implied length is a multiple of the array element's length, you can specify *from* and *to* positions to determine where the array data starts and ends. Then, you specify the name of the array as the field name. This approach will load the same number of array elements as the length of the data you define in the *from* and *to* positions. In addition, on an I-spec, you can specify one element of an array by coding the array name and an index for the field name in parentheses. The index can be a zero decimal-position, numeric field, or it can be a numeric integer literal. Note that because both these techniques require program-described files, they are no longer used much.

More conventional methods of assigning an array element's value involve operation codes in C-specs. You can use array elements in C-specs anywhere you can specify a non-array variable. When addressing one element of an array, operation codes perform the same functions as with non-array fields. You can usually assign one element as either factor of an operation and/or as a Result field. When addressing one entire array, most operation codes perform the operation once for each array element. In this type of array operation, the Result field must specify an array. If an operation is working with two arrays (in Factor 1 or Factor 2 and the Result field) or more (in Factor 1 *and* Factor 2 and the Result field), the operation will occur for the ordinally corresponding entries among the arrays. If the arrays do not have the same number of elements, the operation occurs as many times as there are elements in the shorter array.

If you do not specify a specific element and the operation will occur once for each array element, the following operations can use an array: ADD, ADDDUR, CHECK, CHECKR, DIV, EVAL, EXTRCT, MOVE, MOVEL, MHHZO, MHLZP, MLLZO, MULT, SCAN, SQRT, SUB, SUBDUR, Z-ADD, and Z-SUB. With CHECK, CHECKR, and SCAN, you can specify an array only in the Result field, and the operation will repeat no more times than the number of elements in the array. The operation does not necessarily repeat once for each element, so it can record the positions of up to that many hits.

Operations that can use an element of an array, but cannot use an array as a whole, are BITOFF, BITON, CABxx, CAT, COMP, DO, DOU, DOUxx, DOW, DOWxx, IF, IFxx, MVR, SUBST, TESTB, TESTN, TESTZ, WHEN, and WHENxx. The operations that can reference an entire array, but will act on the entire array rather than repeating the operation for each element, are CLEAR, DEBUG, DEFINE, LOOKUP, PARM, RESET, SORTA, and XFOOT.

Runtime Arrays by Example

Let's expand on the example started earlier in this chapter: using arrays to record monthly totals. Two tasks will show how operation codes with arrays can perform a lot of work with very little code. The two tasks, initializing totals and calculating a standardized commission for each month, are shown on the following page.

```
*...1....+....2....+....3....+....4....+....5....+....6....+....7....+
 * Arrays for monthly totals by department and company
D DpSls           S              11P 2 DIM(12)
D DpCom           S              11P 2 DIM(12)
D CoSls           S              11P 2 DIM(12)
D CoCom           S              11P 2 DIM(12)
 * Arrays to hold standardized commissions calculated
D DpStCom         S              11P 2 DIM(12)
D CoStCom         S              11P 2 DIM(12)
 * Arrays to hold variance between standard and actual commissions
D DpComVar        S              11P 2 DIM(12)
D CoComVar        S              11P 2 DIM(12)
 * Field to hold standardized commission rates for the year
D DpStComRt       S               5P 4
D CoStComRt       S               5P 4


*...1....+....2....+....3....+....4....+....5....+....6....+....7....+
 * Processing for start of new company:
 *   - Clear the company total arrays
 *   - Load the company "standard" commissions rates (not shown in code)
C                 Z-ADD     *ZEROS         CoSls
C                 Z-ADD     *ZEROS         CoCom
   ... other processing
 *
 * Processing for start of new department:
 *   - Clear the department total arrays
 *   - Load the department "standard" commissions rates (not shown in
 *     code)
C                 Z-ADD     *ZEROS         DpSls
C                 Z-ADD     *ZEROS         DpCom
   ... other processing
 *
 * Detail processing:
 *   For each transaction, accumulate the sales and commissions
 *   to the department totals and the company totals
 *   for the month of the transaction.
 *
C                 ADD       TxnSls         DpSls(TxnMo)
C                 ADD       TxnCom         DpCom(TxnMo)
C                 ADD       TxnSls         CoSls(TxnMo)
C                 ADD       TxnCom         CoCom(TxnMo)
   ... other processing
```

CONTINUED

```
*...1....+....2....+....3....+....4....+....5....+....6....+....7....+
*
* Processing for end of department:
*   - Calculate standardized commissions using Department's
*       monthly standard rates
*   - Calculate variance of actual to standard commissions
C     DpSls        MULT (H)  DpStComRt    DpStCom
C     DpCom        SUB       DpStCom      DpComVar
*
* Processing for end of company:
*   - Calculate standardized commissions using company's
*       monthly standard rates
*   - Calculate variance of actual to standard commissions
C     CoSls        MULT (H)  CoStComRt    CoStCom
C     CoCom        SUB       CoStCom      CoComVar
  ... other processing
```

First, this program adds code to the previous example at both the company and department levels to clear out the respective total arrays. (You can accomplish this zeroing faster with the MOVEA operation, but this example will focus on operations that affect multiple elements individually.)

Second, the program must calculate a standardized commission to compare with actual commissions to determine whether commission expense projections are accurate. The standardized commission rate is one value (generated and stored elsewhere in the system) for each company and department. Each department and company uses a single value for every month in a particular year. After calculating the standard commission, the program can calculate the variance of the commissions for each month.

The program uses arrays and operation codes to do a lot of work with a little code. The arrays DpSls, DpCom, CoSls, and CoCom are all from the original example about arrays, and this example adds several arrays. To hold the commissions calculated using standardized or averaged commission rates, this example introduces DpStCom and CoStCom. These arrays hold the commissions calculated on total sales, which will later be compared to the actual commissions. Next, arrays DpComVar and CoComVar will hold the difference between the actual and the standardized commissions to identify the variance between actual and planned (budgeted). Finally, two fields, DpStComRt and CoStComRt, hold the year's standardized commission rate for each department and company. The program will use the rates in these fields to calculate the standardized commissions.

The first new process in this variation of the example is in two parts that perform similar functions. When you get to a new department or company, while the program is reading the records from the database file, you have to clear the total fields for the new department or company. The Z-ADD operation can set each element of the arrays to zero. Notice that this example uses one value in Factor 2 of Z-ADD and an array without a subscript in the Result field. Because 12 elements are in the array for each operation, the Z-ADD will occur 12 times: once for each element in the array that is specified in the Result field. Z-ADDing a value (in this case the figurative constant *Zeros) to an array *without* specifying a particular element through subscription causes that Z-ADD to occur separately for each element of the array. (Many operations that are valid for arrays behave this way.)

At each department and company break, you load the standardized commission rates for the department or company. The example does not include the code for this task, but you load the commission rates from a database file and place them into the arrays DpStComRt and CoStComRt.

Next you see the original code that accumulates the transaction's sales and commission figures in the department- and company-level arrays. Again, because a subscript for the array is in the Result field, the operation occurs for only one element.

Finally, you come to the processing for the end of each department or company. Here, for both the department and the company break, you see the MULT and SUB operations. For both operations, the example uses arrays without subscripts for both Factor 1 and the Result field. The MULT operations have one field in Factor 2, and the SUB operations have an array without a subscript.

Because the arrays are not subscripted and the field is one value, the MULTs will multiply each array element in Factor 1 by the commission rate in Factor 2 (the single value) and then store the result in the corresponding element of the array in the Result field. Because the array has 12 elements, one for each month, the January sales will result in a January commission, February sales in a February commission, and so on. Each calculation will use the single commission rate.

The SUBs work differently because the arrays are not subscripted in all three parts of the operation. The SUBs will subtract the first element of the standardized commission array from the first element of the actual commission array and will put the result in the first element of the commission variance array. This process will repeat with the second element of each array, then the third element, and so on, until the calculation occurs 12 times.

This example demonstrates how to reduce dozens of code lines to very few instructions, thanks to RPG IV standard operations with arrays. You don't have to learn new operation codes for handling arrays.

ARRAY OPERATION CODES

RPG IV supports four operation codes for use specifically with arrays: SORTA (Sort Array), LOOKUP, XFOOT (total the elements of an array), and MOVEA (Move Array). All these operation codes are valid on all array types (compile time, pre-runtime, and runtime).

The array opcodes can reduce program complexity and even size. For example, SORTA lets you sort array elements. Of course, to sort a program array, you can code one of many sorting algorithms, such as a bubble sort or selection sort. However, the complexity of the application will increase with more code. If you can do the job with just one operation code, you're better off.

The SORTA Operation Code

The SORTA (Sort Array) operation code lets you sort an array into ascending or descending sequence by means of the keyword ASCEND or DESCEND, which you specify in positions 44 through 80 of the D-spec that defines the array you want to sort. The default, if you don't specify one of these keywords, is ascending sequence.

You specify SORTA in the C-specs as an opcode in positions 26 through 35. Factor 2 contains the name of the array whose contents you want to sort. The table below summarizes the entries for SORTA.

Factor 1	Opcode	(Extender)	Factor 2	Result	Indicators
Not allowed	SORTA		Required array name	Not allowed	Not allowed

The ASCEND Keyword

The ASCEND keyword has two purposes. The first is checking whether compile-time and pre-runtime arrays load in the correct order. This function dates back to when programs and their tables were all punched in cards. To ensure that the table cards were in the correct order, the ASCEND keyword caused the compiler (in the case of compile-time arrays) or the system (in the case of pre-runtime arrays) to check the order of the table or array as it was loaded. Because you now seldom have to worry about SEU shuffling your array records or a disk file losing its place, this use of the ASCEND keyword is outdated. It's important to know how it functions, however, because if you specify ASCEND on an array that is *not* in ascending sequence, you will get a compiler or system error.

Obsolete as this use of ASCEND is, it can verify source for compile-time arrays. For pre-runtime arrays, the error trapping involved is much more complex than it is worth. You're better off making the application that is responsible for maintaining the pre-runtime array's data verify sort order.

The modern use of ASCEND is to define the sequence for sorting an array using the SORTA operation code. When you specify ASCEND on a runtime array, that function is the only purpose ASCEND will serve. Only on a compile-time or pre-runtime array does ASCEND cause sequence checking.

The DESCEND Keyword

The DESCEND keyword checks for a descending sequence on compile-time and pre-runtime arrays. In addition, DESCEND lets you define a runtime array's sorting sequence as descending.

SORTA by Example

You can handle most data ordering by building logical files over physical files. Occasionally, you need some data in a particular order, but a logical file cannot access the data in that order. Or you sometimes prefer not to incur the overhead of a logical file. In such cases, sorted arrays are the answer.

Consider an analysis report of customers. The marketing division needs a list of all customers and their annual sales reported by year, in descending order of total sales for the last 10 years. For each customer, you need to read through all the invoices, accumulating total sales for the year. Once you calculate each year's total sales, you can store the total and the year in an array. When the array is complete for all customers, you can sort and print it to provide the list the marketing department wants.

Let's look at the code to build and then sort the array, focusing on loading the data into each element of the array, sorting the array, and then extracting the information from each element of the array. The code on pages 241–243 shows how to load, sort, and then preprocess the array CustYrTot to print the data. First is the definition of the array and the fields. Note that the array is 13 digits long, long enough to hold the total sales, a 9.2 field, and the four-digit year for each customer's sales years.

The next three fields, YearSales, SlsYear, and Cur, are important when you're ready to print the array. The program prepares to print each element by dividing an element into its constituent parts: YearSales will hold the sales for the year being printed, SlsYear will hold the year being printed, and Cur will point to the array element currently being processed for printing. All this happens each time the program finishes totaling a customer's invoices.

The program uses three fields during the processing of arrays, as you prepare to place the data in the array for later printing. TotSales is the field that accumulates invoice totals for a given sales year. Year is the year when an invoice was issued. Finally, YrElem holds the index pointing to the element of CustYrTot in which the customer's totals for a given year will be recorded.

The example includes only code related to the creation, sorting, and use of the array. All other steps are pseudocoded.

```
*...1....+....2....+....3....+....4....+....5....+....6....+....7....+....8
D CustYrTot      S            13P 0 DIM(10) DESCEND
D YearSales      S             9P 2
D SlsYear        S             4P 0
D Cur            S             3P 0
D TotSales       S             9P 2
D Year           S             4P 0
D YrElem         S             2P 0
```

```
*...1....+....2....+....3....+....4....+....5....+....6....+....7....+....8
 *
 * Read next customer record, checking for change in customer
 *
 ...
 *
 * For change in customer (including when EOF hit) do for previous customer:
 *  - Sort the sales/year array in descending order
 *  - Print last 10 years of customer's annual sales totals
 *  - clear the CustYrTot array and the TotSales field
 *
 * Sort the sales/year array in descending order
 *
C                 SORTA     CustYrTot
 *
 * Print last 10 years of customer's annual sales totals
 *
C                 DO        10            Cur
 * get sales
C                 IF        CustYrTot(Cur)<>0
C                 EVAL      YearSales=CustYrTot(Cur)/1000000
 * get year
C                 IF        CustYrTot(Cur)=0
C                 EVAL      SlsYear=CustYrTot(Cur)-YearSales*1000000
C                 ELSE
C                 EVAL      SlsYear=(CustYrTot(Cur)-YearSales*1000000)-1
C                 ENDIF
 *
 ... print the current year and sales
 *
C                 ENDIF
C                 ENDDO
 *
```

Continued

```
*...1....+....2....+....3....+....4....+....5....+....6....+....7....+....8
 * Clear the year total array
 *
C                   Z-ADD     *Zeros        CustYrTot
 *
 * For each customer, read through the invoices in date order checking for
 *   change in invoice year and selecting only invoices in last 10 years
 *
 ...
 *
 * If the invoice year changes (including when EOF hit), do for previous yr:
 *   - find the first unused element in the array
 *   - record total for year in the found slot
 *   - clear the total field
 *   - extract the new invoice year into year
 *
 ... find unused element and place element number in variable YrElem
 *
 * Record total for year and the year value in the found slot
 *
C                   EVAL      CustYrTot(YrElem)=(TotSales*1000000)
C                   IF        TotSales=0
C                   EVAL      CustYrTot(YrElem)=CustYrTot(YrElem)+Year
C                   ELSE
C                   EVAL      CustYrTot(YrElem)=CustYrTot(YrElem)-Year
C                   ENDIF
 *
 * Clear the total field
 *
C                   Z-ADD     *Zeros        TotSales
 *
 * Extract the new invoice year into year
 *
 ... extract the new invoice year into year
 *
 * For each invoice,
 *   - accumulate the invoice total for the year in TotSales
 *
 ... accumulate the invoice total for the year in TotSales
 *
```

Continued

```
*...1....+....2....+....3....+....4....+....5....+....6....+....7....+....8
 * Loop to read next invoice
 *
   ... loop for invoice
 *
 * Loop to read next customer
 *
   ... loop for customer
```

The first section of code is executed when you change customers. At this point, you have finished loading data from a previous customer's invoices. The CustYrTot array now has as many of its elements loaded as the customer had years of sales in the last 10 years. A customer who has been active for only three years will have data in only three elements. SORTA on CustYrTot will produce the Sales and Years in descending order by the total sales for each year, and the year associated with each sales volume. The table below shows what is loaded into each array and how sorting provides the data as the user wants it.

Year	Sales	Array Entry	Sorted Array	Sorted Sales	Sorted Year
1995	14,310.24	14310241995	18684071994	18,684.07	1994
1994	18,684.07	18684071994	17984251990	17,984.25	1990
1993	16,309.85	16309851993	16309851993	16,309.85	1993
1992	10,644.17	10644171992	14310241995	14,310.24	1995
1991	10,699.97	10699971991	14078231988	14,078.23	1988
1990	17,984.25	17984251990	10699971991	10,699.97	1991
1989	9,949.96	9949961989	10644171992	10,644.17	1992
1988	14,078.23	14078231988	9949961989	9,949.96	1989
1987	–622.00	–622001987	0	0	0
0	0	0	–622001987	–622.00	1987

As the program encounters each year's sales, the total sales figure is concatenated to the year. Then, by sorting this concatenated value, the program puts both the sales and their associated years in the correct order, descending, as specified on the CustYrTot array's definition.

The next section of code, which is responsible for dividing the sorted array's value back into Sales and Year values, produces the printout of a customer's sorted sales years for the last ten years. A loop reads through the 10 elements of the array and processes those elements that have a non-zero value. Any year that had sales, even if they netted zero through returns, will be a non-zero element because the year will be non-zero.

Notice that the ninth element in the sorted array has a zero entry. Stopping at the first zero entry is not an option because that will prevent you from handling the unique situation of having total sales that are negative for a year. For each non-zero element, you first extract the sales by dividing by 1,000,000, which moves the decimal point six places to the left: four for the year and two for the number of decimal places in the sales figure. Once you extract the sales, you can use the value to extract the year.

The next two EVAL statements handle both negative and positive total sales. The CustYrTot array carries the sign of the total sales for each year. By subtracting the year's total sales after multiplying them by 1,000,000, you get the year, but it can have a negative sign. Therefore, you condition the extraction to multiply by –1 if the year will be negative. You can see the effect in the last array element in the sorted columns above. The sorted array value in 1987 is a negative number (possibly because of special incentives to a first-year customer), so the sorted sales number is negative, but the sorted year is a positive number.

The program prints the array. Then a Z-ADD clears the array, to zero all array elements in preparation for the next customer.

The next section of code is inside a loop that reads the invoices for a given customer. Within that loop, each time the year of the invoices being read changes, you record the total sales for the previous year (the one you just finished reading) in the CustYrTot array. Here, you can see the construction of the array element. Remember that because each element is one value, you have to construct a value that will retain the two pieces of data you need to complete the task: the total sales for a year and the year of the sales. By multiplying the sales by 1,000,000, you shift the decimal place six positions to the right, adjusting for the two decimal positions of the TotSales field and leaving four digits to insert the four-digit year.

Once the sales are in the array element, you need to either add or subtract the year. If the sales are positive, you add the year to the value in the array element. But if the sales are negative, you need to subtract the year. Adding the year when the sales are negative corrupts both the year and the sales figure. Last, after you construct the array element, you clear the TotSales field in preparation for accumulating the next year's sales for the customer.

The LOOKUP Operation Code

In addition to sorting elements, you often need to search array elements for a given value. RPG provides the LOOKUP operation code for this purpose. With an array, LOOKUP, which works with both arrays and tables, compares the value you specify in Factor 1 to the values in the elements of the array you specify in Factor 2. The purpose of the comparison is to find an exact, next-higher, or next-lower match of Factor 1 in one of the elements of the array in Factor 2. That is, the operation uses the value you specify in Factor 1 to search the Factor 2 array. With tables, LOOKUP's function is to activate a particular table element. The section of this chapter that explains tables will cover this use of LOOKUP.

You specify LOOKUP in the C-specs in positions 26 through 35. You supply the search value in Factor 1 and the array name in Factor 2. The table below summarizes the entries for LOOKUP.

Factor 1	Opcode Extender	Factor 2	Result	Indicators		
				High	Low	Equal
Required *search argument*	LOOKUP	Required *array/table name*	Optional *(table name)*	High	Low	Equal

You can specify the starting element for a search by supplying an index with an array name in Factor 2. If the search is successful, the index will be set to the found location. If you use a variable and the search is unsuccessful, the index will be set to 1. If you use a literal or name constant, the index cannot, of course, be changed.

You can check whether a search is successful by examining the resulting indicator, which is set on only if a search is successful. The resulting indicator(s) you specify can determine the type of search to perform. For example, the HI indicator finds an element with a value greater than but not equal to the search value. The table below summarizes the relationship between resulting indicators and the search type.

High	Low	Equal	Search Type
X			Find any element that contains a value greater than but not equal to the value in the search value.
X		X	Find any element that contains a value greater than or equal to the value in the search value.
	X		Find any element that contains a value less than but not equal to the value in the search value.
	X	X	Find any element that contains a value less than or equal to the value in the search value.
		X	Find any element that contains a value equal to the value in the search value.

LOOKUP by Example

If you specify the D-spec keyword ASCEND or DESCEND to sort the contents of an array in ascending or descending order and you want only equal matches, you can use HI for an ascending array and LO for a descending array to ensure a halt of the search once you reach the equal search key value. If you use this technique, be sure the array definition has the ASCEND or DESCEND keyword specified. Otherwise, unpredictable or undesirable results can occur during program execution.

To show how this technique can speed your searches, consider an application that schedules the current day's orders for fulfillment the next morning. Some products can be backordered. You can accelerate the process by loading a list of backordered products into an array and searching the array each time an order item is considered, rather than querying the database.

This example shown below shows how a little extra work can improve performance. The definition of the BkOrdItem array specifies that it is a descending array. Up to 1000 items can be backordered, but you will rarely have that many. Because you hope that the number of backordered items is ordinarily small, you have to assume a lot of blank entries will usually be in the array. By sorting it in descending order, you push all the backordered items to the front of the array when you execute the SORTA operation. The loop that loads the data (code not shown) can load items in any order, and the SORTA operation puts the array in

```
*...1....+....2....+....3....+....4....+....5....+....6....+....7....+.
D BkOrdItem       S              7A   DIM(1000) DESCEND

*...1....+....2....+....3....+....4....+....5....+....6....+....7....+.
 *
 * Loop to load BkOrdItem array from database by
 *   finding all backordered items
 *
   ... Load BkOrdItem array
 *
 * Sort the BkOrdItem array after fully loaded with backordered items
C                 SORTA     BkOrdItem
 *
   ... other processing
 *
 * Order item processing:
 *   Check whether the order item is backordered.
 *
C     OrItmId     LOOKUP    BkOrdItem                         9190
C                 IF        *IN90
 *
   ... processing of items backordered
 *
C                 ELSE
 *
   ... processing of items not backordered
 *
C                 ENDIF
   ... other processing
```

the proper order (remember that the system checks order when loading the array only for compile-time and pre-runtime arrays).

The LOOKUP operation uses a low/equal search, which you specify by putting an indicator in both the low and equal positions for resulting indicators. (Note: The OrItmId field in the LOOKUP comes from the database, so its definition is not on the D-specs.) Because you are interested only in equal results (backordered items), you need a different indicator for low and equal. Indicator 90 will tell whether an item ID is found in the backordered item array. Indicator 91's purpose is solely to stop the search as soon as possible, and the array element's value when this indicator turns on is irrelevant. The indicator stops the LOOKUP operation and tells you that the item is not in the array. Using indicator 90 for both tests will produce false results, as both equal and low hits will turn on the same indicator.

To understand the performance advantage of defining the array as descending and then doing a low/equal LOOKUP, consider the data in the table below. Suppose you have five items backordered. After you load the array and sort it, the data is as shown in the table.

Element	ID
1	96B450
2	96A225
3	95B500
4	95A250
5	95A100
6 - 1000	blanks

You will always get a quick response if you look up any one of the five backordered item IDs, whether you use the low indicator or not. Because the data you are searching for is in one of the first five elements, the search will never look through more than five entries (actually, it never looks past the element that contains the desired entry). But consider what happens if you look for an item that is *not* in the array. In fact, this is the most prevalent case — if the assumption is true that you ordinarily have few backordered items. Without the low indicator, an equal lookup using an ID for an item not in the array looks through all 1000 entries for an equal-valued entry before quitting and reporting no match. Naturally, this approach is wasteful and slow because only five elements require examination.

To eliminate the wasted checks, the LOOKUP specifies that the search also needs to stop if you find an element that is lower than the value you want. Because the sixth element (and all later elements) in the sample data is blank, it will always be lower than any item ID you can use in the LOOKUP. By stopping the LOOKUP's search if a lower value is found, you guarantee that the comparisons will never proceed past the sixth element in this set of data. For instance, the search for item ID 95A900 will stop after comparison to the fourth element because the fourth element is lower than the ID in the LOOKUP. Indicator 91 will be turned on, and 90 off. A LOOKUP using an item ID of 93A100 will stop after comparison of the sixth element because blanks are lower than the ID. Again, 91 will be on, and 90 will be off.

Without the test for lower values to stop the search, both these examples result in a complete search of all 1000 array elements. Consider the implications if you have to allow for even more backordered items, which is a worst-case scenario for a company with a *lot* of products. In that case, 2000, 3000, or even 5000 entries can be necessary. But for practical purposes, any given run will probably use fewer than 50 or 100 elements. The savings in limiting the LOOKUP scope are obvious.

The XFOOT Operation Code

The XFOOT (Cross foot elements of an array) operation code lets you sum the content of all elements of an array. Factor 2 must contain the name of the array whose elements you want to sum. The Result field contains the total of the summing. Resulting indicators can let you check whether the sum from the XFOOT operation is positive, negative, or zero. The table below summarizes the entries for XFOOT.

Factor 1	Opcode	Extender	Factor 2	Result	Indicators		
					plus	minus	zero
Not allowed	XFOOT		Required array name	Required sum	plus	minus	zero

The code below is an example of how to specify the XFOOT operation.

```
*...1....+....2....+....3....+....4....+....5....+....6....+....7....+
D MnthTot         S              5  0 DIM(12)
D YearTot         S              7  0 INZ(0)
D ...

*...1....+....2....+....3....+....4....+....5....+....6....+....7....+
* Sum the packed-numeric array and store the total into the result
* field YearTot
C                   XFOOT     MnthTot       YearTot
```

One method you can use with XFOOT is to keep one extra element in class numeric arrays so that you can maintain an array total in the last element. This approach keeps the total with the array so that you don't have to remember which field contains the total for which array. A drawback is that before you do an XFOOT on the entire array, you must zero out that last array element. If you don't, the value of this total element will be in the sum.

```
*...1....+....2....+....3....+....4....+....5....+....6....+....7....+
D MnthTot          S              5  0 DIM(13)
D* ...


*...1....+....2....+....3....+....4....+....5....+....6....+....7....+
C* Sum the packed-numeric array and store the total in the last
C* element of array MnthTot
C                   Z-ADD     0            MnthTot(13)
C                   XFOOT     MnthTot      MnthTot(13)
```

The code above shows this technique. This example adds one element to the array MnthTot so that you can store the total in the last element of the array instead of in a separate field. The Z-ADD operation zeros out element 13 of MnthTot so XFOOT will calculate the correct sum. The XFOOT places the total in the sum element, as indicated by the index value in the array reference in the Result field; both Factor 2 and the Result field contain the same array name. To show which element will receive the result, Factor 2 is not indexed, but the Result field is. Just remember to zero your sum element before executing XFOOT.

The MOVEA Operation Code

The MOVEA (Move Array) operation code copies values into or out of one or more contiguous array elements. MOVEA works with numeric, character, and graphic class data, but only if both the source and target of the move are the same data class.

You specify MOVEA in the opcode positions (26 through 35) of the C-specs. Factor 1 is not allowed. Factor 2 can be a literal, a constant, a figurative constant, a field, an entire array (no subscript), or an array element (subscript provided).

The Result field can be a field, an entire array, or an array element. Resulting indicators are allowed only when the Result field is a field (not an array). If you specify the indicators with a numeric MOVEA, like most other math operations, MOVEA lets you test for a positive (position 71 to 72), negative (position 73 to 74), or zero (position 75 to 76) result.

Padding via the P operation code extender is allowed with MOVEA. The table below summarizes the entries for MOVEA.

Factor 1	Opcode	Extender	Factor 2	Result	Indicators		
Not allowed	MOVEA	(P)	Required *source*	Required *target*	plus	minus	zero

MOVEA supports three actions: moving one or more contiguous array elements into a single field, moving one field into one or more contiguous array elements, and moving one or more contiguous elements of one array into one or more contiguous elements of another array. You can access all or part of an array by specifying where you want to start your reference. Then the operation includes the entire remainder of the array. When referencing an array with MOVEA, you will always reference everything from the starting point you specify to the end of the array. Depending on the size of the Result field/array, you might not use the entire remainder array, but you will have it available. The simplest way to think of MOVEA is as a MOVEL (Move Left) that lets you use one or more contiguous array elements as a single field. MOVEA accesses these contiguous array elements by ignoring element boundaries after the starting point is established.

Some examples of how MOVEA accesses the contents of an array can illustrate how it works. Consider a 10-element array, ARR, where each element uses 5 bytes of storage. (The array's data type is irrelevant for this part of the discussion.) An index value of 1 references the entire array. If you reference an array without a subscript, you reference the entire array. In this case, because you reference the entire array, you are really referencing a 50-character string.

If you use a subscript to reference an array, you reference only the portion of the array starting at the element the subscript identifies. For example, if you reference ARR(4), because the reference starts at element four, you are referencing only the last seven elements, which gives you access to a 35-character string. In both cases, you reference a portion of the array that starts at a given or implied element in the array and then always includes the entire remainder of the array. Notice, though, that you don't have to use or affect that entire part of the array; you are merely referencing it.

As with a MOVEL operation, you can move the referenced portion of the array to a larger or smaller target. If you move it to a smaller target, only the referenced part needed to fill the target will be used. If you move it to a larger target, the entire referenced portion will be used, but the target will be affected only up to the specified number of characters of the array.

Of course, the referenced array can also be the result. In that case, you can affect only a portion of the array (say, elements 4, 5, and 6) by moving something that uses 15 bytes of storage to the array, starting at element 4.

Numeric Moves with MOVEA

MOVEA can perform numeric and non-numeric moves. Numeric moves are easier to understand because they are the more restrictive of the two.

On numeric MOVEA operations, both the source and target fields and array elements must be the same length. They can have different decimal positions, and they can even use different data types, but they must have the same defined length. For instance, Factor 2 can be 7.2 packed and the Result field 7.4 zoned. As long as the two have the same defined length (in this case, 7), you can use them together in a MOVEA operation. Why can you have different class numeric data types in numeric moves, when different data types take up different amounts of storage? The AS/400 will convert different data types to the same data type (the compiler default of packed decimal), perform the move, and then convert the result back to the correct data type for the Result field.

The reason for this requirement is that MOVEA treats the portion of the array that it is working with as one value and ignores element boundaries. This approach can wreak havoc with numeric moves if the two fields are different lengths. With unequal lengths, the signs of the fields go into the wrong positions of the numeric result, and you get decimal data errors (the nasty errors you get when you accidentally get numerically invalid data in a numeric field). To prevent such results, the compiler enforces the equal length restriction.

If equal field sizes are necessary, MOVEA for numeric operations does little when you have one field in either Factor 2 or the Result field. Because of this restriction, when either part of the MOVEA is not an array in a numeric move, you are better off using MOVE or MOVEL. You can't really use or affect more than one array element at a time because the non-array part of the move must be the same size as the array element. So, the affected portion of the array is always exactly the same size as the non-array participant.

This situation leaves you with only array-to-array moves, the third action you can perform with MOVEA. When you're working with numeric arrays, MOVEA's real benefit comes from the ability to move portions of arrays quickly. Recall that Z-ADDs, MOVEs, and MOVELs will always use either one array element (if you provide a subscript) or each element in the array starting at the first element (if you do not provide a subscript). Even if you want to use every element in both arrays in a move, MOVEA is a faster way to move one array to the other if both arrays' elements have the same length. The other operation codes will do the job, but they result, internally, in as many moves as necessary to move each element of the source array to the corresponding element in the target array. MOVEA, on the other hand, will perform the equivalent operation with one move. Additionally, you can ask MOVEA to start at a specific element. Using a subscript on those other operations means that only the identified element is the source for multiple moves into a target array.

You can specify padding, the (P) operation extender, on numeric array-to-array moves. As a result, any array elements in the target array that do not have corresponding elements in the source array are set to zero.

Numeric MOVEA by Example

MOVEA for numeric arrays can ease some coding burden. Imagine a function that performs rate analysis for a life insurance company. Typically, you calculate the rates for a policy for several years into the future so you can provide payment schedules for the company's policyholders. This company's actuaries have requested a report that shows data in 10-year segments and that starts at intervals of every five years. A 10-year picture helps spot trends for planning the company's profitability, but the actuaries need a fresh look at that picture, starting every five years. The report must always project 30 years into the future, based on the rates established so far.

You can start the process at the current year, calculate 10 years' worth of information (rates, premiums, policy value, commissions, etc.), print that information, and then restart the entire process beginning at the next five-year interval. You will handle the first five years and the last five years once, but you will handle each of the intervening 20 years twice: once for being in the end of a 10-year period and once for being in the beginning of a 10-year period.

A better solution is to process each year only once, as in the code on pages 253 and 254. Arrays let you handle 10 years of premiums, commissions, and so on; print them; move the last five of the 10 years into the first five of the next 10 years; calculate the next five years of data; and then keep repeating this process until you have handled all 30 years of the analysis. In this way, you never calculate a year more than once. Rather, you calculate each year and then save the data for the next round of processing. Arrays make this process easy to code, and MOVEA can make the transition from one 10-year period to the next even easier.

This example starts with the definition of four arrays, Comm, Rate, Prem, and Value. Each has 10 elements that will hold the 10 years of data you need to print on the analysis report for each period of years reported. Next you define four temporary arrays, CommTmp, RateTmp, PremTmp, and ValueTmp. Each temporarily holds five years of data. These arrays have the same element definition as the corresponding permanent arrays. Finally, you define the other fields — a year in which analysis begins, AnzYr; a year to start loading into the arrays, StrYr; and a field to specify which array element to begin loading into, StrIdx. (The routines for loading data from the database and for printing the data are in pseudocode form because they have no bearing on this use of MOVEA.)

The program sets the year to begin loading and the index to put the data into and then calls the routine to load five years' worth of data. You can assume that the AnzYr value has been provided as a parameter, as a read from another database, or some other such means of communication. StrYr will tell the loading routine which year to load first. StrIdx will specify the starting point for loading the data, beginning in the sixth element of each array, thereby loading the sixth through tenth element.

```
*...1....+....2....+....3....+....4....+....5....+....6....+....7....+....8
 * Arrays to hold each 10-year interval
D Comm            S             7P 2 DIM(10)
D Rate            S             7P 2 DIM(10)
D Prem            S             7P 2 DIM(10)
D Value           S             9P 2 DIM(10)
 *
 * Temp arrays for moves
D CommTmp          S             7P 2 DIM(5)
D RateTmp          S             7P 2 DIM(5)
D PremTmp          S             7P 2 DIM(5)
D ValueTmp         S             9P 2 DIM(5)
 *
 * Control fields
D AnzYr            S             4P 0
D StrYr            S             4P 0
D StrIdx           S             2P 0

*...1....+....2....+....3....+....4....+....5....+....6....+....7....+....8
 ... setup processing
 *
 * Load first 5 years
 *   - Set year to start loading for first 5-year period
 *   - Set starting index for arrays to 6 (first element for first 5 years;
 *     data will be shifted to first 5 elements when loading next 5)
 *   - Call routine to load 5 years of data to 5 elements of array
C                 Z-ADD     AnzYr          StrYr
C                 Z-ADD     6              StrIdx
   ... call routine to load 5 years of data using StrYr and StrIdx
 *
 * Build loop to execute 5 times, once for each 10-year period to analyze
 *   - Move last 5 years of data to first 5 years
 *   - Load next 5 years of data to last 5 elements of arrays
 *   - Print data for current 10-year period
 *   - loop back to get next 5 years
 *
C                 DO        5
 *
C                 MOVEA     Comm(6)        CommTmp
C                 MOVEA(P)  CommTmp        Comm(1)
C                 MOVEA     Rate(6)        RateTmp
C                 MOVEA(P)  RateTmp        Rate(1)
```

Continued

```
*...1....+....2....+....3....+....4....+....5....+....6....+....7....+....8
C                   MOVEA     Prem(6)        PremTmp
C                   MOVEA(P)  PremTmp        Prem(1)
C                   MOVEA     Value(6)       ValueTmp
C                   MOVEA(P)  ValueTmp       Value(1)
  *
C                   ADD       5              StrYr
C                   Z-ADD     6              StrIdx
   ... call routine to load 5 years of data using StrYr and StrIdx
  *
   ... call routine to print data in
C                   ENDDO
```

A loop will have to execute five times: once to process each 10-year interval. The next step is to move the last 10 years from the previous iteration into the first 10 years for the current iteration. Note that the first pass will move the first five years to the front of the array, which was the reason for the original load starting at the sixth element.

MOVEA cannot use the same array as both Factor 2 and the Result field. To get around this limitation, you can use temporary arrays that house only five elements each. These arrays are only holding areas for the movement of the five years of data.

The first MOVEA starts at the sixth element of the array Comm, moving it and all the remaining elements to the array CommTmp, starting at the first element. Not specifying a subscript when referencing an array in a MOVEA implies that you want the array reference to start at the first element. The last half of the Comm array, which is the same size as the entire CommTmp array, will replace the entire CommTmp array. This is an illustration of addressing part of an array from a specified point to the end, Comm(6), and also of addressing an entire array, CommTmp.

The next line of code performs a similar task. However, now the roles are reversed between Comm and CommTmp. Here, as in the previous MOVEA, you reference the entire CommTmp array by not specifying an index. However, you also reference the entire Comm array by using an index of 1. While you are referencing the entire array Comm, the move will affect only the first five elements, the part of the array that is the same size as the source array. The numbers in the CommTmp array are transferred into the first five elements of Comm.

The numbers in the sixth through tenth elements of Comm are zeroed out because this example specifies padding on the MOVEA. Any element that you reference in the target but that the move does not directly affect is zeroed out after the move. The result is zeros in the last half of the Comm array. A wise idea is to clear these zeros to ensure that the numbers are zero if the routine that loads the data forgets to zero the elements when it fails to find a rate. A policy that terminates before the end of the 30-year analysis needs to report zero in all the parts of the report for the years after policy termination. Padding just makes the zeroing easy.

The example code continues a similar transfer for all three of the other arrays. Imagine the amount of code and, more important, the amount of processing necessary to move these elements one by one. Although you can construct a loop to handle the job in not many more lines of code, you don't have to address each element directly, which requires 10 moves. The MOVEA technique cuts the program's work by a factor of five. Of course, performance gains depend on how the compiler implements these instructions, but you can be sure the MOVEA technique is faster than looping a set of MOVEs or Z-ADDs.

Non-Numeric Moves with MOVEA

You can think of the MOVEA as a MOVEL, especially when you're working with non-numeric moves. The source and target work as one field, whether you *are* working with a field or you are working with an array. The array appears to be one field that starts at the first byte of the specified element when you subscript the array reference, or at the beginning of the array if you do not subscript the reference.

MOVEA ignores element boundaries once you establish a starting point. The only exception to the ignored-boundary idea with a non-numeric MOVEA is that the part of the array that you reference must always start at the beginning of an element. The beginning boundary of the first element is always honored, but no other boundaries are, until you reach the end of the array.

Let's look at several examples of a non-numeric MOVEA. First, consider moving a field or literal into an array to work with multiple, same-sized substrings from a primary string. Say you have a 62-byte character field that contains a series of 2-byte codes because this data comes from an outside source that uses a two-character status code for each day of the month. You can define the file for this data as 31 fields that are 2-bytes long and work with the data as if it is in a 31-element array. The easiest way to get the data into that array is to read the entire 62-byte string into the program as one field and then use MOVEA to divide it up.

The code on page 256 performs this move. The definitions include the 62-byte field in the D-specs, although it will probably be defined on the database file's definition.

This example can work without the MOVEA if you define the DaySts field to overlay the MonthSts field. The field and the array then occupy the same storage, so you do not need the MOVEA. However, if you don't want the two structures (the array and the field) to share the same storage, MOVEA is the easiest

```
*...1....+....2....+....3....+....4....+....5....+....6....+....7....+
 * Field holding 31 2-byte codes (one per day of month)
D MonthSts        S             62A
 *
 * Array to hold each day's status in separate element
D DaySts         S             2A 2 DIM(31)

*...1....+....2....+....3....+....4....+....5....+....6....+....7....+
 *
 * Separate status fields
C                     MOVEA     MonthSts      DaySts
```

way to copy the data from one to the other. Some sample data, such as what you see below, will help explain.

```
MonthSts

ACACAVAVAVAVAVDNDNOPOPOPOPOPOPOPOPACACACACOPDNDNNANANANANANANA


DaySts before MOVEA

 |   |   |   |   |   |   |   |   |   |   |   |   |   |   |   |   |   |   |   |   |   |   |   |   |   |   |   |   |   |   |


DaySts after MOVEA

|AC|AC|AV|AV|AV|AV|AV|DN|DN|OP|OP|OP|OP|OP|OP|OP|OP|AC|AC|AC|AC|OP|DN|DN|NA|NA|NA|NA|NA|NA|NA|
```

You move field MonthSts into the DaySts field. Each 2 bytes of the Month-Sts field is now a separate element of DaySts. You can access any day's status by using the day of the month as a subscript to the DaySts array.

The data still lines up with the element boundaries. Suppose you have an application that conditionally divides any one of several fields into 3-byte segments and presents the data to users. You have to show how long the field was so that the user can see not only the characters in the field, but what part of the displayed data is *not* part of the field selected. The user sees only one field at a time, and a code on the file signals which field to display now. The fields requiring the breakdown are of varying lengths, and some have sizes that are multiples of three. A reflex thought is to use multiple arrays to break the data down: a different-dimensioned array for each differently sized field. But MOVEA without the padding option will handle the situation with one array — if it is large enough to handle the largest field you have to analyze.

Let's say you have to examine the following fields: Char10, Char12, Char22, and Char25. With one work array, SubFld, you can use MOVEA to load the correct field into the array and then display or print the array. The following example provides the data values on the D-specs. One field, Char25, is too large for the target array. This is probably a programming error, but it illustrates the effect of using a field longer than the combined length of the available array elements. The field FldSlct contains a code that tells which field to select. The example does not provide a value for it because it will change with each pass, and its value is not relevant to the use of MOVEA.

```
*...1....+....2....+....3....+....4....+....5....+....6....+....7....+
 * Fields requiring breakdown into 3-byte segments
D Char10          S              10A   INZ('AAAAAAAAAA')
D Char12          S              12A   INZ('BBB  BBBB B ')
D Char22          S              22A   INZ('CCCCCCCCCCCCCCCCCCCCCC')
D Char25          S              25A   INZ('DDDDDDDDDDDDDDDDDDDDDDDDD')
 *
 * Field Selector to identify which field is to be broken down
D FldSlct          S               1A
 *
 * Array to break data fields into 3-byte segments
D SubFld          S               3A   DIM(8)

*...1....+....2....+....3....+....4....+....5....+....6....+....7....+
 *
 * Fill array with asterisks
C                 MOVEA     *ALL'*'       SubFld
 *
 * Place field in array
C                 SELECT
 *
C                 WHEN      FldSlct = 'A'
C                 MOVEA     Char10        SubFld
 *
C                 WHEN      FldSlct = 'B'
C                 MOVEA     Char12        SubFld
 *
C                 WHEN      FldSlct = 'C'
C                 MOVEA     Char22        SubFld
 *
C                 WHEN      FldSlct = 'D'
C                 MOVEA     Char25        SubFld
 *
C                 ENDSL
 *
```

When this code executes, the first step is to fill the array with asterisks. MOVEA with the figurative constant *ALL('*') moves a string of asterisks into the array. The system will generate a string of asterisks equal to the length of the elements being affected — in this case, 24 bytes, because the entire array is involved. If you specify a subscript of 2, for instance, the generated string is only 21 bytes long, and only elements 2 through 8 are filled with asterisks.

The value of FldSlct changes on each pass through this code, and the data from one of the four character fields (Char10, Char12, Char22, Char25) will go into the elements of array SubFld. In all cases here, the move starts at the first element of the array because no subscript is present. The point of this exercise is to show that the move can end at a place other than a boundary of an element, which is what all previous examples have shown.

The effects of each of these moves is in the examples below. In each example, SubFld is filled with asterisks to start.

```
SubFld
    before MOVEA of Char10   |***|***|***|***|***|***|***|***|
    after MOVEA              |AAA|AAA|AAA|A**|***|***|***|***|
```

The MOVEA puts the data in Char10 into the array, starting at the first byte of the first element. Because Char10 is only 10 bytes long and no padding is specified, MOVEA affects only the first 10 bytes of the array. The operation replaces each of the first three elements completely but affects only 1 byte of the fourth element.

```
SubFld
    before MOVEA of Char12   |***|***|***|***|***|***|***|***|
    after MOVEA              |BBB| B|BBB| B |***|***|***|***|
```

The asterisks in the array help users see the length of the field that goes into the array. Char12 is a 12-byte field, but the last byte is a blank. If you do not have the asterisks in the array to identify positions the field does not use, you cannot tell where the original field stops. The user can erroneously believe that the data stops after only 11 bytes. If you replace the asterisk mask with the characters in the string, blanks correctly show the field's size. Of course, an asterisk in the data in Char12 can cause this logic to fall apart. If you need to give users this type of information in this manner, you need to identify a character that is the least likely to occur in your data. Better yet, you can require that a particular character never occur in that data and use that character to stand for blanks.

```
SubFld
    before MOVEA of Char22   |***|***|***|***|***|***|***|***|
    after MOVEA              |CCC|CCC|CCC|CCC|CCC|CCC|CCC|C**|
```

Like the example involving Char10, the above example again shows that Char22 will affect only the first 22 bytes of the 24-byte array. The affected portion of the array does not terminate on an element boundary. It terminates in the first byte of the last element of the array.

```
SubFld
     before MOVEA of Char25   |***|***|***|***|***|***|***|***|
     after MOVEA              |DDD|DDD|DDD|DDD|DDD|DDD|DDD|DDD|
```

In the example above, the field Char25 is 1 byte longer than the array. The move affects every byte of the array because you start at the first element, and the source string is longer than the referenced part of the array. The last character of the source field Char25 is truncated as this move takes place.

The similarity between MOVEA and MOVEL holds true no matter where you put the array in the MOVEA operation — in the source, target, or both. The only point you need to be well aware of is which part of the array the move involves. The subscript tells you which part.

The second action of MOVEA is moving one or more contiguous elements of an array into a field. Let's revisit the original non-numeric MOVEA example and work it in reverse to illustrate how MOVEA can handle certain aspects of non-normalized databases.

This example includes a 31-element array in a data record. The easiest way to access the array is at the database level as one 62-byte field. Only your programs know to divide that field into a 31-element array after reading the data. To update that array, you reverse the original process.

```
*...1....+....2....+....3....+....4....+....5....+....6....+....7....+
 * Field holding 31 2-byte codes (one per day of month)
D MonthSts        S             62A
 *
 * Array to hold each day's status in separate element
D DaySts          S              2A 2 DIM(31)

*...1....+....2....+....3....+....4....+....5....+....6....+....7....+
 *
 * Separate status fields
C                 MOVEA     MonthSts      DaySts
 *
   ... manipulate status fields as array elements
 *
 * Recombine status fields for updating database
C                 MOVEA     DaySts        MonthSts
```

MOVEA lets you separate the daily status values. Then, once your program finishes updating each daily status value as necessary (which you can now easily do by specifying a subscript with the DaySts array), you can move the entire updated array back into the MonthSts field to update the database. You can see how MOVEA can help you handle data from foreign or legacy databases with ease when you find this type of a repeating structure in a database record.

Finally, let's look at the array-to-array move for non-numeric moves. The non-numeric MOVEA is more versatile in the way it handles moves, because it doesn't have the limitation that numeric moves have. You can use arrays of differing element sizes.

To demonstrate the use of MOVEA in a non-numeric move from one array to another, let's consider a report of the months, quarters, trimesters, half years, and years in which a given department met all monthly sales goals. The data file you are reading contains the monthly sales goals and actual monthly sales, both expressed in dollars. The program can read that data starting at a particular year and construct an array of months when goals were or were not met. Then the program can use that array to populate other arrays and divide the results into quarters, trimesters, and half years. Now you can quickly test for periodic achievement. You can also use that array to populate a field to check achievement for the entire year.

```
*...1....+....2....+....3....+....4....+....5....+....6....+....7....+
 * Arrays to break annual data into defined periods
D MonGoal         S              1A   DIM(12)
D QtrGoal         S              3A   DIM(4)
D TriGoal         S              4A   DIM(3)
D SemiGoal        S              6A   DIM(2)
 *
 * Field to analyze entire year
D YrGoal          S             12A
 * Field to identify a period within a period type
D Per             S              2P 0

*...1....+....2....+....3....+....4....+....5....+....6....+....7....+
 *
 * Loop to read monthly sales data for year into an array
C                   DO        12            Per
 ... read data file for current month
 *
 * If monthly goal met or exceeded, flag month
C                   IF        MonthSls = MonthGoal
C                   MOVE      'X'           MonGoal(Per)
```

CONTINUED

```
*...1....+....2....+....3....+....4....+....5....+....6....+....7....+
C                     ELSE
C                     MOVE      *BLANK         MonGoal(Per)
C                     ENDIF
 *
C                     ENDDO
 *
 * Check each month for goal met and print

C                     DO        12             Per
 *
C                     IF        MonGoal(Per) = 'X'
 ... print notice that month met goal
C                     ENDIF
C                     ENDDO
 *
 * Check each quarter for all goals met and print
C                     MOVEA     MonGoal        QtrGoal
C                     DO        4              Per
C                     IF        QtrGoal(Per) = 'XXX'
 ... print notice that quarter met goal
C                     ENDIF
 *
C                     ENDDO
 *
 * Check each trimester for all goals met and print
C                     MOVEA     MonGoal        TriGoal
C                     DO        3              Per
C                     IF        TriGoal(Per) = 'XXXX'
 ... print notice that trimester met goal
C                     ENDIF
 *
C                     ENDDO
 *
 * Check each half year for all goals met and print
C                     MOVEA     MonGoal        SemiGoal
C                     DO        2              Per
C                     IF        SemiGoal(Per) = 'XXXXXX'
 ... print notice that half year met goal
C                     ENDIF
 *
C                     ENDDO                              CONTINUED
```

```
*...1....+....2....+....3....+....4....+....5....+....6....+....7....+
 *
 * Check each half year for all goals met and print
C                   MOVEA     MonGoal        SemiGoal
C                   DO        2              Per
C                   IF        SemiGoal(Per) = 'XXXXXX'
 ... print notice that half year met goal
C                   ENDIF
C                   ENDDO
 *
 * Check entire year for all goals met and print
C                   MOVEA     MonGoal        YrGoal
C                   IF        YrGoal = 'XXXXXXXXXXXX'
 ... print notice that entire year met goal
C                   ENDIF
 *
```

This code segment relies on two assumptions. The first is that you are examining data for only 12 months. The second is that the dates for which you need the data are available when the program reads data for the current month.

The example starts by defining four arrays for examining the four partial-year periods. The first array, MonGoal, serves a second purpose, storing the month flags for each of the following three arrays.

A flag goes into the MonGoal array to signal whether each month's sales goals were reached. MonGoal has twelve 1-byte elements to represent each month of the year. QtrGoal contains four 3-byte elements that can contain three month flags for the months in each quarter of the year. TriGoal contains three 4-byte elements that correspond to the four month flags that represent the months in each trimester of the year. Finally, SemiGoal contains two 6-byte elements, the six month flags representing the months in each half of the year. Each array takes 12 bytes of storage and provides a different grouping of the data.

Following the array definitions is one 12-byte field, YrGoal. Each byte represents one month in the year. YrGoal serves the same purpose as the four arrays: It lets you look at several months at once.

The last field is Per. This working field tracks which period you are processing. Because you are working with only one period type at a time, you use one field. To work with multiple period types at a time, you have to create a separate field to track each period type.

The C-specs execute a DO loop 12 times: once for each month. The program reads each month's data, comparing the database fields MonthSls and MonthGoal. If the sales for the month meet or exceed the goal, the program stores an X in the MonGoal element corresponding to the month. If not, the program stores a blank in that month's element. This process builds a string consisting of Xs and blanks that represent the results for the entire year. Then you can analyze each period type.

The next step is to run through the MonGoal array (which the previous DO loop loaded), using a 12-pass DO loop. Field Per is the Result field for the DO operation so you can track the iteration of the loop and use this field's value as the index for accessing the proper element of the arrays. This specification explains the use of Per on each DO loop in the example.

Each DO iteration checks the corresponding month element for an X. If an X is present, the month met the sales goals, so you print the information. After the month loop, you prepare for another one to examine the quarters of the year. By moving the 12 bytes of information from the MonGoal array into the QtrGoal array, you can restructure the periods you are examining in one operation. The MOVEA from MonGoal to QtrGoal has no subscripts, which means the move will start at the first byte of the first element for both arrays. Because, in this case, the two arrays represent storage of the same size, each month from MonGoal moves into the appropriate quarter of the QtrGoal array.

With the quarters populated, you can execute a four-pass loop to check each quarter. Because each quarter has three months, you can test each element of the QtrGoal array to see whether it contains three Xs. If an element has three Xs, all three months of the quarter met or exceeded their sales goal.

Next, you twice repeat moving the MonGoal array into other arrays to regroup the months into larger periods. This repetition occurs in the next two sections of code, which look at the trimesters and half years. In each case, you load the array for the period you want to examine. MOVEA puts the MonGoal data into the other arrays, TriGoal and SemiGoal. The TriGoal loop checks each element for four Xs, and the SemiGoal loop checks each element for six Xs.

Finally, a MOVEA moves the MonGoal array into the field YrGoal. You don't need an array for YrGoal because it will always look at all twelve months. Now you can test YrGoal for twelve Xs.

Let's look at how the data is moved and how MOVEA easily divides the data into the groups you need to perform the periodic analysis.

```
MonGoal       |X|X| |X|X|X| | |X|X|X|X|   MOVEA
QtrGoal       |X X  |X X X|   X|X X X|
TriGoal       |X X   X|X X   |X X X X|
SemiGoal      |X X   X X X|   X X X X|
YrGoal        |X X   X X X    X X X X|
```

As this code shows, each MOVEA makes the MonGoal data overlay the twelve positions that each other array or field occupies. MOVEA's ability to cross the boundaries of the array elements lets you work with the data in whatever groupings you want.

You can easily expand this example to handle multiple years. Instead of using a field for YrGoal, you can specify an array of as many 12-byte elements as necessary. You handle each year as the previous example did. The loading routine takes one year at a time, and the other code always works with one year.

```
*...1....+....2....+....3....+....4....+....5....+....6....+....7....+
 * Arrays to break annual data into defined periods
D MonGoal         S              1A   DIM(12)
D QtrGoal         S              3A   DIM(4)
D TriGoal         S              4A   DIM(3)
D SemiGoal        S              6A   DIM(2)
 *
 * Array to store each year to analyze
D YrGoal          S             12A   DIM(3)
 * Field to identify a period within a period type within a year
D Per             S              2P 0
 * Field to identify which year is being processed
D Year            S              1P 0
```

```
*...1....+....2....+....3....+....4....+....5....+....6....+....7....+
 * Loop to load each of 3 years
C                   DO        3             Year
 * Loop to read monthly sales data for year into an array
C                   DO        12            Per
 ... read data file for current month
 *
 * If monthly goal met or exceeded, flag month
C                   IF        MonthSls = MonthGoal
C                   MOVE      'X'           MonGoal(Per)
C                   ELSE
C                   MOVE      *BLANK        MonGoal(Per)
C                   ENDIF
 * end of month loop
C                   ENDDO
 * put monthly data in to the current year
C                   MOVEA     MonGoal       YrGoal(Year)
 * end of year loop
C                   ENDDO
 *
 * Loop to analyze each of 3 years
C                   DO        3             Year
```

CONTINUED

```
*...1....+....2....+....3....+....4....+....5....+....6....+....7....+
 * Load current year into array to process a single year
C                     MOVEA     YrGoal(Year)  MonGoal
 *
 * Check each month for goal met and print
C                     DO        12            Per
 *
C                     IF        MonGoal(Per) = 'X'
 ... print notice that month met goal
C                     ENDIF
 * end of month loop
C                     ENDDO
 *
 * Check each quarter for all goals met and print
C                     MOVEA     MonGoal       QtrGoal
C                     DO        4             Per
C                     IF        QtrGoal(Per) = 'XXX'
 ... print notice that quarter met goal
C                     ENDIF
 * end of quarter loop
C                     ENDDO
 *
   ... trimester and half year processing
 *
 * Check entire year for all goals met and print
C                     IF        YrGoal(Year) = 'XXXXXXXXXXXX'
 ... print notice that entire year met goal
C                     ENDIF
 * end of year loop
C                     ENDDO
```

This code includes the basic modifications to illustrate how MOVEA works with multiple years. You do not need to multi-define the same storage location, so you can easily understand what is happening as MOVEA proceeds.

The YrGoal field is now a three-element array, and each element is 12 bytes long, so the program can handle three years at once. Next, this example creates a field, Year, to track which of the three years the program is processing at any given time. Note that the program identifies the relative year, one to three, not the actual year. The print routine can convert the relative year into the year. Next a three-iteration loop goes around the original loop that loads the MonGoal array.

Now, after the program loads the MonGoal array, MOVEA stores it in one element of the YrGoal array. This code shows how that move functions when you are working on the second year.

```
MonGoal
   |X|X|  |X|X|X|X|  |X|X|  |

MOVEA  MonGoal  YrGoal(2)

YrGoal
   |X X     X X     X X X  |X X   X X X X   X X  |                        |
```

When Year has a value of 2, YrGoal(Year) references both the second and third elements of YrGoal (the remainder of the array, starting at element 2). However, because you are moving the entire MonGoal and not specifying padding, only the 12 bytes of the second element are affected. This technique lets you work with each year independently and then store the data in the YrGoal array.

The next change is to wrap the analysis code (all the original period loops) inside a three-iteration loop to handle each year. You move the current year's element to the MonGoal array. Now, you can examine each period type. (This example shows only the monthly and quarterly code.) The last alteration is to compare the twelve-X string to the current element of YrGoal rather than to one field, as in the previous example. Because you already have a structure that contains all twelve months in one field (the current element of the YrGoal array), you no longer need to move the MonGoal array into one field. Instead, you just check the current element of YrGoal. The key to making all this work is the movement of one element of YrGoal into the MonGoal array at the top of the year loop.

```
YrGoal
   |X X     X X     X X X  |X X   X X X X   X X  |X X X X     X X   X X X|

   MOVEA  YrGoal(2)  MonGoal

MonGoal
                |X|X|  |X|X|X|X|  |X|X|  |
```

For the second year, MOVEA uses a subscripted array. Because the source string (elements 2 and 3 of YrGoal) is longer than the target string (all 12 elements of MonGoal), the data will be truncated and MonGoal will contain only the data from element 2 of YrGoal.

These examples model a process that lets you handle several two-dimensional arrays. Because RPG IV supports only single-dimension arrays (one subscript), moving an element of one array into another array to subdivide it is generally the closest you can come to simulating a multi-dimensional array. Though the approach here makes handling multiple dimensions easy, understanding the program can become difficult as you nest arrays.

OVERLAY ARRAYS

RPG IV lets you use the new OVERLAY keyword with arrays. Without creating a new array in storage, OVERLAY lets you define a new array based on an existing (base) array. The new array, or overlay array, does not take on the attributes of the base array, but you can access all or part of this array in any format you want. This capability is analogous to creating a logical file over a physical file: You can define one array that contains data and then define multiple arrays that can view the data in different parts of the base array.

The impressive capability with overlay arrays is that by sorting any overlay array, you can sort the base array. This capability synchronizes all overlay arrays over the same base array. You can access multiple sort orders for an array because you can sort the underlying array in ascending or descending order, by the entire value, or by a substring in the array.

OVERLAY has two parameters. When you define an overlay array, the first parameter is the name of the array you want to overlay, or the base array. The second parameter is optional, and you can specify it after a colon following the first parameter. The second parameter specifies the position in bytes in the storage of the base array where you want the overlay array to begin. If you omit the second parameter, the default starting position for the overlay array is 1.

The OVERLAY keyword is allowed only when you're working within a data structure and its subfields. You cannot manipulate standalone fields with OVERLAY, so you cannot use standalone arrays to create overlay arrays. You must define a data structure to house the base array. You do not have to name the data structure. In fact, you can define a separate unnamed data structure for each set of overlay arrays you want to create. A set of overlay arrays consists of a base array (the one that you specify DIM on) and all the overlay arrays that reference the base array.

To specify overlay arrays, you define a data structure. To define the base array, you specify a data structure subfield with the DIM keyword. Then, to define the overlay array, you specify another data structure subfield with the OVERLAY keyword. As OVERLAY's parameter value, you enter the name of the subfield that contains the base array.

Now you have a data structure that contains two arrays. Each array has the same dimension and the same elements. Both arrays access the same storage, and each element accesses the same data.

At first, this concept can be a difficult to grasp. A generic example helps explain the basic concept. Then we can rebuild the example from the SORTA operation and take advantage of the new overlay array capability. The code below defines a data structure that contains one array with an overlay array.

```
*...1....+....2....+....3....+....4....+....5....+....6....+....7....+
 * Array of names sorted both ascending and descending
D                   DS
D NameDsc                        15A    DIM(100) DESCEND
D NameAsc                        15A    OVERLAY(NameDsc)


*...1....+....2....+....3....+....4....+....5....+....6....+....7....+
 *
 * Sort the names in ascending order
C                   SORTA    NameAsc
 *
 * Sort the names in descending order
C                   SORTA    NameDsc
```

The first subfield in the unnamed data structure is the array NameDsc. The DIM keyword defines it as an array with 100 elements, so the unnamed data structure is a character string, 1500 characters long (100 elements times 15 characters per element). The next subfield is NameAsc. Because it has the OVERLAY keyword specified to point to an array, NameAsc is also an array. It will inherit the dimension of NameDsc, which is the parameter value of OVERLAY and is thus the base array. Each element of the NameAsc array will come from the corresponding element of NameDsc. The two arrays access the same storage, and each element accesses the same data. The difference is the sorting order: The base array definition includes the DESCEND keyword, so NameDsc will be sorted in a descending order. The overlay array will be sorted in the default, ascending, order.

To work with the names in the base array in ascending order, you specify the SORTA (Sort Ascending) operation on NameAsc. To work with the names in descending order, you need to sort the NameDsc array. You can work only with the array that identifies the last sorted order, so you have to remember the order in which you last sorted the array.

This example shows how an overlay array looks in storage.

```
Data Structure:
           123456789012345 678901234567890 ... 123456789012345 678901234567890
no name    |Adams           Bennet          ... Wentmayer       Zabada          |
NameAsc    |_____/|_____/|...|_____/|_____/|
NameDsc    |_____/|_____/|...|_____/|_____/|
```

The first element of each array in the data structure contains the same value, although the two arrays have opposing sort orders. Both the base array and all the overlay arrays are sorted in the order you specify on the array you name in the SORTA operation. This example uses NameAsc on SORTA to sort the arrays in ascending order. You can access the first element by using a subscript; either NameAsc(1) or NameDsc(1). Both will yield the name Adams.

SORTA on the NameDsc array orders the data as below. Notice that now both arrays will access the name Zabada if you use element 1.

```
Data Structure:
             123456789012345 678901234567890 ... 123456789012345 678901234567890
no name      |Zabada          Wentmayer        ... Bennet          Adams          |
NameAsc      |_____/|_____/|...|_____/|_____/|
NameDsc      |_____/|_____/|...|_____/|_____/|
```

Note one requirement of overlay arrays: Like all overlaying subfields, the overlay array cannot be larger than the base array. Because the elements in the overlay array are over the corresponding elements of the base array, the element size of the overlay array cannot be larger than the elements of the base array. If you are not overlaying the entire base array, the size of the overlay array's element cannot exceed the size of the base array's element minus the starting point in the element, minus 1.

The code below is the example from the SORTA operation, revamped to use overlay arrays. First, note that this example does not use the overlay arrays to provide multiple sort orders. Rather, it gives you access to multiple arrays, and you can keep their elements synchronized by sorting one of the set of arrays.

```
*...1....+....2....+....3....+....4....+....5....+....6....+....7....+.
 * Structure to house base and overlaying arrays
D                   DS
D CustYrDta                      8A   DIM(10)
D   CustYr                       4P 0 OVERLAY(CustYrDta:1)
D   CustSls                      9P 2 OVERLAY(CustYrDta:4)
 *
 * Standalone fields
D YearSales       S              9P 2
D SalesYear       S              4P 0
D Cur             S              3P 0
D TotSales        S              9P 2
D Year            S              4P 0
D YrElem          S              2P 0
```

CONTINUED

```
*...1....+....2....+....3....+....4....+....5....+....6....+....7....+.
*
* Read next customer record, checking for change in customer
*
  ...
*
* For change in customer (including when EOF hit) do for previous
*   customer
*    - Sort the sales array
*    - Print last 10 years of customer's annual sales totals
*    - clear the CustYrTot array, and the TotSales field
*
* Sort the sales array
C                   SORTA     CustSls
*
* Print last 10 years of customer's annual sales totals
* by reading through the array backwards, using 11-complement
* of current iteration produces indexes 10 through 1.
*
C                   DO        10            Cur
* get sales
C                   IF        CustYr(11-Cur)<>0
C                   EVAL      YearSales=CustSls(11-Cur)
* get year
C                   EVAL      SalesYear=CustYr(11-Cur)
*
... print the current year and sales
*
C                   ENDIF
C                   ENDDO
*
* Clear the Year and Total arrays    *
C                   Z-ADD     *Zeros        CustSls
C                   Z-ADD     *Zeros        CustYr
*
* For each Customer read through the invoices in date order checking
*   for change in Invoice year and selecting only invoices in last 10
*   years
*
  ...
*
```

CONTINUED

```
*...1....+....2....+....3....+....4....+....5....+....6....+....7....+.
 * If the Invoice year changes (including EOF hit) do for previous
 *  year
 *  - find the first unused element in the array
 *  - record total for year in the found slot
 *  - clear the total field
 *  - extract the new invoice year into Year
 *
 * find unused element and place element number in variable YrElem
C     *ZERO         LOOKUP    CustYr(YrElem)                        30
 *
 * record total for year and the year itself in the found slot
 *
C                   EVAL      CustYr(YrElem)=Year
C                   EVAL      CustSls(YrElem)=TotSales
 *
 * clear the total field
 *
C                   Z-ADD     *Zeros       TotSales
 *
 * extract the new invoice year into Year
 *
  ... extract the new invoice year into Year
 *
 * For each of the invoices
 *  - accumulate the invoice total for the year in TotSales
 *
  ... accumulate the invoice total for the year in TotSales
 *
 * Loop to read next invoice
 *
  ... loop for invoice
 *
 * Loop to read next customer
 *
  ... loop for customer
```

Let's walk through the changes to see how overlay arrays make this code segment easier to understand than the previous SORTA example. The first change is to define an unnamed data structure to house the arrays. Unnamed data structures are not required, but because the program will not reference the data structure directly, you have no need to name it. Within the data structure, the first subfield is the CustYrDta array. It must be large enough to hold all the data you want in the base array. You can think of this subfield's size as being like the record size in a file: You define an array that represents multiple records and then lay new arrays over the base array to extract the fields.

	Positions							
	1	2	3	4	5	6	7	8
Zone	0	9	5	0	1	3	0	4
Digit	1	9	F	0	4	1	2	F

The table above shows the value in one element of the CustYrDta array. The four-digit year uses positions 1 through 3 of the eight-character array element, and the nine-digit total uses position 4 through 8. This fact is important to understand because it will dictate how you define the overlay arrays in the next step. (Note that packed decimal numbers are always stored as odd-length fields because an odd number of digits is necessary to round out the bytes of storage: The system stores the year field as a five-digit field, but the program can access only four digits if you use a four-digit field to view that storage.)

Next you define two subfields for arrays, CustYr and CustSls. The DIM keyword does not appear on these array definitions. Instead, the OVERLAY keyword specifies that each element of each new array accesses some part of the base array, which is the parameter value of the OVERLAY keyword. The CustYr overlay array's definition specifies that it is a four-digit packed decimal number. OVERLAY(CustYrDta:1) says that each element of CustYr will start in the first position of each element of CustYrDta. Likewise, the CustSls array's definition defines a nine-digit packed decimal number. OVERLAY(CustYrDta:4) means that each element of CustSls will start in the fourth position of each element of CustYrDta. You must know how the data is to be stored so you can effectively select your starting point in the base array element and have your overlay array element access the correct part of the base array element.

Because you cannot have a DESCEND keyword on the CustSls array (OVERLAY makes any other keywords illegal), you have to sort CustSls in the default ascending order. Note that this order slightly changes the example program's functionality. The original program sorts both the year and the total sales in descending order. The new version sorts by total sales only; a small price to pay for the benefits of the changes you're making.

Additionally, because this code sorts ascending rather than descending, you have to work backward through the array rather than forward, working from element 10 through element 1. You do that step when you print the array's contents: You access each array element by building a loop that starts at 1 and increments by 1 on each iteration. Because the loop works from 1 to 10, you subtract the current index from 11 on each pass (11s complement) to get the values 10 to 1.

If you sort the CustSls array, you also sort the base array. Naturally, this situation means the entries in the CustSls and CustYr arrays remain synchronized because corresponding elements from the two arrays always reference the same element of the base array.

Let's look at how the overlay arrays relate to the base array. The table below depicts each element of the base array, and the next table shows the storage for the first four elements of the arrays. Both tables include the same data as in the original SORTA example and show how the data appears after sorting. The tables use hexadecimal to show where the data is in the data structures. This format is necessary because the data is in packed format.

	CustYR 1 to 10	CustSls 1 to 10
CustYrData(1)	01994F	001868407F
CustYrData(2)	01990F	001798425F
CustYrData(3)	01993F	001630985F
CustYrData(4)	01995F	001431024F
CustYrData(5)	01988F	001407823F
CustYrData(6)	01991F	001069997F
CustYrData(7)	01992F	001064417F
CustYrData(8)	01989F	000994996F
CustYrData(9)	00000F	000000000F
CustYrData(10)	01987F	000002200D

	CustYr (1)	CustSls (1)	CustYr (2)	CustSls (2)	CustYr (3)	CustSls (3)	CustYr (4)	CustSls (4)
CustYRDta	(1)		(2)		(3)		(4)	
Data	01994F	001868407F	01990F	001798425F	01993F	01630985F	01995F	001431024F

Let's discuss how the data will look in CustYrDta, which holds the data; you will not access the data via this array. The access will be through the overlay arrays. The two fields on each record are the year and the sales for that year. The year field is four digits, and the sales total is nine digits, two of which are decimal positions. Because you are storing them in packed format, the four-digit year will take up three bytes of storage, and the nine-digit sales figure will take up five bytes of storage. By separating the zone and digit of each byte, the table above shows how the 1995 record will look for total sales $14,310.24.

Now let's consider the highlights of what you change in the C-specs. They become much simpler to understand. First, you sort only the CustSls array to order all the data. Next, you print the data. The previous version of this program requires some unusual mathematical tricks to extract the year and total sales from the array element. Now, though, the two overlay arrays access the necessary year and sales. You specify the same subscript on each array.

Next you have to clear both arrays by moving *Zeros to each element. With the availability of MOVEA, why does this code use Z-ADD (which will result in a separate move for each element)? The answer is that you cannot use MOVEA on an overlay array if the element size of the overlay array is smaller than the base array's size. This restriction makes sense when you realize that the elements in the overlay array are not stored contiguously, but they are distributed throughout the storage for the base array. (The storage tables on page 273 show that the data for each overlay array is noncontiguous.)

Next a LOOKUP operation locates the first non-zero element of CustYr. Any year that has sales will result in a non-zero value in one of CustYr's elements. Again, because each element of CustSls refers to the same element of CustYrDta, as do the corresponding elements of CustYr, this LOOKUP operation also points to the available element in CustSls.

The final changes in this example come in the code that loads the data into the arrays for the current year. In the first approach to the problem, you had to multiply by 1,000,000 and then add or subtract the year from the result. Storing data for sorting was cumbersome and not exactly intuitive. However, overlay arrays make the entire process intuitive.

Overlay arrays let you have multiple arrays and synchronize their corresponding elements. The most significant benefit of this new technique is that you can have as many arrays as needed to contain as many data elements as needed and synchronize them all — possibly by specifying multiple sort orders by defining multiple arrays with SORTA. In fact, nothing stops you from having those overlay arrays overlap each other and thereby gaining access to techniques for sorting by partial fields. However, you'll want to restrict the partial-field techniques to character data because the storage of signs of numeric data is not exactly conducive to the substringing or concatenation of numeric values.

TABLES

Tables and arrays perform similar functions in RPG IV. Tables were available in RPG before arrays, which provide increased function over tables. Perhaps the best way to explain RPG tables is to discuss how they differ from arrays. You must load tables at compile time or pre-runtime; runtime tables are not available. To tell the RPG compiler that the structure you are defining is a table, you must prefix table names with the string TAB. Indexes are not permitted with RPG tables, because the table name refers to a particular table element, which means that only one element of a table is active at any time. You must use the LOOKUP operation to set, or activate, an element. To change the active element, you issue another LOOKUP.

If you need to choose between tables and arrays, our advice is always to select an array. One major reason is readability: When you refer to an array element, the index identifies the element. In contrast, tables allow no index, so identifying that a reference is to a table element is difficult. Besides readability, a reason for preferring arrays is that future enhancements to RPG functionality will focus on arrays. Finally, other languages, such as Pascal and C, provide syntax for arrays and not tables. This support will become important if you need to convert programs from RPG to such languages.

Specifying RPG Tables

To define a table, in the D-specs, you name the table, specify the number of elements it has, and enter the type and size of the elements. The name of a table must begin with TAB. For example, the code below shows the definitions of two tables, TABCTY and TABDIF.

```
*...1....+....2....+....3....+....4....+....5....+....6....+....7....+
D TABCTY          S             10A   DIM(6) CTDATA PERRCD(1)
D TABDIF          S              1S 0 DIM(6) CTDATA PERRCD(1) ASCEND
```

As with array definitions, you specify the table name (prefixed with the obligatory TAB) in positions 7 through 21. In position 24, an S defines a standalone field (like array elements, table elements are standalone fields). In positions 33 through 39, you specify element length, and the data type is in position 40. Array keywords are also valid for tables, so you specify the number of elements for a table by means of the DIM keyword. You can define a compile-time table by specifying the CTDATA keyword (and the **CTDATA record at the bottom of the source) and determine the number of elements per record by using PERRCD. ASCEND and DESCEND are also valid. If you define a pre-runtime table, you can use FROMFILE and, optionally, TOFILE, to identify the associated file, instead of using CTDATA.

LOOKUP with Tables

The LOOKUP operation is essential with tables. Because RPG tables do not permit indexes, the table name refers to a particular table element, which means that only one element of the table is active at any given time. To determine which element the table name is referring to (i.e., which element is active), you need the LOOKUP operation. To change the active element, you issue another LOOKUP operation.

The syntax for LOOKUP with tables is slightly different from its syntax with arrays. As with an array, you specify the value to look up in Factor 1. You specify which table you want to look in as Factor 2. Indicators determine the type of match that will cause the LOOKUP to select a particular element, and indicators signal success or failure of the LOOKUP. No index is allowed in Factor 2 because the table name will reference the currently active element. The most significant distinction in syntax, however, is that a table LOOKUP lets you put a second table name in the Result field, so you can set a particular element in two tables at the same time. When the LOOKUP identifies the active element in the Factor 2 table, the operation will also set the corresponding element of the table in the Result field to be the active element for that table.

Tables by Example

The LOOKUP on table TABDyAbbr finds a value that matches the value of field DyOfWkAbbr. If LOOKUP finds a match to the entry you are looking for, the corresponding entry in TABDyFull will be activated. When TABDyAbbr's active entry is TUE, TABDyFull's active entry will be Tuesday. However, when the value you use in the LOOKUP does not match an entry in TABDyAbbr, indicator 30 will be turned off. You can use that indicator to trigger an error message saying that the entered abbreviation is invalid. This approach illustrates how a LOOKUP on a table can validate and translate user entries in one search operation.

```
*...1....+....2....+....3....+....4....+....5....+....6....+....7....+.
 *
 * Tables for abbreviated and full day names
D TABDyAbbr       S              3A   DIM(7) CTDATA
D TABDyFull       S              9A   DIM(7) CTDATA
 *
 * Standalone fields
D DyOfWkAbbr      S              3A
D DayName         S              9A


*...1....+....2....+....3....+....4....+....5....+....6....+....7....+.
 *
 * Translate day of week abbreviation to full day of week name
C     DyOfWkAbbr    LOOKUP    TABDyAbbr    TABDyFull               30
 * If found, load to field
C                   IF        *IN30
C                   MOVE      TABDyFull    DayName
 * If not found, issue an error
C                   ELSE
```

Continued

```
*...1....+....2....+....3....+....4....+....5....+....6....+....7...|.+.
 ... error processing
 *
C                   ENDIF

*...1....+....2....+....3....+....4....+....5....+....6....+....7...|.+.
**CTDATA TABDyAbbr
MON
TUE
WED
THU
FRI
SAT
SUN
**CTDATA TABDyFull
Monday
Tuesday
Wednesday
Thursday
Friday
Saturday
Sunday
```

When you move TABDyFull to DayName, you reference the name of the table instead of using a subscript. This means of reference is another distinction between tables and arrays. An array reference in that same move requires you to specify an index. You can see a similarity between the definition of compile-time tables and compile-time arrays. In fact, the only way to identify a table definition rather than an array is that the name of the table starts with the obligatory TAB.

When you use related tables in this manner, you must keep the data that is loaded into them synchronized. That data is at the bottom of the code. You have to manually ensure the proper order of data between the two tables. A mistake in ordering this code can result in correctly functioning LOOKUPs that result in errors.

ARRAYS AND TABLES: MAKING THE CHOICE

This chapter explains the three types of arrays RPG IV supports. To decide what type of array you want, you have to consider the efficiencies and program steps required for each solution. The type of array you're defining (i.e., compile-time, pre-runtime, or runtime) determines when an array is filled, so the type of array you choose depends on when you have the data you want to load. If you have the data at compile time, you declare a compile-time array. From a performance perspective, compile-time arrays are most efficient because no data is moved during program initialization (in contrast to pre-runtime arrays) or during program execution (in contrast to runtime arrays). If the data is in a file, the choice is a pre-runtime array. Finally, if you know the data will be loaded only at runtime, you need a runtime array.

You will probably use runtime arrays most often. As programmers move away from hardcoded data in programs, compile-time arrays and tables are dropping by the wayside. Pre-runtime arrays and tables are preferable to compile-time arrays and tables because you can update the data without changing the program. This elimination of program changes can facilitate such tasks as language translation: You can change data such as day names simply by using a different set of data each time the program runs (you can use a different library list with different libraries containing the same file with different translations). However, runtime arrays are the most commonly used array type because they are the most flexible. Pre-runtime arrays are specific to RPG and are not compatible with other languages or architectures. Porting such applications to other languages for multiple platforms can be more difficult than if you simply load data in the array at runtime.

This chapter also explains how to recognize and code a table definition. We recommend that you avoid tables and use arrays instead. Arrays provide more functionality and flexibility than tables and are a more modern programming tool. Bear in mind, though, that there is seldom one correct solution for any programming problem, so choose the solution that fits the problem.

CHAPTER 9

String-Handling Operation Codes

String handling occurs in many business applications, for such purposes as combining multiple fields for printing. For example, you can combine a customer's first, middle, and last name to print an attractive salutation on a bill. Or, partial string searches let a user key in a word or a phrase and have the system return a description field that lists all records that include the entered word or phrase. Another application for string handling is translating strings from lowercase to uppercase to allow case-insensitive searches. Verifying that valid characters appear in strings and parsing free-format data to break it down for storage in a database are further ways string handling works for business programmers.

RPG IV string-handling operations make these capabilities possible. The following table lists and describes these operations.

Operation	Description
SCAN	Scans for one or more occurrences of one string inside another
CAT	Concatenates two strings
SUBST	Extracts one string from another
XLATE	Converts selected characters in a string into another character
CHECK	Locates one or more characters in a string that are not members of a given set of characters
CHECKR	Performs like CHECK but processes the string from end to beginning rather than beginning to end

In addition to these operations, RPG IV has several built-in functions and operators for free-form expressions that can perform other string-handling operations. The next table describes those built-in functions and operators.

Operation/ Function	Description
+	Concatenates strings; similar to CAT operation
%SUBST(source:start:length)	Returns a string that is extracted from a source string; starts in a given position and returns a given number of characters or identifies a portion of a string to be changed
%TRIML(source)	Returns a string after removing all leading spaces
%TRIMR(source)	Returns a string after removing all trailing spaces
%TRIM(source)	Returns a string after removing all leading and trailing spaces

This chapter will discuss each of these operations and built-in functions. At the end of the chapter is a demonstration of several uses for string handling, including case-insensitive searches and reformatting data.

SCANNING

String-handling operations and functions naturally require strings as their operands. Those operands can be either character strings of standard SBCS (Single-Byte Character Set) characters or graphic strings of DBCS (Double-Byte Character Set) characters. You cannot mix the two different types of data on one operation. For operations that require multiple strings (such as SCAN, which requires a string to look for and a string to look in), all the strings must be the same type, character or graphic. This chapter will specifically discuss character strings, but the examples also apply to graphic strings.

The SCAN Operation Code

The SCAN operation looks for one string inside another. Factor 1 identifies the *search* string, the string you want to look for. Factor 2 identifies the *base* string, the string you want to look in to find the search string. The Result field records the position or positions in the base string where SCAN finds the search string. The table below summarizes the entries for SCAN.

Factor 1	Opcode	(Extender)	Factor 2	Result	Indicators		
Required *search string: length*	SCAN		Required *base string: start*	Required *position of find*	N/A	Error	Match Found

Any string field, literal, or named constant can be the search string in Factor 1. Ordinarily, you search the entire string, including any leading or trailing blanks. A different approach is to enter the search string followed by a colon and then enter a *search length*. The search length can be a numeric integer field, literal, or named constant. The search length will cause the operation to consider only the specified number of characters in the search string.

This approach is helpful if you know the search string contains trailing blanks and you want a search to ignore them. If the search string field is a 10-character field and only the first four characters have nonblank data, you can specify a search length of 4 to search only the four nonblank characters. If you do not specify a search length, the search includes all 10 characters, and matches occur only if all 10 characters (including trailing blanks) are in the base string. Note that the search is case sensitive and requires an *exact* match.

A string field, literal, or named constant can be the base string in Factor 2. By default, the search starts at the first character of the base string. You can request that the search start later in the string; you enter a colon and a *start position* following the string. The start position can be a numeric integer field, literal, or named constant. The start position will begin the search at the position you specify.

If you know that the string you are searching for must start at or after, but not before, a certain position in the base string, you can speed the process slightly by starting the search at the appropriate position. In fact, this approach is generally more a necessity than a convenience. If you are searching for several characters in a string in a particular order, you will frequently use the output of a previous SCAN to determine the starting position of the current SCAN. Perhaps you know that the search string occurs several times in the base string, but you want to work your way through one occurrence at a time. By specifying the start position, you prevent SCAN from finding the first occurrence of the search string over and over.

The Result field, which must be a numeric field or array, records the position or positions of the search string in the base string. If you code a field or a single array element (subscript provided), the Result field contains the position of the first found occurrence of the search string in the base string. You are likely to use this information in a SUBST operation later to extract a string starting at that point. This information can also determine the starting point of the next SCAN. If you are performing multiple SCANs on the same base string with a different search string on each SCAN, this is the way to work your way through the string.

If you are using the same search string on each such SCAN, you can choose an even easier way to find all the occurrences of the search string in the base string in one SCAN operation. You can specify an unsubscripted array in the Result field, and SCAN will record the position of the first occurrence of the search string in the first array element, the second position in the second element, and so on. If you have a greater number of elements in the array than occurrences in the string, all subsequent array elements will be set to zero. If you have more occurrences than array elements, you will receive as many positions as you have array elements. Whether you use a field or array element to capture a single position or you use an array to capture multiple positions, the Result field or array elements will be set to zero if the search string is not found in the base string.

SCAN supports two resulting indicators. You can check for an error by coding an indicator in positions 73 and 74. You can get an error if the search string is longer than the base string, which can happen if you are using variables for the search length and starting position parameters on Factor 1 and 2. You can also get an error if the search length is longer than the search string or if the starting position number is larger than the number of positions in the base string.

You can specify an indicator in positions 75 and 76. It will turn on when SCAN finds a match. If it finds no match, the indicator turns off. Because the

Result field is required, you have to decide whether you want an indicator to signal a match or whether you want to check for zero as the value of the Result field. We recommend working with fields instead of indicators and recommend the latter method for determining success or failure of the SCAN.

Note that you cannot specify figurative constants as the strings in this operation. Figurative constants have no defined length and, therefore, have no set value that the operation can reference or include. Additionally, the Result field cannot overlap with either the Factor 1 or Factor 2 field in a data structure.

The SUBST Operation Code

The SUBST (Substring) operation returns a designated portion, or substring, of the base string (i.e., the source string from which you will extract the substring). SUBST is beneficial when you need to parse data from an incoming field and store that data in separate fields. Suppose you receive information from outside vendors, and they supply customer names in one field, such as "Mr. Tom Jones". You must divide that string into the constituent parts, "Mr.", "Tom", and "Jones", and then figure out where to put each part in your database. The constituent parts are a title, a first name, and a last name. Once you determine where in the original string you can find the substrings you need and how long they are, SUBST can extract them and put them in separate fields. (SCAN can help find the starting and ending position of substrings so SUBST can use them.)

With SUBST, Factor 1 can specify the *length* of the string you want to extract from the *base* string. You specify the base string in Factor 2. The operation puts the extracted string in a character field you specify in the Result field.

Factor 1 is optional. It can be a numeric field, literal, or named constant. This field determines how long a string, or how many characters, you want to extract from the base string.

Factor 2, which is required, is where you specify the base string, the string from which you want to extract a substring. The string can be any string field, literal, or named constant. You can specify a *starting position* for the substring by coding a colon immediately after the string and then entering a numeric integer field, literal, or named constant. This numeric value identifies the position in the base string where you want to begin the extraction. When you leave Factor 1 blank, the substring extracted starts at this position and continues up to the length you specify in Factor 1 or through the end of the base string.

The Result field, which is also required, must be a string field. Because SUBST is really just a MOVEL with substring capabilities, you must keep in mind how the data goes into the Result field. The extracted string is left aligned with the start of the Result field, and the characters go into the Result field until it contains as many characters as the length of the extracted string. Unless you do something about it, this placement means that when the extracted string is shorter than the Result field, some data in the Result field is not replaced. You can use this situation to your advantage if you want to replace some but not all of the characters in the Result field. If the extracted string is longer than the Result field, the extra characters from the extracted string are truncated at the right. The table below shows a summary of the SUBST operation code's syntax.

Factor 1	Opcode	(Extender)	Factor 2	Result	Indicators		
Optional Length	SUBST	(P)	Required base string: start position	Required result string	N/A	Error	N/A

If the extracted string is shorter than the Result field and you want nothing in the Result field but the extracted string, you can pad the extracted string with blanks to make it at least as long as the Result field. To do so, you specify the operation extender (P) in the operation field of the C-spec. Padding ensures that old data is not left in the Result field after the SUBST operation. You will want to use the padding facility unless you need to preserve the data beyond the characters that are replaced in the Result field.

Note that you cannot specify figurative constants as the source string in this operation. Figurative constants have no defined length and, therefore, have no set value that the string operations can reference or include. Additionally, the Result field cannot overlap with either Factor 1 or Factor 2 in a data structure.

The %SUBST Built-In Function

The %SUBST built-in function is similar to the SUBST operation. You need %SUBST in free-form expressions with EVAL and DOW, DOU, WHEN, and IF. With each of these operations, the built-in function can let you extract one string from another for a comparison with some other string. Or, in the case of EVAL, you can assign the extracted string to some other string. The built-in function gives you access to a substring without your having to store it in some intermediate variable. Of course, when you specify %SUBST with EVAL, the point might be to assign the substring to a variable.

With EVAL, though, %SUBST can play a different role. In a relational expression on the other operations that support expressions (listed above) or on the right side of an assignment expression on the EVAL operation, %SUBST *extracts* a substring just as the SUBST operation does. But when %SUBST is on the left side of an assignment expression, it *defines the target of the assignment*. The %SUBST built-in function lets you modify any portion of a string variable without having to deconstruct and then reconstruct the value in the variable. With %SUBST, you can directly address, for modification, any part of a string variable, treating the substring defined by the built-in function just as you do any other field to which you are assigning a value.

%SUBST has three parameters: the base string, the start position, and the length. The first two parameters are required. As with all built-in functions, you enclose the three parameters in parentheses immediately following the name of the built-in function and separate the parameters by entering a colon between them. Here is the syntax of %SUBST:

Function	Parameters
%SUBST	(base:start[:length])

You can correlate each part of the %SUBST built-in function with the parts of the SUBST operation. %SUBST's first parameter is the *base* string and serves the same function as the string you specify in Factor 2 of SUBST. The second parameter is the *starting position* where you want to begin extracting the substring. This parameter corresponds to the optional parameter in Factor 2 on SUBST. The third parameter, which is optional, is the *length* of the substring. This parameter has the same purpose as the optional Factor 1 on SUBST.

Note that you cannot specify figurative constants as the string in this built-in function. Figurative constants have no defined length and, therefore, have no set value that string operations can reference or include. Nor can you specify a constant as the base string on the left side of an EVAL operation.

CONCATENATION AND TRIMMING

You've seen how to find a substring, extract a substring, and even modify a substring within another string. Now let's discuss the opposite function, building new strings by combining small strings. This process is concatenation and you do it with the CAT (Concatenate) operation or with the + operator in a free-form expression.

The CAT operation will always assign the result of the concatenation to a string variable. The + operator creates a string, but does not directly assign it to any variable. You can use the string you build with the + operator in other operations in the expression, or you can assign the new string to a variable in an assignment expression on the EVAL operation.

Besides the + operator, this section will discuss three built-in functions for strings: %TRIM, %TRIMR, and %TRIML. These three built-in functions let you remove trailing and leading blanks from a string.

The CAT Operation

CAT (Concatenate) is RPG IV's fixed-form concatenation operation. You can specify two strings (*source string 1* and *source string 2*) and join their values to create a new *result string*.

CAT provides two essential and similar types of concatenation. First is a pure concatenation that appends the value of source string 2 to the value of source string 1 and then stores the combination in the result string. The final string retains all leading and trailing blanks from both original strings, if the Result field is large enough to hold the entire string. The second type of concatenation lets you trim all trailing blanks from the value of source string 1 and then insert zero or more blanks before appending the value of source string 2, again storing the result in the result string. This concatenation retains all leading blanks from both original strings but retains trailing blanks only from the appended string. You control how many intervening blanks to insert.

Factor 1	Opcode	(Extender)	Factor 2	Result	Indicators
Optional *source string 1*	CAT	(P)	Required *source string 2:# blanks*	Required *result string*	Not allowed

The table above summarizes the entries for CAT. Factor 1, which is optional, is where you specify source string 1. Factor 1 can be a string field, literal, or named constant. This string's value will have the value of source string 2 appended to it before the operation stores the concatenated value in the Result field. If you choose not to specify Factor 1, the operation will take the value of the string you specify in the Result field as source string 1. If you are concatenating a person's title and last name, "Mr." and "Jones", source string 1 is the string "Mr.".

Factor 2, a required entry, is where you specify source string 2. Factor 2 can be a string, character field, or named constant. CAT will append the value of this string to the value of source string 1 and then store both in the result string. If you are concatenating a person's title and last name, "Mr." and "Jones", source string 2 is the string "Jones".

Factor 2 has an optional parameter that controls how to handle trailing blanks from source string 1 and how many blanks you want in the result. To specify the optional Factor 2 parameter, which can be a numeric integer field, literal or named constant, you enter a colon after source string 2 and then specify the number of blanks to insert. If you do not include the optional parameter, when building the concatenated value, CAT will retain all the trailing blanks from source string 1. If you include the optional parameter and the value is 0, all trailing blanks will be removed from the value of source string 1, no additional blanks will be inserted, and the value of source string 2 will be concatenated to the trimmed value of source string 1. Leading blanks from source string 2 will be retained.

This difference between not specifying the parameter and specifying it with a value of 0 has confused many a programmer. When you specify the parameter and use a positive, non-zero value, that number of blanks will be inserted after the trimmed value from source string 1 and before the value from source string 2. Again, remember that the leading blanks are retained from the value of source string 2, and those blanks are not included in the count of blanks that CAT inserts.

Finally, the Result field, which is required, is where you specify the string field that will hold the concatenated string. Because you are building a string from other strings, you need to ensure that the Result field is large enough to hold any value you put into it. You can easily forget the number of blanks you're inserting or that the source string may not have any trailing blanks to truncate. These memory lapses let you specify a field that is too small to hold the result of the concatenation. If the Result field is too small, the additional characters are truncated from the right, which leads to the question of what happens when the Result field is larger than the concatenated value.

Like SUBST, CAT is just a glorified MOVEL operation with concatenation capabilities. Because of RPG's MOVEL rules, the data in the Result field is replaced only up to the length of the concatenated value of the result string. Any old data in non-replaced positions remains unless you clear it. By specifying the (P) operation extender after CAT in the operation field of the C-spec, you can blank the remainder of the positions after the concatenated value is in the Result field. CAT does not support resulting indicators.

Note that you cannot specify figurative constants as the strings in this operation. Figurative constants have no defined length and, therefore, have no set value that string operations can reference or include. Additionally, the Result field cannot overlap with either Factor 1 or Factor 2 in a data structure.

The + Operator and the %TRIM, %TRIMR, and %TRIML Built-In Functions

RPG also supports concatenation in free-form expressions. To perform concatenation in an expression, you enter the + operator with two strings (fields, strings, or named constants), *source string 1* and *source string 2*, as the operands. Unlike CAT, the + operator does not directly trim trailing blanks from the end of source string 1. Nor does it insert padding blanks between the two source strings. However, when using expression-style concatenation, you get a little more flexibility in one area while losing a little in another.

Function	Parameters
%TRIM	(string)
%TRIMR	(string)
%TRIML	(string)

This flexibility comes from three new built-in functions, %TRIM, %TRIMR (Trim Right), and %TRIML (Trim Left), which the table above lists. These functions delete leading and trailing blanks from strings. Recall that CAT can trim trailing blanks only from source string 1. With the trimming built-in functions, though, you can trim from both directions, and because trimming occurs directly to a string rather than indirectly via another operation (as with CAT), you can trim both source string 1 and source string 2.

The three built-in functions handle trimming in slightly different ways. %TRIM returns a string with all leading and trailing blanks removed. %TRIMR returns a string with all trailing blanks removed from the right end of the string. %TRIML returns a string with all leading blanks removed from the left end of the string. You get a lot more trimming flexibility when you concatenate with expressions and built-in functions than with CAT.

RPG has no direct support or built-in function to insert blanks between values you're concatenating. Instead, you must include a field, string, or named constant in an expression to concatenate as many blanks as you need into the final string. Of course, this situation means multiple concatenation processes are occurring. Three strings are in the expression: the original two and the third string in the middle, which provides the intervening padding characters.

What about the statement that you lose some flexibility? With the CAT operator, you can specify a variable to determine the number of blanks to insert between the values. (That specification is not an option with expression-level concatenation.) However, inserting these intervening blanks is not a variable process; it is usually fixed at 1 or 2 spaces. An intrepid person can probably rectify this situation by building several fields of varying lengths and then using a pointer-based field in the expression to determine which field is involved in the concatenation at runtime, but the result is probably not worth the effort.

TRANSLATING AND VERIFYING STRINGS

Two other vital capabilities complete the suite of string-handling functions: character translation and string validation. Translation or conversion of characters is not about how to write multi-lingual string-handling routines. This type of translation is a simple replacement translation, where you exchange one character for another. String translation usually converts a string from mixed case to all uppercase or all lowercase. You will recall that the SCAN operation, which lets you perform string searches, is case sensitive. Translating a string to one case before scanning can give you case-insensitive search capability. RPG provides the XLATE operation to perform replacement translation of the type A replaces a, B replaces b, and so on.

The second task is validating a string's content. Suppose you have a user-input field and this field must contain certain characters. RPG provides an easy way to validate the contents of a field against a set of allowed characters. If you require certain characters but not certain patterns (SCAN is used for verifying patterns), verifying all valid character combinations can be time- and code-consuming. However, RPG's CHECK and CHECKR operations make this type of validation a snap. As a bonus, these operations also scan for characters that are not equal to a given character, something SCAN can't do.

The XLATE Operation Code

The XLATE (Translate) operation lets you extract one string from another, apply a set of replacement rules to the extracted string, and create a new string consisting of characters that result from applying the replacement rules to the originally extracted string. The main use for this operation is to provide mixed-case to uppercase or lowercase conversion. However, that is not XLATE's only purpose. For very light security purposes, you can have XLATE encrypt data. The word "encrypt" can be misleading in this case, because this function is only a simple replacement algorithm. Nevertheless, it can keep wandering eyes from getting data they might otherwise pick up too easily.

This discussion will focus on XLATE's case-conversion facility as a way to set up case-insensitive searches. Old databases and programs have data stored and processed in all capital letters. Modern systems output mixed-case information because it is so much more readable.

Mixed case works well for constants and field headings on screen and on reports because programs don't have to interact with such fixed data. The data the users key and that comes out on reports needs to be in mixed case, too.

You can easily allow entry and storage of mixed-case data. OS/400 access path facilities even let you ensure that mixed-case key fields are unique in a case-insensitive way.

However, when programs need to compare and contrast mixed-case data elements, you run into problems. SCANs are case sensitive; relational tests are case sensitive. The CHECK and CHECKR operations are case sensitive. So how do you function in a case-insensitive world with case-sensitive tools? You manipulate the world.

Consider an end-user search facility. When users want to find ACME Arrow in their database, they don't want to be concerned with whether the person who entered the record called it ACME Arrow, Acme Arrow, or Acme arrow. They want to type any one of those variations and have the system find it. Using XLATE, you can convert the text they type (such as "acme arrow") as a search argument into an internal value of "ACME ARROW". Next, as you read through the database searching for the appropriate records, you can convert each entry you read before comparing or scanning the field. When your program hits "ACME Arrow", you just convert it to "ACME ARROW". Now you can SCAN the converted database value using the converted user request and you have a match. This method is not a lot of work; both conversions require one line of code.

The following table shows the syntax of the XLATE operation code. Factor 1, which is required, is where you identify the sets of characters that will replace the original characters. You need two strings, a *from-set string* and a *to-set string*. You separate the from-set string and to-set string with a colon, but you specify both in Factor 1. The two strings can be string fields, literals, or named constants. The two sets must have the same number of characters. During translation, each character in the string you're translating is checked against the characters in the from-set string. If the character is in the set, the corresponding character in the to-set string replaces the character in the string you're translating.

Factor 1	Opcode	(Extender)	Factor 2	Result	Indicators		
Required *from set:to set*	XLATE	(P)	Required *source string: start pos*	Required *result string*	N/A	Error	N/A

The relationship between the characters in the from- and to-set strings is simply ordinal. The first character in the from-set corresponds to the first character in the to-set, the second to the second, and so on. You can see why the two sets must have the same number of characters. The most common sets are "abcdefghijklmnopqrstuvwxyz" and "ABCDEFGHIJKLMNOPQRSTUVWXYZ". You usually set up these characters as named constants. The one-to-one correspondence allows the case translation.

Factor 2, which is required, is where you identify the string to translate, the *source string*. XLATE extracts a string from the field, literal, or named constant in Factor 2 and applies the translation to the extracted string. You must supply a source string to translate. As with SUBST, by entering an optional parameter in Factor 2, you can specify a starting position within the source string to identify the extracted string. You follow the source string with a colon and an integer numeric field, literal, or named constant to supply the starting position within the string.

The Result field, which is required, must be a string field that will hold the translated string. Once you extract and translate the string, it goes into the Result field.

The move of the data follows standard RPG move rules. If the Result field is too small to hold the resultant string, the string is truncated on the right. If the string is shorter than the Result field, only the data up to the length of the resultant string is replaced. Any data after that remains. After the move, by specifying the padding operation extender (P) with XLATE, you can clear the positions that the move of the data does not directly affect.

A resulting indicator is allowed in positions 73 and 74 to handle the possibility that the starting position might be invalid (zero or negative). Note that you cannot specify figurative constants as the strings in this operation. Figurative constants have no defined length and, therefore, have no set value that string operations can reference or include. Additionally, the Result field cannot overlap with either the Factor 1 or Factor 2 field in a data structure.

Note that the term set as used with the XLATE operation refers to the characters you specify as the from-set string and to-set string. Usually, in RPG IV, a string reference is a sequence of characters whose order cannot be disturbed;

whose order has some significant meaning. In the case of the from- and to-sets for XLATE, the strings in the sets have an ordinal relationship, but the order in which the characters are placed in the arrays affects only that ordinal relationship. The order in which the characters are placed in these strings has no significance.

The CHECK and CHECKR Operation Codes

If you specify a set of valid characters to compare with, CHECK and CHECKR can compare every character in a string with that set of characters. CHECK and CHECKR return the first position in the string at which a character does not match any valid character in the set.

A notable difference between CHECK and CHECKR and SCAN is that SCAN finds matches between a search string and a base string, whereas CHECK and CHECKR find *mismatches*. This difference opens up another world of use for CHECK and CHECKR: the ability to find the first character that *doesn't* match another. One of CHECK and CHECKR's most common uses is to find the first or last non-blank character in a string. By specifying a character set that has only a blank in it and then running the CHECK or CHECKR operation, you will get the string's first or last position that is not blank.

Factor 1	Opcode	(Extender)	Factor 2	Result	Indicators		
Required *compare string set*	CHECK		Required *base string:start*	Optional *position not found*	N/A	Error	Match Found
Required *compare string set*	CHECKR		Required *base string:start*	Optional *position not found*	N/A	Error	Match Found

The table above shows the syntax for the CHECK and CHECKR operation codes. In Factor 1, which is required, you specify a string field, literal, or named constant that contains one or more characters. Be cautious when you use a field, because blank positions in a field count as characters in the set. Make sure blanks are allowed in the field you are checking if you are using a field that might not always have a fixed number of characters.

Factor 2, also required, is where you identify the string field, literal, or named constant whose value you want to check. By default, the check will start at the beginning of the field with CHECK and at the end of the field with CHECKR. By specifying a start position, you can control where CHECK or CHECKR starts. To do so, enter a colon immediately after the string you want to check, and then enter the name of a numeric integer field, literal, or named constant. CHECK will validate all characters in the string from the start position to the end of the base string. CHECKR will validate all characters in the string from the start position to the beginning of the the the base string.

CHECK and CHECKR set the value of a numeric field or subscripted array element in the Result field. This value corresponds to the position in the base string relative to the start of the string. As with SCAN, you can also use an unsubscripted array reference to have CHECK and CHECKR report as many invalid characters as possible. When an array is in the Result field, the first position whose character doesn't match one in the set identified in Factor 1 will be placed in the first element of the array. If you have fewer mismatches than array elements, the remaining elements will be set to zero. If you have more mismatches than array elements, you get only as many mismatches as you have array entries. If multiple mismatches occur, the array entries will contain the positions in ascending order for CHECK and in descending order for CHECKR. The array is not sorted either way, but the array elements, which are loaded starting at element 1 for either operation, contain the mismatched entries in the order in which they are found. You can specify an error indicator in positions 73 and 74 to check for errors such as the starting position in Factor 2 being invalid.

Note that you cannot specify figurative constants as the strings in these operations. Figurative constants have no defined length and, therefore, have no set value that string operations can reference or include. Additionally, the Result field cannot overlap with either Factor 1 or Factor 2 in a data structure.

String-Handling APPLICATIONS

One string operation often accompanies another. String-handling operations often complement one another. One will locate data in a string, and another will extract that data. To demonstrate the power of bringing these commands together, this series of examples highlights the major tasks a sophisticated search facility must handle.

One main feature of RPG string operations is to let you perform case-insensitive searches. The first example examines the steps necessary to allow case-insensitivity. The second extracts a phrase that's within a set of delimiters. The third locates, extracts, and searches for text within a string while ignoring leading and trailing blanks. The last example formats some data to make it easy to read.

XLATE by Example

In the following code sample, XLATE enables a case-insensitive search. You need to convert all characters in the search and searched string to the same case. This conversion lets you compare the contents of both fields.

The LIKE keyword defines SrchParm and DataValue as having the same attributes as the external fields ScrnFld and DBFld. The XLATE operation, using the two named constants, goes through the field in Factor 2, examining each character to see whether it matches a character specified in Factor 1. If such a

```
*...1....+....2....+....3....+....4....+....5....+....6....+....7....+
D LCase           C                    'abcdefghijklmnopqrstuvwxyz'
D UCase           C                    'ABCDEFGHIJKLMNOPARSTUVWXYZ'
D SrchParm        S                    LIKE(ScrnFld)
D DataValue       S                    LIKE(DBFld)

*...1....+....2....+....3....+....4....+....5....+....6....+....7....+
C       LCase:UCase   XLATE    DBFld           DataValue
C       LCase:UCase   XLATE    ScrnFld         SrchParm
```

character is found, the corresponding character in the second field in Factor 1 takes that character's place in the Result field. If no such match occurs, the original character from Factor 2 is used without modification. After the operation, the Result field will have the converted value, an uppercase string.

Notice that this example does *not* use the padding option with XLATE. In this case, the work fields that hold the uppercase version of the data are based on the sizes of the fields being translated. Therefore, the resultant string will always be the same size as the original string, so you do not need padding.

SCAN and %SUBST( ) by Example
The routine in the following example lets you extract data from a string between delimiter characters that you supply. Because this code is a generic string processor, it imposes some restrictions. You have to load three things each time you call the subroutine. You must specify a delimiter character by placing it into the field ExtDlm, the string to search must be in the field ExtSrc, and the field PrvLoc must be set to 0 the first time you call the subroutine. If you call the subroutine several times, the routine automatically stores the previous location of the last delimiter and, by iteratively calling the routine, lets you extract several strings if they occur between the delimiter characters. This code can let you extract comma-delimited data from a string, for instance.

The data this subroutine returns is in two fields: ExtTxt and ExtFnd. The first field contains the extracted string and the second is a flag that signals whether a string is extracted. Because an extracted string can be blank, you must use a separate flag to record a blank string. The routine will even return a zero-length string as blanks if the previous delimiter location and the newly found delimiter are in adjacent positions in the string being examined.

You need 10 fields in this routine to extract a string between particular delimiter characters. ExtFnd indicates whether a delimited string is found (extracted). ExtDlm is where you load the delimiter character for defining the start and end of the string to extract. ExtSrc is where you load the string in which you are searching for the delimited string. ExtTxt is the text of the delimited string after you extract it. ExtLen is the length of the string that is extracted

```
*...1....+....2....+....3....+....4....+....5....+....6....+....7....+.
D ExtFnd          S              1
D ExtDlm          S              1
D ExtSrc          3            256
D ExtTxt          S                        LIKE(ExtSrc)
D ExtLen          S              3  0
D ExtStr          S                        LIKE(ExtLen)
D Pos1            S                        LIKE(ExtLen)
D CurLoc          S                        LIKE(ExtLen)
D PrvLoc          S                        LIKE(ExtLen)

*...1....+....2....+....3....+....4....+....5....+....6....+....7....+.
 **********************************************************************
 * Extract string up to next delimiter
 **********************************************************************
C     ExtString     BEGSR
 *
 * If the previous Delimiter is after end of field,
 * no delimited string is available
C                   IF        PrvLoc > 256
C                   EVAL      ExtFnd = 'N'
C                   GOTO      EExtString
C                   ELSE
 * otherwise note that a delimited string will be found
C                   EVAL      ExtFnd = 'Y'
C                   ENDIF
 *
 * Scan for the next delimiter character
C                   EVAL      Pos1 = PrvLoc + 1
C     ExtDlm        SCAN      ExtSrc:Pos1    CurLoc
 *
 * If no delimiter found, delimited string ends at last byte of field
C                   IF        CurLoc = 0
C                   EVAL      CurLoc = 256 + 1
C                   ENDIF
 *
 * Calculate length of delimited string
C                   EVAL      ExtLen = CurLoc - PrvLoc - 1
 *
 * If delimited string has a non-zero length, extract the delimited
 * string
C                   IF        ExtLen > 0              CONTINUED
```

```
*...1....+....2....+....3....+....4....+....5....+....6....+....7....+.
C                       EVAL      ExtStr = PrvLoc + 1
C                       EVAL      ExtTxt =
C                                 %SUBSTR(ExtSrc:ExtStr:ExtLen)
C                       ELSE
 * Otherwise, set the exracted string to blank
C                       EVAL      ExtTxt = *BLANKS
C                       ENDIF
 *
 * Record new previous location as current location
C                       EVAL      PrvLoc = CurLoc
 *
C         EExtString    ENDSR
```

(which can be zero if the two delimiters are next to each other or at either end
of the string). ExtStr marks the start of the string to extract. The start is right
after the opening delimiter but must be recorded because the opening delimiter
can be the beginning of the string rather than a character in the string. Pos1 is a
temporary field whose only function is to give you a shorter field name to
squeeze both a string and a positioner into the Factor 2 when you perform a
SCAN later. Finally, CurLoc and PrvLoc note the positions of the ending delimiter on the last extraction (the beginning delimiter for the current extraction)
and the ending delimiter on the current extraction.

This subroutine ExtString is a generic routine you can call to extract a
string that is between delimiters. Here, you have some examples of scanning
and substringing. The routine starts by checking whether the last delimiter's
position is at the end of the string. If the position is greater than the size of the
field that houses the string, you can conclude that the last time this routine was
used, it extracted a string up to the end of the string. In that case, you do not
have a string to extract, and you immediately set the value of ExtFnd to N and
use a GOTO to exit the subroutine. If not, you know that you will find a string.
Remember, this function will return a zero-length string as a blank string. It will
also return a non-zero length string that has only blanks as a blank string.
Because RPG does not support variable-length fields, you need a flag to indicate whether you find a string (of any length) to extract; you cannot directly
test the field that contains the extracted string.

Next, starting at one position past the last delimiter (which you must have
set to zero on the first call to the subroutine), you start searching for the next
delimiter. Because SCAN has no free-form version, you must calculate a temporary field to hold the position that is one to the right of the previous delimiter. Pos1 holds this value, and is the starting position with the ExtSrc field for
the SCAN to start searching. The next delimiter, if found, will have its position

recorded in CurLoc. If no delimiter is found, indicated by a zero CurLoc, the end of the string is the end of the string (and, logically, the next delimiter), so you record the delimiter position as being 1 byte to the right of the string's length. You will use this value to calculate the length of the delimited string, so a value outside the range of possible positions within the string is allowed.

Now you calculate the length of the delimited string, using the positions of the two delimiters. If you have a non-zero length, you can now extract the string by first calculating its starting position, which is 1 byte to the right of the leading delimiter. Then, using the built-in function %SUBST( ), you extract the string from ExtSrc, starting at ExtStr and extracting ExtLen characters, the length of the string. If the string length is zero, you set the string to *Blanks.

Finally, you take the current position of the terminating delimiter you just found on this pass. You record its position as being the new previous position for the next pass through this routine.

You can use this routine to load any data value up to the size of that field (here, 256 bytes) into the ExtSrc field and load any delimiters and extract a string based on those delimiters. Although you indicate that the important data being returned is the extracted string and the *found* flag, you can also use the fields that contain location information about the extracted string. ExtLen will provide the length of the string, ExtStr will indicate the start of the extracted string in the original string, and PrvLoc will always indicate the position of the last delimiter in the original string.

SUBST, CHECK, and CHECKR by Example

The next routine lets you feed it the data from a field that is to be scanned for a character string that matches the contents of a search-value field. Like the previous example, this one imposes some requirements on the code that executes the subroutine. The calling code must set the field that contains the text to be searched, DataValue, and the field that contains the search text, SrchParm. The routine will return a flag in the SchTrue field to signal whether the text in the SrchParm field is found in the DataValue field.

The function works by stripping the leading and trailing blanks from an incoming search field's text. Then the function uses the text to SCAN and see whether the text is in the data field value that is passed in. To perform the SCAN effectively, you must extract the text found in the search field, and put it into a temporary field that can be the basis for a SCAN.

This routine uses two fields that you must set before executing the subroutine. SrchParm holds the text that you are searching for, and DataValue holds the data from the field that is being analyzed. The routine will return a flag in the SchTrue field. It will be set to N when the search value is not found in the analyzed value. It will be set to Y when the search text is found in the data being analyzed.

```
*...1....+....2....+....3....+....4....+....5....+....6....+....7....+
D Srch            S            256
D DataValue       S                      LIKE(Srch)
 *
D SchTrue         S              1
 *
D Txt             S            256
D TxtLen          S              3 0
D TxtStr          S                      LIKE(TxtLen)
D TxtEnd          S                      LIKE(TxtLen)
D TxtPos          S                      LIKE(TxtLen)

*...1....+....2....+....3....+....4....+....5....+....6....+....7....+.
 *
 *****************************************************************************
 * Test to see if phrase is found in data (Leading/trailing blanks
 * ignored; embedded blanks retained)
 *****************************************************************************
 *
C     ProcPhr      BEGSR
 *
 * Assume failure until success proven
C                  EVAL      SchTrue = 'N'
 *
 * A blank phrase string always evaluates to true
C                  IF        DataValue = *BLANKS
C                  EVAL      SchTrue = 'Y'
C                  GOTO      EProcPhr
C                  ENDIF
 *
 * Find start and end of phrase in string; calculate length
C     ' '          CHECK     Srch          TxtStr
C     ' '          CHECKR    Srch          TxtEnd
C                  EVAL      TxtLen = TxtEnd - TxtStr + 1
 *
 * Extract the text from the phrase string
C     TxtLen       SUBST (P) Srch:TxtStr   Txt
 *
 * Scan for the prase text being in the data field being analyzed
C     Txt:TxtLen   SCAN      DataValue     TxtPos
 *
```

CONTINUED

```
*...1....+....2....+....3....+....4....+....5....+....6....+....7....+.
 * If the phrase text was found, set success for search
C                     IF      TxtPos > 0
C                     EVAL    SchTrue 'Y'
C                     ENDIF
 *
C         EProcPhr    ENDSR
```

The next four fields find, record the position of, and extract the text from the search value to eliminate the effect of any leading and trailing blanks. In order, they store the text, the length of the text, the start of the text in the search field, and the end of the text in the search field. The fifth field records the location of the search text in the data value being analyzed. The routine uses this information to determine whether you get a hit when you scan for the text you are trying to find.

The routine ProcPhr analyzes a data value by finding the first and last character in the search string, extracting the string, and then searching for that extracted string in the DataValue field. First, the routine assumes that the search text is not found in DataValue or that the comparison of the search text to the string is false. Next, you make sure that you return a successful search if the search field is blank (which is equivalent to not making a selection).

The CHECK and CHECKR operations on SrchParm find the first and last non-blank characters of the search string text. If you have a blank as the only character to check in the CHECK and CHECKR operations, the first and last non-blank character positions will be reported as the positions that have failed the CHECK and CHECKR operations. The starting and ending positions are recorded in the TxtStr and TxtEnd fields, respectively. With this information, you can calculate the length of the text in the search string and store it in the TxtLen field. Note that this approach preserves any embedded spaces while trimming off the leading and trailing spaces.

After you record the starting position and the length, you can extract the text from the search string and store it in Txt. You need the SUBST operation — or you can use %SUBST( ). Note that the example includes padding to make certain that any data already in the field Txt is cleared in positions after the end of the text that you just extracted. Once you extract the search text, you can use it and the known length to scan the DataValue field to see whether the text is found. Note here that the example uses the optional length argument to specify that you want only the first TxtLen characters of the Txt field in the SCAN operation. If you do not use that technique, SCAN includes all trailing blanks in the Txt field, and the SCANs will probably never find a match.

If the operation finds the search text in the DataValue (SCAN reports a non-zero TxtPos), you can set the SchTrue flag to Y to override the original assumption of false and signal that the search for the phrase text was successful.

CAT, %TRIMR, and + by Example

One capability that the previous examples don't demonstrate is concatenation and trimming. Often, you need to format data so users can read it or to make it appear in a natural format. An example is formatting the first and last names from a data record in the last-name-comma-first-name format. The following code shows how to do that in both fixed-form and free-form forms.

```
*...1....+....2....+....3....+....4....+....5....+....6....+....7....+
C     LastName     CAT      ',':0          FmtdName
C                  CAT      FirstName:1    FmtdName


C                  EVAL     FmtdName = %TRIMR(LastName) + ', ' +
C                                       FirstName
```

The two sets of code here are equivalent. The first example uses two CAT operations to build the formatted name in the field FmtdName. The first CAT concatenates the LastName field with a comma. The :0 in Factor 2 of the CAT operation means you want to trim the trailing spaces on the LastName and then insert zero spaces before appending the comma. This specification puts the comma immediately after the last character of the last name. Next, you concatenate the value in FirstName onto the previously created value and store it back into the same field. Here, the :1 in Factor 2 of CAT truncates the trailing blanks that follow the comma and then inserts one blank before appending the First-Name field to the string. Note that this code does not suppress any leading blanks that happen to be in the FirstName field.

The second example performs the same operation but uses free-form operations. The result is again stored in the FmtdName field, but you do not have to build the string step by step. Although you have only one operation, EVAL, you are performing two concatenations with the + operators. To trim any trailing blanks from the LastName field, you specify the built-in function %TRIMR(). The value ', ' (a comma and a space) is then appended to the last name. Note that you have to explicitly specify the number of spaces as a literal (or do an additional concatenation of some field or constant that is exactly one space long). There is no method for specifying a variable number of insertion characters with free-form concatenation. To round out the expression, the first name is concatenated after the blank, which, in turn, follows the comma.

CHAPTER 10

Date, Time, and Timestamp

Although IBM introduced AS/400 date, time, and timestamp data types before RPG IV, RPG is just now gaining the capabilities to let you do anything with these important data types. The AS/400 has let you store these data types in the database, and basic OS/400 facilities such as OPNQRYF (Open Query File) and CPYF (Copy File) have supported them for a while. But RPG has limited its support to converting these data type references to character fields that you then had to handle carefully to avoid incurring a runtime error, or worse, an error that corrupts your data.

Up to now, date processing with RPG has required complex routines that you kept in a copy library or accessed through called programs. Now you can forget all that, thanks to RPG IV's new date manipulation capabilities, which work with RPG's other, existing date capabilities.

In many applications, you face the problem of manipulating dates, times, and timestamps. An example is an application for invoicing customers and notifying them when they pass their payment due date. The application must find today's date and calculate the due date for each invoice. RPG now provides tools to manipulate date and time fields in such applications and to retrieve the date in different formats: To access a job's job date, RPG has the sets of special words UDATE, UMONTH, UYEAR, UDAY, and *DATE, *YEAR, *MONTH, *DAY; to access the system time and date, RPG IV has the TIME operation code.

The job date is when a job starts. This date does not roll over at midnight, so it remains constant for the job's duration, no matter how long it runs. In contrast, the system time and date are the real-world clock time and calendar date. The system time and date change at midnight, whereas the job date remains the same as long as the job is running.

The new date, time, and timestamp capabilities work with data types of the same names. These types let you define a field specifically as a date or time field and then format and manipulate it appropriately. The new ADDDUR (Add Duration), SUBDUR (Subtract Duration), TEST, and EXTRCT (Extract data from a date or time field) operation codes let you manipulate date and time fields.

DATE SPECIAL WORDS AND EDITING OUTPUT

Until recently, to retrieve the job date, RPG had only four special words: UDATE, UYEAR, UMONTH, and UDAY. UDATE gets the entire date, with two-digit month, day, and year. Because UDATE is an RPG special word, RPG automatically defines it with a preset length of six. UYEAR, UMONTH, and UDAY

Strinfskr

Info seeker

ILE RPG

retrieve the job year, month, and day, respectively. As with UDATE, RPG sets the size of each of these fields as two characters.

OS/400 Version 2, Release 2 (V2R2) introduced four new RPG special words, *DATE, *YEAR, *MONTH, and *DAY, for accessing the job date. They perform the same function as the old special words but the *DATE and *YEAR words return the century portion of the date, in addition to the year. So UDATE returns a date like 051797, and *DATE returns 05171997. Likewise, *YEAR returns 1996, as opposed to UYEAR's 96. RPG predetermines the size of these new special words as variables. The complete list of RPG's special date and time words and their sizes is in the table below.

U-words	Size	*-words	Size
UDATE	6	*DATE	8
UYEAR	2	*YEAR	4
UMONTH	2	*MONTH	2
UDAY	2	*DAY	2

Although these special words access the job date and return a value that represents that date in a form similar to a named constant, these dates are *not* date data type fields. These dates are just two-, four-, six-, or eight-digit, class numeric named constants. This table shows an example of the date value that each special word represents.

Special Word	Value
*DATE	05171997
UDATE	051797
*YEAR	1997
UYEAR	97
*MONTH	05
UMONTH	05
*DAY	17
UDAY	17

Values represented by the date
special words on May 17, 1997
(assuming system is using the
default *MDY date format)

You can use special-word date fields in C-specs. You can enter them only in Factor 1 or Factor 2 because they are constants; placing them in the Result field implies that they will receive a value, which is not possible for constants. The special words, which reference only the job date, are read only: You cannot modify them. This restriction limits you further than just keeping you from using a date special field in the Result field on a C-spec. In addition, you cannot specify these special fields as Factor 1 of a PARM (Parameter) operation code, as the

Factor 2 index of LOOKUP operations, with BLANK AFTER in the O-specs, as input fields, or anywhere the field will receive a value.

Remember that the user date fields contain the job date, not the system date. For an interactive program, the job date is set when the job starts running. For a batch program, it is set when the job goes to the job queue. In either case, the user date fields are not updated when the program runs past midnight (when the system date changes). To access the system date from a program, you cannot rely on the the the *-word and U-word facilities, such as *DATE and UDAY.

Editing Dates and Times

These values are just numbers. They are not formatted to differentiate the month from the day from the year. If you use these special words on a program's O-specs, you get the class numeric scalar values in the previous table. Of course, users want to see a separator, a character such as a dash, to split up the parts of the date and make it readable. Such editing of date special-word fields involves specifying that you want formatting and specifying the separator character. In addition, you need to tell the system the order you want the date parts in; for example, 13-01-96, or 1996-10-13.

You can edit these fields' printed or displayed appearance by specifying an edit code in position 44 of the O-specs. Usually, you will specify the Y edit code to put a separator character between the month, day, and year. The Y edit code puts the separator character you specify (or the default slash) where you need it so that the month, day, and year will appear as separate parts of the date. Without this edit code, you can still print or display the date values from the special date words, but the date will not be formatted. You can specify a different separator character for the whole program, on the DATEDIT (Date Edit) keyword on the H-spec.

The DATEDIT Keyword

The DATEDIT keyword, which you can specify only on the H-specs, lets you determine the order of the date parts you get from the *DATE and UDATE keywords, the location of the separator character when you specify the Y edit code, and the separator character and where it will appear between the date's parts when the Y edit code is present. The separator character can be any character except the ampersand (&). Specifying this special character results in a space as the separator. The table on page 302 lists the formats you can specify with DATEDIT.

DATEDIT is a direct replacement for the values you used to code in the H-spec positions 19 and 20. Because the H-specs are now free form, you can specify this keyword anywhere on the H-specs. The DATEDIT keyword's syntax is DATEDIT (fmt{separator}). The fmt parameter establishes the date format.

Date Formats	DATEDIT value	Examples (using Y edit code and default / as separator character)	
		*DATE	UDATE
Month/Day/Year	*MDYx	05/17/1997	05/17/97
Day/Month/Year	*DMYx	17/05/1997	17/05/97
Year/Month/Day	*YMDx	1997/05/17	97/05/17

x can be any valid character and is optional. The character you specify will be the separator (except for &, which will cause a space). The default separator character is /.

Within parentheses, immediately following the DATEDIT keyword, you enter the format code (e.g., *MDY, *YMD) that establishes the order of the parts of the *-word and U-word dates. After the value of this fmt parameter, you provide the character (e.g., dash, slash) you want as the separator between the month, day, and year. If you do not specify DATEDIT, the default date format is *MDY/ (month/day/year).

The output format of date fields depends on whether you enter the Y edit code, the value you specify with the DATEDIT keyword on the H-specs, and the length of the date field you're editing. The table below shows how the Y edit code will format a date field, depending on the combination of the DATEDIT value and the length of the date field. Note that you can specify the Y edit code not only on any date word, but you can also enter it for any three- to nine-digit numeric field because all the *-words and U-words produce nothing more than two-, four-, six-, or eight-digit numeric named constants that the compiler initializes.

DATEDIT value	3-digit	4-digit	5-digit	6-digit	7-digit	8-digit	9-digit
*MDYx	99x9	99x99	99x99x9	99x99x99	999x99x99	99x99x9999	999x99x9999
*DMYx	99x9	99x99	99x99x9	99x99x99	999x99x99	99x99x9999	999x99x9999
*YMDx	99x9	99x99	99x99x9	99x99x99	999x99x99	9999x99x99	99999x99x99

In all examples, x represents any character you want to use as a separator, or a space (specified as an ampersand on the DATEDIT code but manifested as a space in the formatted result)

Note that you can specify the Y edit code in an RPG program only for a program-described file. If you use externally described printer files, the DATEDIT keyword only orders the date parts in the date words but does nothing about separators — neither identifying the separator character nor positioning the separators.

DATEDIT with User Date Constants by Example
If you work for a company with branches in Europe, you know that you need a different date format when you're dealing with those branches. In Europe, the

standard date format is day.month.year, and the period (.) character is the separator. The code below will output the job date in the European standard format.

```
*...1....+....2....+....3....+....4....+....5....+....6....+....7....+
H DATEDIT(*DMY.)
```

```
*...1....+....2....+....3....+....4....+....5....+....6....+....7....+
0                                          121 'DATE:'
0                        *DATE         Y   132
```

The DATEDIT keyword on the H-spec specifies how to construct the content of *DATE (or UDATE). For this program-described file, DATEDIT also establishes the formatting for the Y edit code. If this code is in your program and you execute it on May 17, 1997, the contents of *DATE will be 17051997 (UDATE will be 170597), and the formatted output of the *DATE field will be 17.05.1997; the period as the separator comes from the character that you specify on DATEDIT.

The TIME Operation Code

The user date special words retrieve the job date. To get the system date and time at any point during program processing, you need the TIME operation code. You specify TIME in the C-specs as the operation code (positions 26 through 35). In the required Result field, you must enter the name of the numeric field where you want to put the time. The table below summarizes the entries for TIME.

Factor 1	Opcode	Extender	Factor 2	Result	Indicators
Not allowed	TIME		Not allowed	Required numeric	Not allowed

The size of the Result field tells the compiler what portion of the system time and date you want. A 6-byte class numeric Result field means you want only the time. To access both the time and date, you must specify the Result field's length as 12 for a two-digit year (96) or 14 for a four-digit year (1996).

Regardless of the format you specify, for any TIME operation, the system always returns the time in the Result field's first six positions. The hours are in 24-hour format, with midnight appearing as 000000.

TIME Versus Date Special Words

When requesting the system date with the TIME operation, to manipulate the Result field's content, you must be aware of the format you'll get. Take care not to confuse how TIME works with how DATEDIT on the H-specs and the *-word and U-word date words function. DATEDIT has no effect on the format of the value the TIME operation returns. Instead, TIME returns the date in the format that the job's DATFMT attribute specifies. This value can be *MDY, *DMY, *YMD, or *JUL (Julian).

Before using the date from the TIME operation, make sure you understand your program's environment, or interrogate the system's runtime environment to find out what format you'll get, so you can handle the returned value appropriately. For instance, if you expect the date to be in *MDY format, include program code to convert from other formats if the job is using any other format than the one the program is expecting. This way, you can protect your application from errors during execution.

Beyond the date format, don't forget the other difference between the date you get with *DATE (or UDATE) and the date you get from TIME. Use TIME when you need the *system* time and date, the time and date when the TIME operation code is executed. *DATE (or UDATE) is the *job* date, the date when the job begins. Remember that the job date does not change when the system date changes, even if the job lasts past midnight.

RPG lets you access the time only by means of the TIME operation. But the availability of the date with the TIME operation brings up the question of when to get the date from the TIME operation or from the date words.

Because the values of the special date words don't roll over at midnight, you must ask whether the job(s) that the program will run in will ever be executing across that boundary and whether you want the date value to change. Or, if you have batch jobs, will you sometimes submit them before midnight but not start running them until after midnight?

If you always need the current date for recording logs or for setting an update date in a database record, you need the date from the TIME operation to ensure that you have a valid date. This consideration becomes even more important if you are storing the date and time of an operation. Something you're updating in a job that crosses the midnight boundary can appear to have occurred 24 hours before its actual occurrence. One frequent mistake is to forget that an interactive job that runs past midnight never gets its job date reset. This fact can cause unpredictable results if you are relying on the date special words and have interactive jobs running around the clock.

TIME by Example
Suppose you have an order entry application that runs 24 hours a day. When users enter an order, the entry needs to include both the date and time of the order's entry. That information also needs to be on the printed order entry transaction register. The code below is part of a subroutine to get the current date and time when you need it.

```
*...1....+....2....+....3....+....4....+....5....+....6....+....7....+
 *
C     GETCURDTTM     BEGSR
 *
 * Get the current date and time
 *
C                    TIME                SysDtTm          12 0
 *
 * Convert the system date and time to the expected format
 *
                                                     ○○ ○ ○○ ○

C                    ENDSR
```

The TIME operation retrieves both the system time and date because the Result field is 12 digits long. The field SysDtTm holds the time in its first six digits and the date in the last six digits. The time will be in the HHMMSS format, and the date can be in one of several formats (MMDDYY, DDMMYY, YYMMDD, YYDDD0), depending on the current setting of the job's DATFMT attribute, which you cannot see in a program.

DATE, TIME, AND TIMESTAMP DATA TYPES AND OPERATIONS

Once you retrieve the date and time, you sometimes need to manipulate the date and time values. Business programming often depends on incrementing, decrementing, and comparing dates and times. To perform such date- and time-specific calculations and processes, RPG IV introduces the new D (Date), T (Time), and Z (Timestamp) data types and the operation codes, ADDDUR (Add Duration), SUBDUR (Subtract Duration), EXTRCT, and TEST.

The D (Date) Data Type

The D (Date) data type defines a date field. Subfields support date manipulation operations. The D data type for date fields is as important as a type of alphanumeric for character fields and packed, zoned, or binary for numeric fields. If you declare character, the compiler will stop you from using it in arithmetic operations such as ADD, SUB, or Z-ADD. Analogously, only if you declare a date field will the compiler let you specify operations such as ADDDUR, SUBDUR, and EXTRCT.

To declare a date field, you specify D in position 40 (internal data type) on the D-specs. The RPG IV compiler declares these D fields internally with a pre-set field length. The following code shows how to specify a field as data type D.

```
*...1....+....2....+....3....+....4....+....5....+....6....+....7....+
D CurDt          S              D
 *
```

Field CurDt is a date field. This field will have the default date format of *ISO: YYYY-MM-DD, with a dash as the separator character. The field's size is automatically 10 bytes. You can move this date field into a 10-byte character field for displaying or printing, and the value will be formatted and ready for presentation.

The compiler determines a D type field by checking whether you've specified the DATFMT (Date Format) keyword on the D- or H-specs

The DATFMT Keyword

The DATFMT keyword lets you format the data in date data type fields. You can enter DATFMT in two places. First, you can specify DATFMT on the H-spec to establish a program-wide format for all date fields. Second, when you need various date fields in different formats, you can also specify DATFMT and a different format on a D-spec. This specification will affect only the field you're defining on that D-spec. The syntax for the DATFMT keyword is DATFMT (fmt{separator}).

When the compiler determines the format of a date field, any DATFMT keyword on a D-spec takes precedence over the DATFMT in the H-spec. If no DATFMT keyword is on a D-spec, the DATFMT on the H-spec applies to all date fields. If no DATFMT is on the H-spec, the default format is *ISO.

The date data type gives you flexibility. You can store a date in a date field in any valid format shown in the table on page 307. You can choose among several arrangements of the month, day, and year parts and among several separators. The value you specify for the fmt and separator parameter can be any valid date format and separator. Even if two dates have different formats, you can perform operations on them without worrying about the format; the compiler's runtime converts the date fields from one format to another, without destroying the date and time value, so the operations work correctly.

You can store a date field in YY/MM/DD format by adding the DATFMT(*YMD/) keyword to either the D-spec where you define the field or to the H-specs to provide a program-wide default. Better programming practice is to specify DATFMT on the H-spec to reflect your project or shop standards and then enter DATFMT at the D-spec level only if a particular field deviates from that standard. Of course, if your shop standard is ISO, you do not have to specify the DATFMT keyword at all, because *ISO is the default.

Date Formats	RPG Name	Format (Default Separator)	Valid Separator	Length	Example	*LOVAL	*HIVAL
Month/Day/Year	*MDY	mm/dd/yy	/ - . , &	8	01/29/95	01/01/40	12/31/39
Day/Month/Year	*DMY	dd/mm/yy	/ - . , &	8	29/01/95	01/01/40	31/12/39
Year/Month/Day	*YMD	yy/mm/dd	/ - . , &	8	95/01/29	40/01/01	39/12/31
Julian	*JUL	yy/ddd	/ - . , &	6	95/029	40/001	39/365
IBM USA Standard	*USA	mm/dd/yyyy	/	10	01/29/1995	01/01/0001	12/31/9999
IBM Euro Standard	*EUR	dd.mm.yyyy	.	10	29.01.1995	01.01.0001	31.12.9999
International Standard Organization	*ISO	yyyy-mm-dd	-	10	1995-01-29	0001-01-01	9999-12-31
Japanese Industrial Standard Christian Era	*JIS	yyyy-mm-dd	-	10	1995-01-29	0001-01-01	9999-12-31

One interesting point about the *MDY, *DMY, *YMD, and *JUL formats is that the date range is limited to dates between January 1, 1940, and December 31, 2039. The reason is that IBM chose to represent this range of 100 years as two-digit years. All the other formats can contain any dates because they all support four-digit years. In fact, that limitation is the primary reason why we do not suggest using any of the formats that have a two-digit year. It's better to begin using the four-digit year sooner rather than later.

The following code shows how to specify DATFMT on a D-spec. This field's value will be in *MDY format, using a separator (/) character: MM/DD/YY.

```
*...1....+....2....+....3....+....4....+....5....+....6....+....7....+
D CurDt          S              D   DATFMT(*MDY/)
 *
```

After you add DATFMT to the definition of date field CurDt, it is an 8-byte field, containing the date and separating slashes. You can now use the field for program-described output to a printer or data file, or you can move the value to an 8-byte character field for printing or displaying via an externally described printer or display file or for passing to another program as a parameter.

MOVE with Date (and Time) Data Types

You need to force the format of a date (or time) field only if you want to use the field in some process. Suppose you need to put the date into a character field so you can load it into a field defined in an externally described display file. To get the date out of the date field and into a character or numeric field in any of the allowed formats, you can specify MOVE and the format you want, regardless of the format specified with the date field. For example, suppose your shop standard for storing dates is *ISO, but you want to display a date in the familiar MM/DD/YY format. The code below loads the date to a character field in that format. If the date value in IntrnlDt is 1996-06-17, the result of the MOVE operation will be 06/17/96.

```
*...1....+....2....+....3....+....4....+....5....+....6....+....7....+
D IntrnlDt        S                   D   DATFMT(*ISO)
D DsplyDt         S             8A
```

```
*...1....+....2....+....3....+....4....+....5....+....6....+....7....+
C     *MDY/       MOVE      IntrnlDt     DsplyDt
```

Using the MOVE operation to convert a field from a numeric or character field to a date data-type field can be just as powerful. You can convert to USA standard format so that you can begin capturing century data. To keep your users happy, for an interim time, you want to let them continue keying the familiar two-digit year and let the program convert the date to a four-digit year before storing it in your database. The code below will convert the users' numeric six-digit date to a 10-character date data-type field in IBM USA standard date format.

```
*...1....+....2....+....3....+....4....+....5....+....6....+....7....+
D ExpDate         S                   D   DATFMT(*USA)
D InputDate       S             6P 0
```

```
*...1....+....2....+....3....+....4....+....5....+....6....+....7....+
C     *MDY        MOVE      InputDate    ExpDate
```

If a user keys 120495 into field InputDate, the expanded date in ExpDate will be 12/04/1995. This type of MOVE operation, using Factor 1 to define the format, will work with time and date fields.

The D Data Type by Example

The discussion of the TIME operation talks about accessing the system date. Once you get the system date, you can put it into a date field and then manipulate it. The result of the TIME operation is a 12- or 14-digit number representing the system date. You can specify the MOVE operation to transfer the system date into a date data type field.

```
*...1....+....2....+....3....+....4....+....5....+....6....+....7....+
D SysDtTm         S             12P 0
D CurDt           S                   D   DATFMT(*YMD/)
```

```
*...1....+....2....+....3....+....4....+....5....+....6....+....7....+
 *
C      GETCURDTTM     BEGSR
 *
 * Get the current date and time
 *
C                     TIME                    SysDtTm
 *
 *
 * Convert the system date to the expected format
 *
C      *JOBRUN        MOVE      SysDtTm       CurDt
 *
C                     ENDSR
```

The code above shows date fields and their automatic conversion capabilities. A D-spec defines the field CurDt as a date field with the format YY/MM/DD; the slashes are part of the stored value. The definition of SysDtTm is also in the D-specs.

You can specify a date format identifier, such as *MDY, *DMY, and *YMD, on Factor 1 on a MOVE operation to define the format of a character or numeric field that contains date data. The discussion of the TIME operation said that the date from this operation is in a format controlled by the attributes of the job in which the program is running. The special value *JOBRUN on the MOVE operation causes RPG's runtime to obtain the format attribute of the job in which this program is executing. And because the value the TIME operation returns depends on this job attribute, this MOVE statement converts the system date from whatever format it is received in to the format that you want to store it in, as defined on the D-spec for the CurDt field. Because the CurDt field uses a date data type, the field is now formatted and ready for printing. You can move it into another character field for display. (DDS does not support date data type fields on externally described display files.)

The T (Time) Data Type

Another new data type is T (Time), which tells the compiler that the field you are defining is a time field. The T data type determines what operations are possible on this field.

To define a field as data type T, you specify a T in position 40 (internal data type) on the D-specs. In all formats for time, the system automatically specifies an internal field length of eight characters.

The TIME operation code cannot load the time directly into a time data type field. TIME outputs only to numeric fields. To format the time value in such a field, you can MOVE that numeric field into a time data type field.

When you define a time data type field, the default storage format is *ISO (HH.MM.SS). To store the time in a different format, you can use the TIMFMT (Time Format) keyword.

The TIMEMT Keyword

The TIMFMT keyword controls the format of the data in time data type fields. You can specify TIMFMT in two places. First, you can specify it on an H-spec to establish a program-wide format for all time fields. In addition to this global specification, because you occasionally need various time fields in different formats, you can specify TIMFMT on a D-spec, where it will affect only the field you are defining.

To determine the format of a time field, the compiler's runtime checks first for a TIMFMT keyword on the D-spec that defines a particular time data type field. If a TIMFMT keyword is not on the D-spec, the TIMFMT keyword on the H-spec is in effect. If TIMFMT is not on the H-spec, the default format is *ISO.

The syntax for the TIMFMT keyword is TIMFMT (fmt{separator}). The values you specify for fmt and separator can be any time format and separator shown in the following table.

Time Formats	RPG Name	Default Separator	Valid Separators	Length	Example	*LOVAL	*HIVAL
Hours:Minutes:Seconds	*HMS	:	: . , &	8	14:00:00	00:00:00	24:00:00
International Standard Organization	*ISO	.	.	8	14.00.00	00.00.00	24.00.00
IBM USA Standard	*USA	:	:	8	02:00 PM	00:00 AM	12:00 AM
IBM Euro Standard	*EUR	.	.	8	14.00.00	00.00.00	24.00.00
Japanese Industrial Standard Christian Era	*JIS	:	:	8	14:00:00	00:00:00	24:00:00

You can store a time field in HH:MM:SS format (replacing *ISO's periods with colons) by adding the TIMFMT(*HMS:) keyword to either the D-spec where you define the field or on an H-spec to provide a program-wide default. The preferred alternative is TIMFMT on the H-spec to reflect your project or shop standards, and then TIMFMT at the D-spec level only if a particular field deviates from that standard. Of course, if your shop standard is ISO, you do not have to specify TIMFMT because *ISO is the default.

```
*...1....+....2....+....3....+....4....+....5....+....6....+....7....+
D CurTm           S              T   TIMFMT(*HMS:)
 *
```

The code above shows TIMFMT on a D-spec, so this field will be in *HMS format with a colon separator character: HH:MM:SS. TIMFMT makes the time field CurTm an 8-byte field containing the time with separating colons. You can now use the field for program-described output to a printer or data file, or you can move it to an 8-byte character field for printing or displaying via an externally described printer or display file or for passing to another program as a parameter.

The T Data Type by Example

The time data type makes RPG IV time manipulation a lot easier than in RPG III. This data type lets you store times as values that can't be corrupted with non-time values.

The TIME operation gives you access to the system time, which you can manipulate if you can get it into a time field. The result of a TIME operation is a number that represents the system time. To transfer the system time into a field of data type time, you need the MOVE operation code.

```
*...1....+....2....+....3....+....4....+....5....+....6....+....7....+
D SysDtTm          S              12P 0
D CurDt            S               D   DATFMT(*YMD/)
D CurTm            S               T   TIMFMT(*HMS:)

*...1....+....2....+....3....+....4....+....5....+....6....+....7....+
 *
C     GETCURDTTM    BEGSR
 *
 * Get the current date and time
 *
C                   TIME                    SysDtTm
 *
 *
 * Convert the system date and time to the expected format
 *
C     *JOBRUN       MOVE      SysDtTm        CurDt
C     *JOBRUN       MOVEL     SysDtTm        CurTm
 *
C                   ENDSR
```

Returning to the example with the TIME operation and the discussion of the date data type, the code above explores time fields and their automatic conversion capabilities. A new D-spec defines CurTm as a time field in the format HH:MM:SS; the periods are part of the stored value. A *JOBRUN entry is not necessary because you are moving from a numeric field, so the format must be HHMMSS. *JOBRUN is here for consistency's sake. Because the CurTm field is a time data type, the field is now formatted and ready for printing. You can also move the time value into a character field for display (DDS does not support time data type fields on externally described display files).

The Z (Timestamp) Data Type

If you need to be precise about when an event happens, RPG IV gives you the Z (timestamp) data type, which combines both date and time in one field. As with date and time fields, you define timestamp fields on the D-specs. To specify the timestamp data type, you enter a Z in position 40 (internal data type) of the field's definition.

Timestamp fields have a predetermined size and format: The size is 26 characters, and the format is YYYY-MM-DD-HH.MM.SS.UUUUUU (four-digit year, two-digit month, two-digit day, two-digit hour, two-digit minute, two-digit second, six-digit microsecond). Microseconds are optional for timestamp literals. If you do not provide the microseconds, the system will pad the field on the right with zeros.

The code below demonstrates the definition of a timestamp field. Unlike date and time data types, you have no control over the format of a timestamp data type field, so this data type has no equivalent to the DATFMT and TIMFMT keywords.

```
*...1....+....2....+....3....+....4....+....5....+....6....+....7....+
D CurDtTm         S                 Z
  *
```

This data type is not particularly useful for printing and display. Instead, timestamp fields are helpful in complex duration analysis processing, where you need to calculate time intervals that require date rollover. By constructing a starting time in a timestamp field, you can use date math functions to perform sophisticated date calculations. You can perform date calculations on date data type fields and time calculations on time data type fields, and you can do both types of calculations on timestamp fields. And only timestamp calculations can provide an adjusted date when you add and subtract time units rather than date units.

Timestamp by Example

The timestamp data type provides flexibility for working with durations. Calculations that involve durations that span multiple units of date and time are common and irritating to program. The following example shows how to build a timestamp field to perform duration calculations involving both date and time.

```
*...1....+....2....+....3....+....4....+....5....+....6....+....7....+
D SysDtTm        S              12P 0
D CurDt          S                D   DATFMT(*YMD/)
D CurTm          S                T   TIMFMT(*HMS:)
D CurDtTm        S                Z


*...1....+....2....+....3....+....4....+....5....+....6....+....7....+
 *
 * Retrieve the current data and time
 *
C                   EXSR      GETCURDTTM
 *
 * Construct a timestamp with the retrieved date and time
 *
C                   MOVE      CurDt        CurDtTm
C                   MOVE      CurTm        CurDtTm
 *
 *********************************************************
 *
C     GETCURDTTM    BEGSR
 *
 * Get the current date and time
 *
C                   TIME                   SysDtTm
 *
 *
 * Convert the system date and time to the expected format
 *
C     *JOBRUN       MOVE      SysDtTm      CurDt
C     *JOBRUN       MOVEL     SysDtTm      CurTm
 *
C                   ENDSR
```

This routine uses the subroutine GETCURDTTM from the examples of the TIME operation and the date and time data types. The routine retrieves the values necessary to construct a timestamp field that represents the current date and time. A new field called CurDtTm is in the D-specs. Like CurDt and

CurTm, this is a standalone field. The data type is Z (timestamp), which creates a fixed-format, 26-character field that can store both a date and a time.

Of course, the code will need to assign a value to this timestamp field for it to be of much use. So you first call the GETCURDTTM subroutine to retrieve the current date and time and store it in the date and time fields, CurDt and CurTm. Once the GETCURDTTM subroutine executes, you can use the retrieved values to load the timestamp field, CurDtTm. First, you MOVE CurDt to CurDtTm, and then you move CurTm to that same field.

Notice that you don't have to worry about the formats of the three fields. The MOVE operation understands these data types and automatically handles the format conversions and placement of the data in the Result field. The CurDtTm field is now ready for use in other calculations.

THE **ADDDUR** AND **SUBDUR** OPERATION CODES

In the context of a program, the TIME operation and the *-words and U-words perform distinctly different functions. The special words for dates and TIME *retrieve* the values for dates and times. But to *manipulate* those values or use them in any calculations, you need date, time, and timestamp data type fields.

The usefulness of these data types comes when you combine them with operations to add durations, subtract durations, and find the duration between two dates or times. Such operations let you easily calculate due dates, delivery times, and days late, for example.

ADDDUR

The ADDDUR (Add Duration) operation code lets you add a period, such as years, months, days, hours, minute, seconds, or microseconds, to a starting date or time and get the resulting date or time. This operation works with fields of date, time, or timestamp data type.

Timestamps provide the most flexibility with ADDDUR. With a date data type field, you can add only durations of date units (years, months, or days). Time data type fields limit you to durations of time units (hours, minutes, and seconds). But ADDDUR with timestamp fields lets you use any date or time units allowed with date and time data type fields, and you can use microseconds. More important, with timestamp data types, you can add time units to a starting date and time to calculate the resulting date and time. No more modulus math is necessary to compute the number of days between two dates or to add a number of days to a date.

Duration calculations simplify many business calculations. For example, in an invoicing application, you can obtain today's date and add 30 days to get the date 30 days from now to figure out the payment due date.

The following table shows the syntax of ADDDUR. You specify it in the operation code positions, 26 through 35, in the C-specs. In Factor 1, you specify

Factor 1	Opcode (Extender)	Factor 2	Result	Indicators		
Optional *start date/time*	ADDDUR	Required *duration:code*	Required *result date/time*	N/A	Error	N/A

the starting date, time, or timestamp to which you want to add some duration. The value can be a date, time, or timestamp data type field, subfield, array, array element, literal, or constant. If you do not specify Factor 1, the duration is added to the field you specify as the Result field.

Factor 2 contains two subfactors, the duration and a valid duration code, separated by a colon. The duration can be a numeric field, an array element, or a constant with zero decimal positions. If the duration is negative, it is subtracted from the date. The second subfactor, a valid duration code, defines the type of duration in the first subfactor of Factor 2. The valid duration codes are *YEAR or *Y, *MONTH or *M, *DAYS or *D, *HOURS or *H, *MINUTES or *MN, *SECONDS or *S, and *MSECONDS or *MS. Naturally, the type of fields you are working with limits the type of duration you can specify. You can specify date unit durations only with date and timestamp data types. You can specify time unit durations only with time and timestamp data types. The table below shows the valid codes with examples of how to use them.

Duration Codes

Duration Type		Code	Abbreviation	Example
Date Units	Year	*YEARS	*Y	LoanYrs:*YEARS or LoanYrs:*Y
	Month	*MONTHS	*M	9:*MONTHS or 9:*M
	Day	*DAYS	*D	60:*DAYS or 60:*D
Time Units	Hour	*HOURS	*H	WrkHrs:*HOURS or WrkHrs:*H
	Minute	*MINUTES	*MN	NmMin:*MINUTES or NmMin:*MN
	Second	*SECONDS	*S	45:*SECONDS or 45:*S
	Microsecond (millionths of a second)	*MSECONDS	*MS	Qtr:*MSECONDS or Qtr:*MS

The Result field must be a date, time, or timestamp data type field, subfield, array, or array element. The Result field must be of the same type as the field or data in Factor 1.

You can specify a resulting indicator in positions 73 and 74. This indicator will turn on if invalid data is in the field in either Factor 1 or the Result field before the calculation begins, or if the calculation results in a value that is invalid for the Result field's data type. For any error, the value of the Result field remains unchanged.

The SUBDUR Operation Code

The SUBDUR (Subtract Duration) operation code lets you subtract a duration from a date, time, or timestamp, or lets you subtract one date, time, or timestamp from another to calculate an elapsed duration. In the first case, the type of duration you want to subtract can be either date or time units. In the second case, the type of duration can be date and time units. For example, you can compute how many days a customer is past the due date for payments so that you can calculate late payment interest rate charges. The following table shows the syntax of the two variations of the SUBDUR operation code.

Factor 1	Opcode	(Extender)	Factor 2	Result	Indicators		
Optional *start date/time*	SUBDUR		Required *duration:code*	Required *result date/time*	N/A	Error	N/A

Factor 1	Opcode	(Extender)	Factor 2	Result	Indicators		
Required *end date/time*	SUBDUR		Required *start date/time*	Required *duration:code*	N/A	Error	N/A

You specify SUBDUR in the operation code field (positions 26 through 35) in the C-specs. Factor 1, which is optional when you're calculating a date but required when you're calculating a duration, can contain a date, time, or timestamp from which you want to subtract some duration or a date, time, or timestamp. You can specify the value in Factor 1 as a date, time, or timestamp data type field, subfield, array, array element, literal, or constant. In a calculation to determine a starting date or time by subtracting a duration, you specify the date you are starting from. In a calculation to find an elapsed duration, you enter the ending date or time of the time span.

Suppose you need to calculate a starting date and time for a shipment with a required delivery date and time, and you have an accurate estimate of the time required to ship. You can specify the required delivery date and time in Factor 1 as the base for the calculation. If you are analyzing existing shipments to determine the delivery times your shipping department is experiencing, you specify the delivery date and time of completed shipments in Factor 1, as the date from which you subtract the starting date and time of the shipment. Whether you are calculating a date or a duration, this factor will probably contain the later of the dates in question.

Factor 2 can take two different forms. It can represent a duration if you are calculating date and time, or Factor 2 can represent a date and time if you are calculating a duration. Either way, Factor 2 is required. When you are calculating a date, this factor represents a duration, just as it does with ADDDUR.

If you are calculating a duration, Factor 2 must contain a date, time, or time-stamp data type field, subfield, array, array element, literal, or constant. The value must be compatible with the entry in Factor 1. For instance, you can subtract a date, time, or timestamp from a timestamp; a date from a date; and a time from a time, but you cannot subtract a time from a date, or vice versa.

Like Factor 2, the Result field for SUBDUR can be either a date and time or a duration. If you are calculating a date (a duration is in Factor 2), the Result field must contain a date, time, or timestamp data type field, subfield, array, or array element. If you are calculating a duration, the Result field must contain two subfactors to identify the field to place the duration in and the type of duration to calculate. The field must be a numeric, zero-decimal field. The duration can be any valid duration type. The duration type must be compatible with the field types you specify in Factors 1 and 2.

You can specify a resulting indicator in positions 73 and 74. This indicator will turn on if invalid data is in either Factor 1 or the Result field before the calculation begins, or if the calculation result is invalid for the Result field data type. For any error, the value of the Result field remains unchanged.

ADDDUR and SUBDUR by Example

This example will build on the previous example but focus on dates because you most frequently encounter them in business-oriented programming. Suppose you are working for a telemarketing firm and users need to identify and automatically schedule follow-up calls. The rules for follow-up calls require users to schedule a date of five days later than the initial call. For statistical analysis of the sales force, users must log the time they spend on each transaction. You can assume that the start and end time of the transaction is recorded at the appropriate points in the program. The following code shows the duration calculations to find the follow-up call date and the duration of the transaction.

```
*...1....+....2....+....3....+....4....+....5....+....6....+....7....+
D SysDtTm        S              12P 0
D CurDt          S                 D   DATFMT(*YMD/)
D CurTm          S                 T   TIMFMT(*HMS:)
D CurDtTm        S                 Z
D TxnStTm        S                 T
D TxnEnTm        S                 T
D FollowDt       S                 D
D TxnSecs        S               7P 0
```

```
*...1....+....2....+....3....+....4....+....5....+....6....+....7....+
 *
 * Retrieve the current data and time
 *
C                   EXSR      GETCURDTTM
 *
 * Construct a timestamp with the retrieved date and time
 *
C                   MOVE      CurDt          CurDtTm
C                   MOVE      CurTm          CurDtTm
 *
 * Calculate a date 5 days from today for a follow-up call
 *
C     CurDt         ADDDUR    5:*D           FollowDt
 *
 * Calculate the duration in seconds for this transaction
 *
C     TxnEnTm       SUBDUR    TxnStTm        TxnSecs:*S
 *
 ***********************************************************************
C     GETCURDTTM    BEGSR
 *
 * Get the current date and time
 *
C                   TIME                     SysDtTm
 *
 * Convert the system date and time to the expected format
 *
C     *JOBRUN       MOVE      SysDtTm        CurDt
C     *JOBRUN       MOVEL     SysDtTm        CurTm
 *
C                   ENDSR
```

This example has just a few lines of code because it builds on the previous example. The D-specs have two new time data type fields, TxnStTm and TxnEnTm. The first field is the time a transaction starts, such as when the telemarketer first views the screen. The second field is the time the transaction ends, such as when the telemarketer assigns a disposition to the person or company they are calling. In this example, assume that these times are loaded appropriately at the proper processing points. The point here is calculating the durations of the transaction, which you store in another newly defined field, TxnSecs. It is a seven-digit, packed numeric field. The D-specs also define a new date data type field to record the next date for follow-up.

In the C-specs, after you determine the current date, you issue ADDDUR, specifying CurDt in Factor 1 and a duration of five days in Factor 2. This produces the follow-up date, to be stored in the field FollowDt.

Try comparing that code to the code you need without date data types. Just the thought of handling month and year rollover can make the most fearless programmer shudder.

The code to calculate the transaction duration is similar. Again, you can assume that the start and end times of the transaction are in TxnStTm and TxnEnTm. You need only one line of code to calculate the number of elapsed seconds. TxnEnTm is in Factor 1, and TxnStTm is in Factor 2. The difference is calculated as specified in the Result field, where the :*S duration type means that you want the elapsed seconds in the field TxnSecs.

Date Manipulation

The code below demonstrates how to perform various operations on three dates. The first date is January 30, 1996. To find the last day of the following month, you can issue ADDDUR to add one month to the date. In this case, because 1996 is a leap year, the result of adding one month is February 29, 1996.

```
*...1....+....2....+....3....+....4....+....5....+....6....+....7....+
D FEB             S              D
D JAN             S              D    INZ(D'1996-01-30')
D MAY             S              D    INZ(D'1995-05-31')
D JUN             S              D    INZ(D'1995-06-05')
D DAYS            S             2S 0  INZ(0)
D MONTHS          S             2S 0  INZ(0)

*...1....+....2....+....3....+....4....+....5....+....6....+....7....+
C     JAN             ADDDUR    1:*M          FEB
C*
C     JUN             SUBDUR    MAY           DAYS:*D
C*
C     JUN             SUBDUR    MAY           MONTHS:*M
```

In the second example, SUBDUR subtracts the date May 31, 1995, from June 5, 1995. The interesting part of this operation is that the dates are very close together, although in different months. If you subtract the May date from the June date and ask for the number of days' difference, you get five days. In contrast, if you do the same calculation and ask for the difference in months, the answer is zero months because June 5, 1995, and May 31, 1995, are only five days apart.

The code below illustrates how to subtract two dates and get the result in number of years, months, and days. The D-specs define two dates, January 30, 1996, and February 28, 1997.

```
*...1....+....2....+....3....+....4....+....5....+....6....+....7....+
D TmpDate         S               D
D Jan96           S               D   Inz(D'1996-01-30')
D Feb97           S               D   Inz(D'1997-02-28')
D Years           S              2S 0 Inz(0)
D Months          S              2S 0 Inz(0)
D Days            S              2S 0 Inz(0)

*...1....+....2....+....3....+....4....+....5....+....6....+....7....+
C     Feb97           SUBDUR    Jan96         Years:*Y
C     Jan96           ADDDUR    Years:*Y      TmpDate
C     Feb97           SUBDUR    TmpDate       Months:*M
C                     ADDDUR    Months:*M     TmpDate
C     Feb97           SUBDUR    TmpDate       Days:*D
```

This code uses the duration operations to calculate the number of elapsed whole years, whole months, and whole days. The code must

- calculate the number of whole years between the two dates
- adjust the original starting value by that number of years
- calculate the number of whole months between the adjusted date and the end date
- adjust the starting value by the number of whole months again
- and calculate the number of days left in the duration

Alternating SUBDUR and ADDDUR, using the result of each SUBDUR to feed the next ADDDUR, moves the starting date forward in time by whole date units, calculating the remaining duration in whole date units of the next smaller type. A temporary date field is necessary to manipulate the date through time. The following example shows the result of this code.

```
DIFFERENCE IS    01 YEAR    0 MONTHS  29DAYS
```

THE EXTRCT AND TEST OPERATION CODES

In addition to ADDDUR and SUBDUR, RPG IV provides two more date, time, and timestamp operation codes: EXTRCT (Extract) and TEST. EXTRCT lets you remove a specific portion of a date or time field. TEST ensures that the time or date is in the correct format.

The EXTRCT Operation Code

The EXTRCT operation code isolates the year, month, or day portion of a D or Z data type field; the hours, minutes, or seconds portion of a T or Z data type field; or the microseconds part of a Z data type field. This operation replaces the arduous task of coding MOVE and MOVEL operations or including data structures for all date fields.

You specify EXTRCT in the operation code field (positions 26 through 35) of the C-specs. Factor 1 must be blank. Factor 2 contains the date, time, or timestamp field from which to extract the date and time information. The duration code tells the compiler what date or time part to extract. Valid duration codes are *Y (year), *M (month), *D (day), *H (hours), *MN (minutes), *S (seconds), and *MS (microseconds).

The Result field can be any numeric or character field, subfield, or array or table element. Only the error indicator is allowed for EXTRCT. The table below summarizes the entries for EXTRCT.

Factor 1	Opcode	(Extender)	Factor 2	Result	Indicators		
Not allowed	EXTRCT		Required *date/time source*	Required target	N/A	Error	N/A

The TEST Operation Code

The TEST operation code validates the contents of a date, time, or timestamp data type field. However, TEST is most useful with fields that are not of those data types. Display files do not support date, time, or timestamp data types, so you must use character or numeric fields on displays and then convert (MOVE) them to fields of the appropriate data type for manipulation. TEST lets you check character and numeric fields to determine whether they contain valid dates. Imagine just pulling a six-digit field from the screen and then, with one line of code, being able to validate whether the user entered a correct date — no subroutines to write, no programs to call. Even if you have no intention of implementing date, time, and timestamp data types immediately, TEST's ability to perform such validity checking is worth the time you need to learn about RPG IV's new date and time capabilities. The table on page 322 summarizes the valid entries for TEST.

You specify TEST in the operation code (positions 26 through 35) part of the C-specs. TEST can have an operation extender. The extender is either required or not allowed, depending on the type of field you are testing. If the field you are testing has a date, time, or timestamp data type, the operation extender is not allowed. The field's data type determines the type of testing to perform. However, if the field you are testing is a numeric or character field, the operation extender is required. In that case, it instructs the TEST operation

Factor 1	Opcode	(Extender)	Factor 2	Result	Indicators		
Optional *date format*	TEST	(D)	Not allowed *field to be tested*	Required	N/A	Error	N/A
Optional *time format*	TEST	(T)	Not allowed *field to be tested*	Required	N/A	Error	N/A
Not allowed	TEST	(Z)	Not allowed *field to be tested*	Required	N/A	Error	N/A
Not allowed	TEST		Not allowed *date, time, timestamp field*	Required	N/A	Error	N/A

to perform a date, time, or timestamp test. You code the operation extender in parentheses after the operation code as (D), (T), or (Z).

Factor 1 is optional and sometimes not allowed. It determines what date or time format (e.g., *YMD, *HMS, *ISO) to test a numeric or character field for. Like the opcode extender, Factor 1 is not allowed when the field is a date, time, or timestamp data type. You cannot specify Factor 1 if you are testing a numeric or character field for valid timestamp data because only one format is valid for a date, time, or timestamp data type field, and only one format is valid for a numeric or character field containing timestamp data. Factor 1 becomes optional when you're testing a numeric or character field for a valid date or time. You must tell the TEST operation what data format to test for. You can specify any date and time format that is valid on the DATFMT and TIMFMT keywords. Of course, the date and time format must be compatible with the test type you specify in the operation extender. If you do not specify a date or time format, the default will be the value on the DATFMT and TIMFMT keywords on the H-specs, if you specify them. If not, the default, *ISO, will be used. Factor 2 is not allowed.

The Result field is where you specify the field to test. The field can be any character, numeric, date, time, or timestamp data type. Keep in mind that numeric fields will be tested for valid digits, and character fields will be tested for valid digits and valid separator characters. That distinction means that if you have a character field that holds just the digits of a date, you will have to move those digits to a numeric field or add in the separators before testing it. Date, time, or timestamp data type fields will be tested for a valid date or time, depending on their data type.

The TEST operation requires a resulting indicator in positions 73 and 74. It will be set on if the data in the tested field is not valid the type of test you're performing. The indicator will be set off if the data is valid.

EXTRCT and TEST by Example

One frequent request from users is to reformat the date on the screen into plain English. This request generally involves translating the month from a number to a name. With EXTRCT, you can easily get the month portion of a date and then use it as an index to an array that contains the names of the months. But first you need to validate the field. Because of the limitations of display-file DDS, the program must receive any date or time the user enters, in a numeric or character field. The TEST operation allows easy validation of the date and, if no errors occur, ensures that you can confidently proceed with the EXTRCT operation. The code below demonstrates this validation, extraction, and translation.

```
*...1....+....2....+....3....+....4....+....5....+....6....+....7....+
D OrderYrA       S              4A
D OrderMo        S              2P 0
D OrderDyA       S              2A
D WorkDate       S               D
D Month          S              9A   DIM(12) PERRCD(6) CTDATA

*...1....+....2....+....3....+....4....+....5....+....6....+....7....+
 * Validate order date from screen to be valid MDY field
 *  If invalid, set general error indicator and
 *      error indicator for Order Date specifically
 *  Else, convert month and build formatted date
 *
C     *MDY          TEST (D)                  OrderDate          99
 *
C                   IF        *IN99=*ON
C                   EVAL      *IN87=*ON
 *
C                   ELSE
C     *MDY          MOVE      OrderDate    WorkDate
C                   EXTRCT    WorkDate:*Y  OrderYrA
C                   EXTRCT    WorkDate:*M  OrderMo
C                   EXTRCT    WorkDate:*D  OrderDyA
C                   EVAL      FmtdDate=%TRIMR(Month(OrderMo))
C                                       + ' ' + OrderDyA
C                                       + ', ' + OrderYrA
 *
C                   ENDIF
```

```
*...1....+....2....+....3....+....4....+....5....+....6....+....7....+
**CTDATA MONTH
January  February March     April    May      June
July     August   SeptemberOctober   November December
```

The D-specs define all the fields the program needs to validate and format the date. Two fields, OrderDate and FmtdDate, are not defined on the D-specs and you can assume they are defined on the display file. OrderYrA is a four-character field to hold the year portion of OrderDate. OrderDyA is similar and will hold the day portion of the value of OrderDate. Both are defined as character to simplify concatenation, later. OrderMo holds the month portion of the order date. It is numeric so the program can use it as an index to an array to find the name of the month. Month is a 12-element array loaded from data in the source at compile time. Each record has six entries in the source records. WorkDate is a date field that will temporarily hold the value converted from the display file.

All the screen preparation and I/O are not in this sample code, but you can see how the date the user enters into the OrderDate field can quickly be edited. Because you require MMDDYY data entry, you will specify TEST(D) to validate the OrderDate field for a valid date, specifying *MDY in Factor 1 as the expected date format. If OrderDate fails the TEST, the error indicator (99) in positions 73 and 74 will be set on. Next, you test the value of the indicator to see whether it is turned on. If so, EVAL sets indicator 87 on, too. That indicator will condition error attributes on the display file.

If the date passes muster, you will convert it into a D data type field by issuing a MOVE operation that specifies the same date format as in the TEST operation. Next, you extract OrderYrA, OrderMo, and OrderDyA. Finally, you construct a formatted date by concatenating the pieces of the date and inserting separators. The final format is mmmmmmmmm dd, yyyy. At the end of the source, you can include the data records for the month array.

This is all the code necessary to validate a date and put it into a format the user is comfortable with. Before the TEST operation, the date validation used to make this a tedious job. Thanks to EXTRCT, you can avoid building data structures from which you have to pluck the date parts, and you avoid any strange math to extract the portions of the date.

CHAPTER 11

Programming Display Files and Subfiles

The AS/400 has a strong reputation as a database machine. Two inevitable needs for any database are the ability to display data and the ability to maintain data in database programs. To meet these two needs, you need display files so the RPG program's users can view and manipulate data.

Take careful note of the term "display *file*." RPG programs interact with the display as they do with any externally described file. The program must write and read display file record formats to display and accept data from the user. The display file manages field placement and field attributes on the screen. You have to worry only about what data is in which fields and when to write and read the records containing that data.

You define AS/400 display files by means of Data Definition Specifications (DDS). You code a DDS description of the display file and specify a display device. (All RPG display file support is fully compatible with a 5250 terminal.) Usually, AS/400 data is in a physical file, and programs often access it through a logical file. So you need a database file to provide the data the display file will display. The database file and the display file are separate entities. (To learn about DDS, see IBM's *AS/400 Programming: Data Description Reference* manual.)

Display files let you format data for display (output), accept input that an RPG program can then use for updating a database, and manage screens (e.g., by refreshing displayed data after user interaction, overlaying fields with new data, and erasing fields from the screen). Display files also communicate with terminals attached to the AS/400 without your having to know the details of the data stream and instructions the system uses to manage the physical display. An RPG program that uses the display file lets you display and update data in any file instead of restricting data access to a particular file or set of files.

Formatting output means you can retrieve data from an AS/400 database file and determine how to display that information for the end user. Through display files, you can select which information to present; determine where (in which row and column) it appears on the screen; and define special display attributes such as highlighting, blinking, and reverse image. To let you show fields and their attributes on a screen, DDS lets you describe fields as being output capable.

In addition to being output capable, a display file's fields must accept input from users if your programs are interactive. Just as you can format output through display files, you can also format user input. DDS lets you define fields as input capable. When users enter data through the display file, input fields map that data so that an RPG program can use it. DDS lets you position such input fields, use validity checking to specify information such as what type of data users can input, and enforce entry into must-fill fields. DDS can preinitialize input fields so you can reduce the number of user keystrokes if the input data will frequently be identical. Of course, you need not preinitialize an input field. If you don't, it will appear in the chosen row-column screen positions as blank.

Occasionally, you need fields that are both output and input capable, so you can define a field on the screen as being a *both* field that supports both output and input of data. In this case, an RPG program passes the field value to the display. Then the program passes the field value from the display.

Another function of display files is to support the display terminal. The display data stream handles the display and input of data, the formatting of data on the screen, the placement of data on the screen, and the data's visual characteristics such as color and field intensity. Display files shield you from such details and allow interaction on the record level. The display file's role is to convert your RPG program's record-style input and output requests into the data stream necessary to communicate with an AS/400 terminal, so your program sees the display as a record-based device, much like a data file.

Finally, the fact that display files let you access any data in any database means you can decide which database you want to access from an RPG program. Display files are not a database-specific solution.

Once you define a display file in DDS and create it by issuing the CRTDSPF (Create Display File) command, you can use the display file in RPG IV programs. You have to identify the file to an RPG program. In the RPG source, to declare a display file, you specify its name on an F-spec.

A display file can include subfiles, a special way to display data records. Subfiles are useful for data entry. To take advantage of display files and subfiles in RPG programs, you need to know what RPG code makes display files accessible and lets you manipulate them. Display files let an RPG program display one record from a database file, and subfiles let an RPG program display multiple records of a physical database file.

DECLARING DISPLAY FILES

RPG IV terminology calls a display file a workstation (WORKSTN) file. To incorporate a workstation file into an RPG IV application, you need to declare the display file in the program's F-specs. The following F-spec declares workstation file DISPLAY.

```
*...1....+....2....+....3....+....4....+....5....+....6....+....7....+
FDISPLAY   CF   E               WORKSTN
  *
```

The display file name is in positions 7 through 16. In position 17, you enter a C if the display file is a combined (input/output) file, the predominant definition of workstation files. This designation means input and output records can have different layouts, which is usually so with display files. (In contrast, with an update file, which is not an allowed type for WORKSTN files, the input and output records have the same layout and share the same buffer.) With a WORKSTN device, you can alternatively enter either I, for input, or O, for output. These types are rare because display files let programs interact with users.

An F (Full Procedural) in position 18 means the C-specs, instead of the RPG cycle, will control all I/O from and to the display file. Alternatively, if you're using primary and secondary files, P in position 18 for file designation or S in the same position tells the compiler to rely on the RPG program cycle. The cycle, especially for WORKSTN processing, is a very old means of interacting with users. An E (for external file description) in position 19 means the compiler will retrieve the external (DDS) description for this workstation file. Most programs that use a display file will declare the file as a combined, full procedural, externally described file, as in the F-spec above.

USING DISPLAY FILES

To demonstrate how to use display files and acquaint you with the RPG operations necessary when a program requires a display file, this chapter will step through two examples that illustrate the basic display file techniques: single-record screens and multiple-record (subfile) screens. Both examples use inquiries, requiring input from the user and display of the data.

The first example asks the user to enter an item number. Then the program verifies the item's existence and displays the item's details. The second example is similar, but instead of asking the user for an item number, this program displays a subfile containing a list of valid item numbers. The user must select one to get a display of detailed information.

Each example requires some DDS to describe the display file. Each example includes the DDS code and a brief explanation of how to spot the records to read and write and how to understand what fields will be available in the input records and the output record.

Example 1: The DDS

The application is a typical inquiry program that displays a screen asking for an item code or number. After validating the code, the program displays the

information about that item. This program needs a display file that contains two
formats. One requests the item code, and the other displays the item detail.

The DDS is shown below. At the file level, notice the INDARA (Indicator
Area) keyword. It passes the indicators that the DDS references directly to an
indicator array in the program. As a result, the input and output record for each
format won't have a separate field defined for each indicator.

Then the DDS defines the two record formats, ITEMSELR and ITMDTLR.
The top record format, ITEMSELR, is for input from the user, whereas the
ITEMDTLR record format outputs information to users. The organization of
information in display file definitions — formats and fields — is similar to the
organization of information in a database file. ITEMSELR has two fields,
D1ITEM and D1ERR. D1ITEM has a B (for Both input and output capable) in
position 38 meaning that this field provides data for both display and processing in the program. The next field, D1ERR, is an output (O in position 38) field
that lets you display an error message. The CF03 (Command Function Key xx)
keyword activates F3 on the keyboard. Because of the 03 following the keyword in parentheses, pressing F3 turns on indicator 03 in the program after the
format is read. The text string F3=Exit is a literal defined in the DDS to document the function key on the screen so that users know what functions are
available. The input format for this record will contain one field, D1ITEM. The
output format for this record will contain two fields, D1ITEM and D1ERR, so a
program needs to process the file as a combined file.

```
*...1....+....2....+....3....+....4....+....5....+....6....+....7....+
A                                       INDARA
A           R ITEMSELR                  CF03(03)
A                                     2 35'Item Inquiry'
A                                     5 20'Type and Item Code and +
A                                          press Enter...'
A                                     7 30 'Item Code:'
A             D1ITEM        6A  B  7 42
A                                    23  5 'F3=Exit'
A             D1ERR        78A  O 24  2
  *
  *
A           R ITEMDTLR
A                                       CF03(03)
A                                     2 35'Item Inquiry'
A                                     7 30'Item Code:'
A             D2ITEM        6A  O  7 42
A                                     9  3'Size . . . :'
```

Continued

```
*...1....+....2....+....3....+....4....+....5....+....6....+....7....+
A              D2SIZE         4A  O   9 17
A                                   10  3'Description:'
A              D2DESC        50A  O  10 17
A                                   11  3'Qty On Hand:'
A              D2QTOH         7Y  OO 11 17EDTCDE(J)
A                                   11 29'Qty on Order:'
A              D2QTOO         7Y  OO 11 44EDTCDE(J)
A                                   11 56'Qty Sold:'
A              D2QTSL         7Y  OO 11 67EDTCDE(J)
A                                   23  5'F3=Exit'
```

The second record format is ITMDTLR. It also includes the CF03 keyword for the same purpose as in the previous format. ITMDTLR's fields are all output fields. The input format for this record will not contain any fields, but the output format will contain six fields. Although the EDTCDE (Edit Code) keyword won't affect the program, it is on the three numeric fields, D2QTOH, D2QTOO, and D2QTSL. This keyword inserts commas in appropriate positions in these fields on the display; the program need not be concerned with inserting commas when displaying the information. If you define these fields as input fields, you do not have to strip out the commas; the system handles that task, and the program sees only data.

In an explanation of how to display the information in a data file, you need to see the definition of the data file. The DDS below describes a physical file that is uniquely keyed and has six fields. The file's key is the item code, ITITEM.

```
*...1....+....2....+....3....+....4....+....5....+....6....+....7....+
A                                   UNIQUE
A          R ITEMMASTR
A            ITITEM         6
A            ITSIZE         4
A            ITDESC        50
A            ITQTOH         7   O
A            ITQTOO         7   O
A            ITQTSL         7   O
A          K ITITEM
```

The RPG Program

After you declare a display file, the program needs to display and read the record formats that let the program communicate with the terminal. The EXFMT (Execute Format) operation handles this task.

The EXFMT Operation

The EXFMT (Execute Format) operation code writes a display record format to the screen and then waits for a user to press Enter or a function key. The operation then reads the display record. While EXFMT is running, the program waits at that operation. EXFMT is sometimes called a "put-get." It *puts* the record to the screen and then waits to *get* a response.

You enter EXFMT in the operation code portion (positions 26 through 35) of the C-specs. Factor 1 is not allowed. Factor 2 must contain a format name from a display file. You can specify an error indicator in positions 73 and 74. This operation's syntax is shown below.

Factor 1	Opcode	Extender	Factor 2	Result	Indicators		
Not allowed	EXFMT		Required display file format name	Not allowed	N/A	Error	N/A

How the Program Works

The program opens by declaring the two files to display. ItemInqry is a combined, full-procedural, externally described file. The WORKSTN device type identifies it as a display file. The second file is ItemMast. It contains the items you want to display and is an input, full-procedural, externally described database file that will be processed by key. This program has no D-specs. All the fields it needs are from externally described files, and no working fields are necessary.

First, the program prepares the screen by loading the database fields into the screen fields. Then the program turns off any response indicators you are expecting from the screen.

The mainline code executes a subroutine to display and process the program's first screen. The subroutine, SelectItem, lets users select the item to display. This subroutine will loop infinitely (using DO *HIVAL), so users can request one item after another. The process will be to display the screen, accept input, display the detail screen, accept input, and then start again.

In the continuous loop, the program prepares the screen for display. When a user presses F3, indicator 03 is set on. You will probably never have to set it off because it is on only when the user exits the program. However, good programming practice dictates that you always initialize any return indicators before displaying the screen, so you set off indicator 03 here.

Next, EXFMT lets the program display and then read the ItemSelR format from the ItemInqry display file. This operation will display the screen to let users enter an item code. When a user presses Enter, control will go to the next line of code.

```
*...1....+....2....+....3....+....4....+....5....+....6....+....7....+
FItemInqry CF   E               WORKSTN
FItemMast  IF   E             K DISK


*...1....+....2....+....3....+....4....+....5....+....6....+....7....+
 * Execute subroutine to handle display of item code entry screen
C                   EXSR      SelectItem
 *
 *******************************************************************
 * Subroutine to handle display of item code entry screen
 *   - Loop continuously displaying and responding to screen
 *     - Prepare screen for display
 *     - Write/read the screen
 *     - If user requested exit, call exit routine
 *     - Call routine to validate and load the selected record
 *     - If validation routine does not return error, call
 *       function to display detail screen
 *   - Next iteration
 *******************************************************************
C     SelectItem    BEGSR
 *
C                   DO        *HIVAL
C                   SETOFF                                        03
C                   EXFMT     ItemSelR
C                   EVAL      D1ERR=*BLANKS
 *
C                   IF        *IN03
C                   EXSR      ExitPgm
C                   ENDIF
 *
C                   EXSR      ValidItem
 *
C                   IF        D1ERR=*BLANK
C                   EXSR      ShowDetail
C                   ENDIF
 *
C                   ENDDO
C                   ENDSR
 *
```

CONTINUED

```
*...1....+....2....+....3....+....4....+....5....+....6....+....7....+
********************************************************************
* Subroutine to validate existence of item and read the record
*  - Chain with item code to see if it exists
*  - If item does not exist, prepare error message
********************************************************************
C     ValidItem     BEGSR
*
C     D1ITEM        CHAIN      ItemMastR                              30
*
C                   IF         *IN30
C                   EVAL       D1ERR='Item ' +
C                                     %TRIMR(D1ITEM) +
C                                     ' not found'
C                   ENDIF
C                   ENDSR
*
********************************************************************
* Subroutine to display item detail screen
*  - Load data to the item detail screen
*  - Read/write the display
*  - If user requests exit, call exit routine
********************************************************************
C     ShowDetail    BEGSR
*
C                   EVAL       D2Item=ITItem
C                   EVAL       D2Size=ITSize
C                   EVAL       D2Desc=ITDesc
C                   EVAL       D2QTOH=ITQTOH
C                   EVAL       D2QTOO=ITQTOO
C                   EVAL       D2QTSL=ITQTSL
C                   SETOFF                                            03
*
C                   EXFMT      ItemDtlR
*
C                   IF         *IN03
C                   EXSR       ExitPgm
C                   ENDIF
C                   ENDSR
```

CONTINUED

```
*...1....+....2....+....3....+....4....+....5....+....6....+....7....+
 ********************************************************************
 *  Subroutine to handle exit of program
 *    - Set on LR to do a complete termination
 *    - Exit the program
 ********************************************************************
C       ExitPgm       BEGSR
 *
C                     SETON                                        LR
C                     RETRN
 *
C                     ENDSR
```

Now, in preparation for validating the new data from the user, the program tests whether the user pressed F3 (which will turn on indicator 03). If so, the program executes ExitPgm, the subroutine that handles cleanup and exits the program by setting on LR.

If the user did not request an exit (F3), the program executes subroutine ValidItem to validate the item code the user entered. The ValidItem routine issues a CHAIN to the ItemMastR record format to validate the item's existence. If the record isn't found, indicator 30 comes on. The next section of code uses that indicator to condition creation of an error message. The program builds the error message by concatenating the item code the user entered and a text message.

If the item is valid, processing returns to the SelectItem subroutine, which determines whether D1ERR is blank, to check for creation of an error message. If D1ERR is blank, no error occurred, and the subroutine can execute the ShowDetail subroutine to display the item details. The only two options the user has from the detail screen are to press Enter to leave the screen or to press F3 to exit the program. To handle the F3 possibility, which will turn on indicator 03, you again test for 03 being on. If it is on, you execute the routine to exit the program. If a user presses Enter, processing falls through to the end of the subroutine, which takes you back to the subroutine where the item selection screen reappears, because this subroutine is in an infinite loop.

Finally, the ExitPgm subroutine handles any cleanup necessary on an exit from the program. This subroutine sets on LR and the RETURN operation exits the program.

This example demonstrates how easily programs communicate with an AS/400 terminal through the display file and that the process is similar to database file manipulation: The program writes and reads record formats, but in this case, one operation, EXFMT, combines the two operations. Most programs that have display files use EXFMT instead of READ on a display file. However, programs frequently WRITE to a display file, as in the next example, which uses subfiles. This example introduces a new operation exclusively for subfiles, READC (Read Changed Record).

SUBFILES

Putting multiple records out to a screen for display, modification, and input is the purpose of subfiles. This example demonstrates how to code an RPG subfile program that lets users interact with multiple database records at once from the display device.

What Are Subfiles?

A subfile is a special type of display file format that lets users interact with multiple records on one screen. Subfiles support RPG input-output operations and have special characteristics allowing interaction between a program and a display device, such as a 5250 terminal, during program execution.

One definition of a subfile brings these characteristics together: A subfile is a group of data elements that are held in main memory and that you can treat as a file. Specifically, a subfile is a special display file record format that lets you display a series of records, or from the users' perspective, a list of information. Each record in the series, or item in the list, has all the same fields as every other record in the subfile. In the subfile definition, you describe only one record that equates to a single line or set of lines of the display. The program writes and reads one record at a time to the subfile, but one operation sends the set of records to or retrieves it from the display.

Using Subfiles

You define subfiles in a DDS display file. An RPG program brings together the display device, the subfile, the data, and program control.

To incorporate a subfile into a program, you declare the subfile with the SFILE (Subfile) keyword on the WORKSTN file definition in the program's F-specs. The F-spec below declares a display file called ItemInqryS that includes a subfile.

```
*...1....+....2....+....3....+....4....+....5....+....6....+....7....+
FItemInqrySCF   E             WORKSTN SFILE(ItemListR:CurrRRN)
 *
```

The SFILE Keyword

The new RPG IV SFILE (Subfile) keyword on an F-spec that declares a display file tells the compiler that the display file contains a subfile. Because a display file can have multiple formats (and must have them to use subfiles), you need to tell the program which format is a subfile. SFILE accepts two parameter values separated by a colon. SFILE's format parameter identifies the subfile format in the display file. In the example F-spec above, ItemListR is the subfile record format in display file ItemInqryS. SFILE's second parameter value, which follows the colon, names a field that will hold the Relative Record Number (RRN) of a record in a data file. This field will automatically be updated with the subfile's current RRN when you issue a READC (Read Changed Record) or CHAIN operation to the subfile to read a record. You must also use this field to control which record you want to write when you WRITE a record to the subfile.

Each subfile that a program uses must have a SFILE entry in the F-specs. Because a display file can have up to 12 subfiles and you can display multiple subfiles at once, you need to provide a different field for the RRN for each subfile. This field lets you track the current position in each subfile independently.

The READC Operation

You need the READC (Read Changed Record) operation to access records in a subfile. READC is valid only with subfiles. It lets the program read through the subfile records, retrieving only records that a user has changed. This operation lets a program handle only records that need attention, instead of reading many records that require no processing.

You enter READC in the operation code portion (positions 26 through 35) of the C-specs. A resulting indicator is required in positions 75 and 76 to signal when no more changed records are available to read. You can specify an error indicator in positions 73 and 74. A syntax diagram for READC is shown below.

Factor 1	Opcode	Extender	Factor 2	Result	Indicators		
Not allowed	READC		Required subfile format name	Not allowed	N/A	Error	End of subfile

Subfile Processing by Example

A variation on the example for single-record display files can illustrate multiple-record display file technique. One problem with the previous example is that the users have to know the code for any item they want to inquire about. Instead, you can give users a list of items to select from.

Subfiles let you display a list of records so users can select one or more to see its details. Not only do users not need to know the item code to review an item, but they can see multiple item codes at once and select multiple items for review. Users can position the subfile to any item, enter a partial item code to position the list, and scroll through the list.

You must keep in mind two basic concepts. First, handling a subfile is like handling a database file that you are accessing by RRN. Second, to display a subfile, you must use a subfile control record. So, if you have a subfile, you will always have at least two formats in the display file. Also, because two formats cannot overlap on the screen, you can have additional formats, such as the list of function keys users can press.

The example display file and RPG program that begins on page 340 loads several records in memory for display, giving the users access to multiple records at once. Users can scroll through the data and position the cursor at any item.

In line 1 of the RPG program, the display file declaration identifies the sub-file format and RRN field. The file is ItemInqryS (the S is for subfile). The SFILE keyword identifies the ItemListR format as a subfile and assigns CurrRRN as the field to hold the active record's RRN. This value controls which record any I/O operations to the subfile will affect. You must assign this field a value before attempting to write or update a subfile record. The system will report the RRN (position in the subfile) that a READC or CHAIN accesses on the subfile.

Next are the work fields. SaveItem lets you test whether a user has keyed a different code to position the item list. Each time the program fills a page of the subfile, LastItem records the key value of the last item master record read from the database. This technique lets the program resume filling the subfile pages from the proper point in the subfile when users request additional pages. PosItem sets the starting point for reading the data file each time you need to load a page. The value from LastItem will be copied to PosItem when a user presses the Page down key. At other times, such as initial load of the subfile or when a user requests reloading the subfile, PosItem will be filled with blanks or a positioning item number that the user keyed. ThisPageCt counts the subfile records written to the page when you are loading a new subfile page. LastRRN is the number of the last record in the subfile and the number of records in the subfile.

The mainline begins with three setup tasks: It clears the subfile, positions the database file to the first record, and then loads the first page of the subfile. Separate subroutines perform each task. After loading the screen, the program calls the SelItem subroutine to display the subfile screen and handle any actions the user requests (view an item or exit the program). Because the user needs to return to this screen after the display of a detail record, an infinite loop begins. It ends only when the user exits the program.

In preparation for displaying the screen, you first turn off any response indicators (for F3 and Page down) and turn off the indicator that must be off to display the subfile control record and the subfile. Now you must WRITE out the footer format that contains the function key descriptions. Then you execute the ItemHdrR subfile control format to display the subfile control record and the subfile. The EXFMT will wait until the user responds by pressing F3, Page down, or Enter. If the user requests an exit from the program, the program calls the exit routine.

Next you check whether the user has changed the positioning information in the subfile control record. Remember from the DDS that one input field on the control record lets the user specify the list's starting point. If the user changes this information, you clear the subfile, position it to the item requested, and then the necessary subroutines load the first page of data. You also reset the saved field value to test the next time around.

If the user does not request a reposition, you check whether the user pressed the Page down key. If indicator 26 is on, you execute the PosFile routine to reposition the file cursor on the item master file, using the key of the last item read during the last page load. Then you execute the PageLoad routine to load the next page. This ability to reuse part of the processing is why the program includes separate routines. This routine will add one more page to the screen. Any selections the user makes are preserved in the subfile but not yet processed (unlike when a user requests a reposition, which clears the subfile).

Finally, if the users didn't exit, page down, or reposition, you call the ProcSel routine to process any selections they have made. After returning, you loop back around and redisplay the subfile screen.

The ProcSel routine starts looking for the records the user has requested to process. READC helps you find which records the program needs to process. It searches the subfile records and returns the next one that the user has changed by pressing any key while the cursor is on an input-capable subfile record.

The program reads for the first changed record and then drops into a loop, processing each changed record it finds. First the program sets the PageRRN equal to the record number just read. When the program redisplays the subfile, it will show the page containing the record last processed.

Next you check whether the user selected this record. Users must not only change the record (which is why you use READC to read it), but they must also select it. The program considers a record changed if the user types a space in the selection field — which happens more often than you want: Users press the space bar to go down the list, or they select a record, change their minds, and clear the selection field. Either way, you get a changed record. Verifying the selection value before processing the record is therefore prudent. Once you verify the selection, you call a routine to display the details of the selected record.

The next step is to clear the selector field on the subfile record. Remember, the subfile record still contains the value the user keyed. Here, you set the selector field, DLSEL, to blanks and then UPDATE the subfile record. After updating, you read for the next changed record and loop back up to process it. This loop continues until no more changed records are in the subfile.

Incidentally, once you READC a changed record, the program no longer considers it changed. DDS provides some techniques and keywords that let you read the record again later as a changed record.

Now you load the subfile. The LoadPage routine handles that task. This routine sets the current page record count to zero to build a new page. Next the routine reads the next record in the ItemMast file via the ItemMastR format. Then a loop executes as long as you have read a record and you haven't filled the current page.

Inside the load loop, you increment the counter for the current page and the counter for the total number of records in the subfile. Then, in preparation for the WRITE to create the subfile record, you set the RRN field for this subfile (specified on the SFILE keyword in the F-spec) to the new record's RRN, which is now 1 greater than the value previously in the subfile. Next you set the value of each of the subfile's fields: the selector, the item code, and the item description. Finally, you WRITE the subfile record to the subfile. Note that when the program is working with the subfile format, the system never writes anything to the display or reads from the display.

After you write a record to the subfile, you can turn on the indicator that tells whether any records are in the subfile. This approach lets the subfile display only when it has records in it. Displaying an empty subfile causes an ugly error. You read the next record in the file and loop back to process it.

Once you break out of the loop, either because you run out of records or you fill up the subfile page, you set the field that controls which page to display. The field's new value is the number of the last record in the subfile. This value ensures that the new page will display after the page-down processing and redisplay of the subfile.

Now you can check why you broke out of the loop. If indicator 30 is on, processing left the loop because you hit the end of the file. Note that the loop always tries to read 11 records but puts only 10 of them in the subfile. This method lets you tell whether more records are in the file that are not yet loaded to the subfile. Reading that eleventh record determines whether to have the subfile display tell the user whether more records are in the file to display.

You can use indicator 30 to turn on the end-of-file indicator. Additionally, if indicator 30 is not on, you need to tell the user that more records are available to display. If indicator 30 is on, you turn on indicator 33 to signal that the end of the file is reached. If 30 is not on, you turn off indicator 33. Also, remember that this indicator controls the activation of the DDS PAGEDOWN keyword. Finally, if you have not hit end of file, you store the key of the last record read (which will be the eleventh read when loading the page). This step is necessary to let the next load proceed normally. This step is unnecessary at the end of the file because you don't have any more loads.

Next you turn to the subroutine that displays the detail record for a selected item. This subroutine is similar to the one from the previous example except that this subroutine moves the CHAIN to the ItemMastR format. The last example validates the record's existence and retrieves the record you need. This example re-reads the record when you request it. The record already exists because it is in the list. (A real application needs error-handling code in case the record has been deleted since the list was built but before the user got a chance to view it.) This subroutine, then, reads the record, loads the data to the screen, displays the screen, and then handles an exit request from the user if needed. Otherwise, processing returns to the previous routine, which redisplays the subfile.

Next comes routine ClearSFL, which clears the subfile at the initial load of the subfile and each time a user requests repositioning of the subfile. The first requirement is to turn on the indicator that conditions the SFLCLR DDS keyword. Next, with the indicator on, you WRITE the subfile control file. Because the same indicator in its "not" state enables the display of the subfile control and subfile formats, they will not be displayed now. It seems odd to write the format and not have anything go to the screen, but this is how you clear the subfile.

Then (for safety), you set off the indicator that clears the subfile and set off the indicator that lets the subfile display. You have two conditions for the subfile to display: You must not be clearing the subfile, and the subfile must have some records in it. Because the subfile no longer has any records, you turn off the indicator that lets it display. Finally, you have cleared the subfile, so you also set the LastRRN field to zero because it tracks the number of records in the subfile, which is now zero.

The PosFile routine positions the database file to the first record you need when you load a list. This routine requires that you load the field PosItem with the value to position the database file before you execute it. The LoadPage routine reads the next record available, which is what makes that routine generic enough to handle both the first and subsequent page loads. The PosFile subroutine will be executed only when the program starts, when you have a reposition request, and when the user presses the Page down key. Finally, the same ExitPgm routine from the last example sets on LR, and the RETURN opcode terminates the program.

Subfiles require care in screen handling, managing the records in the subfile, controlling what to display when, and, usually, working with three or more formats. This example demonstrates several operations involved in displaying the subfile. The program uses WRITE to put records in the subfile and to write control information to the subfile control format to clear the subfile. WRITE lets you put the footer format on the screen. Although WRITE is not directly involved with the subfile format, you must write that format out before using EXFMT to display the subfile. The UPDATE operation lets you rewrite the subfile record after changing the selector field the user keys data into. The EXFMT operation lets you display and then read the subfile control format (displaying the subfile at the same time). Finally, the READC operation reads the changed records in the subfile.

```
*...1....+....2....+....3....+....4....+....5....+....6....+....7....+..
A            R ITEMLISTR               SFL
A              DLSEL        1A  B 10   2VALUES(' ' 'X')
A              DLITEM       6A  O 10   4
A              DLDESC      50A  O 10  12
 *
A            R ITEMHDRR                SFLCTL(ITMLSTR)
A N35                                  SFLDSPCTL
A N35 36                               SFLDSP
A  35                                  SFLCLR
A  33                                  SFLEND(*MORE)
A                                      SFLSIZ(11) SFLPAG(10)
A N33                                  PAGEDOWN(26)
A                                      CF03(03)
A                                      OVERLAY
 *
A              PAGRRN       4S  0H     SFLRCDNBR
A                                      2 35'Item Inquiry'
A                                      4  4'Item Code:'
A              DHITEM       6A  B  4 15
A                                      6  2'Type ''X'' to select +
A                                         items and press Enter.'
A                                      8  5'Item'
A                                      9  5'Code'
A                                      9 12'Description'
 *
A            R ITEMFTRR
A                                     23  5'F3=Exit'
 *
A            R ITEMDTLR
A                                      CF03(03)
A                                      2 35'Item Inquiry'
A                                      7 30'Item Code:'
A              D2ITEM       6A  O  7 42
A                                      9  3'Size . . . .:'
A              D2SIZE       4A  O  9 17
A                                     10  3'Description:'
A              D2DESC      50A  O 10 17
A                                     11  3'Qty On Hand:'
A              D2QTOH       7Y 0O 11 17EDTCDE(J)
A                                     11 29'Qty on Order:'
```

CONTINUED

```
*...1....+....2....+....3....+....4....+....5....+....6....+....7....+..
A             D2QTOO          7Y 00 11 44EDTCDE(J)
A                                   11 56'Qty Sold:'
A             D2QTSL          7Y 00 11 67EDTCDE(J)
A                                   23  5'F3=Exit'
```

```
*...1....+....2....+....3....+....4....+....5....+....6....+....7....+..
FItemInqrySCF   E              WORKSTN SFILE(ItemListR:CurrRRN)
FItemMast  IF   E         K DISK
```

```
*...1....+....2....+....3....+....4....+....5....+....6....+....7....+..
*
D SaveItem        S                   LIKE(ITITEM)
D LastItem        S                   LIKE(ITITEM)
D PosItem         S                   LIKE(ITITEM)
D ThisPageCt      S              5P 0
D LastRRN         S              5P 0
D CurrRRN         S              5P 0
```

```
*...1....+....2....+....3....+....4....+....5....+....6....+....7....+..
 *
 * Prepare subfile for initial display
 *  - Clear it
 *  - Position the file at the beginning
 *  - Load a single page in to the subfile
 *  - Call routine to handle display and processing of screen
C             EXSR      ClearSFL
C             EVAL      PosItem=*Blanks
C             EXSR      PosFile
C             EXSR      LoadPage
C             EXSR      SelItem
 ******************************************************************
 * Routine to handle display and processing of subfile
 *  - Execute loop to continually display screen (user must request exit)
 *  - Turn off the response indicators and the indicator that causes
 *    display of subfile control and subfile records
 *  - Write the footer record and then display and wait for subfile
 *  - If the user requests exit, call exit routine.
 *  - If user changes positioning criteria, clear and reload the subfile
 *  - Otherwise, if there was a page down request, load the next page
 *  -   Otherwise, call routine to process the user selections
 ****************************************************************** CONTINUED
```

```
*...1....+....2....+....3....+....4....+....5....+....6....+....7....+..
C     SelItem      BEGSR
 *
C                  DO         *HIVAL
 *
C                  SETOFF                                          0326
C                  SETOFF                                          35
 *
C                  WRITE      ItemFtrR
C                  EXFMT      ItemHdrR
 *
C                  IF         *IN03
C                  EXSR       ExitPgm
C                  ENDIF
 *
C                  IF         DHITEM>SaveItem
C                  EXSR       ClearSFL
C                  EVAL       PosItem=DHITEM
C                  EXSR       PosFile
C                  EXSR       LoadPage
C                  EVAL       SaveItem=DHITEM
 *
C                  ELSE
C                  IF         *IN26
C                  EVAL       PosItem=LastItem
C                  EXSR       PosFile
C                  EXSR       LoadPage
 *
C                  ELSE
C                  EXSR       ProcSel
C                  ENDIF
 *
C                  ENDIF
C                  ENDDO
C                  ENDSR
 ****************************************************************
 * Routine to handle processing of user-selected subfile records
 *   - Read the first changed record in the subfile (the user keyed
 *     a selection)
 *   - Loop while a change record was read
 *   - Set the page to display to show the last record processed
```

CONTINUED

```
*...1....+....2....+....3....+....4....+....5....+....6....+....7....+..
 *   -  If the user keyed an 'X', call routine to display details of Item
 *   -  Clear the selection field and update the field on the subfile
 *      record
 *   -  Read for the next changed record an loop back
 ********************************************************************
C     ProcSel      BEGSR
 *
C                  READC     ItemListR                              30
 *
C                  DOW       Not *IN30
 *
C                  EVAL      PageRRN=CurrRRN
 *
C                  IF        DLSEL='X'
C                  EXSR      ShowDetail
C                  ENDIF
 *
C                  EVAL      DLSEL=*BLANK
C                  UPDATE    ItemListR
 *
C                  READC     ItemListR                              30
C                  ENDDO
 *
C                  ENDSR
 ********************************************************************
 * Routine to load a single page to the subfile
 *   - Clear the counter that indicates how many records are loaded
 *     to the current page
 *   - Read the next Item record
 *   - Loop while a record was read and we have not filled the page
 *   -   Increment the current page record count and the total record count
 *   -   Set the current record number to the new record so we can point
 *       the right record number to write out the subfile entry
 *   -   Move the Item fields to the subfile record fields
 *   -   Insert (WRITE) the record into the subfile
 *   -   Turn on the indicator that says there is at least one record in
 *       the subfile
 *   -   Read the next record and loop
 *   - After loop, set the RRN of page to display to the last record in
 *     the subfile
```

CONTINUED

```
*...1....+....2....+....3....+....4....+....5....+....6....+....7....+..
 *  - If we encountered the last record in the data file
 *  - Turn on the indicator that controls the end of file indicator
 *  - on the subfile
 *  - Else
 *  - Turn the indicator off
 *  - Record the item number of the last item read so we can start with
 *    it on the next page load.
 *****************************************************************
C     LoadPage     BEGSR
 *
C                  EVAL      ThisPageCt=*ZERO
 *
C                  READ      ItemMastR                            30
 *
C                  DOW       Not *IN30 and ThisPageCt*
C                  ADD       1              ThisPageCt
C                  ADD       1              LastRRN
C                  EVAL      CurrRRN=LastRRN
 *
C                  EVAL      DLSEL=*BLANKS
C                  EVAL      DLITEM=ITITEM
C                  EVAL      DLDESC=ITDESC
 *
C                  WRITE     ItemListR
 *
C                  SETON                                          36
 *
C                  READ      ItemMastR                            30
C                  ENDDO
 *
C                  EVAL      PageRRN=LastRRN
 *
C                  IF        *IN30
C                  SETON                                          33
C                  ELSE
C                  SETOFF                                         33
C                  EVAL      LastItem=ITITEM
C                  ENDIF
 *
C                  ENDSR
```

CONTINUED

```
*....1....+....2....+....3....+....4....+....5....+....6....+....7....+..
 ******************************************************************
 * Routine to display Item detail screen
 *  - Read the selected record from the database
 *  - Load data to the item detail screen
 *  - Read/Write the display
 *  - If user requests exit, call exit routine
 ******************************************************************
C     ShowDetail    BEGSR
 *
C     DLITEM        CHAIN     ItemMastR                              99
 *
C                   EVAL      D2ITEM=ITITEM
C                   EVAL      D2SIZE=ITSIZE
C                   EVAL      D2DESC=ITDESC
C                   EVAL      D2QTOH=ITQTOH
C                   EVAL      D2QTOO=ITQTOO
C                   EVAL      D2QTSL=ITQTSL
 *
C                   EXFMT     ItemDtlR
 *
C                   IF        *IN03
C                   EXSR      ExitPgm
C                   ENDIF
 *
C                   ENDSR
 ******************************************************************
 * Routine to handle clearing of subfile
 *  - Seton the indicator that controls clearing of subfile
 *  - Write subfile control format to clear the subfile
 *  - Turn the clearing indicator back off
 *  - Turn off the indicator that allows subfile to be displayed
 *    since it is empty
 *  - Set the subfile record counter to zero
 ******************************************************************
C     ClearSFL      BEGSR
 *
C                   SETON                                            35
C                   WRITE     ItemHdrR
C                   SETOFF                                           35
C                   SETOFF                                           36
```

CONTINUED

```
*...1....+....2....+....3....+....4....+....5....+....6....+....7....+..
C                   EVAL      LastRRN=0
 *
C                   ENDSR
 ********************************************************************
 * Routine to position data file according to a given key value
 *  - Use SETLL to position on data file
 ********************************************************************
C     PosFile       BEGSR
 *
C     PosItem       SETLL     ItemMastR
 *
C                   ENDSR
 ********************************************************************
 * Routine to handle exit of program
 *  - Seton LR to do a complete termination
 *  - Exit the program
 ********************************************************************
C     ExitPgm       BEGSR
 *
C                   SETON                                        LR
C                   RETURN
 *
C                   ENDSR
```

CHAPTER 12

Printing

Sooner or later, every RPG programmer has to write a report program. If you are a new programmer, you'll get this task sooner, because RPG report programs are easy to write. RPG's original purpose was as a report writing mechanism. In fact, you probably know that RPG stands for Report Program Generator.

The language has changed a lot since its origins in the punchcard days of data processing. You no longer need to rely on RPG's mysterious program cycle when you design reports, so this chapter will ignore cycle processing. Instead, this chapter will show how to print a report in today's RPG.

As the chapter on database programming stressed, good programming style forbids program-described data files. The same philosophy applies to program-described printer files. Unfortunately, program-described printer files are still the norm in many AS/400 shops. Externally described printer files are finally coming into widespread use, and we urge you to follow this trend. However, bowing to advocates of program-described printer files, we will also cover this method.

First we will present the basic coding techniques for both approaches. Then we will point out the differences. The discussion will culminate in an example that shows how both methods produce the same report.

SPECIFICATIONS FOR PRINTING

To write an RPG program that produces printed output, you have three main tasks. First, as with all files in an RPG program, you must declare the printer file on an F-spec. Program-described and externally described printer files have different F-spec entries.

Second, the program must write the data to the printer file. When you leave behind the infamous RPG cycle, you handle program-described printer output with the EXCEPT operation. If you choose externally described printer files, you can leave EXCEPT behind and turn to the WRITE operation. (Although you *can* specify EXCEPT with externally described printer files, it defeats the purpose of external description, so you won't want to.) You can also use WRITE with a program-described printer file if you build the print image (including any formatting) in a data structure; however, this approach is poor technique for general printing tasks.

Third, you must describe how the printed output will appear. For program-described printer files, you format output in the O-specs to control line spacing, placement of the data, formatting of numeric data, etc. For externally described printer files, you ordinarily do not use O-specs. Instead, you WRITE the format you describe in the printer file DDS. You can use O-specs with EXCEPT, but you will not want to because only the named fields are printed, and others use default values — which is not usually your goal when you print a report. Again, you'll be much happier if you choose externally described printer files and WRITE.

These three tasks are all it takes to print a report in RPG IV. Let's discuss the details of each task.

The File Specification

Whether you choose program- or externally described files, you have to declare the printer file by naming it on an F-spec. The name you specify must be the name of the printer device file (an OS/400 object) you want to use. For an externally described file, you enter the name of a DDS-defined file. For program-described files, you will probably enter the name of a system-supplied file (e.g., QPRINT or QSYSPRT).

Because the printer device file that you declare on the F-spec controls such attributes as lines per inch, characters per inch, and overflow line, you can see the advantages of defining printer files to match your needs, instead of accepting the system's printer device files. You create printer device files by entering DDS source and issuing the CL CRTPRTF (Create Printer File) command to compile it. Or, if you don't want to use QPRINT or QSYSPRT, to create a printer device file for use with a program-described file, you can issue CRTPRTF with no DDS source.

RPG allows up to eight printer files in a program. You enter the printer file's name in positions 7 through 16 of the F-spec that declares the file to your program. In position 18, you specify the file type, which can be only O (output). The file format, E for externally described or F for program described, is in position 22. For a program-described file, you must specify the record length (positions on a single printed line) in positions 23 through 27. These positions are blank for externally described files. Finally, the device type is PRINTER, which you enter in positions 36 through 42.

```
*...1....+....2....+....3....+....4....+....5....+....6....+....7....+
FItemInv   O   E                PRINTER OFLIND(*IN20)
FQPRINT    O   F    80           PRINTER OFLIND(*INOF)
```

The above lines of code are example F-specs for an externally described printer file and for a program-described printer file. Each F-spec includes a keyword, OFLIND (Overflow Indicator). Several keywords are available for printer files. OFLIND is the most commonly specified one. It specifies the indicator to turn on when the printer file reaches the overflow line, which the printer device file determines. By default, this line is ordinarily one inch above the end of the page.

If you print past that point, the indicator on the OFLIND keyword is turned on. For externally described files, you can use any numeric indicator from 01 to 99. For program-described files, you must use the special indicators OA through OG and OV. The most commonly used indicator for this purpose on program-described files is OF, for overflow. If you have more than one printer file in the program, the overflow indicator must be unique for each.

A special note about these indicators and the differences between externally described and program-described printer files: The indicator you select for a program-described file will automatically be turned off when you generate output that goes to the next page. For externally described files, the indicator stays on until you turn it off. As an alternative to the overflow indicator with an externally described printer file, you can specify a resulting indicator in positions 73 to 74 on the WRITE statement. This alternative has the benefit of turning off the indicator if the line being written doesn't cause overflow. However, that benefit means you must specify the indicator on every WRITE to that file. Additionally, the indicator is in the position for detecting errors. Any type of error, not just reaching the overflow line, will cause the indicator to come on. You are better off using the F-spec to declare the indicator and turning it off after you use it.

One last difference between overflow indicators for program- and externally described printer files is when the overflow indicator turns on. The program-described file will turn it on any time you print on or past the overflow line. The externally described file will turn the indicator on for the same reason, but also if you space or skip past the overflow line and only if the printer file DDS doesn't specify an absolute line number (such as, the record always prints on line 64).

Two other F-spec keywords for printing are FORMLEN (Form Length) and FORMOFL (Form Overflow), which let you control the printed page's length and the line at which overflow occurs. If you specify one of these keywords, you must also specify the other. The line number you specify in FORMOFL triggers the indicator you specify on OFLIND.

You also define form length and form overflow line in the printer device file. Usually, you want to use the values on the printer device file instead of specifying these keywords. They require you to specify an exact number (from 1 to 255 for each, and the FORMOFL entry must be less than or equal to the FORMLEN entry), which means that your program is locked in to that form size. If you stick with the printer device's entries instead, you can vary the form length and overflow without having to recompile your program.

The last keyword specifically for printer files is PRTCTL (Printer Control). It lets you name a data structure that contains information to set the skipping and spacing values as you print. PRTCTL is valid only for program-described printer files and is hardly ever used. Other keywords that are not printer-file specific, such as INFSR and INFDS, are also allowed.

C-Spec Print Operations

The two approaches to defining printer files require different operations for generating output. The externally described file usually takes the WRITE operation: You specify WRITE in positions 26 through 35, and in Factor 2 you enter the name of the printer file format you are printing. You can also put an error/overflow indicator in positions 73 to 74. Factor 1 and the Result field are not allowed when you're writing to an externally described file. No O-specs are involved with WRITE and an externally described file. Of course, you can have conditioning indicators. Here is the syntax for the WRITE operation code.

Factor 1	Opcode	Extender	Factor 2	Result	Indicators		
Not allowed	WRITE		Required *format name*	Optional *data structure*	N/A	Error	N/A

You can use the WRITE operation with a program-described printer file. You specify a data structure name in the Result field. The data is then written directly from the data structure to the printer file — no O-specs are involved. This approach requires that all formatting occur in the program so that the data structure's contents produce the correct printed output. When you use WRITE this way, the default spacing control is used, providing a space-after value of 1. You can override the default by naming another data structure on the PRTCTL keyword on the printer file's F-spec. You set the printer skipping and spacing values there. This technique is not one we recommend.

With program-described files in a cycle-free implementation, you usually rely on the EXCEPT operation. Its interaction with O-specs makes it more complicated than the WRITE operation with an externally defined printer file.

You specify EXCEPT in the C-spec operation code field (positions 26 through 35). You cannot enter a value in Factor 1 or the Result field. No resulting indicators are allowed, either. You can specify conditioning indicators.

Factor 2 is optional. In Factor 2, you specify a name that will be matched up with O-specs to select which O-specs to execute. The O-specs that are considered when an EXCEPT operation occurs are those that have a type of E (Exception) in position 17 on their record-level O-spec. Each such O-spec is checked for the exception name you specify on the EXCEPT operation. If that name is specified on an O-spec, it is considered for output.

If you leave Factor 2 blank, only exception output records that do not have exception names specified are considered for output. Because EXCEPT is not file specific, but EXCEPT-name specific, you can mix printer output and database output in a single operation by giving multiple O-specs the same exception name. That capability can be good or bad, depending on your purpose. The following table shows the syntax for EXCEPT.

Factor 1	Opcode	Extender	Factor 2	Result	Indicators
Not allowed	EXCEPT		Optional *EXCEPT name*	Not allowed	Not allowed

The O-Specs: Record and Field Identification and Control

O-specs are ordinarily only for program-described files, such as program-described printer files. Each set of O-specs describes one line of output. A set of O-specs has one record-level O-spec and one or more field-level O-specs. The record-level O-spec is where you identify the file the output comes from (the printer file you name in the F-spec), the type of output (exception output), any skipping and spacing information for that line, and the exception name. You can also specify conditioning indicators to condition whether to print the record.

On the field-level O-spec, you identify the field or literal you want to print. Here is a sample O-spec set including record-level and field-level O-specs.

```
*...1....+....2....+....3....+....4....+....5....+....6....+....7....+
OQPRINT    E          HEADER    1  3
O                                        17 'Program: ITEMLIST'
O                                        46 'Item Inventory'
O                     UDATE        Y     70
```

On the record-level O-spec entry, the file name starts in position 7 and can continue through 16. You can leave the name blank if the set of O-specs you are defining is for the same file as the previous set of O-specs. In position 17, you specify the record type, which, for exception output, will always be E.

If you have conditioning indicators, you enter them in positions 21 through 29, and you can have more than one O-spec to hold the indicators. In that case, you must specify the relationship between the indicators on the current O-spec and the previous O-spec. You can put an AND in positions 16 through 18 to specify that the condition on the current line must be true and the condition on the previous line must be true. You can enter OR to specify that either set can be true. You can build large sets of conditioning indicators this way, but that hard-to-maintain technique is strongly discouraged. Instead, include such logic in the C-specs and specify multiple EXCEPT operations to control what to print.

You enter the EXCEPT name in positions 30 through 39. This name is not required, but O-spec sets are matched with the name specified on the EXCEPT operation. If the EXCEPT operation does not specify an except name, only those exception O-specs that do not have a name are printed.

Finally, you can specify before and after line spacing values in positions 40 through 42 and 43 through 45, respectively, and before and after line skipping values in positions 46 through 48 and 49 through 51, respectively. Spacing refers to the number of lines you want the printer to advance before or after printing the current line. Skipping identifies a specific line number to which you want the printer to move before or after printing the current line. Spacing values can be from 0 to 255, and skipping values can be from 1 to 255. This specification is how you control the advancement of the paper in the printer. Precedence rules specify this order: skip before, space before, print the line, skip after, space after.

A field-level O-spec belongs to the record-level O-spec before it. All field-level O-specs will be in the same set until a new set starts when you enter a new record-level O-spec or processing encounters the end of the O-specs.

You can use conditioning indicators to condition the output of each field or literal. Such conditioning occurs more frequently than conditioning indicators at the record level. Unlike at the record level, at the field level, you cannot have more than one O-spec ANDed or ORed together.

If you are printing a field from a program, the field name goes in positions 30 through 43. If you are printing a numeric field, you can specify an edit code in position 44. Also, if you are printing a field, you can put a B in position 45 to set the field to blank or zero after you print it. Don't use this specification; it can be very hard to track down in a program.

To position the data on the printed form, you specify the ending position for the field or literal in positions 47 through 51. This entry is optional, and if you don't enter it, the data will print in the next position to the right of the last field or literal printed. Additionally, you can use an offset value such as + 2 to cause the current field or literal to start three positions after the end of the previous field, leaving 2 blank spaces. (You can even specify negative offsets, but that gets really nasty looking and is not recommended.) Using the positive offset from the previous field saves you the bother of calculating the ending positions of every field. Note that you enter the + in position 47, and the number must end in position 51 .

To identify date and time fields, you can enter a D or a T in position 52. If you enter one of these values in position 52, you must then enter the DATEFMT (Date Format) or TIMFMT (Time Format) keyword in position 53 to 80. You specify the format for a date field using the DATFMT keyword and the format for a time field using the TIMFMT keyword. The hierarchy the compiler uses when determining the external date and time format is as follows:

1. the date format and separator specified in positions 53 through 58

2. the DATFMT or TIMFMT specified for the current printer file

3. the DATFMT or TIMFMT specified on the H-spec

4. the default, *ISO

Positions 53 through 80 let you print one of three things. First, you can print a literal if you have not specified a field in positions 30 through 43. In these positions, you enter the literal value enclosed in single quotes. Second, you can enter an edit word. Third, if you specify a D or T in position 52, you can specify the date or time format keyword in positions 53 through 80 .

EDIT CODES AND EDIT WORDS

When you print numeric fields, you can make them easy to read by marking them as positive or negative, suppressing zeros, inserting decimal points, and supplying separator characters. Such formatting is called editing a numeric field.

RPG provides two ways to edit numeric fields: edit codes and edit words. Edit codes let you edit numeric fields by specifying a one-character code in position 44 of an O-spec. This code represents a predefined (usually by the system) editing rule. Edit words are literals or named constants that you enter in positions 53 through 80 of the O-spec. They give you more advanced editing facilities than edit codes and let you directly specify editing patterns.

Edit Codes

In RPG, edit codes have three different categories: *simple codes*, which provide or remove the negative and positive sign and edit date fields; *combination codes*, which let you combine different editing functions; and *user-defined codes*, which let you create your own edit codes. The following table lists all the valid edit codes.

RPG IV Edit Codes

Simple Edit Codes	Function
X	Adds hexadecimal F sign for positive fields
Y	Edits 3- to 9-digit date fields; suppresses leftmost zeros up to the digit preceding first separator
Z	Removes the sign from a numeric field, suppresses leading zeros; no decimal point in the field

Combination Edit Codes	Function
1	Prints grouping separator and zero balance — No sign for negative numbers
2	Prints grouping separator but no zero balance — No sign for negative numbers
3	Prints no grouping separator but prints zero balance — No sign for negative numbers
4	Prints no grouping separator or zero balance — No sign for negative numbers
A	Prints grouping separator and zero balance with CR for negative numbers
B	Prints grouping separator but no zero balance with CR for negative numbers
C	Prints no grouping separator but does print zero balance with CR for negative numbers
D	Prints no grouping separator or zero balance with CR for negative numbers

CONTINUED

Combination Edit Codes	Function
J	Prints grouping separator and zero balance with – for negative numbers
K	Prints grouping separator but no zero balance with – for negative numbers
L	Prints no grouping separator but does print zero balance with – for negative numbers
M	Prints no grouping separator or zero balance with – for negative numbers
N	Prints grouping separator and zero balance with floating minus for negative numbers
O	Prints grouping separator but no zero balance with floating minus for negative numbers
P	Prints no grouping separator but does print zero balance with floating minus for negative numbers
Q	Prints no grouping separator or zero balance with floating minus for negative numbers

User-Defined Edit Codes	Function
5, 6, 7, 8	Supply edit assigned by user. The user-assigned values are applied at the system level

You select from these codes and enter the one you want in column 44 of the O-specs. Each edit code category provides specific edits.

Simple Edit Codes

Simple edit codes let you edit numeric fields without having to specify any punctuation. The three simple edit codes are X, Y, and Z. The X code ensures a hexadecimal F sign for positive fields. You do not have to specify X in your program because the system does so by default, if you do not specify an edit code or word for the field you are printing. The Y edit code lets you edit three- to nine-digit date fields. It suppresses the leftmost zeros of date fields, up to but not including the digit preceding the first separator. You specify the DATEDIT (Date Edit) and DECEDIT (Decimal Edit) keywords on the H-specs to alter the edit formats. The Z edit code removes the sign from a numeric field and suppresses the leading zeros. The decimal point is not placed in the field, nor is it printed.

Combination Edit Codes

Combination edit codes let you specify editing combinations by entering a single character that represents a predefined set of editing rules. For example, specifying an A in column 44 of the O-spec tells the compiler that you want to print the number with a grouping separator, print zero balances, and print the negative sign as CR.

Grouping Separator	Zero Values	No Sign	CR for Sign	– for Sign	Floating Minus
Yes	Yes	1	A	J	N
Yes	No	2	B	K	O
No	Yes	3	C	L	P
No	No	4	D	M	Q

The table above illustrates the other combinations you can use to punctuate numeric fields. The first column, printing with grouping separator, adds a comma after every three digits. For example, after the system edits the number 123456.88, the result is 123,456.88. A yes in the second column means the compiler will print zero instead of a blank if the field contains a zero. The following four columns determine how to print a negative number. The first one instructs the compiler to print no negative sign. This edit is similar to getting the absolute value of a negative number. The second one tells the compiler to print CR (for credit) after a negative number. The third column is for printing the negative number with the minus sign. The fourth column allows a floating negative sign with the number, depending on its length. The negative sign prints in the position just to the left of the first digit printed after zero suppression has been handled.

These edits are called combination editing because RPG lets you choose the combination that best suits your application. For example, if you put an L in position 44 of the O-spec, the edited field will have no grouping separator, it will print a zero balance, and the sign printed for a negative value is –. On the other hand, if you select the M edit code, everything is similar to the L editing code except that zero balances are not printed: If the field contains a zero, a blank appears on the printout.

You can perform two other special functions when you use one of the 16 combination edit codes. If you need a floating currency sign, you can put your currency symbol in single quotes in positions 53 through 55 of the same O-spec where you specify the edit code. The currency symbol is, by default, the dollar sign unless you change it in the H-spec by specifying the CURSYM (Currency Symbol) keyword with a different symbol.

Another option is to specify asterisk protection. The asterisk character will appear instead of blanks as the leading character when you have zero suppression. This option is handy for printing checks if you want to leave the printed value right justified in a given space on the form, but you do not want to leave preceding positions empty. You cannot combine the two facilities to print a dollar sign in front of the asterisk character, but you can simulate that effect with edit codes by printing a dollar sign as a literal in the position before the field and then specifying asterisk to fill in the leading positions of the printed value. Of course, this combination requires two O-specs. The following tables show the results of the edit codes on various numbers.

Zero value, 2 decimals

	No special function	*fill	Floating $
1	.00	*********.00	$.00
2		***********	
3	.00	*******.00	$.00
4		*********	
A	.00&&	*********.00&&	$.00&&
B		***********&&	
C	.00&&	*******.00&&	$.00&&
D		*********&&	
J	.00	*********.00&	$.00&
K		***********&	
L	.00&	*******.00&	$.00&
M		*********&	
N	.00	*********.00	$.00
O		***********	
P	.00	*******.00	$.00
Q		***********	

Negative value, 1600.22

	No special function	*fill	Floating $
1	1,600.22	****1,600.22	$1,600.22
2	1,600.22	****1,600.22	$1,600.22
3	1600.22	***1600.22	$1600.22
4	1600.22	***1600.22	$1600.22
A	1,600.22CR	****1,600.22CR	$1,600.22CR
B	1,600.22CR	****1,600.22CR	$1,600.22CR
C	1600.22CR	***1600.22CR	$1600.22CR
D	1600.22CR	***1600.22CR	$1600.22CR
J	1,600.22–	****1,600.22–	$1,600.22–
K	1,600.22–	****1,600.22–	$1,600.22–
L	1600.22–	***1600.22–	$1600.22–
M	1600.22–	***1600.22–	$1600.22–
N	–1,600.22	****–1,600.22	–$1,600.22
O	–1,600.22	****–1,600.22	–$1,600.22
P	–1600.22	***–1600.22	–$1600.22
Q	–1600.22	***–1600.22	–$1600.22

CONTINUED

Positive value, 1600.22

	No special function	*fill	Floating $
1	1,600.22	****1,600.22	$1,600.22
2	1,600.22	****1,600.22	$1,600.22
3	1600.22	***1600.22	$1600.22
4	1600.22	***1600.22	$1600.22
A	1,600.22&&	****1,600.22&&	$1,600.22&&
B	1,600.22&&	****1,600.22&&	$1,600.22&&
C	1600.22&&	***1600.22&&	$1600.22&&
D	1600.22&&	***1600.22&&	$1600.22&&
J	1,600.22&	****1,600.22&	$1,600.22&
K	1,600.22&	****1,600.22&	$1,600.22&
L	1600.22&	***1600.22&	$1600.22&
M	1600.22&	***1600.22&	$1600.22&
N	1,600.22	*****1,600.22	$1,600.22
O	1,600.22	*****1,600.22	$1,600.22
P	1600.22	****1600.22	$1600.22
Q	–1600.22	****1600.22	$1600.22

User-Defined Edit Codes

RPG and the system let you define four edits and assign them to codes 5 through 8. User-defined edit codes are for editing that you can't get with the combination codes.

You use the OS/400 CRTEDTD (Create Edit Description) command to create user-defined edit codes. The screen on the following page lists the parameters for this command.

The combination of these parameters creates the edit. For example, the *Decimal point character* parameter lets you specify a character as a decimal point to separate the integer (INTMASK parameter) and fraction (FRACMASK parameter) portions of the edited result. If the field has no decimal places, this character is not used and is not considered in the width of the edited results. Another example is the *Fill character* parameter, which lets you specify the character to use in each position of a result that is zero suppressed. The specified character replaces all leading zeros that are to the left of the first significant digit in the integer mask (or a forced zero). For negative values, you use the *Negative status characters* parameter to specify the character string that immediately follows the body of the edited result if the field is negative. If the field is positive, blanks are substituted for the length of the string unless a value is also specified for the *Positive status characters* prompt (POSSTS parameter). If you need more information about these parameters, refer to the *OS/400 Command Reference* manual.

```
                        Create Edit Description (CRTEDTD)
 Type choices, press Enter.
 Edit description . . . . . . . .   _                5, 6, 7, 8, 9
 Integer mask . . . . . . . . . .   *NONE
 Decimal point character . . . .   '.'              Character value, ., *NO
 Fraction mask . . . . . . . . .   *NONE
 Fill character . . . . . . . . .  *BLANK           Character value, *BLANK
 Currency symbol  . . . . . . . .  *NONE
 Edit zero values . . . . . . . .  *YES             *YES, *NO
 Negative status characters . . .  *NONE
 Positive status characters . . .  *NONE
 Left constant characters . . . .  *NONE
 Right constant characters  . . .  *NONE
 Text 'description' . . . . . . .  *BLANK
```

Programmers rarely create their own edit codes. You can consider doing so if you have an edit word you're using repeatedly. The next section covers edit words. Becoming familiar with edit words will help you understand the various parts of a user-defined edit code and the parameters that make up the code.

The simple edit codes, X, Y, and Z are the easiest way to edit numeric fields. If these simple codes don't satisfy your needs, the next step is to use the combination codes. As with simple codes, RPG defines combination codes for you. If simple codes and combination codes do not give you the editing functionality you need, you can create your own code using the CRTEDTD command and one of the reserved numbers, 5 through 8. Unless you will need a user-defined edit code often, you will be better off using an edit word. Only four user-defined edit codes are available, and they are global, not local to your program.

Edit Words

An edit word is a character literal or a named constant that you specify in positions 53 through 80 of a program's O-specs. You can specify an edit word directly on the O-specs in positions 53 through 80, or you can define a named constant on the D-specs and enter that name in positions 53 through 80, instead.

An edit word describes the editing pattern for a numeric field and lets you directly specify blank spaces, commas and decimal points, suppression of unwanted zeros, leading asterisks, a currency symbol, addition of constant characters, and output of a negative number. Edit words give you all the combinations and functionality available to edit a numeric field and let you custom design your editing. In contrast, combination codes are preset combinations of the most-used edits. All the function you can get from combination codes, you can also get with edit words — but not the other way around. For example, with edit words, but not with edit codes, you can specify the currency symbol as any character you want.

An edit word consists of three parts: the body, the status, and the expansion. The body is the space for the digits transferred from the source data field to the output record. The body begins at the leftmost position of the edit word. The rule to remember about edit words is that the number of blanks in the edit word body must be equal to or greater than the number of digits in the source data field to be edited. If you have more blanks in the edit word than characters to print, you must remember that the value is *not* decimal aligned when the edit word is applied. If the value you are printing has two decimal positions and the edit word you use has three blanks after the decimal position, your value will appear to have been divided by 10. The value to print is moved into the blanks from right to left. You can have additional blanks at the beginning of the body.

Some special rules apply to the characters that go into the body of an edit word. Let's discuss each rule for the various characters.

Blank: Blank is replaced with the character from the corresponding position of the source data field specified by the field name in positions 30 through 43 of the O-specs. A blank position is referred to as a digit position. Remember that these positions are filled from right to left and that all blank positions (plus a few others, detailed below) are considered replaceable characters.

Decimals and Commas: Decimals and commas are placed in the same relative position in the edited output field as they are in the edit word unless they appear to the left of the first significant digit in the edit word. In that case, they are blanked out or replaced by an asterisk. This means that you can include both these characters, but each character will print only if at least one digit prints to the left of it. This rule includes digits printed because of termination of zero suppression.

Zeros: The first zero in the body of the edit word is interpreted as an end-zero-suppression character. You put this zero where you want zero suppression to end. Subsequent zeros in the edit word are treated as constants. Any leading zeros in the source data are suppressed, up to and including the position of the end-zero-suppression character. Significant digits that would appear in the end-zero-suppression character position, or to the left of it, are output.

If the leading zeros in the value you are printing include, or extend to the right of, the end-zero-suppression character position, that position is replaced with a blank. This means that if you want the same number of leading zeros to appear in the output as are in the source data, the edit word body's replaceable characters must be wider than the source data, and the zero suppression character must appear to the left of the first position in which you want the leading zeros to print.

Asterisk: The first asterisk in the body of an edit word also ends zero suppression. Subsequent asterisks put into the edit word are treated as constants. Any zeros in the edit word following this asterisk are also treated as constants. You can have only one end-zero-suppression character in an edit word, and that character is the first asterisk or the first zero in the edit word.

If you specify an asterisk as an end-zero-suppression character, all leading zeros that are suppressed are replaced with asterisks in the output. Otherwise, the asterisk suppresses leading zeros in the same way as described above for zeros.

Currency Symbol: A currency symbol followed directly by a first zero in the edit word (end-zero-suppression character) is said to float. Floating means that all leading zeros are suppressed in the output, and the currency symbol appears in the output immediately to the left of the most significant digit. However, if the currency symbol is in the first position of the edit word, it will always appear in that position in the output. This symbol is called a fixed currency symbol.

Ampersand: The ampersand character causes a blank in the edited field. You can use this symbol to provide a blank as a separator in your numbers.

Constants: All other characters entered into the body of the edit word are treated as constants. If the source data is such that the output places significant digits or leading zeros to the left of any constant, that constant appears in the output. Otherwise, the constant is suppressed in the output. Commas and the decimal point follow the same rules as for constants.

The status portion defines a space to allow for a negative indicator. The negative indicator can be the two letters CR or the minus sign. The negative indicator is printed only if the value of the field is negative. You enter the status after the last blank in the edit word. The status portion of the edit word begins with the first character following the last blank of the body. Other characters can appear between the body and the negative indicator, but such characters are subject to the following rules. The rules for the negative indicator are included.

Ampersand: As in the body, an ampersand causes a blank in the edited output field. As you may have guessed by now, you cannot include an ampersand in the printed output when using an edit word, because ampersands always represent a blank.

CR or minus symbol: The CR and minus sign are the only values allowed as the negative indicator. If the sign in the edited output is plus (+), these positions are blanked out. If the sign in the edited output field is minus (–), these positions remain undisturbed: The negative indicator is printed. One special note: You can use the minus symbol as a negative indicator only if it is the last character in the entire edit word (you cannot have an expansion part to the word if you need to use the minus symbol).

Constants: Any other characters between the end of the body and the negative indicator are considered constants. These characters will print only if the field is negative; otherwise, blanks will print in these positions. Constants (including commas and decimal point) that you put to the right of the end-zero-suppression character are output, even if there is no source data. Constants to the left of the end-zero-suppression character are output only if the source data has significant digits that would be placed to the left of these constants.

The last part of an edit word is the expansion, a series of ampersands and constant characters that you enter after the status. In the output, blank spaces replace ampersands; constants are printed as is. The expansion part of the edit word will always be printed, no matter what the value of the field to which the edit word is applied. You can have only a body and expansion if you do not specify the CR version of the status portion. (Remember that you can't have an expansion if you use the minus symbol as the negative indicator, so you can have an expansion only if you use the CR version or if you don't supply a status portion at all).

The following table shows examples of edit words and their effect on numeric data. Blanks are represented by a lowercase b with strike through ($\not b$).

Edit Word	Data	Internal Format	Formatted Data
'$\not b\not b\not b\not b\not b$'	000345	N6.0	345
$\not b\not b\not b$'	0239	N4.1	23.9
$\not b0\not b\not b\not b\not b$'	000345	N6.0	0345

CONTINUED

Edit Word	Data	Internal Format	Formatted Data
ƀoƀ,ƀƀƀ.ƀƀ'	00000324	N8.2	0,003.24
ƀƀƀƀƀ*ƀ.ƀƀ**'	000012345	N9.2	****123.45
ƀƀ,ƀƀƀ,ƀ$0ƀƀ'	000123456	N9.2	$1,234.56
ƀ,ƀƀ0.ƀƀ&CR&NET'	000542–	N6.2	5.42 CR NET

PRINTING BY EXAMPLE

To demonstrate both the similarities and the differences between working with externally described printer files and program-described files, this example will show two programs. They produce the same inventory report but use the two different approaches. First is the externally described file version and next is the program-described one. The report lists the items a company sells and includes an item code, a description, a quantity on hand, and a quantity on order.

Externally Described Printer File Example

Before you can write the report using the externally described printer file, you need to code the DDS printer file below and compile it. This printer file contains two records formats, ITEMHDR and ITEMDTL. The report has no conditioning indicators.

ITEMHDR has no fields in the format. Everything is either a literal or special keyword. The DATE and TIME keywords print the date and time on the report header. The PAGNBR (Page Number) keyword automatically numbers the pages. Though three lines of information are in the report header (the title line, the page number line, and the column headings), you have just one format. The SPACE and SKIP keywords in the DDS let you start printing on the line you want. The program writes this format to the printer file, and all the headings will print in the format you want.

The second format contains the four fields you want to print. The program sets the values of these fields before you WRITE this format.

```
*...1....+....2....+....3....+....4....+....5....+....6....+....7....+
A           R ITEMHDR                  SKIPB(3)
A                                       1'Program: ITEMLIST'
A                                      33'Item Inventory'
A                                      63DATE EDTCDE(Y)
A                                      73TIME EDTWRD(' : : ')
A                                         SPACEA(1)
 *
A                                       1'PAGE:'
A                                       7PAGNBR EDTCDE(Z)
A                                         SPACEA(2)
 *
```

CONTINUED

```
*...1....+....2....+....3....+....4....+....5....+....6....+....7....+
A                                   2'Item'
A                                  10'Description'
A                                  61' On Hand'
A                                  71' On Order'
A                                    SPACEA(2)
 *
 *
A            R ITEMDTL                SPACEA(1)
A              PRITEM      6          2
A              PRDESC     50         10
A              PRQTOH      7 Ø       61EDTCDE(J)
A              PRQTOO      7 Ø       71EDTCDE(J)
```

In the program below, the F-specs declare the printer file ItemInv. It is an externally described output file, as specified in positions 17 and 22. To declare that it is a printer file, you enter the device type PRINTER. Finally, the keyword OFLIND identifies indicator 20 as the overflow indicator for this file. Any time you print on, space over, or skip over the overflow line, this indicator will turn on to let you know. The program will use that indicator later to start a new page by reprinting the report headings.

In the C-specs, the program WRITEs the first format of the externally described file to print the report headings. The DDS contains a SKIPB(3) keyword on this format to move printing of the report to line 3 of the current page (or of the next page if the printer is already past line 3 on the current page). Next the program READs the first ItemMast record in the ItemMastR record format. Indicator 30 will signal an end-of-file (EOF) condition.

After the program reads the record, processing drops into a loop that will process the current record, retrieve the next, and continue until EOF. Inside this loop, you check whether the overflow indicator is on. If so, you start a new page by reprinting the heading format. Checking here, rather than immediately after the WRITE, lets you start a new page only if you have a record to print on it.

```
*...1....+....2....+....3....+....4....+....5....+....6....+....7....+.
FItemMast  IF   E          K Disk
FItemInv   O    E             Printer OFLIND(*IN20)

*...1....+....2....+....3....+....4....+....5....+....6....+....7....+.
 *
 * Write initial headings
C                 WRITE     ItemHdr
 *
```

Continued

```
*...1....+....2....+....3....+....4....+....5....+....6....+....7....+.
 * Read first record
C                   READ      ItemMastR                               30
 *
 * Loop through existing records (while not at EOF)
C                   DOW       Not *IN30
 *
 * If the last output caused the overflow indicator to come on
 * - Turn the indicator off
 * - Write new headings (page break)
C                   IF        *IN20
C                   SETOF                                             20
C                   WRITE     ItemHdr
C                   ENDIF
 *
 * Set the printer format's fields to the data in current item record
C                   EVAL      PRItem=ITItem
C                   EVAL      PRDesc=ITDesc
C                   EVAL      PRQTOH=ITQTOH
C                   EVAL      PRQTOO=PRQTOO
 *
 * Write the current item record
C                   WRITE     ItemDtl
 *
 * Read the next Item record and loop back
C                   READ      ItemMastR                               30
C                   ENDDO
 *
 * When done, exit the program
C                   SETON                                             LR
C                   RETRN
```

This step prevents you from printing a blank page if the last record in the file is the one that turns on the overflow indicator. A frequent error is to check for overflow and print headings immediately after printing each detail line, but that practice leads to this problem.

After printing overflow headings (if necessary), you move the current record's data to the PRxxx fields in the detail format, ItemDtl. After loading the fields, you can WRITE the detail format.

In the DDS, the two numeric fields you are printing have the EDTCDE (Edit Code) keyword with a value of J. That keyword causes zero suppression, prints negative signs, and inserts commas. The external file also handles the field positioning. You can change all these edits without having to recompile the program. For example, you can move fields to different positions or lines or apply different edit codes or words. You can also add and remove literals. If the record format for the raw data doesn't change, you can alter the DDS for the externally described printer file and recompile to change the appearance of the report — all without having to recompile the program.

At the end of the loop, you read the next ItemMast record and return to process and print it. Once you finish the loop, processing drops to the end, sets on the LR indicator, and exits.

When you write this program, you have no data formatting to worry about. You can write the DDS for the file or use a printer file that someone else prepared. Perhaps one programmer in your shop is responsible for external interfaces, and you are responsible only for implementing the business logic. Using externally described files, this division of labor can be very efficient. Add to that the printer file's ability to store specific attributes, such as where the report is printed, the number of copies, and whether it is deleted immediately after print, and you can see the compelling reasons for using externally described files.

Program-Described Printer File Example

The program-described file version of the report program is on the following page. This discussion will focus just on the differences in the programs.

The first difference is the F-spec for the printer file. It specifies a system-supplied, generic printer file for use with program-described output. This example uses QPRINT, but we strongly urge you to make a new printer file by issuing the CRTPRTF command with no DDS source.

The next difference is the F in position 22 and the 80 in column 26 to 27. These specifications are for a program-described file with a record length of 80 characters.

Another difference is that the overflow indicator is changed from *IN20 to *INOF. Program-described files require one of the eight special overflow indicators rather than numeric indicators.

Next comes an added work field, PTime. Whereas the externally described file has the DDS TIME keyword to print the time, with program-described printer files, you have to retrieve the time for printing.

Another difference is the output operation. For the program-described printing solution, EXCEPTs replace all three WRITEs in the externally described printer file solution. Correspondingly, EXCEPT names of Header and Detail replace the record format names.

Two other changes are notable. First, you do not have to set off the overflow indicator when you print overflow headings. RPG automatically sets it off. The second change is that you are no longer moving data from the data file fields to other fields for printing. You just use the data file fields on the O-specs.

```
*...1....+....2....+....3....+....4....+....5....+....6....+....7....+.
FItemMast  IF   E           K Disk
FQPRINT    O    F   80         Printer OFLIND(*INOF)


*...1....+....2....+....3....+....4....+....5....+....6....+....7....+.
D PTime          S              6 0


*...1....+....2....+....3....+....4....+....5....+....6....+....7....+.
 *
 * Get the current time to print on the report
C                   TIME                      PTime
 *
 * Write initial headings
C                   EXCPT     Header
 *
 * Read first record
C                   READ      ItemMastR                              30
 *
 * Loop through existing records (while not at EOF)
C                   DOW       Not *IN30
 * If the last output caused the overflow indicator to come on
 *   - Write new headings (page break)
C                   IF        *INOF
C                   EXCPT     Header
C                   ENDIF
 *
 * Write the current item record using fields from the file read
C                   EXCPT     Detail
 *
 * Read the next Item record and loop back
C                   READ      ItemMastR                              30
C                   ENDDO
 *
 * When done, exit the program
C                   SETON                                            LR
C                   RETRN
 *
```

Continued

```
*...1....+....2....+....3....+....4....+....5....+....6....+....7....+.
OQPRINT     E              HEADER          1  3
O                                            17 'Program: ITEMLIST'
O                                            46 'Item Inventory'
O                         UDate           Y  70
O                         Ptime              80 ' : : '
     *
O           E              Header          2
O                                             5 'Page:'
O                         Page            Z  10
     *
O           E              Header          2
O                                             5 'Item'
O                                            20 'Description'
O                                            69 ' On Hand'
O                                            79 ' On Order'
     *
O           E              Detail          1
O                         ITItem              7
O                         ITDesc             59
O                         ITQTOH          J  70
O                         ITQTOO          J  80
```

Because this is a program-described file, you have to describe its layout in the program's O-specs. The O-specs contain all the elements that are in the DDS for the externally described file. Of course, one set of O-specs cannot include multiple print lines, so you have four sets of O-specs. (In contrast, the externally described printer file has only two formats.) The first three sets of O-specs print the report's page headings. The same literals are here as are in the externally described file's DDS .

Note that only one O-spec set has the name of the file specified. All subsequent sets belong to the same file unless you specify a different file name. Each record-level O-spec has an except name. The first three have the same name, so they will all be processed as a group when EXCEPT Header is executed. This specification is analogous to the header format from the externally described file. One operation can still perform the action in the C-specs because the EXCEPT name ties the three sets together. This is a common practice for printing several lines of text at a time.

For the record-level O-specs, notice that the same values for spacing and skipping that you specify by keyword in the externally described file's DDS are represented here positionally. The first header record has a skip-before value of

3 and a space-after value of 1. The next two header records have a space-after value of 2. The detail records have a space-after value of 1.

You specify a print position for each field and literal in the field-level O-specs. They are different from what you specify in the externally described file's DDS. O-specs require the ending position for the field or literal, whereas DDS uses the beginning position. Both these reports have the data positioned in the same places.

As the last note on the O-specs, notice the J edit code in position 44. This is the same edit code as in the EDTCDE keyword in the DDS for the externally described file.

You can now see both the similarities and the differences between using externally described files and program-described files for printing. You will benefit greatly from using externally described files. You can make cosmetic changes to them without having to recompile your programs. This capability assures that nothing can happen to the business logic when a programmer opens up your program source to make minor formatting changes. Of course, neither approach can prevent you from ever having to recompile a program.

CHAPTER 13

The Integrated Language Environment

When IBM redesigned the AS/400 programming environment and created the Integrated Language Environment (ILE), the designers set out to incorporate all existing AS/400 programming languages in this new environment. With OS/400 Version 3 Release 1, RPG became an ILE language and a full participation in ILE, just like the first language designed for this new environment, ILE C. RPG IV is the new version of the language that is fully consistent with ILE and can take advantage of all ILE functionality.

Unlike RPG, C, or COBOL, ILE is not a language. Rather, it is the underlying environment that lets all the newly introduced ILE languages work together. But ILE is not an environment in the same sense as the S/36 environment, for example. Unlike such environments, ILE will let you mix all your old applications written in, say RPG/400, with all new applications written in ILE RPG.

To create interlanguage ILE applications, you can write code in any ILE-supported high-level language (e.g., ILE RPG/400, ILE COBOL, ILE CL, or ILE C/400) and then include modules written in different ILE languages, such as ILE RPG and ILE C, in one program object. ILE compilers translate source code for each language into an intermediate language, and create an object of type *MODULE when you issue a new command, CRTxxxMOD (Create*xxx* Module, where *xxx* stands for a particular ILE language, such as RPG). When you execute the new CRTPGM (Create Program) command, you call the ILE optimizer and binder to link all your *MODULE objects and create a program (*PGM object). It includes all the module objects you specify on the CRTPGM command. Because all ILE languages are compiled into the same intermediate language, you can easily bind ILE RPG, C, and COBOL modules within one application. ILE improves application, performance and code reusability in mixed-language and call-intensive applications.

Consider the following example: Suppose you have a payroll application with some functions written in ILE RPG and a numeric function written in ILE C to do some arithmetic calculation. You can create each function as a separate module object and bind them into one program object. You first compile the ILE RPG code using the CRTRPGMOD (Create RPG Module) command to produce the first program module. Second, you execute the CRTCMOD (Create C Module) command to produce the C module. Finally, you execute the CRTPGM command to bind these pieces together and produce an executable program (of object type *PGM) that contains both modules.

When you're ready to perform arithmetic calculations, the RPG module can call the C module by executing a new RPG operation code, CALLB (Call Bound). This operation calls the modules that are bound together, so the call's performance is quicker and more efficient than the old CALL operation. With CALL, one *PGM object calls a separate *PGM object.

PROGRAMMING ENVIRONMENTS BEFORE ILE

Before ILE, the first AS/400 programming environment was the Original Program Model (OPM); then came the Extended Program Model (EPM). To set the stage for a detailed discussion of ILE program creation, reviewing program compilation in the AS/400's previous programming environments is helpful. Then you can compare the new process for ILE program compilation.

The OPM example in Figure 13.1 is equivalent in function to the ILE example in Figure 13.2. The code for the old environment consists of two source members, MAIN and TAX. Program MAIN will use an RPG CALL operation code to call program TAX, which computes Canadian federal and provincial tax amounts. The CALL operation code is a *dynamic call*, which means the system resolves the pointer to the called program during execution of the calling program: The system finds the program CALL wants, while the program containing this CALL is executing.

FIGURE 13.1
Program-to-Program CALLs in the OPM Model

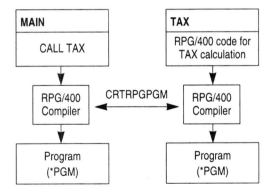

Figure 13.1 shows the steps for compiling and executing this application in the OPM environment. You execute the CRTRPGPGM (Create RPG Program) command for each program to compile source members MAIN and TAX as separate executable programs. The result of each compile is an object of type *PGM.

The order of compilation in the OPM/EPM environment is irrelevant because MAIN issues a dynamic call to program TAX during runtime. The

FIGURE 13.2
Mixing RPG and C in an ILE Application

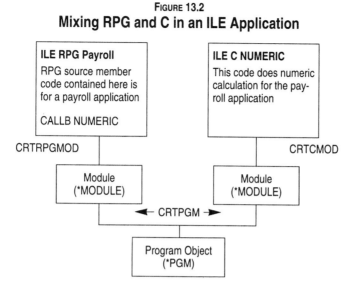

existence of TAX is not important to the compilation of source program MAIN because the system will resolve the pointer to TAX during execution, as is always the case with dynamic calling.

WHAT'S DIFFERENT IN ILE?

With this brief review of OPM/EPM program creation in mind, let's look at the process of program creation in ILE. Figure 13.3. shows the same programming example as above, but in ILE RPG IV.

In ILE, the program creation process differs from the one-step OPM/EPM process, in which you execute CRTRPGPGM to compile each of two executable programs, one of which calls the other. With ILE, you first execute the new CRTRPGMOD command to compile two nonexecutable RPG program *modules*, both of which you will include in one program. Only after you execute the new CRTPGM command, will these modules become executable as part of the resulting *PGM object.

Instead of *program* MAIN calling *program* TAX, *procedure* MAIN in *module* MAIN can call *procedure* TAX in *module* TAX. This call within one *PGM object is possible because of the ILE RPG CALLB opcode. (Note that all ILE languages provide specific syntax for bound calls.)

Modules

Figure 13.3. shows ILE's new CRTRPGMOD command. You issue this command for each source member, MAIN and TAX, to invoke the ILE RPG compiler. This

FIGURE 13.3
ILE's CRTRPGMOD Command

```
┌─────────────────┐            ┌──────────────────────┐
│ MAIN            │            │ TAX                  │
├─────────────────┤            ├──────────────────────┤
│ CALLB "TAX"     │            │ ILE RPG/400 code     │
│                 │            │ for tax calculation  │
└─────────────────┘            └──────────────────────┘
         │                               │
         ▼                               ▼
  ┌────────────┐   CRTRPGMOD     ┌────────────┐
  │ ILE RPG    │◄──────────────►│ ILE RPG    │
  │ Compiler   │                │ Compiler   │
  └────────────┘                └────────────┘
         │                               │
         ▼                               ▼
  ┌────────────┐                  ┌────────────┐
  │ Module     │                  │ Module     │
  │ (*MODULE)  │                  │ (*MODULE)  │
  └────────────┘                  └────────────┘
         │          CRTPGM                │
         └──────────◄────►────────────────┘
                     │
                     ▼
          ┌──────────────────┐   "link" or
          │ Optimizing       │   "bind" step
          │ Translator       │
          └──────────────────┘
                     │
                     ▼
          ┌──────────────────┐
          │ Program Object   │
          │ (*PGM)           │
          └──────────────────┘
```

command produces nonexecutable module objects of type *MODULE. Such objects are not executable until they go through the bind process (initiated through the CRTPGM command) that attaches them to and lets them execute as part of the *PGM object that results from CRTPGM. You cannot execute a *MODULE from the command line. You have to bind modules into a program object before you can run them.

If an application consists of one source member, you can follow the same steps as in Figure 13.3. Or you can use the CRTBNDxxx (Create Bound xxx) command to compile and bind the source directly into a program, skipping the intermediate step of module creation.

Be careful not to confuse objects of type *MODULE with those of type *PGM. Remember, ILE *PGM objects consist of one or more *MODULE objects that you can reuse in multiple *PGM objects. Because of their reusability, modules are the basic building blocks of ILE programs.

Binding

As you see in Figure 13.4, after you create *MODULE objects, you issue the new CRTPGM command to create an executable program object (*PGM) that contains both modules, MAIN and TAX. (In fact, in ILE, only two commands,

CRTPGM and CRTBNDxxx, can create an executable program object.) A parameter of the CRTPGM command lets you list all the modules that comprise the application program.

FIGURE 13.4
Example of CALLB Operation

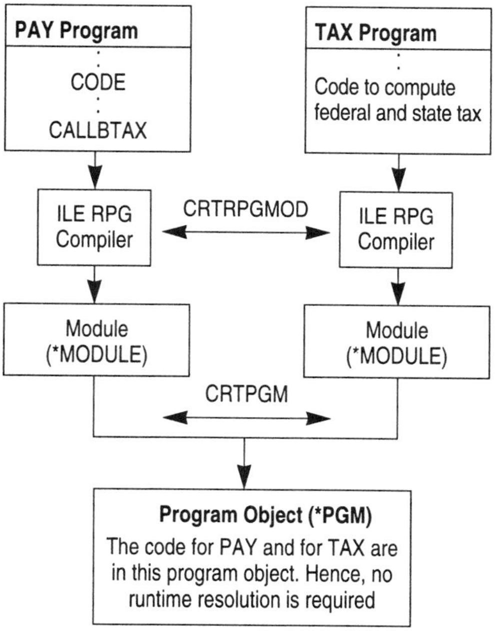

Unlike the resolution for program calls in OPM/EPM, resolution for program calls in ILE is not restricted to runtime, but occurs when you issue the CRTPGM command. Binding refers to associating program modules with each other to form one application. When you issue the CRTPGM command, the resulting bind step resolves all module references and copies all the modules into the executable *PGM object.

Binding also identifies the main, or starting, entry point for the application. Because an ILE application can contain more than one module, the operating system must know the main module to call first when you execute the CALL command to start the program. Therefore, an entry point is necessary. The CRTPGM command has a parameter that identifies that point as the Program Entry Procedure (PEP).

The distinction between OPM/EPM's runtime resolution and ILE's bind-time resolution is important. Runtime resolution for program objects is expensive in terms of performance. Binding procedures or global data items is a major contributor to the performance gains ILE provides. ILE can improve performance for call-intensive applications.

When you execute the CRTPGM command, ILE's binder locates the module that contains the TAX program and copies it into the *PGM as part of the binding process. As the figure shows, when the program executes, the code for the TAX module is part of the *PGM object, so no resolution is required when you call TAX. In contrast, with OPM/EPM resolution of called programs must happen at runtime.

You use the CALLB operation code in a bound program. However, be sure to remember that this is not the only program type available in ILE. ILE supports three types of programs: unbound OPM/EPM programs, bound ILE programs, and ILE service programs.

1. *Unbound programs*: An unbound program is an OPM/EPM program that you create outside ILE, with a non-ILE compiler. A CRTxxxPGM command compiles an unbound program. An unbound program does not include *MODULE objects. An example of an unbound program is an RPG III or COBOL/400 program that you create with CRTRPGPGM or CRTCBLPGM and call from the OPM/EPM environment. Such programs contain one entry point.

2. *Bound programs*: You compile a bound program by using the CRTPGM or CRTBNDxxx command. Bound programs consist of one or more module objects (object type *MODULE) compiled with an ILE language compiler by means of a CRTxxxMOD command and bound together with CRTPGM. Figures 13.3 and 13.4 illustrate bound programs.

3. *Service programs*: A service program is a program of object type *SRVPGM that you create with the CRTSRVPGM (Create Service Program) command. A service program consists of one or more module objects (object type *MODULE) compiled with an ILE language compiler by means of a CRTxxxMOD command and bound together with CRTSRVPGM. A service program is similar to a subroutine library or procedure library. Service programs provide services such as communications or math routines that several ILE objects can access.

This brief introduction to some fundamental ILE concepts will help you understand the subjects of the next two chapters. First, Chapter 14 provides some details about using CALL and CALLB in RPG IV programs. Then, Chapter 15 introduces the new pointer data type.

Manpower Technical
COMPUTER PROGRAMMER
Cedar Rapids, Iowa

Position Title/Code
Computer Programmer, JO #21

Skills Desired:
* Image
* RPG

Duties/Responsibilities:
2-10 years experience AS-400, IMAGE PLUS, RPG.

Compensation/Benefits:
Salary is commensurate with qualifications and experience.

How to Apply:
Please reference the above listed position title and code.
You may fax or send resumes to:

Manpower Technical
Attn: Scott M. Fisher
1113 2nd Ave, SE, Dept NJN
Cedar Rapids, IA 52403

Fax: 319-297-7435

Please Be Sure To Tell Them That You Saw
This Opportunity On The NationJob Network!

if sctnbr changes
put out heading - need to
have read next 2 sctnbr.
write detail lines = pre sctnbr

Credits Taken   Earned   Overall
                 Credits   GPA

add   if not W,I,F
to
total   ——   accumulate to
                    subtotal

        Subtotal rollover to
                    total

at subbrk —figure grade
point   roll to total credits
                        earned

if 3.00 or better
put deans list in NOTES

Each detail line accumulate
to subtotal

accum subtotal to grdtotal
    year   ~~~~ 19 constant
    substr   3rd byte =1   =2 =3

CHAPTER 14

CALL and CALLB

Two types of procedure calling are available in ILE RPG. The first is an external call by means of the CALL operation code. The external CALL is familiar to RPG III programmers as the way to call a program from within an RPG program. The second type, a bound call, is new with ILE: A program can consist of module objects that are linked, or bound, into a program object. You issue a CALLB to a procedure in a module that is bound to the executing program or to a service program in the same activation group. This chapter will examine both call operation codes, how to specify them, how to use parameter lists with them, and how to use them.

THE CALL OPERATION CODE

The CALL operation code lets an RPG program execute a different program object. When execution returns from the called program, the original (calling) program continues at the first C-spec following the CALL operation or at any PARM (Parameter) operation associated with the CALL. The CALL operation is available and serves the same purpose in both RPG III and RPG IV.

Factor 1 is not allowed with CALL. Factor 2 is required and names the program you want to call. The Factor 2 specification must be in the form library_name/program_name, where program_name is the name of the program you are calling; the optional library_name is that program's location. If you omit the library qualification, the system will search the library list for the program. Specifying the library name, however, can give you better performance because the system will not have to resolve the entry by searching the library list for the program. CALL does not accept *CURLIB.

Factor 2 can be a field, literal, string constant, or an array element. If you specify a literal, its total length cannot exceed 12 bytes. The length of a string from a field or named constant cannot exceed 21 bytes. When the total length of the library name or program name exceeds 10 characters, the system will right truncate. Any leading or trailing blanks in the name will be ignored.

Case conversion does not occur. That is, if you enter lowercase characters, the compiler will not convert these characters into uppercase. Also, if you enclose the name in quotation marks, the system accepts the quotation marks as part of the name and does not remove them.

The Result field is optional. If you are passing a parameter list to the called program, you place the name of the list in the Result field.

CALL accepts a valid resulting indicator in positions 73 and 74. This indicator will be set on if the called program returns an error. You can also enter a valid resulting indicator in positions 75 and 76. This indicator will be set on if the called program returns to the caller with the last record indicator set on. Here is the syntax of the CALL operation code.

Factor 1	Opcode	Extender	Factor 2	Result	Indicators		
Not allowed	CALL		Required *lib-name/pgm-name*	Optional *parameter list*	N/A	Error	LR

Passing Parameters with CALL

Often you will need to communicate information to and from the called program. For example, the called program can calculate a result that the calling program needs. CALL accepts parameter lists to pass information back and forth between the calling and called program. Unlike other inline operation codes, the CALL operation causes execution control to leave the program at the point at which CALL appears. The called program executes and then control returns to the calling program, where the next statement after the CALL is executed.

Suppose you have a C program that calculates the SINE of any number. You need to communicate the value for which you need a SINE to the called C program. After the C program calculates the SINE, you must pass the result back to the calling program. You use a parameter list to pass a reference to a particular field that the called procedure or program is using to hold the value that the calling program needs.

In most languages, such parameter passing comes in two flavors — by value and by reference. CALL passes parameters by value, so the receiving program gets the field's content. If the receiving program changes that content, the original field remains unchanged. In contrast, in ILE RPG you must pass by-reference, which means the called program passes a pointer to a particular field, not its content. The calling program then looks at the storage location the passed pointer is referencing. When the called program or procedure changes the content of the passed-by-reference field, the change also affects the value for the calling program because it receives a pointer to the value's storage location and not a value itself.

Defining Parameters with PARM

To pass parameters, you need the PARM (Parameter) opcode. It defines one parameter that you will pass between a calling and called program. PARM requires a Result field value that names the parameter. You can also optionally specify Factors 1 (a target field name) and 2 (a source field) on the PARM operation, but you will infrequently need to. The following table summarizes the syntax of the PARM operation code.

Factor 1	Opcode	Extender	Factor 2	Result	Indicators
Optional target field	PARM		Optional source field	Required parameter name	Not allowed

Factor 1 and 2 on the PARM Operation

Factor 1 and Factor 2 on PARM can give you flexibility when passing information between programs. PARM uses the Factor 1 field to receive a value from the Result field. In the called program, the value of the parameter from the calling program will be in both the Result field and the field you specify in Factor 1. In the calling program, the value returned from the called program will be both in the Result field and in Factor 1 when control returns to the calling program.

When you specify Factor 2 on a PARM operation, it is a *source field* for the Result field. When you specify it in the calling program, the value of the field in Factor 2 is copied into the Result field just before the call occurs. When you specify Factor 2 in the called program, the contents of the field in Factor 2 are copied into the Result field just before control returns to the calling program.

Programmers often use this field in a calling program to initialize a parameter that will return a value to the called program. The code below shows how to initialize field ResName to blanks before each call to NameProg.

```
*...1....+....2....+....3....+....4....+....5....+....6....+....7....+
C                   CALL      NameProg
C                   PARM                      FName
C                   PARM                      LName
C                   PARM      *Blanks         ResName
```

Another use for Factor 2 on a PARM operation is to preserve the value of a field that will be a parameter. If, for example, your shop standards require that you never modify database field names, you can specify the database field in Factor 2 and a parameter name in the Result field. Before the CALL occurs, the value of the database field in Factor 2 will be copied to the parameter name in the Result field. The parameter will be passed and the value in the database field will remain unchanged.

To help you understand the movement of data, let's look at each step in the process of calling a program, executing it, and then returning.

Before the call: In the calling procedure, the value in Factor 2 is moved into the Result field entry of the same PARM operation, so the Result field can never be a literal. The type of the Factor 2 entry and the Result field must be the same.

During the call, on entry: In the called procedure, a field in Factor 1 of a PARM operation code will receive a copy of the contents of the Result field associated with the same PARM operation. Factor 1 can never be a literal.

During the call, before exit: If you specify Factor 2 with the PARM operation in the called procedure, Factor 2's contents are copied to the Result field before the return to the calling procedure. This move can result in errors when the called procedure ends abnormally.

After the call: Once execution control returns from the called procedure, the system's runtime will copy the content of the Result field into the Factor 1 field if you specify one on the PARM operation in the calling procedure. Do not depend on this move when the called procedure has ended abnormally.

You can specify a PARM or a group of PARMs immediately after the CALL operation in the calling program, as illustrated below.

```
*...1....+....2....+....3....+....4....+....5....+....6....+....7....+
C                    CALL      NameProg
C                    PARM                    FName
C                    PARM                    LName
C                    PARM                    ResName
```

This example calls a program named NameProg, which concatenates first and last names and returns the result. FName and LName will come from this calling program. ResName will be created in the called program and returned to the calling program

Defining Parameter Lists with PLIST

When you want a list of parameters in more than one location, you need PLISTs (Parameter Lists). The PLIST operation code lets you define the list of parameters to send to a called program and the list of parameters to come from the calling program.

When you specify a list to receive, you put *ENTRY in Factor 1. A program can have only one PLIST declaration with *ENTRY. When you specify a list to pass to another program, you enter a parameter list name in Factor 1. You will specify this name on the CALL opcode to define the parameters to pass.

You can define a PLIST anywhere in the C-specs. If you specify a PLIST operation, at least one PARM operation must follow. This table shows PLIST's syntax.

Factor 1	Opcode	Extender	Factor 2	Result	Indicators
Required list name or *ENTRY	PLIST		Not allowed	Not allowed	Not allowed

CALL with PARM and PLIST

Let's see how CALL, PARM, and PLIST work together. The calling program passes a first name and a last name to the called program. The called program concatenates the two fields and then passes the resulting name field back to the original program.

The example program below calls a program, which, given input strings FName and LName, will provide the concatenated result of those two strings in ResName. FName and LName are defined in the D-specs as fields of type character and length 15.

```
*...1....+....2....+....3....+....4....+....5....+....6....+....7....+
D FName           S              15A
D LName           S              15A
D ResName         S              30A
```

```
*...1....+....2....+....3....+....4....+....5....+....6....+....7....+
C* Build the parameter list
C*
C       Names           PLIST
C                       PARM                      FName
C                       PARM                      LName
C                       PARM                      ResName
C*
C* Now call NameProg, which in turn will concatenate FName and LName,
C* returning a new character string ResName
C*
C                       CALL      NameProg        Names
```

The PLIST operation defines a parameter list called Names. Names includes the parameters that the three PARMs that follow that PLIST define. If you want to pass all three parameters, you have to specify only the PLIST name, Names. This approach is convenient, especially if you refer to the same list of parameters in more than one place in the same RPG source. Besides saving source space by eliminating the need to repeat the same list of parameters for each CALL operation, the PLIST also enhances readability and maintainability of the calling program. In the code above, CALL's Factor 1 names the program to call, NameProg. The Result field contains the name of the parameter list to pass, Names.

The called program, NameProg, is below.

```
*...1....+....2....+....3....+....4....+....5....+....6....+....7....+
D FName           S              15A
D LName           S              15A
D ResName         S              30A
```

```
*...1....+....2....+....3....+....4....+....5....+....6....+....7....+
*
C       *ENTRY       PLIST
C                    PARM                        FName
C                    PARM                        LName
C                    PARM                        ResName
C*
C* Concatenate the two input name strings and return to the caller.
C*
C                    EVAL       ResName = FName + Lname
 *
C                    RETURN
```

The first difference between this called program and the calling program is on the PLIST operation. The *ENTRY value in Factor 1 identifies what follows as a list of parameters that the calling program will pass into this program. For convenience, you can name the parameters in the called procedure the same as in the caller, but you don't have to.

When this program receives the parameters, the + operator in an EVAL concatenates the content of FName with that of LName, producing a new string that contains the entire name. At the RETURN operation, when control returns to the calling program, all three fields in the PLIST, including the modified ResName field, are passed back to the calling program.

THE CALLB OPERATION CODE

The CALLB (Call Bound) operation code lets you execute a function or procedure that is bound (or compiled) into the application that issues the CALLB. When execution returns from the called function or procedure, the first C-spec following the CALLB or any PARM associated with the CALLB will execute.

CALLB is a *static call*, as opposed to CALL's *dynamic call*. The difference between a static call and a dynamic call rests in how name resolution occurs. *Resolution* lets the system's runtime obtain the physical storage location to the code segment being called. Resolution also can be system activity such as paging and loading all or some of the executable instructions of the called code. Resolution can occur at one of three times — during bind time, during activation, or during execution.

Bind time is when the system links all specified modules containing one or more entry points and thus produces one callable program. Binding occurs when you issue commands such as CRTBNDRPG (Create Bound RPG) and CRTPGM (Create Program) to compile an RPG IV program. This type of resolution is *static binding*. Because CALLB accesses statically bound objects, CALLB is a static call.

CALL's *Dynamic binding,* in contrast, has the system's runtime use a program name to find the physical storage address of a called program. The AS/400 searches a job's library list to find a match for the program name you specify with CALL. This type of resolution is *dynamic binding.* Because CALL causes a dynamic binding at runtime, CALL performs a dynamic call.

CALLB's static calling within a program object is more efficient than the dynamic CALL, which references a separate program object. With dynamic calls, for resolution to occur, the system's runtime has to obtain a pointer, or handle, to the program being called. In contrast, for a bound call, procedure references are resolved when you compile the program, during bind time. Because the AS/400 loads all bound procedures (or addresses to those bound procedures) into random access memory during application startup, static calling has little impact on execution-time performance.

You sometimes need dynamic calls. One example is a call from an ILE program object to a non-ILE program object that you cannot convert to ILE RPG IV. In this situation, only a dynamic CALL will work.

You'll find few differences in the specification of a CALLB and CALL operation. CALLB is available only in ILE programs that you compile by means of the CRTPGM (Create Program) or CRTSRVPGM (Create Service Program) command and that have module objects bound into them.

CALLB Specification

CALLB accepts a valid resulting indicator in positions 73 and 74. This indicator is set on if the called procedure returns in error. You can also enter a valid resulting indicator in positions 75 and 76. It will be set on if the called procedure returns to the caller with the last record indicator set on.

Factor 1 is not allowed with CALLB. Factor 2 is required to provide the reference to the procedure being called. The Result field can provide a PLIST name. The table below shows a summary of the syntax for CALLB.

Factor 1	Opcode	Extender	Factor 2	Result	Indicators		
Not allowed	CALLB	(D)	Required name or procedure pointer	Optional PLIST name	N/A	Error	LR

Factor 2 Specification Details

You can specify the Factor 2 reference by name or by procedure pointer. (Chapter 15 covers pointers and will explain CALLB with procedure pointers.) If you specify Factor 2 by name, you enter a field, array element, named constant, or literal containing the name of the procedure you want to statically call. This name can be greater than 10 bytes and no more than 255 bytes long. The string in a Factor 2 field will be right truncated if it exceeds 255 bytes.

The CALLB operation is essential for referencing bindable system APIs. In the Factor 2 value, you must enter a prefix of CEE or an underscore for all APIs. This entry lets the compiler know that you want to call a bindable system API. To avoid confusion, be sure you do not name your own procedures with these prefixes.

CALLB and Parameter Lists

Like CALL, CALLB accepts parameter lists. To use a parameter list, you enter the PLIST operation code with the name of the parameter list as Factor 1, followed by a list of up to 399 PARM operations.

You can specify PLISTs anywhere in the C-specs. A program can have only one PLIST declaration with *ENTRY. Note that once you specify a PLIST operation, at least one PARM operation must follow.

The PARM operation for a CALLB is the same as for a CALL. You can specify Factors 1 and 2. PARM uses the Factor 1 field to receive a value from the Result field in the called procedure. The contents of the Factor 2 field are copied into the Result field after normal termination of the procedure or program that the CALL or CALLB operation called.

The program below uses a CALLB instead of a CALL. The called procedure is bound to the same program object as the calling procedure.

```
*...1....+....2....+....3....+....4....+....5....+....6....+....7....+
D FName           S               15A
D LName           S               15A
D ResName         S               30A

*...1....+....2....+....3....+....4....+....5....+....6....+....7....+
C* Build the Parameter List
C*
C       Names           PLIST
C                       PARM                          FName
C                       PARM                          LName
C                       PARM      *BLANKS             ResName
C*
C* Now call NameProg, which in turn will concatenate FName and LName,
C* returning a new character string ResName
C*
C                       CALLB     ProgName            Names
```

Calling Functions with *OMIT

RPG III programmers are familiar with the concept of omitting parameters on a CALL operation. The same concept applies for a CALLB. If you are not going to pass a parameter that the called program expects, you can specify the *OMIT figurative constant as the Result field for a PARM operation for CALLB. *OMIT lets you pass a null address to the called program or procedure, providing the same capability as omitting parameters for CALL while making your code much more readable.

Suppose you have a subprogram that provides a utility function to your application programs. If some programs that call the subprogram pass two parameters, but others can pass only one, you have to tell the called program to expect only one parameter.

```
*...1....+....2....+....3....+....4....+....5....+....6....+....7....+
D UtilProc       S             *    PROCPTR INZ(%PADDR('func2'))
D Ds1            DS
D   SubFld1                80     INZ('ABC')

*...1....+....2....+....3....+....4....+....5....+....6....+....7....+
 *   Call bound utility procedure with second parameter omitted
 *
C                  CALLB     UtilProc
C                  PARM                    SubFld1
C                  PARM                    *OMIT
```

The code above shows how to use *OMIT. The second PARM specifies the *OMIT figurative constant as the Result field value. As a result, a null address is passed to the called program or procedure.

Operational Descriptor

The CALLB operation code accepts the operational descriptor (D) to provide detailed information about the parameters the call is passing in. Often, programs contain more than one call to a program or procedure, and the data type or content can vary from call to call. An example is calling a procedure that requires passing class numeric data as parameters. The type of numeric data can be zoned decimal, packed decimal, or binary. If the data type or field length is important to the called program or procedure, you want to specify the operational descriptor, in the form CALLB(D). Specifying an operational descriptor has no effect on the parameters the call is referencing.

You can obtain the operational descriptor information by means of the system APIs CEEDOD (Retrieve Operation Descriptor Information) and CEESG (Get Descriptive Information About a String). The CEEDOD API finds out about whether the class numeric field is zoned-decimal, packed-decimal, or binary, and learns the length of the parameter passed.

Below is a call to this API. The name of the API (CEEDOD) is in Factor 2 of the CALLB operation. Following are seven parameters that the API requires, beginning with the number of parameters. This call specifies a 1 in Factor 2 of the first PARM operation. This value will be moved into field num_parm just before the call. For a detailed explanation of each parameter, see the *System API Reference*.

```
*...1....+....2....+....3....+....4....+....5....+....6....+....7....+
C*        Calling system API 'CEEDOD' to retrieve
C*           operational descriptor information.
C*
C                     CALLB     'CEEDOD'
C                     PARM      1              num_parm
C                     PARM                     dsc_type
C                     PARM                     data_type
C                     PARM                     info_1
C                     PARM                     info_2
C                     PARM                     Len_HEX
C                     PARM                     *OMIT
```

Although operational descriptors can be useful, we do not encourage you to use them. Not all platforms and languages support operational descriptors, so RPG code with operational descriptions written for ILE will not translate to VisualRPG on an OS/2 platform, for example. Operational descriptors change the logic of a function or procedure, so they affect portability.

CALLB to a C Function

Suppose you want to call a C function to tokenize a character string. C has a very powerful function, strtok, that you can specify with delimiting characters to tokenize a given character string. RPG has no equivalent string-related operation code. However, ILE RPG IV lets you write the C code for this purpose, bind it into your application at compile time, and then use a CALLB to execute the function when your program is ready for it. Below is the C function that makes the call to library function strtok.

```
#include <stdlib.h>
#include <math.h>
#include <stdio.h>

extern void cfunc( char *value,      /* String to tokenize.*/
               char *delim,          /* Delimeters.*/
                  char *rv )         /* Return value. */
 {
```

CONTINUED

```
        rv = strtok(str, delim) ; /* Tokenize.*/
        return;                   /* Return to caller. */
}
```

The ILE RPG compiler passes all values by reference (by address with a pointer) rather than by value. When you pass by reference, because you are passing the address and not the value, the called program can change the content of the passed field before returning to the caller. In contrast, if you pass by value, changing the content of the field in the calling program or procedure is not possible because you receive only a copy of the data in that field and not a pointer to that field. Because the RPG compiler passes all values by reference, for each parameter in the parameter list for this C function, the system passes pointers to values instead of the values. The C syntax * means the variable contains a pointer rather than the data.

Now let's look at the RPG procedure that calls that C function. Some explanation of the data structure in this example is necessary. All character strings in C must be null terminated. For this reason, the RPG code simulates the null termination by appending X'00' at the end of each string that cfunc uses. The data structure subfield n_term2 causes null termination of both the string you want to tokenize and the delimiting character string.

```
*...1....+....2....+....3....+....4....+....5....+....6....+....7....+
D Const1          C               CONST('cfunc')
 *
D FuncArg         DS
D   S1                      19A    INZ('This dog has fleas.')
D   NTerm_1                  1A    INZ(x'00')
D   S2                       4A    INZ(' ')
D   NTerm_2                  2A    INZ(x'0000')
D ResStr S                  10A    INZ(*BLANKS)

*...1....+....2....+....3....+....4....+....5....+....6....+....7....+
 *    Tokenizing Strings with strtok.
 *
 *  Build the Parameter List
 *
C     ArgList        PLIST
C                    PARM                  S1
C                    PARM                  S2
C                    PARM                  ResStr
 *
```

Continued

```
*...1....+....2....+....3....+....4....+....5....+....6....+....7....+
 * Now call cfunc, which in turn will call strtok to tokenize our
 * character string.
 *
C                   CALLB     Const1      ArgList
```

With each call to cfunc, the field ResStr will contain the next token in character string S1. The output resulting from the execution of this program is shown below.

```
This
dog
has
fleas.
```

CHAPTER 15

Pointer Variables

A new data type that RPG IV supports is the pointer. A pointer is a field whose value is a system address for a particular structure, function, program, register, or field. As a field of type character contains a character value and a field of type numeric contains a numeric value, a field of type pointer contains an address as its value.

The AS/400 has long supported the capability that pointers represent, but until the new ILE language definition, the RPG compiler supported pointers only under the covers. For example, when a program calls another program and passes parameters to it, RPG uses pointers to pass the parameters.

Using pointers to pass parameters is called *pass by reference*, as opposed to *pass by value*, which copies the value and sends it when the program is called. Pointers copy the address, not the content, of the parameters to the called program. Because the system passes the physical address of the parameter to the called program, pass by reference causes the calling program to reflect any change in the field's value in the called program. If the pass of parameters is by value, the field in the calling program will not reflect any change in the value in the called program.

With the new pointer data type, RPG IV supports basing pointers and procedure pointers. A basing pointer accesses dynamically allocated storage and formats that storage's layout based on the definition of a field that has the BASED keyword on its definition A procedure pointer is a field of the pointer data type, and it lets you access by reference any procedures or functions bound into an RPG IV program.

This chapter explains the new pointer data type and gives examples of how to use it in application situations. How to define a pointer type field precedes a discussion of the basing pointer and how, when, and why to use it. This discussion includes how to allocate storage for a dynamic array using pointer fields to save the address of the storage. The next section shows how to create dynamic data structures using pointers. Then comes an explanation of the procedure pointer, how to define it, and how to take advantage of it for programming efficiency.

THE POINTER DATA TYPE

You define a field of data type pointer in a program's D-specs. The definition is similar to the definition of any standalone field. What identifies a pointer is an asterisk as the data type specification in position 40.

You specify a pointer field's name in positions 7 through 21 and an S (standalone field) in position 24. Because addresses on the AS/400 are 16 bytes long, the size of pointer fields is automatically 16 bytes, so you don't have to specify a length.

Like the D-specs for other standalone fields, the D-specs for fields of data type pointer let you specify keywords. The three keywords you use most often with the pointer data type are INZ (to initialize the field to a value), BASED (to define a field as being described by a basing pointer), and PROCPTR (to define a procedure pointer). The BASED keyword is not for a pointer type field; instead, this keyword specifies that a non-pointer field will refer to a pointer field to find and define its data. You specify BASED on non-pointer field definitions, but its parameter always names a pointer field that contains the storage location of the field you're defining.

```
*....1....+....2....+....3....+....4....+....5....+....6....+....7....+
D NUMP            S              4P 0 INZ(200)
D NUMZ            S              5S 2 INZ(22.5)
D NAME            S             15A   INZ('AnnaLisa Farr')
D POINTON         S               *   INZ(%ADDR(NAME))
D POINTER         S               *   INZ(*NULL)
```

The D-specs above define several fields, including some pointer data type fields. The definitions all include the INZ keyword to provide an initial value for the field. The definitions are for a packed-numeric field, NUMP, that contains an initial value of 200; a zoned-numeric field, NUM, that contains the value 22.5; and a character field, NAME, that contains the initial value of 'AnnaLisa Farr'.

In addition, two definitions contain the value * in position 40 to define two fields as type pointer. Each of these pointer type fields contains an address for an entity in storage. Like the other fields, the pointer fields have initial values. The first pointer field, POINTON, is pointing to the address of the field NAME. The second pointer field has an initial value of *NULL, which means it initially points to no entity. A *NULL value for a pointer is similar to initializing a character field to blanks or a numeric field to zeros.

A pointer field contains the address of a space in memory. When accessed, this address yields a value of some given data type other than the pointer type. The following diagram shows how the alpha field NAME looks in storage if it is assigned to address 47.

..... 47	48	49	50	51	52	53	54	55	56	57	58	59	60	61	62	63	64	65	66 .....
	A	n	n	a	L	i	s	a		F	a	r	r						

The character field NAME contains the value 'AnnaLisa Farr', and the pointer field POINTON contains the address of the field NAME. In this case, the pointer field POINTON has a value of 47. So, POINTON is pointing to the address of the first byte of the character value 'AnnaLisa Farr'.

BASING POINTERS

A basing pointer lets you access dynamically allocated storage. Such storage is system space allocated to a program during execution time. In contrast, finite static storage is associated with declared fields and data structures at compile time. These different types of storage mean that a reference to storage can be direct (referencing static storage) or indirect (referencing dynamic storage). A direct reference is one that contains a value the program can immediately use during execution. An indirect reference, the kind of reference available with a basing pointer, contains the memory address to a space that contains a value the program can use during its execution. To access this storage, you must provide a field to format the storage.

The basing pointer lets you create and use based data structures. The term based means that the data structure contains a format, or template, with which the program can view storage. When you specify the BASED keyword on a data structure or standalone field definition, the system associates this definition with a basing pointer that you specify as the BASED keyword's parameter. This basing pointer holds the address or storage location of data in the based data structure or standalone field being defined. So the name PFirst in positions 7 through 21 on the field definition below refers to the data stored at the location that the basing pointer points to.

```
*...1....+....2....+....3....+....4....+....5....+....6....+....7....+
D Ptr1             S                 *   INZ(*NULL)
D PFirst           S                8A   BASED(Ptr1)
```

This code shows how to define a basing pointer. Field Ptr1 is data type pointer, and it is initialized to NULL, so it points to no storage location. Field PFirst is like a template that tells the compiler to create an alphanumeric field 8 bytes long, but to not allocate any storage to it because its storage is BASED on pointer field Ptr1. Once the program modifies pointer Ptr1 to contain a valid storage location, PFirst will be able to reference, examine, and modify the data at that location. Ptr1 is the pointer to storage, and PFirst gives a format to that storage.

The %ADDR Built-In Function

Before you can use a based data structure or standalone field, you must assign the basing pointer a valid address by using the %ADDR (Address) built-in function with an EVAL operation in the program's C-specs or in the D-specs' keyword section. Otherwise, a runtime error will occur.

The %ADDR built-in function moves an address to a pointer. On an EVAL operation, in the extended Factor 2, you specify the name of the pointer that you want to assign an address. Then you enter the = operator followed by %ADDR. After this built-in function, in parentheses, you give the name of the data structure or field whose storage location you want the pointer to access. Alternatively, on the D-spec where you define a basing pointer, you can enter %ADDR with a data structure or field name in parentheses, both following the INZ keyword and enclosed in an outer set of parentheses.

This program segment defines one based data structure, BDS_A. Let's look at the situation before the first C-spec executes and after setup of all initial values for the program, including storage allocation for all fields and structures defined in the program. BDS_A is defined and has no storage associated with it; the data structure DS_1, which does have automatic storage associated with it, is defined; and the pointer P1, although defined, does not point to any valid storage because it is initialized to *NULL.

```
*...1....+....2....+....3....+....4....+....5....+....6...+....7....+
D DS_1            DS
D    A_Stor_1              1024      INZ(*Blanks)
 *
D P1              S            *      INZ(*NULL)
 *
D BDS_A           DS                 BASED(P1)
D    SF_A_1               512
D    SF_A_2               512

*...1....+....2....+....3....+....4....+....5....+....6....+....7....+
 *
C                 EVAL      P1 = %ADDR(DS_1)
 *
```

When execution of the C-specs begins, storage is associated with a based data structure once the program executes the EVAL. This operation uses %ADDR to move the address of DS_1 to the pointer P1. At that point, the pointer P1 points to the storage allocated for DS_1 and BDS_A is a template over that storage so that subfields SF_A_1 and SF_A_2 refer to valid program data.

Basing Pointers and Dynamically Allocated Storage

The ability to dynamically allocate storage is important. In RPG III, when you define a size for an array or a multiple-occurrence data structure that will contain records for customers, you probably guess at a number big enough to hold all the records the program will require. You probably declare an array of size 10,000 although you are using just the first 1000 elements. When you do that, the system allocates the entire amount of memory even if you are not using it all.

In RPG III, such guessing is your only choice, but RPG IV lets you allocate memory during processing as you need it. You can allocate storage for an array at runtime instead of allocating storage at compile time. Instead of allocating 10,000 elements in your program, you can allocate 1000 elements first and then request more memory as the program needs it.

Dynamically allocating storage is efficient for applications that frequently change storage requirements at runtime. An example is an airline passenger list. If you maintain this list in alphabetical order in an array, to make room for each new passenger's data in the array, you need to move all passenger records that alphabetically follow a new passenger. This processing requires a loop to copy each data record being moved to the next array element. If you use a dynamic array or data structure (dynamic arrays and data structures expand or contract during program execution, depending on the program's data storage require-ments), you can insert the new passenger data between two existing passenger records, with minimum effort — not to mention with a performance gain and improved efficiency in storage.

In the new ILE model, a program can directly control runtime storage by managing heaps. A heap is an area of storage reserved for allocation of dynam-ic storage. The amount of dynamic storage an application requires depends on the data the program is processing and the procedures that use the heap. You manage heaps by calling ILE-bindable APIs. To allocate storage from the heap, you call the CEEGTST API. To free storage that was previously allocated from the heap, you call CEEFRST. To reallocate storage, you call CEECZST, which changes the storage size of the previously allocated storage from the heap. The following examples show three procedures that perform the three functions of allocating, freeing, and reallocating storage by using the APIs CEEGTST, CEEFRST, and CEECZST.

Allocating Storage

By calling the CEEGTST API, a program asks the system to allocate storage while the program is running. This API requires three parameters and has one that is optional. The heap ID, the size in bytes to be allocated, and the address of the storage you will allocate (you have to declare a pointer to hold this address) are the required parameters. The optional one is the feedback para-meter. To accommodate the API's required parameters, you need to define two fields and the pointer to hold the address, as shown below.

```
*...1....+....2....+....3....+....4....+....5....+....6....+....7....+
D*
D HeapID          S              9B 0 INZ(0)
D Size            S              9S 0 INZ(0)
D ListAddr        S               *   INZ(*NULL)
D AirList         S             15P 0 DIM(32767) BASED(ListAddr)

*...1....+....2....+....3....+....4....+....5....+....6....+....7....+
C*
C                 EVAL      Size=1000*%SIZE(AirList)
C                 CALLB     'CEEGTST'
C                 PARM                HeapID
C                 PARM                Size
C                 PARM                ListAddr
C                 PARM                *OMIT
```

The definition initializes the HeapID field to zero. The pointer ListAddr will contain the system address of the passenger list, and Size will contain the number of bytes you want to allocate. AirList, the last parameter for the feedback, is optional. When you call this API, the program must provide a field to receive each of the API's parameters, including any optional ones. Even if you do not want the optional parameter, you still have to specify a field for it or tell the system you don't want it. If you don't want it, you enter the *OMIT option on the parameter so that on return, the API will not bother updating that parameter. The program will have less overhead and maybe better performance.

Finally, you define the dynamic array that will contain all airline passengers. The DIM keyword determines that this definition is an array and its size (number of elements) is 32,767, the maximum size allowed for an array. No storage is allocated, because the BASED keyword is specified to create a template for an array at the largest size possible and then allocate its storage as you need it.

The next task is to call the allocation API. The Size field needs to contain the number of bytes you want the API to allocate; in this case, enough storage to hold 1000 elements. To get the number of bytes, you use the EVAL operation with the %SIZE built-in function, which returns the number of bytes (stored as a 15-digit packed decimal number) that each element of AirList requires and then multiplies that value by the number of elements to get the total number of bytes required.

After the API call, the field ListAddr will contain the address of the newly allocated storage. At this point, you can access the first 1000 elements by indexing the array AirList as you do with any array.

Freeing Storage

Once the storage is allocated, you can deallocate it when the program no longer needs it: You call the second API, CEEFRST. Like the previous API, this one requires parameters. In this case, they are the address of the storage to be freed and the optional feedback parameter.

Below are the field and pointer definitions for the API's parameters when you deallocate storage. Pointer ListAddr contains the address of the storage to deallocate. It is the first parameter you supply to CEEFRST. Note that the second parameter is the feedback parameter, for which you specify *OMIT, as in the previous example.

```
*...1....+....2....+....3....+....4....+....5....+....6....+....7....+
D SIZE            S              9S 0  INZ(0)
D ListAddr        S               *    INZ(*NULL)
D AirList         S             15P 0  DIM(32767) BASED(ListAddr)


*...1....+....2....+....3....+....4....+....5....+....6....+....7....+
C                 CALLB     'CEEFRST'
C                 PARM                    ListAddr
C                 PARM                    *OMIT
```

Allocating More Storage

As you use the array in the program, when you insert an element, you have to make sure you don't exceed the 1000 elements you allocated. To keep track, you can define a field to count the number of storage locations allocated so far. This code adds a field, TotalMem, for total memory, to the D-specs.

```
*...1....+....2....+....3....+....4....+....5....+....6....+....7....+
D HeapID          S              9S 0  INZ(0)
D TotalMem        S              9S 0  INZ(1000)
D SIZE            S              9S 0  INZ(0)
D ListAddr        S               *    INZ(*NULL)
D AirList         S             15P 0  DIM(32767) BASED(ListAddr)
```

You initialize TotalMem to 1000 because this is the number of elements for which you have allocated storage. The program always needs to check this field before inserting an element into the array to make sure that you have enough storage for more elements. You first increment the index to the next location of the array. If the index is not greater than the TotalMem variable, the array still has room, so you can insert an element at the index location.

If the index is greater than the TotalMem field, the array has run out of storage and a call to the third system API CEECZST is necessary to allocate more storage. As you do when you allocate storage, you use EVAL and %SIZE to calculate the number of bytes you need, and then you call CEECZST.

This API, like the others, requires parameters: the address of the storage that you want to allocate (you need to define a pointer to hold this address) and the number of bytes to be allocated. The feedback parameter is optional. After you define the fields for these parameters, you can call the API, as shown below.

```
*...1....+....2....+....3....+....4....+....5 ...+....6....+....7....+
C* Add element to the array
C*
C                    ADD       1               Index
C                    IF        Index > TotalMem
C                    ADD       1000            TotalMem
C                    EVAL      Size=TotalMem*%SIZE(AirList)
C                    CALLB     'CEECZST'
C                    PARM                      ListAddr
C                    PARM                      Size
C                    PARM                      *OMIT
C                    ENDIF
C* Add element to the array...
C*
```

The %SIZE built-in function returns the number of bytes the array occupies. The parameter of %SIZE can be a literal, named constant, a data structure, a data structure subfield, a field, an array, or a table name. This example uses the array AirList as the parameter to %SIZE to get its size. Because this parameter is an array name (or if it is a table name or multiple-occurrence data structure name), the value returned is the size of one element (or occurrence).

As the code illustrates, you first check whether the index is greater than the number of elements for which you have allocated memory. If so, you call the API to allocate more storage.

This example shows how to create a dynamic array. You first create an array of the maximum number of elements allowed, 32,767, as a template. You specify the BASED keyword to base the whole array on a pointer, which will be set to the address of the storage that is allocated by calls to APIs. You start by allocating 1000 elements for the array, and as the program progresses, you can ask for more memory as the program needs it. You can free storage when the program does not require it any more.

PROCEDURE POINTERS

Procedure pointers, a special category of the pointer class, access any procedures or functions bound into the RPG program in which this pointer occurs. Instead of referencing a function you want to call by specifying its name as Factor 2 of the CALLB (Call Bound) operation, you can enter a procedure pointer name in Factor 2. You set the procedure pointer to the value of a character string, the name of the procedure or function you need.

As with any pointer support, when you define a procedure pointer, you allocate storage only for the pointer, not for the data it will point to. Defining a procedure pointer is similar to defining any pointer except that the keyword PROCPTR (Procedure Pointer) is on the D-spec. The code below shows how to define a procedure pointer and then issue a CALLB operation in an RPG program.

```
*...1....+....2....+....3....+....4....+....5....+....6....+....7....+
D* P2 is a pointer to the statically bound function Func2, used below.
D*
D P2              S              *    PROCPTR INZ(%PADDR('Func2'))
D*
D* Ds1 is a data structure comprising an 80 character string.
D*
D Ds1             DS
D   S_F_A1                      80    INZ('Alpha data')

*...1....+....2....+....3....+....4....+....5....+....6....+....7....+
 *   A statically bound call example in ILE RPG
C                    CALLB     P2
C                    PARM                    S_F_A1
```

In the D-specs, the PROCPTR keyword defines field P2 as a procedure pointer. No length specification is necessary for P2, as it is a pointer. The INZ keyword, with the %PADDR (Procedure Address) built-in function, initializes the procedure pointer to obtain the address of the procedure named as the parameter of %PADDR; this procedure is Func2. %PADDR is similar to %ADDR, but %PADDR returns the address of a procedure instead of a structure.

Procedure Pointers by Example

Procedure pointers are most useful when you want to call a procedure or function that is bound into your RPG IV program. Consider a program that has a function written in C and then bound into it. The C function calculates a power of an integer. You pass the base number and the power, and the function will return the result. This method lets you use CALLB and %PADDR to take advantage of functions available in other programming languages.

You compile the C function by issuing the CRTCMOD (Create C Module) command. Then you compile the RPG program module by issuing CRTRPGMOD. Finally, you bind the functions by entering the functions' names as parameters of the CRTPGM command that you execute to compile the entire program.

The code below is the part of the RPG program that calls the C module.

```
*...1....+....2....+....3....+....4....+....5....+....6....+....7....+
D PTR             S               *    PROCPTR INZ(%PADDR('POWER'))
DI                S              9B 0
DBASE             S              9B 0 INZ(2)

*...1....+....2....+....3....+....4....+....5....+....6....+....7....+
C*
C                 EVAL      I=0
C                 DOW       I <=10
C                 CALLB     PTR
C                 PARM                    BASE
C                 PARM                    I
C                 ADD       1             I
C                 ENDDO
```

This example initializes the field PTR to the POWER address. You then issue CALLB, using the pointer PTR in Factor 2, to get to the POWER function, which is written in ILE C.

You might wonder about the definition of the parameters being passed and the data types of the I and BASE fields. In C, the int data type maps to a 16-bit, or 2-byte, field, whereas a long int maps to a 32-bit, or 4-byte, field. In contrast, in RPG, if you define a binary field anywhere between 1 and 4, it will be allocated 2 bytes; or anything between 5 and 9 binary will be allocated 4 bytes. This code declares the parameters in C as long integers, so you define the RPG parameters as 9 binary with zero decimal positions.

APPENDIX A

RPG IV Compile Listings

Before the advent of user-interactive workstations, programmers had little support for finding syntax and relational errors in source code. However, as workstations became more popular, high-level languages have enhanced user interfaces to meet users' growing need to improve productivity. One important user interface for any compiler is a program listing. If you specify a compiler option, the compiler produces a log of all errors.

COMPILER LISTING OPTIONS

In ILE RPG IV, three commands let you compile module and program objects: CRTBNDRPG, CRTRPGMOD, and CRTPGM. When you compile a program by issuing one of these commands, you can use the new RPG IV debugging utility to examine your source for errors.

To illustrate how to use an RPG IV listing, let's look at how to produce a listing when you issue CRTBNDRPG to compile a program consisting of only one module. You enter CRTBNDRPG on the command line. Then you press the F10 key for additional parameters and you see the following panel.

```
                    Create Bound RPG Program (CRTBNDRPG)

 Type choices, press Enter.

 Program  . . . . . . . . . . .   SF_RPG        Name, *CTLSPEC
   Library  . . . . . . . . .       LISTINGS     Name, *CURLIB
 Source file  . . . . . . . .     QRPGLESRC     Name, QRPGLESRC
   Library  . . . . . . . . .       LISTINGS     Name, *LIBL, *CURLIB
 Source member  . . . . . . .     SF_RPG        Name, *PGM
 Generation severity level  . . .  10            0-20
 Text 'description' . . . . . . .  Farr/Topiwala subfiles sample.

 Default activation group . . . .  *YES          *YES, *NO

                          Additional Parameters

 Compiler options . . . . . . . .                *XREF, *NOXREF, *GEN...
             + for more values    +
  Debugging views  . . . . . . .   *STMT         *STMT,
 *SOURCE, *LIST...
  Output . . . . . . . . . . . .   *PRINT        *PRINT,
 *NONE
                                                 More...
  F3=Exit   F4=Prompt   F5=Refresh   F12=Cancel  F13=How to use this display
  F24=More keys
```

The + character on the *compiler options* parameter lets you enter values in list form. Below is the screen you get when you select the +.

```
                  Specify More Values for Parameter OPTION

  Type choices, press Enter.


                          Additional Parameters

  Compiler options . . . . . . . .   *XREF          *XREF, *NOXREF, *GEN...
                                     *EXPDDS
                                     *SECLVL
                                     *SHOWCPY
                                     *EXT








                                                                   More...
    F3=Exit F4=Prompt F5=Refresh F12=Cancel F13=How to use this display
    F24=More keys
```

After you add such listing options, you get the screen below. The completed first panel of the CRTBNDRPG command includes the listing options specified above.

```
                    Create Bound RPG Program (CRTBNDRPG)

  Type choices, press Enter.

                          Additional Parameters

  Compiler options . . . . . . . .   *XREF          *XREF, *NOXREF, *GEN...
                                     *EXPDDS
                                     *SECLVL
                                     *SHOWCPY
                 + for more values  *EXT
  Debugging views . . . . . . . .    *NONE          *STMT, *SOURCE, *LIST...
  Output . . . . . . . . . . . .     *PRINT         *PRINT, *NONE
  Optimization level . . . . . . .   *NONE          *NONE, *BASIC, *FULL
  Source listing indentation . . .   *NONE          Character value, *NONE
  Type conversion options . . . .    *NONE          *NONE, *DATETIME, *GRAPHIC...
                 + for more values
  Sort sequence . . . . . . . . .    *HEX           Name, *HEX, *JOB, *JOBRUN...
    Library . . . . . . . . . . .                   Name, *LIBL, *CURLIB




                                                                   More...
    F3=Exit F4=Prompt F5=Refresh F12=Cancel F13=How to use this display
    F24=More keys
```

When you press Enter from this screen, the operating system will execute the command and call the ILE RPG compiler. Because you specified that the compiler listing is required, the RPG compiler will place the listing in a spool file under your job.

The program listing that starts below and runs through page 404 is an example. This listing has seven sections: the Prologue section, the Source Section, the Output Buffer Positions Section, the /COPY Member Table Section, the Cross-Reference Section, the External References List, the Message Summary, and the Final Summary.

```
5763RG1 V3R1MØ  940909 RN       IBM ILE RPG/4ØØ       LISTINGS/SF_RPG       1ØØØØØ1TORASØ16   Ø1/Ø8/95 16:21:16       Page     1
  Command  . . . . . . . . . . . . :   CRTBNDRPG
    Issued by  . . . . . . . . . . :   TOPIWALA
  Program  . . . . . . . . . . . . :   SF_RPG
    Library  . . . . . . . . . . . :   LISTINGS
  Text 'description' . . . . . . . :   *SRCMBRTXT
  Source Member  . . . . . . . . . :   SF_RPG
  Source File  . . . . . . . . . . :   QRPGLESRC
    Library  . . . . . . . . . . . :   LISTINGS
    CCSID  . . . . . . . . . . . . :   37
  Text 'description' . . . . . . . :   SubFiles Example. Uses SF_DSP AND SF_PF.
  Last Change  . . . . . . . . . . :   12/3Ø/94  1Ø:Ø6:Ø6
  Generation severity level  . . . :   1Ø
  Default activation group . . . . :   *YES
  Compiler options . . . . . . . . :   *XREF      *GEN      *SECLVL    *SHOWCPY
                                       *EXPDDS    *EXT      *NOEVENT
  Debugging views  . . . . . . . . :   *STMT
  Output . . . . . . . . . . . . . :   *PRINT
  Optimization level . . . . . . . :   *NONE
  Source listing indentation . . . :   '|'
  Type conversion options  . . . . :   *NONE
  Sort sequence  . . . . . . . . . :   *HEX
  Language identifier  . . . . . . :   *JOBRUN
  Replace program  . . . . . . . . :   *YES
  User profile . . . . . . . . . . :   *USER
  Authority  . . . . . . . . . . . :   *LIBCRTAUT
  Truncate numeric . . . . . . . . :   *YES
  Fix numeric  . . . . . . . . . . :   *NONE
  Target release . . . . . . . . . :   V3R1MØ
  Allow null values  . . . . . . . :   *NO
```

CONTINUED

```
5763RG1 V3R1MØ  94Ø9Ø9 RN       IBM ILE RPG/4ØØ        LISTINGS/SF_RPG        TORASØ16    Ø1/Ø8/95 16:21:16        Page    2
Line   <--------------------- Source Specifications --------------------------><---- Comments ----> Do  Page  Change Src Seq
Number ....1....+....2....+....3....+....4....+....5....+....6....+ ....7....+....8....+....9....+...1Ø Num Line  Date   Id Number
                        S o u r c e   L i s t i n g
    1 F******************************************************************                               941231  ØØØ1ØØ
    2 F*ILE RPG Src Mbr:  SF_RPG                                       *                                941231  ØØØ2ØØ
    3 F*Used By:          N/A                                          *                                941231  ØØØ3ØØ
    4 F*Authors:          Farr/Topiwala                               *                                941231  ØØØ4ØØ
    5 F*Purpose:          Use subfiles to provide display program for *                                941231  ØØØ5ØØ
    6 F*                  D.U.H. Consultants.                          *                                941231  ØØØ6ØØ
    7 F*Dependencies:     SF_DSP, SF_PF, SF_COPY                       *                                941231  ØØØ7ØØ
    8 F******************************************************************                               941231  ØØØ8ØØ
    9 FSF_DSP    CF   E            WORKSTN                                                               941231  ØØØ9ØØ
   1Ø F                                 SFILE(TSFDTL:RRN)                                               941201  ØØ1ØØØ
      *---------------------------------------------------------------------*
      *                            RPG name          External name          *
      * File name. . . . . . . . :  SF_DSP           LISTINGS/SF_DSP         *
      * Record format(s) . . . . :  TSFDTL           TSFDTL                  *
      *                             TSFCTL           TSFCTL                  *
      *                             TBOTT            TBOTT                   *
      *---------------------------------------------------------------------*
   11 FSF_PF     IF   E            DISK                                                                 951214  ØØ11ØØ
   12 *                                                                                                 941201  ØØ12ØØ
      *---------------------------------------------------------------------*
      *                            RPG name          External name          *
      * File name. . . . . . . . :  SF_PF            LISTINGS/SF_PF          *
      * Record format(s) . . . . :  C_REC            C_REC                   *
      *---------------------------------------------------------------------*
   13=ITSFDTL                                                                                                      1
      *---------------------------------------------------------------------*
      * RPG record format . . . . :  TSFDTL                                  *                                     1
      * External format . . . . . :  TSFDTL : LISTINGS/SF_DSP               *                                     1
      *---------------------------------------------------------------------*                                     1
   14=I                 A    1   25 FLDØØ1                                                                   1ØØØØØ2
   15=I                 A   26   55 FLDØØ2                                                                   1ØØØØØ3
   16=I                 A   56   7Ø FLDØØ3                                                                   1ØØØØØ4
   17=ITSFCTL                                                                                               2ØØØØØ1
      *---------------------------------------------------------------------*
      * RPG record format . . . . :  TSFCTL                                  *                                     2
      * External format . . . . . :  TSFCTL : LISTINGS/SF_DSP               *                                     2
      *---------------------------------------------------------------------*                                     2
   18=I                 A    1    1 *INØ3                   END OF JOB                                       2ØØØØØ2
   19=I                 A    2    2 *INØ5                   CLEAR SFL                                        2ØØØØØ3
   2Ø=ITBOTT                                                CLEAR SFL                                       3ØØØØØ1
      *---------------------------------------------------------------------*
      * RPG record format . . . . :  TBOTT                                   *                                     3
      * External format . . . . . :  TBOTT : LISTINGS/SF_DSP                *                                     3
      *---------------------------------------------------------------------*                                     3
   21=IC_REC                                                CLEAR SFL                                       4ØØØØØ1
      *---------------------------------------------------------------------*                                     4
      * RPG record format . . . . :  C_REC                                   *                                     4
      * External format . . . . . :  C_REC : LISTINGS/SF_PF                 *                                     4
      *---------------------------------------------------------------------*                                     4
```

CONTINUED

```
5763RG1 V3R1MØ  94Ø9Ø9 RN        IBM ILE RPG/4ØØ        LISTINGS/SF_RPG       TORASØ16    Ø1/Ø8/95 16:21:16      Page    3
Line  <-------------------- Source Specifications --------------------------><---- Comments ----> Do  Page  Change Src Seq
Number ....1....+....2....+....3....+....4....+....5....+....6....+....7....+....8....+....9....+...1Ø Num Line  Date   Id Number
   22=I                         A    1   25 CONTACT                                                                 4ØØØØØ2
   23=I                         A   26   55 COMPANY                                                                 4ØØØØØ3
   24=I                         A   56   7Ø AREA                                                                    4ØØØØØ4
Line  <-------------------- Source Specifications --------------------------------------><---- Comments ---->  Src Seq
Number ....1....+....2....+<--------26 - 35 -------->....4....+....5....+....6....+....7....+....8....+....9....+...1Ø Id Number
   25 C                   Z-ADD                     Ø           RRN       5 Ø                                       ØØ13ØØ
   26 C                   EXSR                      $LODSF                                                          ØØ14ØØ
   27 C                   WRITE                     TBOTT                                                           ØØ15ØØ
   28 C     @REDSP        TAG                                                                                       ØØ16ØØ
   29 C                   EXFMT                     TSFCTL                                                          ØØ17ØØ
   3Ø C     Ø3            SETON                                           LR----                                    ØØ18ØØ
   31 *                                                                                                            ØØ19ØØ
   32 *   CLEAR SUBFILE                                                                                            ØØ2ØØØ
   33 *                                                                                                            ØØ21ØØ
   34 C     *INØ5         IFEQ                      '1'                                                             ØØ22ØØ
   35 C                   |SETON                                          3Ø----                                   ØØ23ØØ
   36 C                   |WRITE                    TSFCTL                                                         ØØ24ØØ
   37 C                   |SETOFF                                         3Ø----                                   ØØ25ØØ
   38 C                   |GOTO                     @REDSP                                                         ØØ26ØØ
   39 C                   END                                                                                      ØØ27ØØ
   4Ø C*                                                                                                           ØØ28ØØ
   41 C/COPY qrpglesrc.sf_copy                                                                 941228              ØØ29ØØ
      *--------------------------------------------------------------------------*
      * RPG member name . . . . . :  SF_COPY                                     *                                 5
      * External name . . . . . . :  LISTINGS/QRPGLESRC(SF_COPY)                 *                                 5
      * Last change . . . . . . . :  12/31/94  Ø9:ØØ:21                          *                                 5
      * Text 'description' . . . . :  SubFiles Example. Uses SF_DSP AND SF_PF.   *                                 5
      *--------------------------------------------------------------------------*

   42+C********************************************************************                                        5ØØØ1ØØ
   43+C*Copy Member:      SF_COPY                                      *                                           5ØØØ2ØØ
   44+C*Used By:          SF_RPG                                       *                                           5ØØØ3ØØ
   45+C*Authors:          Farr/Topiwala                                *                                           5ØØØ4ØØ
   46+C*Purpose:          Provide load routine for subfiles sample pgm. *                                         5ØØØ5ØØ
   47+C*Dependencies:     None.                                        *                                           5ØØØ6ØØ
   48+C********************************************************************                                        5ØØØ7ØØ
   49+C     $LODSF        BEGSR                                                                                    5ØØØ8ØØ
   5Ø+C                   READ                      dF_PF                 ----1Ø                                   5ØØØ9ØØ
------->                                            aaaaaaaaaaaaaa
*RNF5317 3Ø a   ØØØ9ØØ+ Factor 2 entry must be a previously defined name;          LISTINGS/QRPGLESRC(SF_COPY)
                       specification is ignored.
   51+C     *IN1Ø        DOWNE                      *ON                                                            5ØØ1ØØØ
   52+C                   |AxD                      1           RRN                                                5ØØ11ØØ
------->                                            aaa
*RNF5Ø14 3Ø a   ØØ11ØØ+ Operation entry is not valid; specification is ignored.    LISTINGS/QRPGLESRC(SF_COPY)
   53+C                   |MOVEL                    CONTACT     FLDØØ1                                              5ØØ12ØØ
   54+C                   |MOVEL                    COMPANY     FLDØØ2                                              5ØØ13ØØ
   55+C                   |MOVEL                    AREA        FLDØØ3                                              5ØØ14ØØ
   56+C                   |WRITE                    TSFDTL                                                         5ØØ15ØØ
   57+C                   |READ                     SF_PF                 ----1Ø                                   5ØØ16ØØ
   58+C                   ENDDO                                                                                    ØØ17ØØ
   59+C                   ENDSR                                                                                    5ØØ18ØØ
```

CONTINUED

```
5763RG1 V3R1M0  940909 RN       IBM ILE RPG/400       LISTINGS/SF_RPG      TORAS016  01/08/95 16:21:16      Page    4
Line   <--------------------- Source Specifications ------------------------><---- Comments ----> Do  Page  Change Src Seq
Number ....1....+....2....+....3....+....4....+....5....+....6....+....7....+....8....+....9....+...10 Num Line  Date   Id Number
    60=0TSFDTL                                                                                  *                  6000001
      *-----------------------------------------------------------------------------------*                      6
      * RPG record format  . . . . :  TSFDTL                                                *                      6
      * External format  . . . . . :  TSFDTL : LISTINGS/SF_DSP                              *                      6
      *-----------------------------------------------------------------------------------*                      6
    61=0                         *IN14              1A CHAR       1                                                6000002
    62=0                         FLD001            26A CHAR      25                                                6000003
    63=0                         FLD002            56A CHAR      30                                                6000004
    64=0                         FLD003            71A CHAR      15                                                6000005
    65=0TSFCTL                                                                                                    7000001
      *-----------------------------------------------------------------------------------*                      7
      * RPG record format  . . . . :  TSFCTL                                                *                      7
      * External format  . . . . . :  TSFCTL : LISTINGS/SF_DSP                              *                      7
      *-----------------------------------------------------------------------------------*                      7
    66=0                         *IN30              1A CHAR       1                                                7000002
    67=0TBOTT                                                                                                     8000001
      *-----------------------------------------------------------------------------------*                      8
      * RPG record format  . . . . :  TBOTT                                                 *                      8
      * External format  . . . . . :  TBOTT : LISTINGS/SF_DSP                               *                      8
      *-----------------------------------------------------------------------------------*                      8
    * * * *  E N D   O F   S O U R C E  * * * *
```

```
5763RG1 V3R1M0  940909 RN       IBM ILE RPG/400       LISTINGS/SF_RPG      TORAS016  01/08/95 16:21:16      Page    5
              A d d i t i o n a l   D i a g n o s t i c   M e s s a g e s
*RNF7066 00     11 001100  Record-Format C_REC not used for input or output.*RNF7086 00     11 001100  RPG handles blocking for
file SF_PF. INFDS is updated only
                          when blocks of data are transferred.
* * * * *  E N D   O F   A D D I T I O N A L   D I A G N O S T I C   M E S S A G E S  * * * * *

                  O u t p u t   B u f f e r   P o s i t i o n s
Line   Start End  Field or Constant
Number Pos   Pos
   61    1     1  *IN14
   62    2    26  FLD001
   63   27    56  FLD002
   64   57    71  FLD003
   66    1     1  *IN30
* * * * *  E N D   O F   O U T P U T   B U F F E R   P O S I T I O N  * * * *
                      / C o p y   M e m b e r s
Line   Src RPG name  <-------- External name -------> CCSID  <- Last change ->
Number Id            Library  File     Member               Date      Time
   41    5 SF_COPY    LISTINGS QRPGLESRC SF_COPY       37   12/31/94 09:00:21
       * * * *  E N D   O F   / C O P Y   M E M B E R S  * * * *
```

```
5763RG1 V3R1M0  940909 RN       IBM ILE RPG/400       LISTINGS/SF_RPG      TORAS016  01/08/95 16:21:16      Page    6
                  C r o s s   R e f e r e n c e
     File and Record References:
         File             Device        References (D=Defined)
           Record
         SF_DSP           WORKSTN            9D
           TSFDTL                            0     13    56    60
           TSFCTL                            0     17    29    36
                                            65
           TBOTT                             0     20    27    67
         SF_PF            DISK             11D     57
           C_REC                             0     21
     Field References:
         Field            Attributes    References (D=Defined M=Modified)
         $LODSF           BEGSR             26    49D
         *IN03            A(1)              18D
         *IN05            A(1)              19D    34
         *IN10            A(1)              51
         *IN14            A(1)              61
```

CONTINUED

```
            *IN30          A(1)                66
            @REDSP         TAG                 28D     38
            AREA           A(15)               24D     55
            COMPANY        A(30)               23D     54
            CONTACT        A(25)               22D     53
            FLD001         A(25)               14M     53M     62
            FLD002         A(30)               15M     54M     63
            FLD003         A(15)               16M     55M     64
            RRN            P(5,0)              10      25D
     Indicator References:
        Indicator                      References (D=Defined M=Modified)
        03                                  30
         10                                      50D     57D
        30                                      35D     37D
        LR                                      30D
     * * * * *  E N D   O F   C R O S S   R E F E R E N C E  * * * * *
```

```
5763RG1 V3R1M0  940909 RN      IBM ILE RPG/400      LISTINGS/SF_RPG      TORAS016   01/08/95 16:21:16       Page      7
                        E x t e r n a l   R e f e r e n c e s
        Statically bound procedures:
            Procedure                      References
            No references in the source.
        Imported fields:
            Field          Attributes      Defined
            No references in the source.
        Exported fields:
            Field          Attributes      Defined
            No references in the source.
     * * * * *  E N D   O F   E X T E R N A L   R E F E R E N C E S  * * * * *
```

```
5763RG1 V3R1M0  940909 RN      IBM ILE RPG/400      LISTINGS/SF_RPG      TORAS016   01/08/95 16:21:16       Page      8
                        M e s s a g e   S u m m a r y
     Msg id  Sv Number Message text
    * RNF7066 00      1 Record-Format name of Externally-Described file is not used.
                            Cause  . . . . . :   There is a Record-Format name for an
                            Externally-Described File that is not used on a valid
                            input or output operation.
                            Recovery  . . . :   Use the Record-Format name of the
                            Externally-Described File for input or output, or specify
                            the name as a parameter for keyword IGNORE. Compile
                            again.
    * RNF7086 00      1 RPG handles blocking for the file. INFDS is updated only when
                        blocks of data are transferred.
                            Cause  . . . . . :   RPG specifies MLTRCD(*YES) in the UFCB
                            (User-File-Control Block). Records are passed between RPG
                            and data management in blocks. Positions 241 through the
                            end of the INFDS (File-Information-Data Structure) are
                            updated only when a block of records is read or written.
                            Recovery  . . . :   If this information is needed after
                            each read or write of a record, specify the OVRDBF
                            command for the file with SEQONLY(*NO).
    * RNF5014 30      1 Operation entry is not valid; specification is ignored.
                            Cause  . . . . . :   The Operation entry (positions 26 - 35)
                            is not valid. No further checking is done on the
                            specification. The Operation entry (positions 26 - 35)
                            must start with a valid Operation Code left justified in
                            the entry and can be followed by an optional Operation
                            Extender. If specified the Operation Extender must be one
                            of H, N, P, D, T, or Z, and enclosed within parentheses.
                            The Operation Extender can begin anywhere to the right of
                            the Operation Code. Blanks before, after, or within the
                            Operation Extender are allowed.
                            Recovery  . . . :   Specify a valid Operation entry
                            (positions 26 - 35), or omit the specification. Compile
                            again.
```

CONTINUED

```
*RNF5317 30    1 Factor 2 entry must be a previously defined name;
               specification is ignored.
                 Cause . . . . . . :  The Factor 2 entry (positions 36 - 49)
                 must be previously defined.
                 Recovery . . . :  Correct the Factor 2 entry (positions
                 36 - 49). Compile again.
          * * * * *  E N D   O F   M E S S A G E   S U M M A R Y  * * * * *


5763RG1 V3R1M0  940909 RN       IBM ILE RPG/400        LISTINGS/SF_RPG      TORAS016   01/08/95 16:21:16      Page    9
                        F i n a l   S u m m a r y
Message Totals:
  Information  (00) . . . . . . . :       2
  Warning     (10) . . . . . . . :       0
  Error       (20) . . . . . . . :       0
  Severe Error (30+) . . . . . . :       2
  -------------------------------   -------
  Total . . . . . . . . . . . . :        4
Source Totals:
  Records . . . . . . . . . . . :       67
  Specifications  . . . . . . . :       46
  Data records  . . . . . . . . :        0
  Comments  . . . . . . . . . . :       20
     * * * * *  E N D   O F   F I N A L   S U M M A R Y  * * * * *
Compilation stopped. Severity 30 errors found in program.
        * * * * *  E N D   O F   C O M P I L A T I O N * * * * *
```

THE PROLOGUE SECTION

The first section of the listing is the prologue. This section shows general information about the values you specify on the create (CRT) command you issued. This section is repeated below.

```
5763RG1 V3R1M0  940909 RN       IBM ILE RPG/400        LISTINGS/SF_RPG      TORAS016   Page    1
   Command  . . . . . . . . . . . . . :  CRTBNDRPG
      Issued by . . . . . . . . . . :  TOPIWALA
   Program  . . . . . . . . . . . . :  SF_RPG
      Library  . . . . . . . . . . :     LISTINGS
   Text 'description'  . . . . . . . :  *SRCMBRTXT
   Source Member  . . . . . . . . . :  SF_RPG
   Source File  . . . . . . . . . . :  QRPGLESRC
      Library  . . . . . . . . . . :     LISTINGS
      CCSID  . . . . . . . . . . . :     37
   Text 'description'  . . . . . . . :  Subfiles Example. Uses SF_DSP AND SF_PF.
   Last Change  . . . . . . . . . . :  12/30/94  10:06:06
   Generation severity level  . . . :  10
   Default activation group . . . . :  *YES
   Compiler options . . . . . . . . :  *XREF       *GEN       *SECLVL     *SHOWCPY
                                       *EXPDDS     *EXT       *NOEVENT
   Debugging views  . . . . . . . . :  *STMT
   Output . . . . . . . . . . . . . :  *PRINT
   Optimization level . . . . . . . :  *NONE
   Source listing indentation . . . :  '|'
   Type conversion options  . . . . :  *NONE
   Sort sequence  . . . . . . . . . :  *HEX
   Language identifier  . . . . . . :  *JOBRUN
   Replace program  . . . . . . . . :  *YES
   User profile . . . . . . . . . . :  *USER
   Authority  . . . . . . . . . . . :  *LIBCRTAUT
   Truncate numeric . . . . . . . . :  *YES
   Fix numeric  . . . . . . . . . . :  *NONE
   Target release . . . . . . . . . :  V3R1M0
   Allow null values  . . . . . . . :  *NO
```

The prologue section is like a snapshot of the CRTBNDRPG or CRTRPGMOD command that produces the program listing. This section's first line is the page heading, which provides such information as the operating system version, the compiler, and a page number. You can modify all page headings so that they include company-specific information. (See the *ILE RPG/400 Programmer's Guide* for more information on how to customize your page headings with the /TITLE directive.)

After the page heading, the next line in the listing is information about the call to the ILE RPG compiler. The following line shows the compile command issued. This example uses the CRTBNDRPG command, as you can see from the *Command* field. The next line tells you what user ID called that command. The location of the module or program (depending on the command issued, e.g., CRTBNDRPG or CRTRPGMOD) and its associated *Text description* are next in the listing.

The following set of fields are important as they help ensure that you are fixing program errors in the correct source member. A common programming practice is to keep more than one version of source, which can easily lead to confusion about which is the most recent source member. Another important point to remember is that the value in the *Source Member* field can differ from the module or program you're creating if you override values on the CRT command. The *Source File* field gives you the file name. As with the *Source Member* field, if you override values on the CRT command, the name of that overriding source will appear here.

Following the *Text description* and *Last Change* fields for the program source are the compiler options you specified on the command. *Generation severity level* is the maximum severity level for which you want a program or module generated. *Default activation group* tells you the activation group you specified on the CRT command. This is the activation group in which the program will execute. On the listing, this field will contain *user-named*, *system-named*, or *CALLER*. The *CALLER value means the program or module will execute in the activation group belonging to the caller of this program. The *Compiler options* field shows the compiler options you specified on the CRT command. In this example, they are *XREF, *NOXREF, *GEN, *EXPDDS, *SECLVL, *SHOWCPY, and *EXT.

ILE's source-level debugger has improvements over OPM's. ILE introduces source-level debugging for the ILE languages. ILE RPG uses the system support of debugging by introducing different views in which you can debug your RPG program. For example, you can debug your program using a source view or listing view.

The *Debugging* views field tells the compiler which view you want to debug your program with. You can do only source-level debugging using the member source of the RPG program instead of the listing view.

The value *PRINT* on the *Output* field lets you print a program listing. A value of *NONE on this compilation parameter means no program listing will be generated.

Next is the *Optimization level* field, which, in this example, is set to *NONE*. In ILE, you can optimize modules and programs as *FULL, *BASIC, or *NONE*.

The following line shows whether the program has indentation and specifies the *indentation mark* you want to denote indentation to show structure in the source code. The indention mark is a one- or two-character mark that the compiler will use to align any structured operation groups as they appear in the program listing. This example uses the vertical bar (|) character as an indentation mark to enhance the readability of the program listing.

Note that although the *Source listing indentation* field shows an indentation mark, if you specify *LIST* for the debugging view, the indentation character (or characters) will not appear during debugging. Also note that if the program contains errors, you have no guarantee that indentation and the indentation mark will appear correctly.

Often, you need to see the profile and authority level (i.e., the user profile) of the developer who created this listing. For this purpose, you can look at the *User profile* and *Authority* fields.

Frequently, developers generate programs that will be executed on production systems of different releases from the development system. To tell which release of OS/400 this program is intended for, you refer to the *Target release* field. In this case, V3R1MO is the release on which this program is to run.

THE SOURCE SECTION

The main body of the ILE RPG program listing is the source section. This section's major parts are the source heading, DDS information (including generated specifications), file and record information (including /COPY member information, /COPY member records, indentation, and indicator usage), and error messages (including syntax errors and relational errors). The body of the source includes *information boxes* that are set off with dashes and asterisks. These boxes contain additional information that the compiler pulls into your source for the DDS file and record information, external data descriptions, data structures, input specifications, output specifications, and /COPY members.

Source Headings

The first part of this section is the source heading. The compiler adjusts these headings when you specify indentation and when you list data records. This source heading consists of six fields. The *Line Number* field begins numbering the lines of source code with 1 and increments each source line in the listing by 1. The ruler line shows what column each source entry is in. The *Do Number* field helps you desk-check structured operation codes. The listing matches the structured opcode with its corresponding END statement by outputting a vertical bar to the left of all specifications in the body of the structured operation. You can see this vertical bar in statements 52 through 57.

Indentation requires additional space in an RPG listing. Positions 26 through 35 are stretched into 28 spaces rather than the 10 used when you don't request indentation. Note that when you use indentation, the compiler will not output the *Do Num, Change Date*, and *Page/Line* columns in the listing. (The *Do Num* can be useful where the program source contains nested structured operations such as a DO loop within a DO loop. In this case, the compiler will assign a different level number with each DO-END pair to make the program easy to read.)

The *Page Line* field shows you the first five column positions of the source record. The *Source ID* field contains a digit count of the /COPY and DDS members that provide a record the program uses. The starting value is 1, and in this example, this value reaches 8. The *Sequence Number* field contains the SEU sequence number from the source member or a sequential count for generated records.

DDS Information

The DDS information subsection is next. It tells the location of the field and record information that appears in expanded form below it in the listing.

Generated Specifications

This section shows the specifications generated from the DDS. One value you can see in the *Compiler options* field is the *EXPDDS* (Expand DDS) compile listings option. This value means that this listing will include an expanded version of each externally described record format. For example, the expanded TSFDTL record format reveals three subfields. Below, you see this portion of the listing.

```
Line    <-------------------- Source Specifications --------------------><---- Comments ---->
Number  ....1....+....2....+....3....+....4....+....5....+....6....+ ....7....+....8....+....9....+
   14=I                                A    1   25  FLD001
   15=I                                A   26   55  FLD002
   16=I                                A   56   70  FLD003
```

This expansion is not the complete record format pulled in from the DDS source. RPG listings show only information that the program uses. For example, DDS keywords and text fields do not appear in the listing. Field text does appear, but only when indentation is off. However, any fields that the RPG source can use are included.

To reinforce this point, let's look at the DDS for the TSFCTL record format, from which the compiler has pulled in only two specifications. The following example shows the entire record format.

```
A           R TSFCTL                    SFLCTL(TSFDTL)
A N30                                   SFLDSP
A N30                                   SFLDSPCTL
A  30                                   SFLCLR
A                                       SFLSIZ(0006)
A                                       SFLPAG(0005)
A                                       OVERLAY
A                                       CA03(03 'END OF JOB')
A                                       CA05(05 'CLEAR SFL')
A                           3 22'Consultants Client List'
A                           6  1'CONTACT'
A                           6 27'COMPANY'
A                           6 60'AREA'
A                           7  1'----------'
A                           7 27'----------'
A                           7 60'----------'
```

The program listing excludes many DDS specifications for this record format because the RPG program doesn't need to know about them. Here are the two specifications in the compile listing.

```
18=I                A    1    1  *IN03              END OF JOB
19=I                A    2    2  *IN05              CLEAR SFL
```

Notice the equals (=) character to the right of the line number on the *generated specifications*. The meaning of this character is connected with the DDS specifications that you need to see in your RPG source. Here, you need to see how indicators are specified in the DDS, so the only two fields shown for the TSFCTL record are those that contain indicator information. The = character identifies the DDS specifications that come into the RPG program as external descriptions.

File/Record Information

IBM completely redesigned the RPG compiler listing for ILE. If you are used to working with RPG III, you'll notice the changes in such subsections as the one for File/Record Information in the source section. This example reproduces part of one File/Record Information subsection from the sample listing.

```
*--------------------------------------------------------------------------------*
*                          RPG name          External name                       *
* File name. . . . . . . . :  SF_PF          LISTINGS/SF_PF                       *
* Record format(s) . . . . :  C_REC          C_REC                               *
*--------------------------------------------------------------------------------*
13=ITSFDTL 1000001
```

This subsection tells you the file and record format names in both their RPG form and their DDS form. You can easily see each record format quickly and clearly.

/COPY Member Information

In addition to the DDS information and generated specifications, the file/record information subsection's comment area shows you /COPY member information,

/COPY member records, indentation, and indicator usage. The /COPY member information part of the file/record information identifies the /COPY member used and gives any member text. This part also provides date and time information. Good programming practice dictates including any member comments because they are useful to any program using the /COPY member. This example reproduces the /COPY member information portion of the listing.

```
41 C/COPY qrpglesrc.sf_copy                                                                      941228      002900
   *--------------------------------------------------------- -----------------------------------*
   * RPG member name  . . . . . . :  SF_COPY                                                 *      5
   * External name  . . . . . . . :  LISTINGS/QRPGLESRC(SF_COPY)                             *      5
   * Last change  . . . . . . . . :  12/31/94  09:00:21                                      *      5
   * Text 'description'  . . . . . :  SubFiles Example. Uses SF_DSP AND SF_PF.               *      5
   *--------------------------------------------------------------------------------------------*
```

/COPY Member Records
The /COPY member records portion of the file/records information section shows which records from the /COPY member are in the source program. The code below reproduces the /COPY member records portion of the listing. The + character beside each /COPY member record marks an insertion of a record into the original source member.

```
42+C***********************************************************  5000100
43+C*Copy Member:       SF_COPY                               *  5000200
44+C*Used By:           SF_RPG                                *  5000300
45+C*Authors:           Farr/Topiwala                         *  5000400
46+C*Purpose:           Provide load routine for subfiles sample pgm. * 5000500
47+C*Dependencies:      None.                                 *  5000600
48+C***********************************************************  5000700
```

Indentation
The indentation mark to show structure in this example is the vertical line character. The code below shows the effectiveness of the indentation mark in making the code in the listing understandable at a glance. The vertical bar character clearly connects the entire DO loop, setting it off from the rest of the code.

```
   49+C     $LODSF       BEGSR                                                          5000800
   50+C                  READ            dF_PF                    ----10                 5000900
=======>>                               aaaaaaaaaaaaaa
*RNF5317 30 a     000900+ Factor 2 entry must be a previously defined name;   LISTINGS/QRPGLESRC(SF_COPY)
                         specification is ignored.
   51+C     *IN10        DOWNE           *ON                                             5001000
   52+C                  iAxD            1            RRN                                 5001100
=======>>                               aaa
*RNF5014 30 a     001100+ Operation entry is not valid; specification is ignored.   LISTINGS/QRPGLESRC(SF_COPY)
   53+C                  |MOVEL          CONTACT      FLD001                             5001200
   54+C                  |MOVEL          COMPANY      FLD002                             5001300
   55+C                  |MOVEL          AREA         FLD003                             5001400
   56+C                  |WRITE          TSFDTL                                          5001500
   57+C                  |READ           SF_PF                    ----10                 5001600
   58+C                  ENDDO                                                           5001700
   59+C                  ENDSR                                                           5001800
```

Indicator Usage

Another feature of the listing that adds to the code's readability is that the listing clearly marks used and unused portions of the indicator space. For example, look at the READ operation codes above. From the listing, you know that the first and second indicator are not used (as denoted by four dashes). The last one is used.

Error Messages

Two types of error, syntax errors and relational errors, appear in this listing. Let's examine what you see on the listing for each type.

Syntax Errors

The listing shows syntax errors that the compilation process can catch in one pass. One clear case of a syntax-related error is the invalid operation code entry in the sample program. This example shows the section of the listing that points to this error.

```
   52+C            |AxD                    1            RRN                             5001100
------>>           aaa
*RNF5014 30 a   001100+ Operation entry is not valid; specification is ignored.      LISTINGS/QRPGLESRC(SF_COPY)
```

For syntax errors, the listing shows the error, as below. The example program contains a programming error: an undefined format name in the Factor 2 entry of the READ operation. The letter a represents the pointer to the error line. If two errors occur on the same line, the compiler marks the second entry in error with the letter b, and so on.

```
   50+C            READ                   dF_PF                    ----10              5000900
------>>                                  aaaaaaaaaaaaaa
*RNF5317 30 a   000900+ Factor 2 entry must be a previously defined name;            LISTINGS/QRPGLESRC(SF_COPY)
                        specification is ignored.
```

Relational Errors

Relational errors are ones that the compiler cannot catch in one pass. As you can see below, this listing example has two severity zero relational errors. The first one is the record format C_REC, which the program defines but never uses for input or output. This is not a syntax error because the program cannot determine that it does not use C_REC until it processes the entire source. On a *second* pass of the compilation process, where the compiler checks the list of defined or extracted definitions against those the program used, the compiler can detect such an error and issue a message; in this case, message RNF7066. (Most relational messages in ILE are of the 7000 series.)

```
                 A d d i t i o n a l   D i a g n o s t i c   M e s s a g e s
*RNF7066 00      11 001100  Record-Format C_REC not used for input or output.
*RNF7086 00      11 001100  RPG handles blocking for file SF_PF. INFDS is updated only
                            when blocks of data are transferred.
 * * * * *   E N D   O F   A D D I T I O N A L   D I A G N O S T I C   M E S S A G E S   * * * * *
```

Although no *data-type incompatibility* occurs in this sample program, this is a very common relational error. Data-type incompatibility happens when you specify a program field of one data type with an operation code requiring another. An example is attempting a DIV operation with character data.

THE OUTPUT BUFFER POSITIONS SECTION

The next major section of the listing is the output buffer positions section. The example below repeats this portion of the listing.

```
                  O u t p u t   B u f f e r   P o s i t i o n s
Line   Start End  Field or Constant
Number Pos   Pos
   61    1     1  *IN14
   62    2    26  FLD001
   63   27    56  FLD002
```

This section contains any fields that are output. Note that indicators are also in this section if they condition fields on the screen output. For example, you can see the indicators in the TSFDTL and TSFCTL record formats.

THE /COPY MEMBER TABLE SECTION

As you strive for a modular programming style, you realize the usefulness of /COPY members. This feature of RPG encourages modular programming and code reuse and, perhaps most important, improves programmer productivity. This is why the next section of the compiler listing, the /COPY member table section, is important. The example below reproduces this section of the listing.

```
                  / C o p y   M e m b e r s
Line   Src RPG name  <-------- External name -------> CCSID  <- Last change->
Number Id            Library   File      Member              Date      Time
   41    5 SF_COPY   LISTINGS  QRPGLESRC SF_COPY        37  12/31/94 09:00:21
    * * * * *   E N D   O F   / C O P Y   M E M B E R S   * * * * *
```

This section lists all /COPY members that the program uses and provides the source ID, library name, file name, member name, CCSID, and last-change information. This example has only one /COPY member, SF_COPY.

THE CROSS REFERENCE SECTION

This cross reference section of the program listing shows useful file- and field-level information. The following example repeats this section of the listing.

Files in this section are listed under workstation, printer, or disk. The field information is listed in alphabetical sequence. An addition to the field information is the D (defined) or M (modified) references. The M reference tells the programmer where a field has been modified — in other words, where the value of a field has changed. D tells where the field was defined. Fields can be defined on any C-spec, so instead of having to search for where a certain field is defined, you can check the cross reference section of the compile listing. This section also lists indicators and program tags.

```
5763RG1 V3R1M0  940909 RN        IBM ILE RPG/400        LISTINGS/SF_RPG          TORAS016   Page     6
                                C r o s s   R e f e r e n c e
        File and Record References:
           File              Device              References (D-Defined)
              Record
           SF_DSP            WORKSTN                   9D
              TSFDTL                                    0       13      56      60
              TSFCTL                                    0       17      29      36
                                                       65
              TBOTT                                     0       20      27      67
           SF_PF            DISK                       11D      57
              C_REC                                     0       21
        Field References:
           Field             Attributes          References (D-Defined M-Modified)
           $LODSF            BEGSR                      26      49D
           *IN03             A(1)                       18D
           *IN05             A(1)                       19D      34
           *IN10             A(1)                       51
           *IN14             A(1)                       61
           *IN30             A(1)                       66
           @REDSP            TAG                        28D      38
           AREA              A(15)                      24D      55
           COMPANY           A(30)                      23D      54
           CONTACT           A(25)                      22D      53
           FLD001            A(25)                      14M      53M     62
           FLD002            A(30)                      15M      54M     63
           FLD003            A(15)                      16M      55M     64
           RRN               P(5.0)                     10       25D
        Indicator References:
           Indicator                             References  (D-Defined M-Modified)
           03                                         30
           10                                         50D      57D
           30                                         35D      37D
           LR                                         30D
        * * * * *  E N D   O F   C R O S S   R E F E R E N C E  * * * * *
```

THE EXTERNAL REFERENCES LIST

The external references list section shows any external procedures and fields that other modules define or use. You can think of this section as containing any information required at bind time. You can easily tell whether a name in your program will appear in this section: If you access an object by issuing a CALLB or %PADDR, the object will appear in the external references list. This section will also include any fields the program module imports to or exports from other modules.

THE MESSAGE SUMMARY

The message summary section lists all messages issued in the program. This part of the listing shows you message IDs, severity, and message text. Because this example requests second-level text for this listing, both the Cause and Recovery for each message also appear here. You see this section of the listing below. Errors are listed in message-number sequence, sorted within message severity.

```
                        M e s s a g e   S u m m a r y
  Msg id  Sv Number Message text
  *RNF7066 00     1 Record-Format name of Externally-Described file is not used.
                      Cause . . . . . :   There is a Record-Format name for an
                      Externally-Described File that is not used on a valid
                      input or output operation.
                      Recovery  . . . :   Use the Record-Format  name of the
                      Externally-Described File for input or output, or specify
                      the name as a parameter for keyword IGNORE. Compile
                      again.
  *RNF7086 00     1 RPG handles blocking for the file. INFDS is updated only when
                    blocks of data are transferred.
                      Cause . . . . . :   RPG specifies MLTRCD(*YES) in the UFCB
                      (User-File-Control Block). Records are passed between RPG
                      and data management in blocks. Positions 241 through the
                      end of the INFDS (File-Information-Data Structure) are
                      updated only when a block of records is read or written.
                      Recovery  . . . :   If this information is needed after
                      each read or write of a record, specify the OVRDBF
                      command for the file with SEQONLY(*NO).
  *RNF5014 30     1 Operation entry is not valid; specification is ignored.
                      Cause . . . . . :   The Operation entry (positions 26 - 35)
                      is not valid. No further checking is done on the
                      specification. The Operation entry (positions 26 - 35)
                      must start with a valid Operation Code left justified in
                      the entry and can be followed by an optional Operation
                      Extender. If specified the Operation Extender must be one
                      of H, N, P, D, T, or Z, and enclosed within parentheses.
                      The Operation Extender can begin anywhere to the right of
                      the Operation Code. Blanks before, after, or within the
                      Operation Extender are allowed.
                      Recovery  . . . :   Specify a valid Operation entry
                      (positions 26 - 35), or omit the specification. Compile
```

THE FINAL SUMMARY

The final summary is the last section in the program listing. This section is a tabulation of all messages issued to the source. The following example reproduces this section.

```
                        F i n a l   S u m m a r y
  Message Totals:
    Information  (00) . . . . . . . :       2
    Warning      (10) . . . . . . . :       0
    Error        (20) . . . . . . . :       0
    Severe Error (30+) . . . . . . . :       2
   -------------------------------- -------
    Total . . . . . . . . . . . . :       4
  Source Totals:
    Records . . . . . . . . . . . :      67
    Specifications  . . . . . . . . :      46
    Data records  . . . . . . . . . :       0
    Comments  . . . . . . . . . . . :      20
        * * * * *   E N D   O F   F I N A L   S U M M A R Y   * * * * *
  Compilation stopped. Severity 30 errors found in program.
```

Besides providing a total error count by severity, this section also gives some statistics about the program. This information includes records, specifications, data records, and comments. The last line is the result of the compile. In this case, the compiler does not generate a program because compilation stopped with a maximum error severity of 30.

THE COMPILE-TIME DATA SECTION

RPG IV developers have provided useful information for alternate collating sequence tables and array-related information in the compile-time data section. When you specify an alternate collating sequence, the compiler will print a matrix showing the mapping of the characters whose sort order has been changed. This map shows you, in row-column format, exactly which characters have been affected and their new sort value in hexadecimal. For arrays and tables, the listing will give the name of the array or table for which compile-time data is expected and, if defined, the name of the alternate array.

The program listing is an important programmer tool. Without it, you have a difficult time determining the cause of not only syntax and relational errors but also execution time errors.

Error-Handling Data Structures

Adding error-handling code to RPG programs can save time and effort. More important, error handling can spare users from obscure error messages that they don't understand or know what to do about. To help with error handling, RPG supports two data structures, the file status data structure (INFDS) and the program status data structure (PSSR). This appendix explains these data structures and how to use them in your programs.

FILE STATUS DATA STRUCTURE

A file status data structure is a special data structure. It is not a special type of data structure, because you define it just as you define any named data structure. What makes a named data structure a file status data structure is that you associate it with a file that your program opens. Then the compiled program will maintain information about the associated file in the data structure.

Programmers usually include file status data structures among advanced programming methods. To beginning programmers, the volume and detail of data in a file status data structure can be overwhelming. However, all programmers can benefit from these data structures. Just remember that somewhere in this mass of data may be just the information you need to solve a problem.

Using the File Status Data Structure

You associate a data structure with a file by specifying the INFDS (File Information Data Structure) keyword on the F-spec when you declare a file to the program. Each file in the program can have the INFDS keyword to associate a data structure with it, but each file must have a different data structure.

The INFDS keyword has one required parameter, the name of the data structure where you want to put information about the file. The name you specify in this parameter must be the name of a standard data structure, so data area data structures, multiple-occurrence data structures, and program status data structures are not allowed.

Associating the data structure with the file turns the data structure into a file status data structure. Because the system is placing a string of characters into the data structure, you have to construct data structure subfields to divide that string of data so that it correctly formats the information it receives. You can specify *from* and *to* positions that identify which bytes of the string compose one subfield, or you can specify each field's length. You do not have to specify particular subfields; you must do so only if you expect to make any sense of the data!

The POST Operation

What data goes into the file status data structure depends on the type of file you define. The file type can be PRINTER, DISK, WORKSTN, SEQ, or SPECIAL. You'll get some different data for each file type. The type of data also depends on whether you specify a special (rarely used) operation, POST. This operation retrieves the get-attributes feedback area, which you must explicitly load and update. POST can also prevent automatic updating of the I/O feedback areas (command and device dependent) and allow their loading only when you execute POST to do so.

The POST operation uses Factor 1, Factor 2, and the Result field. All are optional, but you must enter either a Factor 2 or a Result field. You can specify an error indicator in positions 73 and 74.

Factor 1 is where you specify the program device name if you're in a display or communications session. When you specify Factor 1, you must execute the operation against a file defined as a WORKSTN device file in the F-specs. An entry in Factor 1 triggers the retrieval of the get-attributes feedback area. The value in Factor 1, which you can specify with a variable, constant, or literal, must be the name of a device that the program is communicating with via the WORKSTN file. If you're using a display file, this value is the name of the terminal where the program is running. You can retrieve this information by means of the open feedback area.

You must specify Factor 2 or the Result field. If you specify Factor 2, you enter the name of a file that has an INFDS keyword on its F-spec. If you specify the Result field, it must contain the name of a file status data structure. If you specify both Factor 2 and the Result field, the file you name in Factor 2 and the file status data structure you name in the Result field must match: They must be associated on the INFDS keyword on the F-specs.

Every file type uses the first 240 bytes of the data structure in the same way. The first 80 bytes are the file feedback area. The next 160 bytes are the open feedback area. The next 126 bytes, if you do not specify the POST operation for this file anywhere in the program, are the input/output (I/O) feedback area. The next area, also available only if you do not specify POST for this file anywhere in the program, is the device-specific feedback area. Its length depends on the file's RPG device type. If you specify POST for this file anywhere in the program, you can replace both the I/O feedback area and device-specific feedback area with the get-attributes feedback area. Like the device-specific feedback area, the get-attributes feedback area's length depends on the device type of the file.

The POST operation causes the file status data structure associated with the file to be updated with the latest I/O feedback area information *if you leave Factor 1 blank*. If Factor 1 is not blank (it contains a program device name), the get-attributes feedback area is retrieved instead.

You need the POST operation to retrieve the I/O feedback area for a file although it is usually loaded automatically and normally refreshed after every file I/O. The reason lies in the second use of POST. If an RPG program has any POST operations with a blank Factor 1, the automatic updating of the I/O feedback area is turned off, and only the execution of a POST that has Factor 1 blank updates the I/O feedback area.

POST with a Factor 1 and either a Factor 2 or a Result field retrieves the get-attributes feedback area for a file. POST without a Factor 1 but with either a Factor 2 or a Result field retrieves the I/O feedback areas (common and device dependent). Having any POST operation in the program with a blank Factor 1 turns off the automatic updating of the I/O feedback areas and requires you to issue the POST operation to retrieve those areas.

With this introduction to POST, you will be able to understand references to this operation in the discussions of the various feedback areas. Let's examine each area.

The File Feedback Area

The file feedback area contains information such as whether the file is open, whether an error has occurred, the error message and routine in which the error appeared, and the type of operation that was executing when the error occurred. If you specify POST (which you will rarely want to do) in the program, the information also includes the size and type of the display and the type of keyboard the program is using.

Table B.1 lists the information in the file feedback area's first 80 bytes. Note that the information in the first 66 positions is always available and is updated after every operation involving the file. The information in positions 67 through 80, however, is updated only if you specify POST on this file, and this information is updated only when you execute POST.

Because programmers frequently need some fields in this section of the data structure, RPG IV provides some special keywords you can specify to pre-define the positions of the data in the data structure. These keywords eliminate the need for you to code the *from* and *to* positions for some of the fields. The keywords all start with an asterisk, which is how you can recognize them in the tables. You enter the special keyword in the D-spec *from/to* positions (left justified), and the compiler will generate the correct *from/to* positions. Tables B.2 through B.4 identify the possible status values that can be in the *STATUS positions (11 through 15) of the data structure. A lot of information is available in just the first 80 bytes.

In contrast to the tables in IBM's manuals, these tables include *from/to* positions for entries that include only offset length in the manuals. In addition, the tables here identify some fields as being for internal system use only; they are meaningless to an RPG program, or they are not available through the file status data structure.

File Feedback Information Available in the INFDS

From	To	Format	Length	Keyword	Information
1	8	Character	8	*FILE	The first 8 characters of the file name.
9	9	Character	1		Open indication (1 = open).
10	10	Character	1		End of file (1 = end of file).
11	15	Zoned decimal	5,0	*STATUS	Status code. For a description of these codes, see Status code tables below.
16	21	Character	6	*OPCODE	Operation code The first five positions (left-adjusted) specify the type of operation by using the character representation of the calculation operation codes. For example, if a READE was being processed, READE is placed in the leftmost five positions. If the operation was an implicit operation (for example, a primary file read or update on the output specifications), the equivalent operation code is generated (such as READ or UPDATE) and placed in location *OPCODE. Operation codes that have 6-letter names will be shortened to 5 letters.
					DELETE DELET EXCEPT EXCPT READPE REDPE UNLOCK UNLCK UPDATE UPDAT
					The remaining position contains one of the following:
					F The last operation was specified for a file name.
					R The last operation was specified for a record.
					I The last operation was an implicit file operation.
22	29	Character	8	*ROUTINE	First 8 characters of the procedure name or zero if the call is by procedure pointer.
30	37	Character	8		RPG IV source listing line number.

CONTINUED

TABLE B.1 *CONTINUED*

From	To	Format	Length	Keyword	Information
38	42	Zoned decimal	5,0		User-specified reason for error on SPECIAL file.
38	45	Character	8	*RECORD	For a program-described file, you put the record-identifying indicator left adjusted in the field; the remaining six positions are filled with blanks. For an externally described file, the first 8 characters of the name of the record being processed when the exception/error occurred.
46	52	Character	7		Machine or system message number.
53	66	Character	14		Unused.
67	70	Zoned decimal	4,0	*SIZE	Screen size (product of the number of rows and the number of columns on the device screen).
71	72	Zoned decimal	2,0	*INP	The display's keyboard type. Set to 00 if the keyboard is alphanumeric or Katakana. Set to 10 if the keyboard is ideographic.
73	74	Zoned decimal	2,0	*OUT	The display type. Set to 00 if the display is alphanumeric or Katakana. Set to 10 if the display is ideographic. Set to 20 if the display is DBCS.
75	76	Zoned decimal	2,0	*MODE	Always set to 00.
77	80	Character	4		Unused.

TABLE B.2
Status Code Normal Codes

Code	Device(1)	RC(2)	Condition
00000			No exception/error.
00002	W	n/a	Function key used to end display.
00011	W, D, SQ	llxx	End of file on a read (input).
00012	W, D, SQ	n/a	No-record-found condition on a CHAIN, SETLL, or SETGT operation.
00013	W	n/a	Subfile is full on WRITE operation.

Note: (1)"Device" refers to the devices for which the condition applies. The following abbreviations are used: P = PRINTER; D = DISK; W = WORKSTN; SP = SPECIAL; SQ = Sequential. The major/minor return codes under column RC apply only to WORKSTN files. (2)The formula mmnn is used to described major/minor return codes: mm is the major and nn the minor.

TABLE B.3

Status Code Exception/Error Codes

Code	Device(1)	RC(2)	Condition
01011	W, D, SQ	n/a	Undefined record type (input record does not match record identifying indicator).
01021	W, D, SQ	n/a	Tried to write a record that already exists.
01022	D	n/a	Referential constraint error detected on file member.
01031	W, D, SQ	n/a	Match field out of sequence.
01041	n/a	n/a	Array/table load sequence error.
01042	n/a	n/a	Array/table load sequence error. Alternate collating sequence used.
01051	n/a	n/a	Excess entries in array/table file.
01071	W, D, SQ	n/a	Numeric sequence error.
01121(4)	W	n/a	No indicator on the DDS keyword for Print key.
01122(4)	W	n/a	No indicator on the DDS keyword for Roll Up key.
01123(4)	W	n/a	No indicator on the DDS keyword for Roll Down key.
01124(4)	W	n/a	No indicator on the DDS keyword for Clear key.
01125(4)	W	n/a	No indicator on the DDS keyword for Help key.
01126(4)	W	n/a	No indicator on the DDS keyword for Home key.
01201	W	34xx	Record mismatch detected on input.
01211	all	n/a	I/O operation to a closed file.
01215	all	n/a	OPEN issued to a file already opened.
01216(3)	all	yes	Error on an implicit OPEN/CLOSE operation.
01217(3)	all	yes	Error on an explicit OPEN/CLOSE operation.
01218	D, SQ	n/a	Record already locked.
01221	D, SQ	n/a	Update operation attempted without a prior read.
01222	D, SQ	n/a	Record cannot be allocated due to referential constraint error
01231	SP	n/a	Error on SPECIAL file.
01235	P	n/a	Error in PRTCTL space or skip entries.
01241	D, SQ	n/a	Record number not found. (Record number specified in record address file is not present .)
01251	W	80xx 81xx	Permanent I/O error occurred.
01255	W	82xx 83xx	Session or device error occurred. Recovery may be possible.
01261	W	n/a	Attempt to exceed maximum number of acquired devices.
01271	W	n/a	Attempt to acquire unavailable device
01281	W	n/a	Operation to unacquired device.
01282	W	0309	Job ending with controlled option.
01284	W	n/a	Unable to acquire second device for single device file

CONTINUED

TABLE B.3 *CONTINUED*

Code	Device(1)	RC(2)	Condition
01285	W	0800	Attempt to acquire a device already acquired.
01286	W	n/a	Attempt to open shared file with SAVDS or IND options.
01287	W	n/a	Response indicators overlap IND indicators.
01299	W, D, SQ	yes	Other I/O error detected.
01331	W	0310	Wait time exceeded for READ from WORKSTN file.

Note: (1)"Device" refers to the devices for which the condition applies. The following abbreviations are used: P =PRINTER; D=DISK; W=WORKSTN; SP=SPECIAL; SQ=Sequential. The major/minor return codes under column RC apply only to WORKSTN files. (2)The formula mmnn describes major/minor return codes: mm is the major and nn the minor. (3)Any errors that occur during an open or close operation will result in a *STATUS value of 1216 or 1217 regardless of the major/minor return code value.

TABLE B.4

Status Code Mapped Values for Major/Minor Return Codes

Major	Minor	*STATUS
00,02	all	00000
03	all (except 09, 10)	00000
03	09	01282
03	10	01331
04	all	01299
08	all	01285(1)
11	all	00011
34	all	01201
80,81	all	01251
82,83	all	01255

Note: (1)The return code field will not be updated for a *STATUS value of 1285, 1261, or 1281 because these conditions are detected before data management is called. To monitor for these errors, you must check for the *STATUS value and not for the corresponding major/minor return code value.

To include the file feedback area in your file status data structure, you code your file and data structure as follows.

```
*...1....+....2....+....3....+....4....+....5....+....6....+....7....+....8....+....9....+....10
FDBaseFile IF   E              DISK      INFDS(DBaseFBK)
```

```
*...1....+....2....+....3....+....4....+....5....+....6....+....7....+....8....+....9....+....10
DDBaseFBK          DS
 *
 * File Feedback area
 *
D File              *FILE                          * File name
D OpenInd              9        9                   * File open?
D EOFInd              10       10                   * File at EOF?
D Status             *STATUS                        * Status code
D Opcode             *OPCODE                        * Last opcode
D Routine            *ROUTINE                       * RPG Routine
D ListNum             30       37                   * Listing line
D SpclStat            38       42S 0                * SPECIAL status
D Record             *RECORD                        * Record name
D MsgID               46       52                   * Error MSGID
D Screen             *SIZE                          * Screen size
D NLSIn              *INP                           * NLS Input?
D NLSOut             *OUT                           * NLS Output?
D NLSMode            *MODE                          * NLS Mode?
```

This code creates a data structure called DbaseFBK (database feedback). You can use this code for any file type because the file feedback area is the same for all file types.

In the definition of the data structure, nothing is special. The only entry that makes this a file status data structure is the reference to its name on the F-spec, which includes the INFDS keyword with the name of the data structure as its parameter.

You have two ways (besides referring to other fields) of defining the size of a data structure subfield: You can specify the size of the field, or you can specify the *from* and *to* positions in the data structure. Because the feedback areas have predefined formats, *from/to* syntax is generally easier when you're defining the subfields for a file status data structure. That option is in the sample code for the definition of OpenInd, EOFSts, ListNum, SpclStat, and MsgID.

As you can see in the previous table, many file feedback area data structure subfields have a special keyword that you can use instead of entering the starting and ending positions of some subfields. These keywords are not variables, and you cannot use them as names to access the data. The keywords are a shorthand for specifying the subfield location in the data structure. You can achieve the same result by specifying the *from/to* positions. Also, although the example shows definitions for all fields, you do not have to specify all the fields; only those that you need in your program.

Open Feedback Area

The open feedback area contains such basic information as the name of the file, the library in which the file resides, the number of lines on a display or printer page, the number of characters on each line of a display or printer device, the overflow line number for a printer file, and much more. It also contains such esoteric information as the file type, the method for accessing the file (arrival, keyed unique, keyed with duplicates allowed), whether the file is a join logical, and whether other programs are sharing the file's ODP. Table B.5 shows the information available. Like the file feedback area, the open feedback area is the same for all file types.

TABLE B.5
Information in the Open Feedback Area

From	To	Data Type	Length	Contents	File Type
81	82	Character	2	Open data path (ODP) type: DS Display, tape, ICF, save, printer file not being spooled, or diskette file not being spooled. DB Database member. SP Printer or diskette file being spooled or inline data file.	All
83	92	Character	10	Name of the file being opened. If the ODP type is DS, this is the name of the device file or save file. If the ODP type is SP, this is the name of the device file or the inline data file. If the ODP type is DB, this is the name of the database file that the member belongs to.	All
93	102	Character	10	Name of the library containing the file. For an inline data file, the value is *N.	All
103	112	Character	10	Name of the spooled file. The name of a database file containing the spooled input or output records.	Printer or diskette being spooled or inline data
113	122	Character	10	Name of the library in which the spooled file is located.	Printer or diskette being spooled or inline data
123	124	Binary	2	Spooled file number.	Printer or diskette being spooled

CONTINUED

TABLE B.5 CONTINUED

From	To	Data Type	Length	Contents	File Type
125	126	Binary	2	Maximum record length.	All
127	128	Binary	2	Maximum key length.	Database
129	138	Character	10	Member name: • If ODP type DB, the member name in the file named at offset 2. If file is overridden to MBR(*ALL), the member name that supplied the last record. • If ODP type SP, the member name in the file named at offset 22.	Database, printer, diskette, and inline data
139	142	Binary	4	Reserved.	
143	146	Binary	4	Reserved.	
147	148	Binary	2	File type: 1 Display 2 Printer 4 Diskette 5 Tape 9 Save 10 DDM 11 ICF 20 Inline data 21 Database	All
149	151	Character	3	Reserved	
152	153	Binary	2	Number of lines on a display screen or number of lines on a printed page. Length of the null field byte map.	Display, printer Database
154	155	Binary	2	Number of positions on a display screen or number of characters on a printed line. Length of the null field byte map.	Display, printer Database
156	159	Binary	4	Number of records in the member at open time. For a join logical file, the number of records in the primary. Supplied only if the file is being opened for input.	Database, inline data
160	161	Character	2	Access type: AR Arrival sequence.	Database

CONTINUED

TABLE **B.5** *CONTINUED*

From	To	Data Type	Length	Contents	File Type
160	161	Character	2	KC Keyed with duplicate keys allowed. Duplicate keys are accessed in first-changed-first-out (FCFO) order. KF Keyed with duplicate keys allowed. Duplicate keys are accessed in first-in-first-out (FIFO) order. KL Keyed with duplicate keys allowed.Duplicate keys are accessed in last-in-first-out (LIFO) order. KN Keyed with duplicate keys allowed. The order in which duplicate keys are accessed can be one of the following: • First-in-first-out (FIFO) • Last-in-first-out (LIFO) • First-changed-first-out (FCFO) KU Keyed, unique.	
162	162	Character	1	Duplicate key indication. Set only if the access path is KC, KF, KL, KN, or KU: D Duplicate keys allowed if the access path is KF or KL. U Duplicate keys are not allowed; all keys are unique and the access path is KU.	Database
163	163	Character	1	Source file indication. Y File is a source file. N File is not a source file.	Database, tape, diskette, and inline data
164	173	Character	10	Reserved	
174	183	Character	10	Reserved	
184	185	Binary	2	System Internal Use. Offset to volume label fields of open feedback area.	Diskette, tape
186	187	Binary	2	Maximum number of records that can be read or written in a block when using blocked record I/O.	All
188	189	Binary	2	Overflow line number.	Printer

CONTINUED

TABLE B.5 CONTINUED

From	To	Data Type	Length	Contents	File Type
190	191	Binary	2	Blocked record I/O record increment. Number of bytes that must be added to the start of each record in a block to address the next record in the block.	All
192	195	Binary	4	Reserved	
196	196	Character	1	Miscellaneous flags	
				Bit 1: Reserved	
				Miscellaneous flags, continued	
				Bit 2: File shareable	All
				0 File was not opened shareable.	
				1 File was opened shareable (SHARE(*YES)).	
				Bit 3: Commitment control	Database
				0 File is not under commitment control.	
				1 File is under commitment control.	
				Bit 4: Commitment lock level	Database
				0 Only changed records are locked (LCKLVL (*CHG)). If this bit is zero and bit 8 of the character at offset 132 is one, then all records accessed are locked, but the locks are released when the current position in the file changes (LCKLVL (*CS)).	
				1 All records accessed are locked LCKLVL (*ALL)).	
				Bit 5: Member type	Database
				0 Member is a physical file member.	
				1 Member is a logical file member.	
				Bit 6: Field-level descriptions	All, except database
				0 File does not contain field-level descriptions.	
				1 File contains field-level descriptions.	

CONTINUED

TABLE B.5 *CONTINUED*

From	To	Data Type	Length	Contents	File Type
196	196	Character	1	Bit 7: DBCS or graphic-capable file	Database, display, printer, tape, diskette, and ICF
				0 File does not contain DBCS or graphic-capable fields.	
				1 File does contain DBCS or graphic-capable fields.	
				Bit 8: End-of-file delay	Database
				0 End-of-file delay processing is not being done.	
				1 End-of-file delay processing is being done.	
197	206	Character	10	Name of the requester device. For display files, this is the name of the display device description that is the requester device. For ICF files, this is the program device name associated with the remote location of *REQUESTER. This field is supplied only when either a device or remote location name of *REQUESTER is being attached to the file by an open or acquire operation. Otherwise, this field contains *N.	Display, ICF
207	208	Binary	2	File open count. If the file has not been opened shareable, this field contains a 1. If the file has been opened shareable, this field contains the number of programs currently attached to this file.	All
209	210	Binary	2	Reserved	
211	212	Binary	2	Number of based-on physical members opened. For logical members, this is the number of physical members over which the logical member was opened. For physical members, this field is always set to 1.	Database

CONTINUED

TABLE B.5 *CONTINUED*

From	To	Data Type	Length	Contents	File Type
213	213	Character	1	Miscellaneous flags	
				Bit 1: Multiple member processing	Database
				0 Only the member specified will be processed.	
				1 All members will be processed.	
				Bit 2: Join logical file	Database
				0 File is not a join logical file.	
				1 File is a join logical file.	
				Bit 3: Local or remote data	Database
				0 Data is stored on local system.	
				1 Data is stored on remote system.	
				Bit 4: Remote System/38 or AS/400 data. Applicable only if the value of Bit 3 is 1.	Database
				0 Data is on a remote System/38 or AS/400 system.	
				1 Data is not on a remote System/38 or AS/400 system.	
				Bit 5: Separate indicator area	Printer, display, ICF
				0 Indicators are in the I/O buffer of the program.	
				1 Indicators are not in the I/O buffer of the program. The DDS keyword, INDARA, was used when the file was created.	
				Bit 6: User buffers	All
				0 System creates I/O buffers for the program.	
				1 User program supplies I/O buffers.	
				Bit 7: Reserved	
				Bit 8: Additional commitment lock level indicator. This is only valid if bit 3 of the character at offset 15 is one.	Database
				If bit 4 of the character at offset 115 is zero:	
				0 Only changed records are locked (LCKLVL(*CHG)).	
				1 All records accessed are locked, but the locks are released when the current position in the file changes (LCKLVL(*CS)).	

CONTINUED

TABLE B.5 *CONTINUED*

From	To	Data Type	Length	Contents	File Type
213	213	Character	1	If bit 4 of the character at offset 115 is one: 　0 All records accessed are locked (LCKLVL(*ALL)). 　1 Reserved.	
214	215	Character	2	Open identifier. This value is unique for a full open operation (SHARE(*NO)) or the first open of a file that is opened with SHARE(*YES). This is used for display and ICF files, but is set up for all file types. It allows you to match this file to an entry on the associated data queue.	All
216	217	Binary	2	The field value is the maximum record format length, including both data and file-specific information such as: first-character forms control, option indicators, response indicators, source sequence numbers, and program-to-system data. If the value is zero, then use the field at offset 44.	Printer, diskette, tape, and ICF
218	219	Binary	2	Coded character set identifier (CCSID) of the character data in the buffer.	Database
220	220	Character	1	Miscellaneous flags	
				Bit 1: Null-capable field file. 　0 File does not contain null-capable fields. 　1 File contains null-capable fields.	Database
				Bit 2: Variable-length fields file. 　0 File does not contain any variable-length fields. 　1 File contains variable-length fields.	Database
				Bit 3: Variable-length record processing 　0 Variable-length record processing will not be done. 　1 Variable-length record processing will be done.	Database

CONTINUED

TABLE **B.5** *CONTINUED*

From	To	Data Type	Length	Contents	File Type
220	220	Character	1	Bit 4: CCSID character substitution 0 No substitution characters will be used during CCSID data conversion. 1 Substitution characters may be used during CCSID data conversion. Bits 5-8: Reserved.	Database
221	226	Character	6	Reserved.	All
227	228	Binary	2	Number of devices defined for this ODP. For displays, this is determined by the number of devices defined on the DEV parameter of the Create Display File (CRTDSPF) command. For ICF, this is determined by the number of program devices defined or acquired with the Add ICF Device Entry (ADDICFDEVE) or the Override ICF Device Entry (OVRICFDEVE) command. For all other files, t has the value off.	All
229	240	Character	12	Internal System Use.	All

The open feedback area uses positions 81 through 240 of the file status data structure. To access this information, you need to code the appropriate subfields in your file status data structure. The sample code on page 431 includes all the possible fields for the open feedback area. So that you can examine it in context, the information has been added to the sample code from the example of the file feedback area.

The F-spec defines a database file (DISK device). Comparing that fact with the intent of some of the fields in this and other feedback areas, you can see that not all fields are relevant to all file types. You will ordinarily specify only the fields you need for the type of device you are working with. In fact, this need to limit the number of fields is exactly the reason why you want to use the *from/to* syntax when defining your subfields. If you use the size syntax, to get the data to fall in the correct place in the data structure, you must always define all fields (or a large fake field) preceding the field you are interested in — far too much work. Of course, you do not need to use the field names specified in this example. You can use any field name you want. Remember, the only entry that makes a file status data structure unique is that you name it on the INFDS keyword on an F-spec.

```
*...1....+....2....+....3....+....4....+....5....+....6....+....7....+....8....+....9....+....10
FDBaseFile IF   E           DISK    INFDS(DBaseFBK)


*...1....+....2....+....3....+....4....+....5....+....6....+....7....+....8....+....9....+....10
DDBaseFBK         DS
 *
 * File Feedback area
D File            *FILE                              * File name
D OpenInd             9      9                       * File open?
D EOFInd             10     10                       * File at EOF?
D Status          *STATUS                            * Status code
D Opcode          *OPCODE                            * Last opcode
D Routine         *ROUTINE                           * RPG Routine
D ListNum            30     37                       * Listing line
D SpclStat           38     42S 0                    * SPECIAL status
D Record          *RECORD                            * Record name
D MsgID              46     52                       * Error MSGID
D Screen          *SIZE                              * Screen size
D NLSIn            *INP                              * NLS Input?
D NLSOut           *OUT                              * NLS Output?
D NLSMode          *MODE                             * NLS Mode?
 *
 *
 * Open Feedback Area
D ODPType            81     82                       * ODP Type
D FileName           83     92                       * File name
D Library            93    102                       * Library name
D SpoolFile         103    112                       * Spool file name
D SpoolLib          113    122                       * Spool file lib
D SpoolNum          123    124B 0                    * Spool file num
D RcdLen            125    126B 0                    * Max record len
D KeyLen            127    128B 0                    * Max key len
D Member            129    138                       * Member name
D Type              147    148B 0                    * File type
D Rows              152    153B 0                    * Num PRT/DSP rows
D Columns           154    155B 0                    * Num PRT/DSP cols
D NumRcds           156    159B 0                    * Num of records
D AccType           160    161                       * Access type
D DupKey            162    162                       * Duplicate key?
D SrcFile           163    163                       * Source file?
D BlkRcds           186    187B 0                    * Max rcds in blk
D Overflow          188    189B 0                    * Overflow line
D BlkIncr           190    191B 0                    * Blk increment
D Flags1            196    196                       * Misc flags
D Requester         197    206                       * Requester name
D OpenCount         207    208B 0                    * Open count
D BasedMbrs         211    212B 0                    * Num based mbrs
D Flags2            213    213                       * Misc flags
D OpenId            214    215                       * Open identifier
D RcdfmtLen         216    217B 0                    * Max rcd fmt len
D CCSID             218    219B 0                    * Database CCSID
D Flags3            220    220                       * Misc flags
D NumDevs           227    228B 0                    * Num devs defined
```

Common I/O Feedback Area

The next part of the file status data structure is the common I/O feedback area. This part contains statistical and detail information about I/O associated with your file. Programmers do not often use this section. It provides information such as the number of reads and writes to the file and basic information about the type of device you are communicating with. That information can come in handy if you must have your program act differently depending on the capabilities of, say, a printer or display device that your program is using. Table B.6 shows the information available via the common I/O feedback area.

The common I/O feedback area uses the positions from 241 to 366 in the file status data structure. This feedback area is updated only when an I/O occurs against the file it is attached to. Note that POST can cause RPG to *not* update this information on every I/O. Specifying POST against the file anywhere in the program will cause RPG to require you to specify POST to have this information updated.

TABLE B.6
Common I/O Feedback Area

From	To	DataType	Length	Contents
241	242	Binary	2	Offset to file-dependent feedback area.
243	246	Binary	4	Write operation count. Updated only when a write operation completes successfully. For blocked record I/O operations, this count is the number of blocks, not the number of records.
247	250	Binary	4	Read operation count. Updated only when a read operation completes successfully. For blocked record I/O operations, this count is the number of blocks, not the number of records.
251	254	Binary	4	Write-read operation count. Updated only when a write-read operation completes successfully.
255	258	Binary	4	Other operation count. Number of successful operations other than write, read, or write-read. Updated only when the operation completes successfully. This count includes update, delete, force-end-of-data, force-end-of-volume, change-end-of-data, release record lock, and acquire/release device operations.
259	259	Character	1	Reserved.

CONTINUED

TABLE B.6 *CONTINUED*

From	To	DataType	Length	Contents
260	260	Character	1	Current operation.

hex 01	Read or read block or read from invited devices
hex 02	Read direct
hex 03	Read by key
hex 05	Write or write block
hex 06	Write-read
hex 07	Update
hex 08	Delete
hex 09	Force-end-of-data
hex 0A	Force-end-of-volume
hex 0D	Release record lock
hex 0E	Change end-of-data
hex 0F	Put delete
hex 11	Release device
hex 12	Acquire device

From	To	DataType	Length	Contents
261	270	Character	10	Name of the record format just processed, which is either:

- Specified on the I/O request, or
- Determined by default or format selection processing

For display files, the default name is either the name of the only record format in the file or the previous record format name for the record written to the display that contains input-capable fields. Because a display file may have multiple formats on the display at the same time, this format may not represent the format where the last cursor position was typed.

For ICF files, the format name is determined by the system, based on the format selection option used. Refer to the ICF Programming book for more information.

From	To	DataType	Length	Contents
271	272	Character	2	Device class:

Byte 1:

hex 00	Database
hex 01	Display
hex 02	Printer
hex 04	Diskette
hex 05	Tape
hex 09	Save
hex 0B	ICF

Byte 2 (if byte 1 contains hex 00):

hex 00	Nonkeyed file
hex 01	Keyed file

CONTINUED

From	To	DataType	Length	Contents
271	272	Character	2	Byte 2 (if byte 1 does not contain hex 00):

		hex 02	5256 Printer	
		hex 07	5251 Display Station	
		hex 08	Spooled	
		hex 0A	BSCEL	
		hex 0B	5291 Display Station	
		hex 0C	5224/5225 printers	
		hex 0D	5292 Display Station	
		hex 0E	APPC	
		hex 0F	5219 Printer	

Byte 2 (if byte 1 does not contain hex 00):

hex 10	5583 Printer (DBCS)
hex 11	5553 Printer
hex 12	5555-B01 Display Station
hex 13	3270 Display Station
hex 14	3270 Printer
hex 15	Graphic-capable device
hex 16	Financial Display Station
hex 17	3180 Display Station
hex 18	Save file
hex 19	3277 DHCF device
hex 1A	9347 Tape Unit
hex 1B	9348 Tape Unit
hex 1C	9331-1 Diskette Unit
hex 1D	9331-2 Diskette Unit
hex 1E	Intrasystem communications support
hex 1F	Asynchronous communications support

Byte 2 (if byte 1 does not contain hex 00):

hex 20	SNUF
hex 21	4234 (SCS) Printer
hex 22	3812 (SCS) Printer
hex 23	4214 Printer
hex 24	4224 (IPDS) Printer
hex 25	4245 Printer
hex 26	3179-2 Display Station
hex 27	3196-A Display Station
hex 28	3196-B Display Station
hex 29	5262 Printer
hex 2A	6346 Tape Unit
hex 2B	2440 Tape Unit
hex 2C	9346 Tape Unit
hex 2D	6331 Diskette Unit
hex 2E	6332 Diskette Unit

CONTINUED

TABLE B.6 *CONTINUED*

From	To	DataType	Length	Contents
271	272	Character	2	Byte 2 (if byte 1 does not contain hex 00):

Byte 2 (if byte 1 does not contain hex 00):

hex 30	3812 (IPDS) Printer
hex 31	4234 (IPDS) Printer
hex 32	IPDS printer, model unknown
hex 33	3197-C1 Display Station
hex 34	3197-C2 Display Station
hex 35	3197-D1 Display Station
hex 36	3197-D2 Display Station
hex 37	3197-W1 Display Station
hex 38	3197-W2 Display Station
hex 39	5555-E01 Display Station
hex 3A	3430 Tape Unit
hex 3B	3422 Tape Unit
hex 3C	3480 Tape Unit
hex 3D	3490 Tape Unit
hex 3E	3476-EA Display Station
hex 3F	3477-FG Display Station

Byte 2 (if byte 1 does not contain hex 00):

hex 41	3279 DHCF device
hex 42	ICF finance device
hex 43	Retail communications device
hex 44	3477-FA Display Station
hex 45	3477-FC Display Station
hex 46	3477-FD Display Station
hex 47	3477-FW Display Station
hex 48	3477-FE Display Station
hex 49	6367 Tape Unit
hex 4A	6347 Tape Unit
hex 4D	Network Virtual Terminal Display Station
hex 4E	6341 Tape Unit
hex 4F	6342 Tape Unit

Byte 2 (if byte 1 does not contain hex 00):

hex 50	6133 Diskette Unit
hex 51	5555-C01 Display Station
hex 52	5555-F01 Display Station
hex 53	6366 Tape Unit
hex 54	7208 Tape Unit
hex 55	6252 (SCS) Printer
hex 56	3476-EC Display Station
hex 57	4230 (IPDS) Printer
hex 58	5555-G01 Display Station
hex 59	5555-G02 Display Station
hex 5A	6343 Tape Unit
hex 5B	6348 Tape Unit
hex 5C	6368 Tape Unit

CONTINUED

TABLE B.6 *CONTINUED*

From	To	DataType	Length	Contents
271	272	Character	2	hex 5D 3486-BA Display Station hex 5F 3487-HA Display Station
				Byte 2 (if byte 1 does not contain hex 00): hex 60 3487-HG Display Station hex 61 3487-HW Display Station hex 62 3487-HC Display Station hex 63 3935 (IPDS) Printer hex 64 6344 Tape Unit hex 65 6349 Tape Unit hex 66 6369 Tape Unit hex 67 6380 Tape Unit hex 68 6378 Tape Unit hex 69 6390 Tape Unit
				Byte 2 (if byte 1 does not contain hex 00): hex 70 6379 Tape Unit hex 71 9331-11 Diskette Unit hex 72 9331-12 Diskette Unit hex 73 3570 Tape Unit hex 74 3590 Tape Unit hex 75 6335 Tape Unit
273	282	Character	10	Device name. The name of the device for which the operation just completed. Supplied only for display, printer, tape, diskette, and ICF files. For printer or diskette files being spooled, the value is *N. For ICF files, the value is the program device name. For other files, the value is the device description name.
283	286	Binary	4	Length of the record processed by the last I/O operation (supplied only for an ICF, display, tape, or database file). On ICF write operations, this is the record length of the data. On ICF read operations, it is the record length of the record associated with the last read operation.
287	366	Character	80	Reserved

The following code demonstrates how to specify the common I/O feedback area of the file status data structure and how to use the information available. Again, both for context and because all file types use this part of the file status data structure, this example includes the common I/O feedback area with the two feedback areas described previously.

```
*...1....+....2....+....3....+....4....+....5....+....6....+....7....+....8....+....9....+....10
FDBaseFile IF   E           DISK      INFDS(DBaseFBK)


*...1....+....2....+....3....+....4....+....5....+....6....+....7....+....8....+....9....+....10
DDBaseFBK         DS
 *
 * File Feedback area
D File              *FILE                        * File name
D OpenInd                   9      9             * File open?
D EOFInd                   10     10             * File at EOF?
D Status             *STATUS                     * Status code
D Opcode             *OPCODE                     * Last opcode
D Routine            *ROUTINE                    * RPG Routine
D ListNum                  30     37             * Listing line
D SpclStat                 38     42S 0          * SPECIAL status
D Record             *RECORD                     * Record name
D Msgid                    46     52             * Error MSGID
D Screen             *SIZE                       * Screen size
D NLSIn              *INP                        * NLS Input?
D NLSOut             *OUT                        * NLS Output?
D NLSMode            *MODE                       * NLS Mode?
 *
 * Open Feedback Area
 *
D ODPType                  81     82             * ODP Type
D FileName                 83     92             * File name
D Library                  93    102             * Library name
D SpoolFile               103    112             * Spool file name
D SpoolLib                113    122             * Spool file lib
D SpoolNum                123    124B 0          * Spool file num
D RcdLen                  125    126B 0          * Max record len
D KeyLen                  127    128B 0          * Max key len
D Member                  129    138             * Member name
D Type                    147    148B 0          * File type
D Rows                    152    153B 0          * Num PRT/DSP  rows
D Columns                 154    155B 0          * Num PRT/DSP cols
D NumRcds                 156    159B 0          * Num of records
D AccType                 160    161             * Access type
D DupKey                  162    162             * Duplicate key?
D SrcFile                 163    163             * Source file?
D BlkRcds                 186    187B 0          * Max rcds in blk
D Overflow                188    189B 0          * Overflow line
D BlkIncr                 190    191B 0          * Blk increment
D Flags1                  196    196             * Misc flags
D Requester               197    206             * Requester name
D OpenCount               207    208B 0          * Open count
D BasedMbrs               211    212B 0          * Num based mbrs
D Flags2                  213    213             * Misc flags
D OpenId                  214    215             * Open identifier
D RcdfmtLen               216    217B 0          * Max rcd fmt len
D CCSID                   218    219B 0          * Database CCSID
D Flags3                  220    220             * Misc flags
```

CONTINUED

```
*...1....+....2....+....3....+....4....+....5....+....6....+....7....+....8....+....9....+....10
D NumDevs                227   228B 0                                    * Num devs defined
*
* Common I/O Feedback area
*
D WriteCnt               243   246B 0                                    * Write count
D ReadCnt                247   250B 0                                    * Read count
D WrtRdCnt               251   254B 0                                    * Write/read count
D OtherCnt               255   258B 0                                    * Other I/O count
D Operation              260   260                                       * Cuurent operatn
D IORcdFmt               261   270                                       * Rcd format name
D DevClass               271   272                                       * Device class
D IOPgmDev               273   282                                       * Pgm device name
D IORcdLen               283   286B 0                                    * Rcd len of I/O
```

This basic data structure layout is valid for any file type in RPG. No special keywords are available to predefine the positions of the subfields for this part of the file status data structure. Such keywords are available only for the file feedback area, in positions 1 through 80.

File-Dependent I/O Feedback Areas

Because each device type on the system has different operational characteristics, the feedback area for each device type has a different layout. Separate layouts exist for ICF and display files, printer files, and disk (or database) files. The following tables describe the three layouts you need to access the different types of data. Some frequently used items are the code for the the function key that the user pressed (in position 369 for ICF and display files), the cursor location (in positions 370 and 371 for display files, though simpler techniques are now available via DDS keywords), major and minor return codes for communications programs (positions 401 through 404 for ICF, printer, and display files), and current page and line number (in positions 367 through 372 for printer files). Table B.7 shows the feedback area for ICF and display files. Table B.8 is the feedback area for printer files, and Table B.9 is for database files.

I/O Feedback Area for ICF and Display Files

From	To	Data Type	Length	Contents	File Type
367	368	Character	2	Flag bits.	Display
				Bit 1: Cancel-read indicator.	Display
				0 The cancel-read operation did not cancel the read request.	
				1 The cancel-read operation canceled the read request.	
				Bit 2: Data-returned indicator.	Display
				0 The cancel-read operation did not change the contents of the input buffer.	
				1 The cancel-read operation placed the data from the read-with-no-wait operation into the input buffer.	
				Bit 3: Command key indicator.	Display
				0 Conditions for setting this indicator did not occur.	
				1 The Print, Help, Home, Roll Up, Roll Down, or Clear key was pressed. The key is enabled with a DDS keyword, but without a response indicator specified.	
				Bits 4-16: Reserved.	
369	369	Character	1	Attention indicator byte (AID). This field identifies which function key was pressed.	
				For ICF files, this field will always contain the value hex F1 to imitate the Enter key being pressed on a display device.	
				For display files, this field will contain the 1-byte hexadecimal value returned from the device.	
				Hex Codes Function Keys	Display,
				hex 31 1	ICF
				hex 32 2	
				hex 33 3	
				hex 34 4	
				hex 35 5	
				hex 36 6	
				hex 37 7	
				hex 38 8	
				hex 39 9	

CONTINUED

TABLE **B.7** *CONTINUED*

From	To	Data Type	Length	Contents		File Type
369	369	Character	1	hex 3A	10	
				hex 3B	11	
				hex 3C	12	
				hex B1	13	
				hex B2	14	
				hex B3	15	
				hex B4	16	
				hex B5	17	
				hex B6	18	
				hex B7	19	
				hex B8	20	
				hex B9	21	
				hex BA	22	
				hex BB	23	
				hex BC	24	
				hex BD	Clear	
				Hex Codes	Function Keys	
				hex F1	Enter/Rec Adv	
				hex F3	Help (not in operator-error mode)	
				hex F4	Roll Down	
				hex F5	Roll Up	
				hex F6	Print	
				hex F8	Record Backspace	
				hex 3F	Auto Enter (for selector light pen)	
370	371	Character	2	Cursor location (line and position). Updated on input operations that are not subfile operations that return data to the program. For example, hex 0102 means line 1, position 2. Line 10, position 33 would be hex 0A21.		Display
372	375	Binary	4	Actual data length. For an ICF file, see the *ICF Programming* book for additional information. For a display file, this is the length of the record format processed by the I/O operation.		Display
376	377	Binary	2	Relative record number of a subfile record. Updated for a subfile record operation. For input operations, updated only if data s returned to the program. If multiple subfiles are on the display, this offset will contain the relative record number for the last subfile updated.		Display, ICF

CONTINUED

TABLE B.7 *CONTINUED*

From	To	Data Type	Length	Contents	File Type
378	379	Binary	2	Indicates the lowest subfile relative record number currently displayed in the upper-most subfile display area if the last write operation was done to the subfile control record with SFLDSP specified. Updated for roll up and roll down operations. Reset to 0 on a write operation to another record. Not set for message subfiles.	Display
380	381	Binary	2	Total number of records in a subfile. Updated on a put-relative operation to any subfile record. The number is set to zero on a write or write-read operation to any subfile control record with the SFLINZ keyword optioned on. If records are put to multiple subfiles on the display, this offset will contain the total number of records for all subfiles assuming that no write or write-read operations were performed to any subfile control record with the SFLINZ keyword optioned on.	Display
382	383	Character	2	Cursor location (line and position) within active window. Updated on input operations that are not subfile operations that return data to the program. For example, hex 0203 means line 2, position 3 relative to the upper-left corner of the active window.	Display
384	400	Character	17	Reserved.	
401	402	Character	2	Major return code. 00 Operation completed successfully. 02 Input operation completed successfully, but job is being canceled (controlled). 03 Input operation completed successfully, but no data received. 04 Output exception. 08 Device already acquired. 11 Read from invited devices was not successful. 34 Input exception. 80 Permanent system or file error. 81 Permanent session or device error. 82 Acquire or open operation failed. 83 Recoverable session or device error.	Display, ICF

CONTINUED

TABLE B.7 *CONTINUED*

From	To	Data Type	Length	Contents	File Type
403	404	Character	2	Minor return code. For the values for a display file, see the *Application Display Programming* book. For the values for an ICF file, see the *ICF Programming* book and the appropriate communications-type programmer's guide.	Display, ICF
405	412	Character	8	Systems Network Architecture (SNA) sense return code. For some return codes, this field may contain more detailed information about the reason for the error. For a description of the SNA sense codes, see the appropriate SNA manual.	ICF
413	413	Character	1	Safe indicator: 0 An end-of-text (ETX) control character has not been received. 1 An ETX control character has been received.	ICF
414	414	Character	1	Reserved.	
415	415	Character	1	Request Write (RQSWRT) command from remote system/application. 0 RQSWRT not received 1 RQSWRT received	ICF
416	425	Character	10	Record format name received from the remote system.	ICF
426	429	Character	4	Reserved	
430	437	Character	8	Mode name	ICF
438	446	Character	9	Reserved	

TABLE B.8
I/O Feedback Area for Printer Files

From	To	Data Type	Length	Contents	File Type
367	368	Binary	2	Current line number in a page.	Printer
369	372	Binary	4	Current page count	Printer
373	400	Character	28	Reserved	

CONTINUED

TABLE B.8 CONTINUED

From	To	Data Type	Length	Contents	File Type
401	402	Character	2	Major return code.	Printer
				00 Operation completed successfully.	
				80 Permanent system or file error.	
				81 Permanent device error.	
				82 Open operation failed.	
				83 Recoverable device error occurred.	
403	404	Character	2	Minor return code. For the values for a printer file, refer to the *Printer Device Programming* guide.	Printer

TABLE B.9

I/O Feedback Area for Database Files

From	To	Data Type	Length	Contents	File Type
367	370	Binary	4	Size of the database feedback area, including the key and the null key field byte map.	Database
371	374	Character	4	Bits 1-32: Each bit represents a join logical file in JFILE keyword.	Database
				0 JDFTVAL not supplied for file	
				1 JDFTVAL supplied for file	
375	376	Binary	2	System Internal Use. Offset from the beginning of the I/O feedback area for database files to the null key field byte map which follows the key value (which begins at offset 34 in this area).	Database
377	378	Binary	2	Number of locked records.	Database
379	380	Binary	2	Maximum number of fields.	Database
381	384	Binary	4	System Internal Use. Offset to the field-mapping error-bit map.	Database
385	385	Character	1	Current file position indication.	Database
				Bit 1: Current file position is valid for get-next-key equal operation.	
				0 File position is not valid.	
				1 File position is valid.	
				Bits 2-8: Reserved.	

CONTINUED

TABLE B.9 CONTINUED

From	To	Data Type	Length	Contents	File Type
386	386	Character	1	Current record deleted indication: Bits 1-2: Reserved. Bit 3: Next message indicator. 0 Next message not end of file. 1 Next message may be end of file. Bit 4: Deleted record indicator. 0 Current file position is at an active record. 1 Current file position is at a deleted record. Bit 5: Write operation key feedback indicator. 0 Key feedback is not provided by last write operation. 1 Key feedback is provided by last write operation. Bit 6: File position changed indicator. Set only for read and positioning I/O operations. Not set for write, update, and delete I/O operations. 0 File position did not change. 1 File position did change. Bit 7: Pending exception indicator. Valid for files open for input only and SEQONLY(*YES N) where N is greater than 1. 0 Pending retrieval error does not exist. 1 Pending retrieval error does exist. Bit 8: Duplicate key indicator. 0 The key of the last read or write operation was not a duplicate key. 1 The key of the last read or write operation was a duplicate key.	Database
387	388	Binary	2	Number of key fields. Use this offset for binary operations. Use the next offset (offset 21) for character operations. These offsets overlap and provide the same value (there can be no more than 32 key fields, and only the low-order byte of offset 20 is used).	Database
388	388	Character	1	Number of key fields	Database
389	392	Character	4	Reserved	*CONTINUED*

TABLE B.9 *CONTINUED*

From	To	Data Type	Length	Contents	File Type
383	394	Binary	2	Key length	Database
395	396	Binary	2	Data member number	Database
397	400	Binary	4	Relative record number in data member	Database
401		Character	*	Key value. Length depends on length of file's defined key.	Database

A lot of information about each file type is available. The following code examples include sample subfield specs for each different available layout. Naturally, you will use only the ones that fit your needs.

```
*....1....+....2....+....3....+....4....+....5....+....6....+....7....+....8....+....9....+....10
FDBaseFile IF   E           DISK    INFDS(DBaseFBK)


*....1....+....2....+....3....+....4....+....5....+....6....+....7....+....8....+....9....+....10
DDBaseFBK          DS
 *
 * File Feedback area
 *
   ... any fields needed
 *
 * Open Feedback Area
 *
   ... any fields needed
 *
 * Common I/O Feedback area
 *
   ... any fields needed
 *
 * Device dependent database file I/O feedback area
 *
D FdbkSize              367    370B 0        * Size of DB fdbk
D JoinBits              371    374B 0        * JFILE bits
D LockRcds              377    378B 0        * Nbr locked rcds
D NbrFlds               379    380B 0        * Max Nbr Flds
D PosBits               385    385           * File pos bits
D DltBits               386    386           * Rcd deleted bits
D NumKeys               387    388B 0        * Num keys (bin)
D KeyLen                393    394B 0        * Key length
D MbrNum                395    395B 0        * Member number
D DbRRN                 397    400B 0        * Relative-rcd-num
D Key                   401   2400           * Key value (max
D                                            *  size 2000)
```

```
*...1....+....2....+....3....+....4....+....5....+....6....+....7....+....8....+....9....+....10
FDspFile   CF   E           WORKSTN INFDS(DspFBK)


*...1....+....2....+....3....+....4....+....5....+....6....+....7....+....8....+....9....+....10
DDspFBK          DS
 *
 * File Feedback area
 *
 ... any fields needed
 *
 * Open Feedback Area
 *
 ... any fields needed
 *
 * Common I/O Feedback area
 *
 ... any fields needed
 *
 * Device dependent display file I/O feedback area
 *
D DspFlag1             367    368           * Display flags
D DspAID               369    369           * AID byte
D Cursor               370    371           * Cursor location
D DataLen              372    375B 0        * Actual data len
D SfRrn                376    377B 0        * Subfile rrn
D MinRRN               378    379B 0        * Subfile min rrn
D NumRcds              380    381B 0        * Subfile num rcds
D ActCurs              382    383           * Active window
D                                           *  cursor location
D DspMajor             401    402           * Major ret code
D DspMinor             403    404           * Minor ret code


*...1....+....2....+....3....+....4....+....5....+....6....+....7....+....8....+....9....+....10
FICFFile   CF   E           WORKSTN INFDS(ICFFBK)


*...1....+....2....+....3....+....4....+....5....+....6....+....7....+....8....+....9....+....10
DICFFBK          DS
 *
 * File Feedback area
 *
 ... any fields needed
 *
 * Open Feedback Area
 *
 ... any fields needed
 *
 * Common I/O Feedback area
 *
 ... any fields needed
 *
 * Device dependent ICF file I/O feedback area
 *
D ICFAID               369    369           * AID byte
D ICFLen               372    375B 0        * Actual data len
D ICFMajor             401    402           * Major ret code
D ICFMinor             403    404           * Minor ret code
D SNASense             405    412           * SNA sense rc
D SafeInd              413    413           * Safe indicator
D Rqswrt               415    415           * Request write
D RmtFmt               416    425           * Remote rcd fmt
D ICFMode              430    437           * Mode name
```

```
*...1....+....2....+....3....+....4....+....5....+....6....+....7....+....8....+....9....+....10
FPrtFile   O   E                 PRINTER INFDS(PrtFBK)


*...1....+....2....+....3....+....4....+....5....+....6....+....7....+....8....+....9....+....10
DICFFBK          DS
 *
 * File Feedback area
 *
   ... any fields needed
 *
 * Open Feedback Area

 *
   ... any fields needed
 *
 * Common I/O Feedback area
 *
   ... any fields needed
 *
 * Device dependent printer file I/O feedback area
 *
D CurLine              367    368B 0              * Current line num
D CurPage              369    372B 0              * Current page cnt
D PrtMajor            401    402                  * Major ret code
D PrtMinor            403    404                  * Minor ret code
```

Get-Attributes Feedback Area

When working with display and ICF files, you have another option for using the feedback areas. Some detailed information is available for display and ICF files when you request get-attributes layout. Only advanced applications, such as generic utility programs, need most of this information, which includes the type of display and the status of the communications sessions. As you can see in Table B.10, an enormous amount of information is available.

TABLE B.10
Get Attributes for Display and ICF Files

From	To	Data Type	Length	Contents	File Type
241	250	Character	10	Program device name.	Display, ICF
251	260	Character	10	Device description name. Name of the device description associated with this entry.	Display, ICF
261	270	Character	10	User ID.	Display, ICF
271	271	Character	1	Device class: D Display I ICF U Unknown	Display, ICF

CONTINUED

TABLE B.10 *CONTINUED*

From	To	Data Type	Length	Contents	File Type
272	277	Character	6	Device type:	Display
				3179 — 3179 Display Station	
				317902 — 3179-2 Display Station	
				3180 — 3180 Display Station	
				3196A — 3196-A1/A2 Display Station	
				3196B — 3196-B1/B2 Display Station	
				3197C1 — 3197-C1 Display Station	
				3197C2 — 3197-C2 Display Station	
				3197D1 — 3197-D1 Display Station	
				3197D2 — 3197-D2 Display Station	
				3197W1 — 3197-W1 Display Station	
				3197W2 — 3197-W2 Display Station	
				3270 — 3270 Display Station	
				3476EA — 3476-EA Display Station	
				3476EC — 3476-EC Display Station	
				3477FA — 3477-FA Display Station	
				3477FC — 3477-FC Display Station	
				3477FD — 3477-FD Display Station	
				3477FE — 3477-FE Display Station	
				3477FG — 3477-FG Display Station	
				3477FW — 3477-FW Display Station	
				525111 — 5251 Display Station	
				5291 — 5291 Display Station	
				5292 — 5292 Display Station	
				529202 — 5292-2 Display Station	
				5555B1 — 5555-B01 Display Station	
				5555C1 — 5555-C01 Display Station	
				5555E1 — 5555-E01 Display Station	
				5555F1 — 5555-F01 Display Station	
				5555G1 — 5555-G01 Display Station	
				5555G2 — 5555-G02 Display Station	
				3486BA — 3486-BA Display Station	
				3487HA — 3487-HA Display Station	
				3487HC — 3487-HC Display Station	
				3487HG — 3487-HG Display Station	
				3487HW — 3487-HW Display Station	
				DHCF77 — 3277 DHCF device	ICF
				DHCF78 — 3278 DHCF device	
				DHCF79 — 3279 DHCF device	
				APPC — Advance program-to-program communications device	
				ASYNC — Asynchronous communications device	
				BSC — Bisynchronous communications device	

CONTINUED

TABLE B.10 *CONTINUED*

From	To	Data Type	Length	Contents	File Type
272	277	Character	6	BSCEL BSCEL communications device FINANC ICF Finance communications device INTRA Intrasystem communications device LU1 LU1 communications device RETAIL RETAIL communications device SNUF SNA upline facility communications device	
278	278	Character	1	Requester device. This flag indicates whether this entry is defining a **REQUESTER device. N Not a *REQUESTER device (communications source device). Y A *REQUESTER device (communications target device).	Display, ICF
279	279	Character	1	Acquire status. Set even if device is implicitly acquired at open time. N Device is not acquired. Y Device is acquired.	Display, ICF
280	280	Character	1	Invite status. Y Device is invited. N Device is not invited.	Display, ICF
281	281	Character	1	Data available. Y Invited data is available. N Invited data is not available.	Display, ICF
282	283	Binary	2	Number of rows on display.	Display
284	285	Binary	2	Number of columns on display.	Display
286	286	Character	1	Display allow blink. Y Display is capable of blinking. N Display is not capable of blinking.	Display
287	287	Character	1	Online/offline status. O Display is online. F Display is offline.	Display
288	288	Character	1	Display location. L Local display. R Remote display.	Display

CONTINUED

TABLE B.10 *CONTINUED*

From	To	Data Type	Length	Contents	File Type
289	289	Character	1	Display type. A Alphanumeric or Katakana. I DBCS. G Graphic DBCS.	Display
290	290	Character	1	Keyboard type of display. A Alphanumeric or Katakana I DBCS keyboard.	Display
291	291	Character	1	Transaction status. All communication types. N Transaction is not started. An evoke request has not been sent, a detach request has been sent or received, or the transaction has completed. Y Transaction is started. The transaction is active. An evoke request has been sent or received and the transaction has not ended.	ICF
292	292	Character	1	Synchronization level. APPC and INTRA. 0 Synchronization level 0 (SYNLVL(*NONE)). 1 Synchronization level 1 (SYNLVL(*CONFIRM)). 2 Synchronization level 2 (SYNLVL(*COMMIT)).	ICF
293	293	Character	1	Conversation being used. APPC only. M Mapped conversation. B Basic conversation.	ICF
294	301	Character	8	Remote location name. All communication types.	ICF
302	309	Character	8	Local LU name. APPC only.	ICF
310	317	Character	8	Local network ID. APPC only.	ICF
318	325	Character	8	Remote LU name. APPC only.	ICF
326	333	Character	8	Remote network ID. APPC only.	ICF
334	341	Character	8	Mode. APPC only.	ICF

CONTINUED

TABLE B.10 *CONTINUED*

From	To	Data Type	Length	Contents	File Type
342	342	Character	1	Controller information.	Display
				N Display is not attached to a controller that supports an enhanced interface for non-programmable workstations.	
				1 Display is attached to a controller (type 1) (1) that supports an enhanced interface for non-programmable workstations.	
				2 Display is attached to a controller (type 2) (1) that supports an enhanced interface for non-programmable workstations.	
				3 Display is attached to a controller (type 3) (1) that supports an enhanced interface for non-programmable workstations.	
343	343	Character	1	Conversation being used. APPC only.	Display
				M Mapped conversation.	
				B Basic conversation	
344	344	Character	1	Color capability of display.	Display
				Y Color display	
				N Monochrome display	
345	345	Character	1	hex 00 Reset state	ICF
				hex 01 Send state	
				hex 02 Defer received state	
				hex 03 Defer deallocate state	
				hex 04 Receive state	
				hex 05 Confirm state	
				hex 06 Confirm send state	
				hex 07 Confirm deallocate state	
				hex 08 Commit state	
				hex 09 Commit send state	
				hex 0A Commit deallocate state	
				hex 0B Deallocate state	
				hex 0C Rollback required state	
346	353	Character	8	LU.6 Conversation Correlator	ICF
354	384	Character	31	Reserved	

CONTINUED

TABLE B.10 *CONTINUED*

From	To	Data Type	Length	Contents	File Type
Note: The following information is only for Integrated Service Digital Network (ISDN) in the ICF or remote display session. Also, not all the information will be available if the area to receive it is too small.					
385	386	Binary	2	ISDN remote number length in bytes.	Display, ICF
				Consists of the total of the lengths of the next three fields: ISDN remote numbering type, ISDN remote numbering plan, and the ISDN remote number. If the ISDN remote number has been padded on the right with blanks, the length of that padding is not included in this total.	
				If ISDN is not used, this field contains 0.	
387	388	Character	2	ISDN remote numbering type (decimal).	Display, ICF
				00 Unknown. 01 International. 02 National. 03 Network-specific. 04 Subscriber. 06 Abbreviated.	
389	390	Character	2	ISDN remote numbering plan (decimal).	Display, ICF
				00 Unknown. 01 ISDN/Telephony. 03 Data. 04 Telex**. 08 National Standard. 09 Private.	
391	430	Character	40	The ISDN remote number in EBCDIC, padded on the right with blanks if necessary to fill the field.	Display, ICF
431	434	Character	4	Reserved	Display, ICF
435	436	Binary	2	ISDN remote subaddress length in bytes.	Display, ICF
				Consists of the total of the lengths of the next two fields: ISDN remote subaddress type and the ISDN remote subaddress. If the ISDN remote subaddress has been padded on the right with blanks, the length of that padding is not included in this total. If ISDN is not used, this field contains 0.	*CONTINUED*

TABLE B.10 *CONTINUED*

From	To	Data Type	Length	Contents	File Type
437	438	Character	2	ISDN remote subaddress type (decimal). 00 NSAP. 01 User-specified.	Display, ICF
439	478	Character	40	ISDN remote subaddress (EBCDIC representation of the original hexadecimal value, padded on the right with zeros).	Display, ICF
479	479	Character	1	Reserved.	Display, ICF
480	480	Character	1	ISDN connection (decimal). 0 Incoming ISDN call. 1 Outgoing ISDN call. Other Non-ISDN connection.	Display, ICF
481	482	Binary	2	ISDN remote network address length in bytes. If the ISDN remote network address has been padded on the right with blanks, the length of that padding is not included. If ISDN is not used, this field contains 0.	Display, ICF
483	514	Character	32	The ISDN remote network address in EBCDIC, padded on the right with blanks, if necessary, to fill the field.	Display, ICF
515	518	Character	4	Reserved.	Display, ICF
519	520	Character	2	ISDN remote address extension length in bytes. Consists of the total of the lengths of the next two fields: ISDN remote address extension type and the ISDN remote address extension. If the ISDN remote address extension has been padded on the right with zeros, the length of that padding is not included. If ISDN is not used or there is no ISDN remote address extension, this field contains 0.	Display, ICF
521	521	Character	1	ISDN remote address extension type (decimal). 0 Address assigned according to ISO 8348/AD2 2 Address not assigned according to ISO 8348/AD2 Other Reserved.	Display, ICF

CONTINUED

TABLE B.10 *Continued*

From	To	Data Type	Length	Contents	File Type
522	561	Character	40	ISDN remote address extension (EBCDIC representation of the original hexadecimal value, padded on the right with zeros).	Display, ICF
562	565	Character	4	Reserved.	Display, ICF
566	566	Character	1	X.25 call type (decimal). 0 Incoming Switched Virtual Circuit (SVC) 1 Outgoing SVC 2 Not X.25 SVC Other Reserved.	Display, ICF

Note: The following information is available only for when your program was started as a result of a received program start request. Also, not all the information will be available if the area to receive it is too small.

From	To	Data Type	Length	Contents	File Type
567	630	Character	64	Transaction program name. Name of the program specified to be started as a result of the received program start request, even if a routing list caused a different program to be started.	ICF
631	631	Binary	1	Length of the protected LUWID field. The valid values are 0 through 26.	ICF
632	632	Binary	1	Length of the qualified LU-NAME. The valid values are 0 through 17.	ICF
633	649	Character	17	Network qualified protected LU-NAME in the form: netid.luname. This field is blank if there is no network qualified protected LU-NAME.	ICF
650	655	Character	6	Protected LUWID instance number.	ICF
656	657	Binary	2	Protected LUWID sequence number.	ICF

Note: The following information is available only when a protected conversation is started on the remote system (when a conversation is started with a SYNCLVL of *COMMIT). Also, not all the information will be available if the area to receive it is too small.

From	To	Data Type	Length	Contents	File Type
658	658	Binary	1	Length of the unprotected LUWID field. The valid values are 0 through 26.	ICF
659	659	Binary	1	Length of the qualified LU-NAME. The valid values are 0 through 17.	ICF

Continued

TABLE B.10 *Continued*

From	To	Data Type	Length	Contents	File Type
660	676	Character	17	Network qualified unprotected LU-NAME in the form: netid.luname. This field is blank if there is no network qualified unprotected LU-NAME.	ICF
677	682	Character	6	Unprotected LUWID instance number.	ICF
683	684	Binary	2	Unprotected LUWID sequence number.	ICF

(1)

Type 1	Controllers available at V2R2 that support such features as windows and continued cursor progression.
Type 2	Controllers available at V2R3. These support all V2R2 functions and menu bars, continued-entry fields, edit masks, and simple hotspots.
Type 3	Controllers available at V3R1. These support all V2R2 and V2R3 functions. They also support text in the bottom border of windows.

As you see from the *from/to* positions for the fields in this layout, the get-attributes feedback area format starts at the same place as the common I/O feedback area. The file status data structure for a file can contain either get-attributes information or I/O feedback information, but you can request the different types of information as you need them, and you can define the subfields in your file status data structure for both types of data. Naturally, you will want to access only the subfields that are relevant at any given time.

POST and Loading the Get Attributes Feedback Area

Unlike the other feedback areas, which are automatically loaded and updated, the get-attributes feedback area requires you to take action to load it. To load the get-attributes feedback area, you can specify POST anywhere in your program's C-specs. You must use POST with a value in Factor 1 (the program name of some device, display, or communications file that you are communicating with) to retrieve the get-attributes feedback area. The sample code below lets you load the get-attributes feedback area into the data structure.

```
*...1....+....2....+....3....+....4....+....5....+....6....+....7....+....8....+....9....+....10
FDspFile   CF   E              WORKSTN INFDS(DspFBK)


*...1....+....2....+....3....+....4....+....5....+....6....+....7....+....8....+....9....+....10
DDspFBK          DS
 *
 * File Feedback area
 *
 ... any fields needed
 *
 * Open Feedback Area
 *
```

Continued

```
*...1....+....2....+....3....+....4....+....5....+....6....+....7....+....8....+....9....+....10
D Requester                  197    206                                   * Requester name
    ... any other fields needed
 *
 * Get Attributes Feedback area for Display file
 *
D PgmDev                      241    250                                   * Program device
D DevDsc                      251    260                                   * Dev description
D UserId                      261    270                                   * User ID
D DevClass                    271    271                                   * Device class
D DevType                     272    277                                   * Device type
D ReqDev                      278    278                                   * Requester?
D AcqStat                     279    279                                   * Acquire status
D InvStat                     280    280                                   * Invite status
D DataAvail                   281    281                                   * Data available
D NumRows                     282    283B 0                                * Number of rows
D NumCols                     284    285B 0                                * Number of cols
D Blink                       286    286                                   * Allow blink?
D LineStat                    287    287                                   * Online/offline?
D DspLoc                      288    288                                   * Display location
D DspType                     289    289                                   * Display type
D KbdType                     290    290                                   * Keyboard type
D CtlInfo                     342    342                                   * Controller info
D ColorDsp                    343    343                                   * Color capable?
D GridDsp                     344    344                                   * Grid line dsp?
D
D* Following fields apply to ISDN...
D ISDNLen                     385    386B 0                                * Rmt number len
D ISDNType                    387    388                                   * Rmt number type
D ISDNPlan                    389    390                                   * Rmt number plan
D ISDNNum                     391    430                                   * Rmt number
D ISDNSlen                    435    436B 0                                * Rmt sub-addr leng
D ISDNStype                   437    438                                   * Rmt sub-addr type
D ISDNSnum                    439    478                                   * Rmt sub-address
D ISDNCon                     480    480                                   * Connection
D ISDNRlen                    481    482B 0                                * Rmt address len
D ISDNRnum                    483    514                                   * Rmt address
D ISDNElen                    519    520                                   * Extension len
D ISDNEtype                   521    521                                   * Extension type
D ISDNEnum                    522    561                                   * Extension num
D ISDNXtype                   566    566                                   * X.25 call type


*...1....+....2....+....3....+....4....+....5....+....6....+....7....+....8....+....9....+....10
... other code
C                  EXFMT     DspFmt
C       Requester  POST      DspFile
... other code
```

When this code executes, it needs two parts of the feedback areas. First it uses the open feedback area to retrieve the program device name of the requester, the display using the program. Next the Requester value is in Factor 1 on POST to request information about that workstation. When you execute POST, the information in the get-attributes feedback area is loaded to the data structure. This example includes all possible fields. You will include only the fields that have information you need in your application.

The following code shows the definition of the file status data structure when you're using a display file and the get-attributes feedback area. The next sample illustrates how to define the fields for an ICF file when you're using the get-attributes feedback area. Each example uses different fields in different cases. Both display files and ICF files require many of the fields.

```
*...1....+....2....+....3....+....4....+....5....+....6....+....7....+....8....+....9....+....10
FDspFile   CF   E                WORKSTN INFDS(DspFBK)


*...1....+....2....+....3....+....4....+....5....+....6....+....7....+....8....+....9....+....10
DDspFBK           DS
 *
 * File Feedback area
 *
   ... any fields needed
 *
 * Open Feedback Area
 *
   ... any fields needed
 *
 * Get Attributes Feedback area for ICF file
 *
D PgmDev               241    250           * Program device
D DevDsc               251    260           * Dev description
D UserId               261    270           * User ID
D DevClass             271    271           * Device class
D DevType              272    277           * Device type
D ReqDev               278    278           * Requester?
D AcqStat              279    279           * Acquire status
D InvStat              280    280           * Invite status
D DataAvail            281    281           * Data available
D SesStat              291    291           * Session status
D SyncLvl              292    292           * Synch level
D ConvType             293    293           * Conversation typ
D RmtLoc               294    301           * Remote location
D LclLU                302    309           * Local LU name
D LclNetID             310    317           * Local net ID
D RmtLU                318    325           * Remote LU
D RmtNetID             326    333           * Remote net ID
D AppcMode             334    341           * APPC Mode
D LU6State             345    345           * LU6 conv state
D LU6Cor               346    353           * LU6 conv
D                                           *    correlator
D* Following fields apply to ISDN...
D ISDNLen              385    386B 0        * Rmt number len
D ISDNType             387    388           * Rmt number type
D ISDNPlan             389    390           * Rmt number plan
D ISDNNum              391    430           * Rmt number
D ISDNSlen             435    436B 0        * sub-addr len
D ISDNStype            437    438           * sub-addr type
D ISDNSnum             439    478           * Rmt sub-address
D ISDNCon              480    480           * Connection
D ISDNRlen             481    482B 0        * Rmt address len
D ISDNRnum             483    514           * Rmt address
D ISDNElen             519    520           * Extension len
D ISDNEtype            521    521           * Extension type
D ISDNEnum             522    561           * Extension num
D ISDNXtype            566    566           * X.25 call type
```

```
*...1....+....2....+....3....+....4....+....5....+....6....+....7....+....8....+....9....+....10
D* Following info is available only when program was started
D* as result of a received program start request... (P_ stands for protected)
D TranPgm                  567     630                          * Trans pgm name
D P_LUWIDln                631     631                          * LUWID fld len
D P_LUNameLn               632     632                          * LU-NAME len
D P_LUName                 633     649                          * LU-NAME
D P_LUWIDin                650     655                          * LUWID instance
D P_LUWIDseq               656     657B 0                       * LUWID seq num
D
D* Following info is available only when a protected conversation
D* is started on remote system... (U_ stands for unprotected)
D U_LUWIDln                658     658                          * LUWID fld len
D U_LUNameln               659     659                          * LU-NAME len
D U_LUName                 660     676                          * LU-NAME
D U_LUWIDin                677     682                          * LUWID instance
D U_LUWIDseq               683     684B 0                       * LUWID seq num
```

THE PROGRAM STATUS DATA STRUCTURE

Another special type of data structure that you can use for error handling is the program status data structure. It is similar to a file status data structure but is simpler to use and understand. Whereas a file status data structure contains information about a specific file, the program status data structure contains information about the entire program or the job the program is running in.

The program status data structure is a special type of data structure because you have to define it in a specific way, with a predefined format. As with a file status data structure, *from/to* notation to define the subfields in a program status data structure is easier than length notation. This method lets you include only the fields you need in your program. As with file status data structures, you can specify some special keywords in place of *from/to* entries. These special keywords provide predefined *from/to* positions automatically. When you specify the keywords, you do not have to worry about the layout of the data structure. Table B.11 lists the keywords in the program status data structure layout. Table B.12 describes all the data available in the program status data structure. Following the listing of available fields, Table B.12 describes each possible value of the status code subfield of the program status data structure.

TABLE B.11
Contents of Program Status Data Structure

From	To	Data Type	Length	Keyword	Contents
1	10	Character	10	*PROC	Procedure name
11	15	Zoned decimal	5,0	*STATUS	Status code
16	201	Zoned decimal	5,0		Previous status code.
21	28	Character	8		RPG IV source listing line number.
29	36	Character	8	*ROUTINE	Name of the RPG IV routine in which the exception or error occurred. This subfield is updated at the beginning of an RPG IV routine or after a program call only when the *STATUS subfield is updated with a nonzero value. The following names identify the routines:

					*INIT Program initialization
					*DETL Detail lines
					*GETIN Get input record
					*TOTC Total calculations
					*TOTL Total lines
					*DETC Detail calculations
					*OFL Overflow lines
					*TERM Program ending
					*ROUTINE Name of program or procedure called (first 8 characters).
					Note: *ROUTINE is not valid unless you use the normal RPG IV cycle. Logic that takes the program out of the normal RPG IV cycle may cause *ROUTINE to reflect an incorrect value.
37	39	Zoned decimal	3,0	*PARMS	Number of parameters passed to this program from a calling program.
40	42	Character	3		Exception type (CPF for a OS/400 system exception or MCH for a machine exception).
43	46	Character	4		Exception number. For a CPF exception, this field contains a CPF message number. For a machine exception, it contains a machine exception number.
47	50	Character	4		Reserved

CONTINUED

Table B.11 Continued

From	To	Data Type	Length	Keyword	Contents
51	80	Character	30		Work area for messages. This area is only for internal use by the RPG IV compiler. The organization of information will not always be consistent. It can be displayed by the user.
81	90	Character	10		Name of library in which the program is located
91	170	Character	80		Retrieved exception data. CPF messages are placed in this subfield when location *STATUS contains 09999.
171	174	Character	4		Identification of the exception that caused RNX9001 exception to be signaled.
175	190	Character	16		Unused
191	198	Character	8		Date (*DATE format) the job entered system. In the case of batch jobs submitted for overnight processing, those run after midnight will carry the next day's date.
199	200	Zoned decimal	2,0		First 2 digits of a 4-digit year. The same as the first 2 digits of *YEAR.
201	208	Character	8		Name of file on which the last file operation occurred (updated only when an error occurs).
209	243	Character	35		Status information on the last file used. This information includes the status code, the RPG IV opcode, the RPG IV routine name, the source listing line number, and record name. It is updated only when an error occurs. Note: The opcode name is in the same form as *OPCODE in the INFDS
244	253	Character	10		Job name
254	263	Character	10		User name from the user profile
264	269	Zoned decimal	6,0		Job number
270	275	Zoned decimal	6,0		Date (in UDATE format) the job was entered in the system (UDATE is derived from this date). In the case of batch jobs submitted for overnight processing, those run after midnight will carry the next day's date.

Continued

TABLE B.11 *CONTINUED*

From	To	Data Type	Length	Keyword	Contents
276	281	Zoned decimal	6,0		Date of program running (the system date in UDATE format).
282	287	Zoned decimal	6,0		Time of program running in the format hhmmss.
288	293	Character	6		Date (in UDATE format) the program was compiled.
294	299	Character	6		Time (in the format hhmmss) the program was compiled.
300	303	Character	4		Level of the compiler
304	313	Character	10		Source file name
314	323	Character	10		Source library name
324	333	Character	10		Source file member name
334	343	Character	10		Program containing procedure
344	353	Character	10		Module containing procedure
354	429	Character	76		Unused

TABLE B.12

Status Codes

Code	Condition
Normal Codes	
00000	No exception/error occurred
00001	Called program returned with the LR indicator on.
Exception/Error Codes	
00100	Value out of range for string operation
00101	Negative square root
00102	Divide by zero
00103	An intermediate result is not large enough to contain the result.
00112	Invalid date, time or timestamp value.
00113	Date overflow or underflow. (For example, when the result of a date calculation results in a number greater than *Hival or less than *Loval.)
00114	Date mapping errors, where a Date is mapped from a 4-character year to a 2-character year and the date range is not 1940-2039.

CONTINUED

TABLE B.12 *CONTINUED*

Code	Condition
Exception/Error Codes	
00120	Table or array out of sequence.
00121	Array index not valid
00122	OCCUR outside of range
00123	Reset attempted during initialization step of program
00202	Called program or procedure failed; halt indicator (H1 through H9) not on
00211	Error calling program or procedure
00221	Called program tried to use a parameter not passed to it.
00222	Pointer or parameter error
00231	Called program or procedure returned with halt indicator on
00232	Halt indicator on in this program
00233	Halt indicator on when RETURN operation run
00299	RPG IV formatted dump failed
00333	Error on DSPLY operation
00401	Data area specified on IN/OUT not found
00402	*PDA not valid for non-prestart job
00411	Data area type or length does not match
00412	Data area not locked for output
00413	Error on IN/OUT operation
00414	User not authorized to use data area
00415	User not authorized to change data area
00421	Error on UNLOCK operation
00431	Data area previously locked by another program
00432	Data area locked by program in the same process
00450	Character field not entirely enclosed by shift-out and shift-in characters
00501	Failure to retrieve sort sequence.
00502	Failure to convert sort sequence.
00802	Commitment control not active.
00803	Rollback operation failed.
00804	Error occurred on COMMIT operation
00805	Error occurred on ROLBK operation
00907	Decimal data error (digit or sign not valid)
00970	The level number of the compiler used to generate the program does not agree with the level number of the RPG IV runtime subroutines.
09998	Internal failure in RPG IV compiler or in runtime subroutines
09999	Program exception in system routine.

To create a program status data structure, you must include a special entry on the D-spec where you define the data structure: You must enter an S in position 23. This entry identifies the data structure as a program status data structure and is the only unique requirement to defining a program status data structure.

Some information programmers need most frequently for error handling are the job name, user ID, and job number of the current job. This information is in positions 244 through 269 of the program status data structure.

In addition to this information, the program status data structure contains valuable information for error handling. If you want a program to handle certain errors, you can code a *PSSR (Program Status Subroutine) in the program. You write this special subroutine, and it will automatically be called any time an error occurs that the program does not handle by means of error indicators (positions 73 and 74 on the C-specs for operations that support error indicators). The *PSSR is similar to a CL message monitor. The information in the program status data structure can help you determine what type of error has occurred in your program. When an error occurs that your program is not handling automatically, you can interrogate the status code in positions 11 through 15 to see what the error is. The *PSSR is where you will usually find or create code to review and process the status code.

You need to know how many parameters were passed to the program when it was called. The number of parameters passed is in positions 37 through 39 of the program status data structure. An RPG program does not require all defined parameters to be passed to it. You can have optional parameters. However, if a program tries to use an unpassed parameter, an error will occur. IF the program checks the number of parameters passed, you can call it with fewer than the defined number of parameters, and your code can use the number of parameters passed to condition the execution of code that might attempt to use an unpassed parameter.

The program status data structure contains a lot of information that can help identify errors in programs. You can log the error to an error file when a failure occurs in a program. Or, a program can automatically handle certain errors. To include a program status data structure in a program, you can use the sample code below.

```
*...1....+....2....+....3....+....4....+....5....+....6....+....7....+....8....+....9....+....10
DPgmStsDS      SDS
D ProcName       *PROC                           * Procedure name
D PgmStatus      *STATUS                          * Status code
D PrvStatus          16     20S 0                 * Previous status
D LineNum            21     28                    * Src 1st line num
D Routine        *ROUTINE                         * Routine name
D Parms          *PARMS                           * Num passed parms
D ExcpType           40     42                    * Exception type
D ExcpNum            43     46                    * Exception number
D*
D PgmLib             81     90                    * Program library
D Excpdata           91    170                    * Exception data
D Excpid            171    174                    * Exception Id
D Date              191    198                    * Date (*DATE fmt)
D Year              199    200S 0                 * Year (*YEAR fmt)
D Lastfile          201    208                    * Last file used
D Fileinfo          209    243                    * File error info
D Jobname           244    253                    * Job name
D User              254    263                    * User name
D Jobnum            264    269S 0                 * Job number
```

CONTINUED

```
*...1....+....2....+....3....+....4....+....5....+....6....+....7....+....8....+....9....+....10
D Jobdate            270    275S 0                                   * Date (UDATE fmt)
D Rundate            276    281S 0                                   * Run date (UDATE)
D Runtime            282    287S 0                                   * Run time (UDATE)
D Crtdate            288    293                                      * Create date
D Crttime            294    299                                      * Create time
D Cpllevel           300    303                                      * Compiler level
D Srcfile            304    313                                      * Source file
D Srclib             314    323                                      * Source file lib
D Srcmbr             324    333                                      * Source file mbr
D Procpgm            334    343                                      * Pgm Proc is in
D Procmod            344    353                                      * Mod Proc is in
```

This example code defines all the available fields. Of course, you can define and use just the fields you need. Note that all the numeric fields here are zoned decimal, not packed. Programmers often accidentally code those fields as packed rather than zoned, so watch out for that potential problem.

Index

Also Published by *NEWS/400*

THE A TO Z OF EDI

By Nahid M. Jilovec

Electronic Data Interchange (EDI) can help reduce administrative costs, accelerate information processing, ensure data accuracy, and streamline business procedures. Here's a comprehensive guide to EDI to help in planning, startup, and implementation. The author reveals all the benefits, challenges, standards, and implementation secrets gained through extensive experience. She shows how to evaluate your business procedures, select special hardware and software, establish communications requirements and standards, address audit issues, and employ the legal support necessary for EDI activities. 263 pages.

APPLICATION DEVELOPER'S HANDBOOK FOR THE AS/400

Edited by Mike Otey, a **NEWS/400** *technical editor*

Explains how to effectively use the AS/400 to build reliable, flexible, and efficient business applications. Contains RPG/400 and CL coding examples and tips, and provides both step-by-step instructions and handy reference material. Includes diskette. 768 pages, 48 chapters.

AS/400 DISK SAVING TIPS & TECHNIQUES

By James R. Plunkett

Want specific help for cleaning up and maintaining your disk? Here are more than 50 tips, plus design techniques for minimizing your disk usage. Each tip is completely explained with the "symptom," the problem, and the technique or code you need to correct it. 72 pages.

AS/400 SUBFILES IN RPG

On the AS/400, subfiles are powerful and easy to use, and with this book you can start working with subfiles in just a few hours — no need to wade through page after page of technical jargon. You'll start with the concept behind subfiles, then discover how easy they are to program. The book contains all of the DDS subfile keywords announced in V2R3 of OS/400. Five complete RPG subfile programs are included, and the book comes complete with a 3.5" PC diskette containing all those programs plus DDS. The book is an updated version of the popular *Programming Subfiles in RPG/400.* 200 pages, 4 chapters.

C FOR RPG PROGRAMMERS

By Jennifer Hamilton, a **NEWS/400** *author*

Written from the perspective of an RPG programmer, this book includes side-by-side coding examples written in both C and RPG to aid comprehension and understanding, clear identification of unique C constructs, and a comparison of RPG op-codes to equivalent C concepts. Includes many tips and examples covering the use of C/400. 292 pages, 23 chapters.

CL BY EXAMPLE

By Virgil Green

CL by Example gives programmers and operators more than 850 pages of practical information you can use in your day-to-day job. It's full of application examples, tips, and techniques, along with a sprinkling of humor. The examples will speed you through the learning curve to help you become a more proficient, more productive CL programmer. 864 pages, 12 chapters.

CLIENT ACCESS TOKEN-RING CONNECTIVITY

By Chris Patterson

Attaching PCs to AS/400s via a Token-Ring can become a complicated subject — when things go wrong, an understanding of PCs, the Token-Ring, and OS/400 is often required. Client Access Token-Ring Connectivity details all that is required in these areas to successfully maintain and trouble-shoot a Token-Ring network. The first half of the book introduces the Token-Ring and describes the Client Access communications architecture, the Token-Ring connection from both the PC side and the AS/400 side, and the Client Access applications. The second half provides a useful guide to Token-Ring management, strategies for Token-Ring error identification and recovery, and tactics for resolving Client Access error messages. 125 pages, 10 chapters.

COMMON-SENSE C
Advice and warnings for C and C++ programmers

By Paul Conte, a **NEWS/400** *technical editor*

C programming language has its risks; this book shows how C programmers get themselves into trouble, includes tips to help you avoid C's pitfalls, and suggests how to manage C and C++ application development. 100 pages, 9 chapters.

CONTROL LANGUAGE PROGRAMMING FOR THE AS/400

By Bryan Meyers and Dan Riehl, **NEWS/400** *technical editors*

This comprehensive CL programming textbook offers students up-to-the-minute knowledge of the skills they will need in today's MIS environment. Progresses methodically from CL basics to more complex processes and concepts, guiding readers toward a professional grasp of CL programming techniques and style. 512 pages, 25 chapters.

DDS BY EXAMPLE

By R S Tipton

DDS by Example provides detailed coverage on the creation of physical files, field reference files, logical files, display files, and printer files. It includes more than 300 real-life examples, including examples of physical files, simple logical files, multi-format logical files, dynamic selection options, coding subfiles, handling overrides, creating online help, creating reports, and coding windows. 360 pages, 4 chapters.

DDS PROGRAMMING FOR DISPLAY & PRINTER FILES

By James Coolbaugh

Offers a thorough, straightforward explanation of how to use Data Description Specifications (DDS) to program display files and printer files. Covers basic to complex tasks using DDS functions. The author uses DDS programming examples for CL and RPG extensively throughout the book, and you can put these examples to use immediately. Focuses on topics such as general screen presentations, the A specification, defining data on the screen, record-format and field definitions, defining data fields, using indicators, data and text attributes, cursor and keyboard control, editing data, validity checking, response keywords, and function keys. A complimentary diskette includes all the source code presented in the book. 446 pages, 13 chapters.

DESKTOP GUIDE TO THE S/36

By Mel Beckman, Gary Kratzer, and Roger Pence, **NEWS/400** *technical editors*
This definitive S/36 survival manual includes practical techniques to supercharge your S/36, including ready-to-use information for maximum system performance tuning, effective application development, and smart Disk Data Management. Includes a review of two popular Unix-based S/36 work-alike migration alternatives. Diskette contains ready-to-run utilities to help you save machine time and implement power programming techniques such as External Program Calls. 387 pages, 21 chapters.

THE ESSENTIAL GUIDE TO CLIENT ACCESS FOR DOS EXTENDED

By John Enck, Robert E. Anderson, and Michael Otey
The Essential Guide to Client Access for DOS Extended contains key insights and need-to-know technical information about Client Access for DOS Extended, IBM's strategic AS/400 product for DOS and Windows client/server connectivity. This book provides background information about the history and architecture of Client Access for DOS Extended; fundamental information about how to install and configure Client Access; and advanced information about integrating Client Access with other types of networks, managing how Client Access for DOS Extended operates under Windows, and developing client/server applications with Client Access. Written by industry experts based on their personal and professional experiences with Client Access, this book can help you avoid time-consuming pitfalls that litter the path of AS/400 client/server computing. 430 pages, 12 chapters.

ILE: A FIRST LOOK

By George Farr and Shailan Topiwala
This book begins by showing the differences between ILE and its predecessors, then goes on to explain the essentials of an ILE program — using concepts such as modules, binding, service programs, and binding directories. You'll discover how ILE program activation works and how ILE works with its predecessor environments. The book covers the new APIs and new debugging facilities and explains the benefits of ILE's new exception-handling model. You also get answers to the most commonly asked questions about ILE. 183 pages, 9 chapters.

IMPLEMENTING AS/400 SECURITY, SECOND EDITION
A practical guide to implementing, evaluating, and auditing your AS/400 security strategy
By Wayne Madden, a **NEWS/400** *technical editor*
Concise and practical, this second edition brings together in one place the fundamental AS/400 security tools and experience-based recommendations that you need and also includes specifics on the latest security enhancements available in OS/400 Version 3 Release 1. Completely updated from the first edition, this is the only source for the latest information about how to protect your system against attack from its increasing exposure to hackers. 389 pages, 16 chapters.

INSIDE THE AS/400
An in-depth look at the AS/400's design, architecture, and history
By Frank G. Soltis

The inside story every AS/400 developer has been waiting for, told by Dr. Frank G. Soltis, IBM's AS/400 chief architect. Never before has IBM provided an in-depth look at the AS/400's design, architecture, and history. This authoritative book does just that — and also looks at some of the people behind the scenes who created this revolutionary system for you. Whether you are an executive looking for a high-level overview or a "bit-twiddling techie" who wants all the details, *Inside the AS/400* demystifies this system, shedding light on how it came to be, how it can do the things it does, and what its future may hold — especially in light of its new PowerPC RISC processors. 475 pages, 12 chapters.

AN INTRODUCTION TO COMMUNICATIONS FOR THE AS/400, SECOND EDITION
By John Enck and Ruggero Adinolfi

This second edition has been revised to address the sweeping communications changes introduced with V3R1 of OS/400. As a result, this book now covers the broad range of AS/400 communications technology topics, ranging from Ethernet to X.25, and from APPN to AnyNet. The book presents an introduction to data communications and then covers communications fundamentals, types of networks, OSI, SNA, APPN, networking roles, the AS/400 as host and server, TCP/IP, and the AS/400-DEC connection. 210 pages, 13 chapters.

JIM SLOAN'S CL TIPS & TECHNIQUES
By Jim Sloan, developer of QUSRTOOL's TAA Tools

Written for those who understand CL, this book draws from Jim Sloan's knowledge and experience as a developer for the S/38 and the AS/400, and his creation of QUSRTOOL's TAA tools, to give you tips that can help you write better CL programs and become more productive. Includes more than 200 field-tested techniques, plus exercises to help you understand and apply many of the techniques presented. 564 pages, 30 chapters.

MASTERING THE AS/400
A practical, hands-on guide
By Jerry Fottral

This introductory textbook to AS/400 concepts and facilities has a utilitarian approach that stresses student participation. A natural prerequisite to programming and database management courses, it emphasizes mastery of system/user interface, member-object-library relationship, utilization of CL commands, and basic database and program development utilities. Also includes labs focusing on essential topics such as printer spooling; library lists; creating and maintaining physical files; using logical files; using CL and DDS; working in the PDM environment; and using SEU, DFU, Query, and SDA. 484 pages, 12 chapters.

OBJECT-ORIENTED PROGRAMMING FOR AS/400 PROGRAMMERS
*By Jennifer Hamilton, a **NEWS/400** author*

Explains basic OOP concepts such as classes and inheritance in simple, easy-to-understand terminology. The OS/400 object-oriented architecture serves as the basis for the discussion throughout, and concepts presented are reinforced through an introduction to the C++ object-oriented programming language, using examples based on the OS/400 object model. 114 pages, 14 chapters.

PERFORMANCE PROGRAMMING — MAKING RPG SIZZLE

By Mike Dawson, CDP

Mike Dawson spent more than two years preparing this book — evaluating programming options, comparing techniques, and establishing benchmarks on thousands of programs. "Using the techniques in this book," he says, "I have made program after program run 30%, 40%, even 50% faster." To help you do the same, Mike gives you code and benchmark results for initializing and clearing arrays, performing string manipulation, using validation arrays with look-up techniques, using arrays in arithmetic routines, and a lot more. 257 pages, 8 chapters.

POWER TOOLS FOR THE AS/400, VOLUMES I AND II

Edited by Frederick L. Dick and Dan Riehl

NEWS 3X/400's Power Tools for the AS/400 is a two-volume reference series for people who work with the AS/400. Volume I (originally titled *AS/400 Power Tools*) is a collection of the best tools, tips, and techniques published in *NEWS/34-38* (pre-August 1988) and *NEWS 3X/400* (August 1988 through October 1991) that are applicable to the AS/400. *Volume II* extends this original collection by including material that appeared through 1994. Each book includes a diskette that provides load-and-go code for easy-to-use solutions to many everyday problems. *Volume I*: 709 pages, 24 chapters; *Volume II*: 702 pages, 14 chapters.

PROGRAMMING IN RPG IV

By Judy Yaeger, Ph.D., a **NEWS/400** *technical editor*

This textbook provides a strong foundation in the essentials of business programming, featuring the newest version of the RPG language: RPG IV. Focuses on real-world problems and down-to-earth solutions using the latest techniques and features of RPG. Provides everything you need to know to write a well-designed RPG IV program. Each chapter includes informative, easy-to-read explanations and examples as well as a section of thought-provoking questions, exercises, and programming assignments. Four appendices and a handy, comprehensive glossary support the topics presented throughout the book. An instructor's kit is available. 450 pages, 13 chapters.

PROGRAMMING IN RPG/400, SECOND EDITION

By Judy Yaeger, Ph.D., a **NEWS/400** *technical editor*

This second edition refines and extends the comprehensive instructional material contained in the original textbook and features a new section that introduces externally described printer files, a new chapter that highlights the fundamentals of RPG IV, and a new appendix that correlates the key concepts from each chapter with their RPG IV counterparts. Includes everything you need to learn how to write a well-designed RPG program, from the most basic to the more complex, and each chapter includes a section of questions, exercises, and programming assignments that reinforce the knowledge you have gained from the chapter and strengthen the groundwork for succeeding chapters. An instructor's kit is available. 440 pages, 14 chapters.

PROGRAMMING SUBFILES IN COBOL/400

By Jerry Goldson

Learn how to program subfiles in COBOL/400 in a matter of hours! This powerful and flexible programming technique no longer needs to elude you. You can begin programming with subfiles the same day you get the book. You don't have to wade through page after page, chapter after chapter of rules and parameters and keywords. Instead, you get solid, helpful information and working examples that you can apply to your application programs right away. 204 pages, 5 chapters.

THE QUINTESSENTIAL GUIDE TO PC SUPPORT

By John Enck, Robert E. Anderson, Michael Otey, and Michael Ryan

This comprehensive book about IBM's AS/400 PC Support connectivity product defines the architecture of PC Support and its role in midrange networks, describes PC Support's installation and configuration procedures, and shows you how you can configure and use PC Support to solve real-life problems. 345 pages, 11 chapters.

RPG ERROR HANDLING TECHNIQUE
Bulletproofing Your Applications

By Russell Popeil

RPG Error Handling Technique teaches you the skills you need to use the powerful tools provided by OS/400 and RPG to handle almost any error from within your programs. The book explains the INFSR, INFDS, PSSR, and SDS in programming terms, with examples that show you how all these tools work together and which tools are most appropriate for which kind of error or exception situation. It continues by presenting a robust suite of error/exception handling techniques within RPG programs. Each technique is explained in an application setting, using both RPG III and RPG IV code. 164 pages, 5 chapters.

RPG IV JUMP START
Moving ahead with the new RPG

*By Bryan Meyers, a **NEWS/400** technical editor*

Introducing the "new" RPG, in which the columnar syntax has been challenged (all the specifications have changed, some vestigial specifications from an earlier era have been eliminated, and new specifications and data types have been added), this book shows you RPG IV from the perspective of a programmer who already knows the old RPG. Points out the differences between the two and demonstrates how to take advantage of the new syntax and function. 193 pages, 12 chapters.

RPG/400 INTERACTIVE TEMPLATE TECHNIQUE

By Carson Soule, CDP, CCP, CSP

Here's an updated version of Carson Soule's *Interactive RPG/400 Programming*. The book shows you time-saving, program-sharpening concepts behind the template approach, and includes all the code you need to build one perfect program after another. These templates include code for cursor-sensitive prompting in DDS, for handling messages in resident RPG programs, for using the CLEAR opcode to eliminate hard-coded field initialization, and much more. There's even a new select template with a pop-up window. 258 pages, 10 chapters.

S/36 POWER TOOLS

Edited by Chuck Lundgren, a **NEWS/400** *technical editor*

Winner of an STC Award of Achievement in 1992, this book contains five years' worth of articles, tips, and programs published in *NEWS 3X/400* from 1986 to October 1990, including more than 290 programs and procedures. Extensively cross-referenced for fast and easy problem solving, and complete with diskette containing all the programming code. 737 pages, 20 chapters.

STARTER KIT FOR THE AS/400, SECOND EDITION

**An indispensable guide for novice to intermediate
AS/400 programmers and system operators**

By Wayne Madden, a **NEWS/400** *technical editor*
with contributions by Bryan Meyers, Andrew Smith, and Peter Rowley

This second edition contains updates of the material in the first edition and incorporates new material to enhance it's value as a resource to help you learn important basic concepts and nuances of the AS/400 system. New material focuses on installing a new release, working with PTFs, AS/400 message handling, working with and securing printed output, using operational assistant to manage disk space, job scheduling, save and restore basics, and more basic CL programming concepts. Optional diskette available. 429 pages, 33 chapters.

SUBFILE TECHNIQUE FOR RPG/400 PROGRAMMERS

By Jonathan Yergin, CDP, and Wayne Madden

Here's the code you need for a complete library of shell subfile programs: RPG/400 code, DDS, CL, and sample data files. There's even an example for programming windows. You even get some "whiz bang" techniques that add punch to your applications. This book explains the code in simple, straightforward style and tells you when each technique should be used for best results. 326 pages, 11 chapters, 3.5" PC diskette included.

TECHNICAL REFERENCE SERIES

Edited by Bryan Meyers, a **NEWS/400** *technical editor*

Written by experts — such as John Enck, Bryan Meyers, Julian Monypenny, Roger Pence, Dan Riehl — these unique desktop guides put the latest AS/400 applications and techniques at your fingertips. These "just-do-it" books (featuring wire-o binding to open flat at every page) are priced so you can keep your personal set handy. Optional online Windows help diskette available for each book.

Desktop Guide to CL Programming

By Bryan Meyers, a **NEWS/400** *technical editor*

This first book of the **NEWS/400** *Technical Reference Series* is packed with easy-to-find notes, short explanations, practical tips, answers to most of your everyday questions about CL, and CL code segments you can use in your own CL programming. Complete "short reference" lists every command and explains the most-often-used ones, along with names of the files they use and the MONMSG messages to use with them. 205 pages, 36 chapters.

Desktop Guide to AS/400 Programmers' Tools

By Dan Riehl, a **NEWS/400** *technical editor*

This second book of the **NEWS/400** *Technical Reference Series* gives you the "how-to" behind all the tools included in *Application Development ToolSet/400* (ADTS/400), IBM's Licensed Program Product for Version 3 of OS/400; includes Source Entry Utility (SEU), Programming Development Manager (PDM), Screen Design Aid (SDA), Report Layout Utility (RLU), File Compare/Merge Utility (FCMU) — *new in V3R1*, and Interactive Source Debugger — *new in V3R1*. Highlights topics and functions specific to Version 3 of OS/400. 266 pages, 30 chapters.

Desktop Guide to DDS

By James Coolbaugh

This third book of the **NEWS/400** *Technical Reference Series* provides a complete reference to all DDS keywords for physical, logical, display, printer, and ICF files. Each keyword is briefly explained, with syntax rules and examples showing how to code the keyword. All basic and pertinent information is provided for quick and easy access. While this guide explains every parameter for a keyword, it doesn't explain every possible exception that might exist. Rather, the guide includes the basics about what each keyword is designed to accomplish. The *Desktop Guide to DDS* is designed to give quick, "at your fingertips" information about every keyword — with this in hand, you won't need to refer to IBM's bulky *DDS Reference* manual. 132 pages, 5 major sections.

Desktop Guide to RPG/400

By Roger Pence and Julian Monypenny, **NEWS/400** *technical editors*

This fourth book in the *Technical Reference Series* provides a variety of RPG templates, subroutines, and copy modules, sprinkled with evangelical advice, that will help you write robust and effective RPG/400 programs. Highlights of the information provided include string-handling routines, numeric editing routines, date routines, error-handling modules, tips for using OS/400 APIs with RPG/400, and interactive programming techniques. For all types of RPG projects, this book's tested and ready-to-run building blocks will easily snap into your RPG. The programming solutions provided here would otherwise take you days or even weeks to write and test. 211 pages, 28 chapters.

Desktop Guide to Creating CL Commands

By Lynn Nelson

In this most recent book in the *Technical Reference Series*, author Lynn Nelson shows you how to create your own CL commands with the same functionality and power as the IBM commands you use every day, including automatic parameter editing, all the function keys, F4 prompt for values, expanding lists of values, and conditional prompting. After you have read this book, you can write macros for the operations you do over and over every day or write application commands that prompt users for essential information. Whether you're in operations or programming, don't miss this opportunity to enhance your career-building skills. 158 pages, 14 chapters.

UNDERSTANDING BAR CODES

By James R. Plunkett

One of the most important waves of technology sweeping American industry is the use of bar coding to capture and track data. The wave is powered by two needs: the need to gather information in a more accurate and timely manner and the need to track that information once it is gathered. Bar coding meets these needs and provides creative and cost-effective solutions for many applications. With so many leading-edge technologies, it can be difficult for IS professionals to keep up with the concepts and applications they need to make solid decisions. This book gives you an overview of bar code technology including a discussion of the bar codes themselves, the hardware that supports bar coding, how and when to justify and then implement a bar code application, plus examples of many different applications and how bar coding can be used to solve problems. 70 pages.

USING QUERY/400

By Patrice Gapen and Catherine Stoughton

This textbook, designed for any AS/400 user from student to professional with or without prior programming knowledge, presents Query as an easy and fast tool for creating reports and files from AS/400 databases. Topics are ordered from simple to complex and emphasize hands-on AS/400 use; they include defining database files to Query, selecting and sequencing fields, generating new numeric and character fields, sorting within Query, joining database files, defining custom headings, creating new database files, and more. Instructor's kit available. 92 pages, 10 chapters.

USING VISUAL BASIC WITH CLIENT ACCESS APIs

By Ron Jones

This book is for programmers who want to develop client/server solutions on the AS/400 and the personal computer. Whether you are a VB novice or a VB expert, you will gain by reading this book because it provides a thorough overview of the pinciples and requirements for programming in Windows using VB. Companion diskettes contain source code for all the programming projects referenced in the book, as well as for numerous other utilities and programs. All the projects are compatible with Windows 95 and VB 4.0. 680 pages, 13 chapters.

**FOR A COMPLETE CATALOG
OR TO PLACE AN ORDER, CONTACT**

NEWS/400

Duke Communications International
221 E. 29th Street • Loveland, CO 80538-2727
(800) 621-1544 • (970) 663-4700 • Fax: (970) 669-3016